Blackface, White Noise

Blackface, White Noise

Jewish Immigrants in the
Hollywood Melting Pot

Michael Rogin

UNIVERSITY OF CALIFORNIA PRESS

Berkeley   Los Angeles   London

University of California Press
  Berkeley and Los Angeles, California

University of California Press, Ltd.
  London, England

First Paperback Printing 1998

Portions of this book have been published in earlier versions as:
"Blackface, White Noise: The Jewish Jazz Singer Finds His Voice,"
  Critical Inquiry 18 (spring 1992): 417–53.
"Making America Home:Racial Masquerade and Ethnic Assimilation
  in the Transition to Talking Pictures," *Journal of American
  History* 79 (Dec. 1992): 1050–77.
" 'Democracy and Burnt Cork': The End of Blackface, the Beginning
  of Civil Rights," *Representations* 46 (spring 1994): 1–34.

Library of Congress Cataloging-in-Publication Data

Rogin, Michael, 1937–
    Blackface, white noise: Jewish immigrants in the Hollywood
  melting pot / Michael Rogin.
      p.   cm.
    "A Centennial book"
    Includes bibliographical references and index.
    ISBN 0-520-21380-7 (pbk : alk. paper)
    1. Afro-Americans in motion pictures.   2. Jews in the motion
  picture industry—United States.   3. Jews—Cultural assimilation—
  United States.   4. Blackface entertainers—United States.
  5. Jewish entertainers—United States.   I. Title
  PN1995.9.N4R64   1996
  791.43'6520396073—dc20   95-44109
                                                              CIP

Printed in the United States of America
9 8 7 6 5 4 3 2 1

To escape from a servile life into the freedom of just conditions.

Wat Tyler memorial, Norwich, England, 1949

*For Ann,
and in memory of James E. B. Breslin,
December 12, 1935–January 6, 1996*

Contents

Illustrations

Acknowledgments

Fred Schaffer assembled the materials from which this analysis began. I am greatly in his debt. Egypt Brown, Christian Galatti, Donna Murch, and Elaine Thomas also undertook research tasks; the Committee on Research, University of California, Berkeley, supplied financial assistance. The Rockefeller Foundation's Bellagio Study and Conference Center provided an extraordinarily supportive and beautiful environment for writing and reflection as the book was nearing completion.

Many readers and listeners responded to portions of the work and left their imprint on its final form: thanks to Norman Jacobson (who first set me on the path he may wish I had never taken), Gordon Hutner, Amy Kaplan, Patrice Petro, and Justin Suran; Kathleen Woodward and the Center for Twentieth Century Studies, University of Wisconsin, Milwaukee; Larry Reynolds and the Interdisciplinary Group for Historical Literary Study, Texas A & M University; W. T. Mitchell and the readers of the essay on *The Jazz Singer* published in *Critical Inquiry;* Fred Hoxie, David Thelen, Casey Blake, Susan Armeny, and the contributers to the special issue of the *Journal of American History,* "Discovering America"; the film scholars who gathered at the Humanities Research Institute, University of California, Irvine, in the fall of 1992, Leo Braudy, Nick Browne, Carol Clover, George Lipsitz, Nita Rollins, David Russell, Tom Schatz, Vivian Sobchack, and Linda Williams; and Stephen Greenblatt and the other members of the *Representations* editorial board. A number of cinephiles besides those named above directed me to movies that have a place in this study; I am particularly grateful to

William Nestrick, to Roland De La Rosa and Randy Beucus of Movie Image, and to Nancy Goldman and Lee Amazonas of the Pacific Film Archive, University Art Museum, University of California, Berkeley. Gaston Alonse Donate, Carol Clover, George Lipsitz, Donna Murch, Keally McBride, Hanna Pitkin, Paul Romano, and Tom Schatz offered indispensable readings of what was, before they saw it, the completed manuscript. Jim Clark was, as always, wonderfully supportive, Anne Canright edited the book with incredible care, Gordon Adams solved all computer problems, and Tim Clark supplied the epigraph. Finally, thanks to Elizabeth Abel, Ann Banfield, James E. B. Breslin, Kim Chernin, Cathy Gallagher, Arlie Hochschild, Kathleen Moran, and Lillian Rubin, upon whose engagement with and detailed responses to my work I have come to depend.

PART 1

Made in America

The elements that went into vaudeville were combed from . . . the four corners of the world. . . . There were hypnotists, iron-jawed ladies, one-legged dancers, one-armed cornetists, mind readers, female impersonators, male impersonators, Irish comedians, Jewish comedians, blackface, German, Swedish, Italian and rube comedians. . . . Vaudeville asked only that you own an animal or an instrument, or have a minimum of talent or a maximum of nerve. With these dubious assets, vaudeville offered fame and riches. It was up to you.

Fred Allen, *Much Ado About Me* (1956)

CHAPTER 1

Uncle Sammy
and My Mammy

I
_____

"Owl Jolson," the hero of a 1936 Warner Bros., Looney Tunes, and Merry Melodies cartoon, is thrown out of his father's house because he wants to sing "jazz." The father, identified by accent and demeanor as an Old World music teacher, had welcomed the hatching of Owl's older siblings—"another Caruso!" "another Kreisler!" "another Mendelssohn!"—but Owl pops out "a crooner." "Shtop! Shtop!" shouts the father as the fledgling bursts into song. Setting off on his own, the self-made American rebel auditions for a radio talent show. Failed contestants drop through a trap door whenever the judge bangs his gavel. But Owl wins the contest, and with it the approval of his entire family, by singing, "With a cheer for Uncle Sammy, and another for my mammy, I love to sing."

This animated film, titled *I Love to Singa,* is in part an ephemeron from the temporary 1930s decline of the most popular entertainer of the first half of the twentieth century. It advertised Al Jolson's effort to revive his flagging career on radio. It also promoted what would turn out to be another in his series of unsuccessful films, *The Singing Kid,* which opens and closes with the song cheering for "Uncle Sammy and my mammy." Yet both the cartoon and the failed feature were situated between two of the most widely seen movies of classic Hollywood, *The Jazz Singer* (1927) and *The Jolson Story* (1946). The paternal "Shtop!" at Owl's birth quotes the famous word with which the jazz singer's cantor father interrupts the son playing piano for his mother, thus returning the first talking picture to silence. Beginning with paternal disapproval and ending with familial embrace, the cartoon bridges the gap between the generational conflict of the 1920s film and the Americanization of the old people as well in the post–World War II, postimmigration, postgenocide *Jolson Story.*

I Love to Singa overrides the details of its historical moment, however, in the way it links art to politics. Popular culture Americanizes Owl Jolson, defeating Old World high culture. How, then, does Uncle Sammy employ "My Mammy" in that process? The film jazz singer had Jewish origins, like Kreisler, Mendelssohn, and Jolson, and, as is attested by the record collections of numerous grandfathers—mine and the protagonist's of Clifford Odets's *Awake and Sing*, for instance—the Italian, Caruso, was also an idol in immigrant Jewish households. The Owl Jolson cartoon subsumed immigrant popular music—opera and *The Jazz Singer*'s cantorial chants—under a European elite label. What took the place of foreign influence, in the cartoon as in the first talking picture, was the sound of the man known as "the mammy singer."

"Uncle Sammy" merged the patriotic icon of Uncle Sam with a familiar figure in American Jewish families—I had one—Uncle Sammy. But that hybridization, too ethnic for universal American appeal, was just another sign of Jolson's foundering for an audience in the 1930s: "Uncle Sammy" was New York provincial.[1] Jolson's act of genius was to gather immigrant Jews and other Americans together under Uncle Sam's banner by invoking a second patriotic icon. Appearing in her Jewish incarnation in the plot of *The Jazz Singer*, she is named in the song Jolson sings in blackface to climax and end the film: "My Mammy."

"The 'mammy' of whom we have so often heard," as NAACP founder, Mary White Ovington, called the African American mother, nursed the master's child as well as her own. In domestic service in millions of American homes (the percentage of black women in paid employment was several times higher than that of whites, and the difference for mothers was even greater), "mammy" bestowed "her loving care" on other families at the expense of "her own offspring"; indeed, Ovington attributed the higher infant mortality rate among African Americans to the fact that "mothers who go out to day's work are also unable to nurse their babies." Even if Ovington's specific interpretation was distorted by progressive maternalism, she understood that "mammy" nurtured whites—that is, supplied material support and a symbolic, imagined community—at the expense of blacks. She knew, too, that the mammy of unconditional love was actually a domestic worker (not least in urban, Jewish households); that forcing her to compensate for immigrant family rupture effaced the distinctive maternal losses imposed by slavery; and that desexualization was the price the black mother paid for public acceptance. Ovington understood that the condition for displays of interracial intimacy was the color line.[2]

Segregation was only half of white supremacy, however, for it coexisted alongside racial cross-dressing. A single image inspired the present

Figure 1.1. Al Jolson sings "My Mammy" in *The Jazz Singer*. Courtesy of the Academy of Motion Picture Arts and Sciences. © 1927 by Warner Bros.

study: Al Jolson, born Jakie Rabinowitz in *The Jazz Singer* and reborn as Jack Robin, singing "My Mammy" in blackface to his immigrant Jewish mother (fig. 1.1). How could blacking up and then wiping off burnt cork be a rite of passage from immigrant to American? To whose mother is the man born in the Old World Pale of Jewish Settlement really singing? "My Mammy" forces us to consider these questions by condensing into a single figure the structures of white supremacist racial integration that built the United States: black labor in the realm of production, interracial nurture and sex (the latter as both a private practice and a unifying public prohibition) in the realm of reproduction, and blackface minstrelsy in the realm of culture.

Minstrelsy was the first and most popular form of mass culture in the nineteenth-century United States. Blackface provided the new country with a distinctive national identity in the age of slavery and presided over melting-pot culture in the period of mass European immigration. While blackface was hardly the only distinctively American cultural form, even in black-white relations and especially for African Americans, it was a dominant practice and it infected others. My subject—for one cannot study everything—is its place in motion pictures. Minstrelsy claimed to speak for both races through the blacking up of one. Jolson's blackface "My Mammy," in the service of Americanizing immigrants, pretended to the absence of conflict between black and white.

After "My Mammy" and a montage of Jolson's other hits opens *The*

Singing Kid, Jolson cheers for Uncle Sammy and his mammy on one New York rooftop as the black bandleader Cab Calloway joins in on another. The separate-but-equal verses on separate-but-equal skyscrapers illustrate Jolson's awkward efforts to incorporate actual African Americans into his 1930s films. The trouble arose not from the question of just whose mammy he was singing about, since segregation was already the long-established tool of racial harmony. By the 1930s, however, whites in blackface were giving way to African American motion picture actors. What disturbs the films where Jolson performs alongside African Americans is that he continues to appear in the burnt cork that had raised him to stardom. The presence of Jolson among the people he was supposedly representing better than they could represent themselves split in two the blackface figure of American unity.

No such problem troubled *The Jazz Singer*. With Jolson cheering for "my mammy" and Uncle Sam, blackface as American national culture Americanized the son of the immigrant Jew. In his 1914 afterword to *The Melting Pot*, a play about Jewish-gentile intermarriage that fixed its title on the United States, Israel Zangwill explained, "However scrupulously and justifiably America avoids physical intermarriage with the negro, the comic spirit cannot fail to note the spiritual miscegenation which, while clothing, commercialising, and Christianising the ex-African, has given 'rag-time' and the sex-dances that go to it, first to white America and thence to the whole white world."[3] Zangwill was naming the exclusion unthinkingly exposed by Fred Allen in the epigraph to this chapter when he listed "blackface" and not black performers among the Irish, Jewish, German, and other vaudevillians allowed to perform under the sign of their own ethnicities. Absent in substance, African Americans made their contribution in spirit. And "spiritual miscegenation" between black and Jew not only appealed to mother; it also sacramentalized under burnt cork the earthly miscegenation between Jewish son and his once taboo object of desire. For the jazz singer was marrying outside his community the figure still "scrupulously and justifiably" forbidden to African American men: the all-American (to distinguish her from mammy) "girl."

II

Jump forward half a century from "Uncle Sammy and my mammy." In mid-November 1993, perhaps in anticipation of Thanksgiving, both *Time* and *Newsweek* published cover stories on the problem of race in the United States. The *Time* cover, visualizing anxiety over the new immigration, placed photographs of real people of various nationalities—"Middle Eastern, Italian, African, Vietnamese, Anglo-Saxon, Chinese, Hispanic"—across the top and down the side of the cover, women along the *x* and men along the *y* axes of a chromosome-linked graph. Computer software, known as "Morph" (for Metamorphosis 2.0), produced at the meeting points of the graph axes a simulation of the results of extensive intermarriage. *Time*'s cover girl, her large image superimposed on the forty-nine small ones (adding up to the number of states in the Union), represented the all-American synthesis.

What might seem a bold depiction of miscegenation in the new melting pot was, however, doubly contaminated. For one thing, the pictorialization of distinctive national origins was a throwback to nineteenth-century theories of pure racial types. Just as earlier "scientific" racism gave precise numerical values to brain size and facial bone structure, so *Time* produced a "new face of America" that was "15% Anglo-Saxon, 17.5% Middle Eastern, 17.5% African, 7.5% Asian, 35% Southern European, and 7.5% Hispanic."[4] This mathematics was doubly imaginary, since the percentages bore no relation to any actual or prospective distribution of nationality groups in the United States.

Time's foray into computer dating might seem to indicate approval of the miscegenation that scientific racism condemned, for the magazine's art directors confessed to falling in love with the cover girl they had created. However—second problem—the price of the attraction was a similar look across all the supposedly different nationalities. In the enlarged living-color chart inside the magazine, all forty-nine faces, even the real people born before computer sex, are rendered in polite, pastel shades of light yellow-brown. (Choosing original pure types of the same, youthful age intensifies the sameness displayed in the name of variety.) Not only are the two photographed "Africans" close in color to the un-morphed Asians, Hispanics, and Anglo-Saxons, but their features are Caucasian as well. The *Time* table not only whitens its Africans; it blots out the two largest racial minorities in the United States by subsuming (dark-skinned) Latinos under "Hispanic" and including no one labeled African American at all. The intermarriage chart purifies African Americans in words (by calling them Africans) as it eliminates the dark majority in images. (They would return in the infamous darkening—blacking up—of O. J. Simpson's face on the *Time* cover half a year later.)[5]

Celebrating the melting pot by whitening its blacks, *Time* is inadvertently faithful to the historic character of assimilation. Since well before *The Melting Pot* and *The Jazz Singer*, marriage across ethnic and religious lines has symbolized the making of Americans. African Americans were excluded from that process, however, legally as well as symbolically: twenty-four states forbade white-and-black intermarriage until the 1967 Supreme Court decision *Loving v. Virginia*. The *Time* cover responds to the changed legal and moral climate by homogenizing all its peoples of color and making the black man and woman virtually invisible. Nevertheless, the repressed returns in the title *Time* gave to its new melting pot: "Rebirth of a Nation." The magazine was invoking (without, one assumes, full consciousness of its meaning) Hollywood's founding motion picture, *Birth of a Nation*, where Ku Klux Klan punishment of the black desire for miscegenation married North to South onscreen and united immigrants and old-stock Americans in the film audience. In "Rebirth" as in *Birth*, moreover, the inclusion of some people is predicated on the violent exclusion of others; for even after restricting marriage partners by age, color, and aesthetic ideal of facial beauty, Morph still produces monsters—only now, in keeping with homophobic demonology, they are sexual instead of racial. Just as *Birth* invented and then lynched a black rapist beast, so Morph generated, and its programmers destroyed, a grotesque alter ego of the cover girl, "a distinctively feminine face—sitting atop a masculine neck and hairy chest." *Time*'s jokey, eugenic-inflected elimination of the monstrous birth stands in for the unacknowledged racial cleansing.[6]

Newsweek made up for *Time*'s erasure of African Americans by illustrating its contemporaneous cover story, "The Hidden Rage of Successful Blacks," with a wary, scowling African American man half hidden behind a smiling black mask. *Newsweek* was showing that blacks were still forced to don blackface, to minstrelize themselves to ward off white retaliation. In giving voice in the issue to several African Americans, *Newsweek* advanced well beyond *Time*.[7] One would not know from the *Newsweek* cover, however, that historically blackface permeated American culture in performances not by blacks, but by whites. Even as *Time* and *Newsweek* made visible, they also falsely separated miscegenation from racial cross-dressing. When these are put back together, the newsmagazine covers expose what they separately covered over: in the making of American national culture, whites in blackface acted out a racially exclusionary melting pot.

Newsweek did feature on an inside page a white man under burnt cork, Ted Danson, who had blacked up at a roast for his then companion, the African American movie star Whoopi Goldberg. Danson's "blackface thing," in the words of Karen Grigsy Bates, his belief that it would be funny to become "a living stereotype that has haunted African Americans for a century," generated near-universal condemnation. Unremarked upon was that Goldberg's stage name was taken from Eddie Cantor's title song, "Making Whoopee," of his Jewish blackface film.[8]

Danson and Goldberg (she wrote his lines) mistakenly thought they could get away with blacking up to mock (or were they exploiting?) racial and sexual stereotypes. The actress's reappropriation of blackface, like her interracial romance, may seem like racial progress. So, too, does the movie that cast Danson with Goldberg, *Made in America,* whose miscegenation theme was forbidden to the screen before the civil rights revolution. Even more up-to-date was the plot device that brings Whoopi and Ted together in the first place: Whoopi's daughter's apparent discovery that a white man was her mother's anonymous sperm donor. Like other recent movies, *Made in America* capitalizes on both the continuing frisson over interracial sex and the enlistment of romance in the quest for racial harmony. But just as *Time*'s computer dating simulation endorses miscegenation by separating it from sex, so *Made in America* celebrates interracial sex by cutting it off from reproduction. The movie that seems to be making fun of the mother's belief that black pride requires racial purity ends up by granting her wish. Although the daughter's search for her biological father allows Ted to "make" her mother, in one meaning of the title, the daughter turns out to be made in America by a black sperm donor after all. Uncle Sam may have moved beyond spiritual miscegenation with the black mother, but he manages to provide the black mother and child with the necessary surrogate white father without violating racial descent.[9]

Made in America brings up-to-date the film tradition, once highly visible and now mostly forgotten, that is the subject of this book. The movie's title is a quadruple entendre, alluding not only to sex, babies, and melting-pot patriotism but also to the product for sale, *Made in America* itself, racialized entertainment as commodity. Blackface and miscegenation were also selling *Time* and *Newsweek,* as they had sold mass culture from its American origins. A sales campaign of the 1993 holiday season capitalized similarly on the "made in America" theme. "We hold these truths to be self-evident," declared a seductive female radio voice, "that all men are created equal, that they are endowed by their creator with certain inalienable rights. Those are life, liberty, and the pursuit of happiness. America built a nation around this idea. Leave it to Club Med to build a vacation around it."[10]

Using the American creed to sell vacations may seem like a perversion of the Declaration of Independence. To be sure, Club Med was more politically enlightened than the founding fathers. When the ad repeated Jefferson's words a second time, it added "and women" to "all men." The female voice-over was promising other women that they, too, could pursue happiness and not just occupy the object-of-pursuit position. Spoken as a female come-on, however, the inclusion of women appears a further profanation, sexualizing as the voice commodifies the sacred text. But the unspoken in the Club Med ad—what is displayed on the *Time* and *Newsweek* covers—brings the copy closer to the original. The Declaration of Independence demanded freedom for a nation built on slavery. Club Med promises mostly upscale white Americans service, to be delivered by—in their native habitats—mostly third world peoples of color. Instead of dismissing the Club Med ad, let it transport us back to Independence Hall.

The racialized foundations of the United States erupt on the surface of the three drafts of the Declaration of Independence. The Declaration has now been rendered a visibly hysterical text by the editors of Jefferson's autobiography (in which Jefferson included the Declaration), who use three typefaces to distinguish between the passages of Jefferson's original that remain in the final document, those excised by the convention, and those added to Jefferson's version. Although the entire Declaration shows the marks of multiple authorship, only the section on slavery is made incoherent by their omnipresence. Jefferson himself sought to blame the king of England for inflicting slavery and the slave trade on the colonies, although the crown's effort to regulate the trade in slaves, sugar, rum, and molasses was actually a cause of the Revolution. But Jefferson's displacement of the crime was too antislavery for other southern delegates, and the final version retains only the accusation against George III of inciting slave insurrection.[11]

The Declaration of Independence, as its multiple drafts expose, bequeathed a Janus-faced legacy to the new nation: the logic (as in the Club Med ad) that the equality to which white men were born could be extended to women and slaves, and the foundation of white freedom on black servitude. Slavery's deep embeddedness in the United States produced the Declaration's slide from condemning slavery for inflicting bondage to blaming slaves for demanding freedom. And—it will come as no surprise to readers of *Time* and viewers of *Made in Amer-*

ica—as that reversal infected Jefferson himself, it took a sexualized turn. Jefferson's *Notes on Virginia* appended to his proposal to emancipate slaves speculations on the natural inferiority of Africans. Because black men desired white women, wrote Jefferson, they could not be freed without "staining the blood" of their former masters.[12] Although the father of the Declaration favored returning slaves to Africa, his twin policies of segregation—the removal of Indians as well as slaves—worked only in Indian policy. Jefferson's wish to "remove [blacks] beyond the reach of mixture," conflicting as it did with actual white dependence on African Americans, issued forth in a quadruple fantasy: that interracial sex was a barrier to emancipation, that it stained blood, that it was driven by black and not white practices, and that colonization in Africa could solve the problem.

Slave owners like Jefferson—including his own father-in-law and nephew, and likely Jefferson himself—produced children whose condition followed that of their slave mothers. Claiming that it was the black desire for white that required the separation of the races, Jefferson inverted a white male desire for black. In his day, that desire took the forms of labor and sex, chattel slavery and miscegenation. As expressive performance—in the form of blackface minstrelsy—white possession of black would help produce a second, cultural, Declaration of Independence during the Age of Jackson.

Nonetheless, there was always a contradiction between the logic of natural rights and white supremacy. Almost from the moment of its inception in the late nineteenth century, the immigrant Yiddish press began to protest against the denial of equality to African Americans. "POGROM IN PENNSYLVANIA" is the headline Alfred Kazin remembers above a 1920s *Jewish Daily Forward* report of a lynching. Lynchings and race riots, pogroms in the promised land, were, in the oft-repeated phrase, "a stain of shame on the American flag." Consciously invoking the Declaration of Independence, the phrase unknowingly reproached Jefferson for blaming the "stain" on victimized black bodies. Many Jews who were entering the melting pot had their own stain of shame, however—burnt cork—for by the turn of the twentieth century Jewish entertainers were the major blackface performers. And their stain is the link between Jefferson's Declaration and blackface Ted Danson's *Made in America*. Jews in the entertainment business— vaudeville, Tin Pan Alley, Hollywood—were creating mass culture for the immigrant, industrial age. In the cultural production of America, Jewish blackface was playing a role.[13]

III

Blackface, White Noise investigates the neglected roots of motion pictures—the dominant popular culture form of the first half of the twentieth century—in the first and most popular form of nineteenth-century mass culture, blackface minstrelsy. Motion picture blackface, I propose, inherited the function of its predecessor: by joining structural domination to cultural desire, it turned Europeans into Americans.

Frederick Jackson Turner began his classic frontier thesis with the words, "The wilderness . . . strips off the garments of civilization and arrays [the colonist] in the hunting shirt and moccasin. . . . The outcome is . . . a new product that is American."[14] Like the myth of the West, blackface was a form of racial cross-dressing.[15] Current writing on gender, race, and popular culture celebrates the subversive character of cross-dressing for allegedly destabilizing fixed identities. Such accounts need to consider history if they are to carry conviction, for far from being the radical practice of marginal groups, cross-dressing defined the most popular, integrative forms of mass culture. Racial masquerade did promote identity exchange, I argue, but it moved settlers and ethnics into the melting pot by keeping racial groups out.

History, not biology, distinguishes ethnicity from race, making the former groups (in the American usage) distinctive but assimilable, walling off the latter, legally, socially, and ideologically, to benefit those within the magic circle and protect the national body from contamination. Although inherent and immutable differences supposedly keep racial groups distinct, the racial label is a shifting one. Anglo-Saxonists postulated a racial divide between old immigrants to the United States and groups that are now called white ethnics. During the period of mass European immigration, roughly the 1840s to the 1920s, the racial status of Irish, Italians, Jews, and Slavs was in dispute. As anti-Semitism racialized Jews in Europe, however, European immigrants to the United States were coming under the banner of a new racial invention: whiteness.

"No one was white before he/she came to America," wrote James Baldwin. "It took generations and a vast amount of coercion before this became a white country. . . . There is an Irish community. . . . There is a German community. . . . There is a Jewish community. . . . There are English communities. There are French communities," Baldwin explained. "Jews came here from countries where they were not white, and they came here in part *because* they were not white. . . . Everyone who got here, and paid the price of the ticket, the price was to become 'white.' " The differentiation of white immigrant workers from colored chattel, a process organic to the creation of race-based slavery at the origins of the United States, was repeated for the waves of European immigrants that came to these shores after slavery had come to an end. Minstrelsy and Hollywood were venues for that sorting-out procedure.[16]

By transubstantiating the forbidden mixture of bodily fluids into a burnt cork–covered white face, blacking up mocks any claim of division between the personal and the political. Blackface is grounded in mammy, since the nurturing figure that deprived black men and women of adult authority and sexuality gave white boys permission to play with their identities, to fool around. Instead of assigning Uncle Sam to political iconography, mammy to a circumscribed domestic space, American national politics and culture, I will argue, issued forth from the "spiritual miscegenation" between the two. Together they provided white Americans with their imagined community, their national home.

This study examines the conjunction between blackface and Americanization, a meeting that hardly exhausts the multiple significances of either term. I will focus neither on Uncle Sam nor on mammy (though both will often appear in these pages), but rather on the acculturating Jewish male entertainers and producers who negotiated between them. Those figures appear in some of the films we will be looking at; they are implicated in various ways in others that have no explicit Jewish theme. Visible Jewish absence is significant not because of some invisible Jewish power operating behind the scenes, but rather because of the already racialized culture that immigrant Jews entered, which they had no role in originally creating. Part One sets that stage. Parts Two and Three, beginning with Al Jolson's jazz singer, examine how Hollywood blackface helped engender white America.

The Hollywood version of the American story is necessarily partial. With respect to Jewish blackface, it picks up the tale at the end of mass immigration, removing it in both space and time from the polyglot immigrant cosmos of New York's Lower East Side. An ethnography of stage blackface, vaudeville, the sheet music business, and Broadway, or a study of early, New York–based silent film, would offer a rawer, more variegated picture of Jewish blackface than the view from Hollywood.[17] Nonetheless, traces of New York, though we cannot take them at face value, are thematized in Jolson's *Jazz Singer* and Cantor's *Whoopee!*, both made from Broadway plays and both featured in the pages that follow.

Those films illustrate Hollywood's reach: no single institution in the first half of the twentieth century had more mass cultural importance than the motion picture business.

Hollywood's importance in making Americans, in giving people from diverse class, ethnic, and geographic origins a common imagined community, is by now a commonplace. What has not heretofore been noticed is that the four transformative moments in the history of American film—moments that combine box office success, critical recognition of revolutionary significance, formal innovations, and shifts in the cinematic mode of production—all organized themselves around the surplus symbolic value of blacks, the power to make African Americans represent something beside themselves.[18]

With Edwin S. Porter's film trilogy of 1902–3, encompassing the West in *The Great American Train Robbery,* the city in *The Life of an American Fireman,* and the South in *Uncle Tom's Cabin,* the history of American movies begins. It begins with race. Porter introduced national narratives and stylistic inventions into the welter of foreign imports, documentary actualities (real and staged), cinematographic tricks, and unmotivated short scenes of comedy and violence that constituted primitive cinema. Bringing the most-performed theatrical spectacle of the late nineteenth century, *Uncle Tom's Cabin,* into the movies marked the transition from popular theater to motion pictures that characterized the prehistory of classic Hollywood. The most lavish and expensive film to date, and the first to use intertitles, *Uncle Tom's Cabin* was the first extended movie narrative with a black character and therefore, since African Americans were forbidden to play serious dramatic roles, the first substantial blackface film. Straddling the border between blackface and motion pictures, and undercutting Stowe's novel, Porter's one-reeler introduced the plantation myth into American movies.[19]

D. W. Griffith's *Birth of a Nation* (1915) originated classic Hollywood cinema in the ride of the Ku Klux Klan against black political and sexual revolution. (Inadvertently underlining the status of the black menace as white fantasy, *Birth's* two rapists and its mulatto seductress were whites in blackface.) "The longest, costliest, most ambitious, most spectacular American movie to date," its technique, expense, length, mass audience, critical reception, and influential historical vision all identify *Birth* as the single most important movie ever made. *Uncle Tom's Cabin,* with Porter at the camera, derived from the artisanal mode of film production; *Birth* confirmed the period of directorial control.[20]

The Jazz Singer (1927) was the founding movie of Hollywood sound, and it introduced the most popular entertainer of his day, the blackface performer Al Jolson, to feature films. *The Jazz Singer* was a pure product of the studio producer system, a production assembly line that turned out film after film. Alan Crosland directed *The Jazz Singer,* but Warner Bros. was in charge. Finally, David O. Selznick's *Gone with the Wind* (1939) was perhaps the first example of the producer unit system, the method of making films that would come to dominate Hollywood, where an entrepreneur assembled the team for a single blockbuster. *Gone with the Wind* established the future of the technicolor spectacular by returning to American film origins in the plantation myth. *Birth* was the most widely seen movie of the silent period, *The Jazz Singer* broke all existing box office records, and Jolson's blackface sequel, *The Singing Fool* (1928), became the leading money-maker of the 1920s. All three were eclipsed by *Gone with the Wind,* Hollywood's all-time top box office success. Far from playing themselves in *Gone with the Wind,* black actors and actresses were assigned roles minstrelsy had already defined.[21]

American literature, critics from D. H. Lawrence to Richard Slotkin have argued, established its national identity in the struggle between Indians and whites. American film was born from white depictions of blacks. The white male hero of so much of our classic literature frees himself from paternal, Old World constraints and declares his American independence against Indians; white over black, to apply Winthrop Jordan's formulation, defines these transformative films.[22] The alternative racial roots are not arbitrary, for just as the frontier period in American history generated the classic American literature, so American film was born in the industrial age out of the conjunction between southern defeat in the Civil War, black resubordination, and national integration; the rise of the multiethnic, industrial metropolis; and the emergence of mass entertainment, expropriated from its black roots, as the locus of Americanization.

On the one hand, however, the frontier myth was hardly confined to the nineteenth century. It flourished in the industrial age, and its multiple uses made the western the most popular film genre in the silent period and during much of the history of sound.[23] On the other hand, racialized sectional conflict, urban immigration, and mass culture originated not with Hollywood but nearly a century earlier, and their most important original cultural progeny was minstrelsy. Indeed, whereas the racialized character of mass entertainment appeared on the blackface surface in the decades surrounding the Civil War, and later in the Hollywood western, very few movies organized themselves around the racial subordination of African Americans. Motion pictures normally buried their racial foundations in white over black. Romances, melodramas, social-problem pictures, westerns and other adventure stories, historical epics, gangster and detective films, comedies—it is rare to find black and white (in the racial sense) at the center of these genre films. But the transformative moments go beneath the marginal, everyday, African American presence on screen—as servants, entertainers, buffoons. When American film takes its great leaps forward, it returns to its buried origins. Then it exposes the cinematic foundations of American freedom in American slavery.[24]

The racial revelations of *Uncle Tom's Cabin, Birth of a Nation, The Jazz Singer,* and *Gone with the Wind* also point to widely popular but now neglected routine films of classic talking-pictures Hollywood—films like Cantor's *Whoopee!* (1930), John Ford's *Judge Priest* (1934), Mickey Rooney and Judy Garland's *Babes in Arms* (1939), Fred Astaire and Bing Crosby's *Holiday Inn* (1942), Larry Parks's *Jolson Sings Again* (1949), and others that will appear in the following pages. These movies continue and comment on the blackface melting-pot tradition, bringing it forward beyond World War II into the early civil rights era. There, as we will see, the blackface tradition infected race relations films, like *Body and Soul* (1947), *Pinky* (1949), and *Home of the Brave* (1949), that wanted to repudiate it.

Hollywood was descended from nineteenth-century forms of American popular culture. Along with vaudeville and Tin Pan Alley, however, it also added something new to American entertainment: the creative presence of immigrant Jews. Jews—Al Jolson, Eddie Cantor, George Jessel, George Burns, Sophie Tucker—had pretty well taken over blackface by the early twentieth century. Jewish songwriters—Irving Berlin, George Gershwin, and Jerome Kern, to name only the most famous—created melting-pot American music in the Jazz Age from African American sources. Jewish moguls invented Hollywood, in Neal Gabler's phrase. The anti-Semitic pamphlet "Jew Stars over Hollywood" charged, "The motion picture industry has become a Jew industry run by and for Jews." Since Gabler is right, one cannot meet such anti-Semitic accusations (brought up-to-date by Louis Farrakhan, Leonard Jeffries, and Khalid Abdul Muhammad) by burying the Jewish presence in the entertainment business.[25]

Just as immigrant Jews were helping to produce a racialized twentieth-century mass culture in the United States, they also led the fight for civil rights. Unlike adherents of the working-class, Irish, Democratic Party milieu of stage blackface, Jewish activists were distinctively allied with African Americans in the struggle for racial equality. Both civil rights and minstrelsy were ways of establishing an American imagined community, making new identities out of the diverse peoples of the Old World. Supporters of civil rights invoked the Declaration of Independence, which founded the new nation politically in natural right. The historian of Jewish support for black causes Hasiah Diner explains that Jews could prove their Americanness by supporting the American creed.[26] Blackface minstrelsy founded the new nation culturally in racial wrong. Jews acquired American credentials by, in this racially divided society, taking control of the black role. Civil rights descended from what Lincoln called "the father of all moral principle," extending to all those not "descended by blood from our ancestors"—the high words of "that old Declaration of Independence." Blackface staged the return of what the document repressed—slavery—by displaying the racialized body whited out beneath the Declaration's universalist claims. The demand for racial justice extended the melting pot to peoples of color, offering an inclusionary alternative to melting-pot blackface. Instead of aspiring upward to a unifying ideal, minstrels dressed down through hierarchical, racial division.[27]

Civil rights called blackface into question, posing—from Wendell Phillips, Frederick Douglass, and Lydia Maria Childs, to W. E. B. Du Bois, Joel Spingarn, and Jane Addams, to A. Philip Randolph, Rosa Parks, and John Lewis (or James Chaney, Michael Schwerner, and Andrew Goodman)—the most fundamental, politically significant challenge ever mounted to racial inequality in the United States. It would be seriously mistaken, from the position either of misguided sympathy for blackface popular culture or of legitimate disappointment at the shortcomings of civil rights politics, to collapse the differences between the two. Such a declaration of political virtue would be fatuous, however, if blackface did not cast its shadow over civil rights as well, for the two forms of Jewish/black identification shared a common world. Targets alike of discrimination and racial prejudice, Jews and African Americans formed a political alliance. As the anthropologist Franz Boas put it in his foreword to Mary White Ovington's "refutation of the claim that the Negro has equal opportunity with the whites, and that his failure to advance more rapidly than he has is due to innate ability," "The Negro of our times carries even more heavily the burden of his racial descent than did the Jew of an earlier period."[28] Under the conditions of white supremacy in politics and entertainment, though, Jews could speak for blacks but not blacks for Jews. Racial hierarchy placed such pressure on the idea of equality, moreover, that even representations intending to include peoples of color within the Declaration of Independence still often reproduced racialized images. These were images embodying desire, finally, not just repulsion, since blackface and civil rights shared an investment in the other side of the racial divide. Although minstrelsy advertised that interest as racial difference, while civil rights presented it as common humanity, the movies we will look at expose a less clearly divided picture.

Michael Roemer, a Jewish refugee from Nazi Germany who directed *Nothing but a Man* (1963), a film about a southern black family, recently explained, "In the 1960s we felt we could cross these racial lines, that we were all one, and I think we were a bit optimistic." Equally fascinated with crossing the racial line, blackface and civil rights often cohabited as secret sharers. This commonality was not universal, however. It was less characteristic of the real-world civil rights struggle, for example, where—in legal challenges and on the streets—African Americans played significant leadership roles, than of Hollywood versions of interracial sympathy, where they did not. Even on the motion picture screen, minstrelsy does not infect *Nothing but a Man*.[29] As director and self-critic, however, Roemer is exceptional. Motion picture blackface, neglected in so many ways, illuminates the prehistory of the current, widely reported troubles between these two historically identified groups, African Americans and Jews.

Hollywood blackface once celebrated America, and we should not avert our eyes from its country. The literal meaning of blackface—blacking up to play the African American role—as used here subsumes two metaphors. One points to white modes of representing blacks that take the form of appropriative identification. The other includes African Americans who, whether or not literally under burnt cork, perform against themselves for white eyes—although to what extent minstrel roles actually constrained blacks in blackface, particularly in front of African American audiences, is a disputed question. Figurative blackface played a role when African Americans got parts in film and as the modern civil rights period began. But black minstrel roles and civil rights, I will argue, are embedded in the long history of literal blackface, which itself requires interpretation. The view through burnt cork places race relations at the center of mass politics and culture in the United States; it displays the peculiar feature of American nationalism, a popular expression that emerged (by way of the frontier myth on the one hand, blackface minstrelsy on the other) not to free oppressed folk but to constitute national identity out of their subjugation; and it opens up the links that have bound Jews and African Americans together, supportively and problematically, in popular culture and liberal politics.

CHAPTER 2

Two Declarations
of Independence

*The Contaminated Origins of
American National Culture*

I

The first white European in recorded history to black her
face was Queen Anne, wife of James I, Stuart king of England. Blackface occupies at its origins a privileged place in the conjoined histories
of the English theater and the English court, imperial politics and Eliz-
abethan culture. Courtiers had masked themselves as Moors since the
early sixteenth century, as had blackface players on the English stage.
Lady Mary, sister of Henry VIII and the future queen of France, had
worn a Moorish costume, but before 1605, the year in which Queen
Anne asked Ben Jonson to write a masque in which she and her ladies
could play black, there had been no actual darkening of skin. *The Masque
of Blackness* and *The Masque of Beauty* were, notably, Ben Jonson's first
court masques, his first collaborations with the theatrical designer and
architect Inigo Jones, and the first court masques with scenery and prepared text. At the apex of a political system where theatricality was a form
of power, the English court was dramatizing the royal imperium.[1]

Blackface is a product of European imperialism, the material and psychological investment in the peoples being incorporated into the capitalist world system of the sixteenth and seventeenth centuries. Curios-
ity about these new peoples, the trying on of their identities as Europeans
imagined them, was part of the exploitive interaction between Europeans, Africans, and inhabitants of the New World. African slavery is the
material base of blackface. Although England was not yet significantly
involved, the Atlantic slave trade was well established by 1600, underpinning the Caribbean, Brazilian, and Mexican export economies. One
route to racial masking lay in the slave trade. But blackface also grew out
of relations, real and imaginary, between medieval Christians and Moors.
And it superimposed itself on a religious and theatrical tradition in which
masks provided access to states of intense experience—holy or satanic,

19

tragic or comic—removed from everyday life. Masks blocked out mundane reality to reveal archetypal substrates. They also often exposed to ridicule either the figures represented or their representatives. When Queen Anne blacked up, she linked the masking method to representations of a particular people, a people in the process of being subjugated and ridiculed, a people who had their own, sacred (African) masks and who would develop, under slavery, their own form of defensive masking.[2]

Queen Anne's desire to play a blacked-up role dramatized a curious sympathy for Africans, an effort to imagine oneself inside the skin of an exotic people. Ultimately that desire produced, in Aphra Behn's late-seventeenth-century novel *Oroonoko*, a protest against the enslavement of African royalty. Queen Anne could hardly impersonate a slave, but there was precedent for the portrayal of dignified black royalty in late-medieval representations of the Moorish magus. Although the black magus worshiped a white Christ, he retained his African identity. Not so the blackface Queen Anne. She and her ladies played princesses from "the blackest nation of the world." However much their father, Niger, praised them, they longed "to leave their blacknesse, and true beautie to receive." The natural sun had turned them black; King James, bringing them to England, had the power to turn them white. Ben Jonson's masques, produced by the white desire to play black, imagined royal blackness as the desire for white.[3]

Jonson's color symbolism conflated three meanings. In the first, classical and Neoplatonist, the dark desire for light moved the ladies of Niger from ignorance to knowledge. The body of touch, a nocturnal blackness that could not be seen—and that, in one of her plays, Aphra Behn associated through a black female character with the "black ace," the invisible female genitalia—gave way to the higher sense of sight. Night yields "to the light, As Blacknesse hath to *Beautie*." Hidden, mysterious, and invisible, the black hole signified absence (or was it engulfing presence?), the dark continent of Freud's later imperial conflation of woman and Africa. The masque turned blackness into the desire to be illuminated by and for the white male gaze. Sexualized, that imaginary desire of lower black for higher white would move with the slave trade to the British colonies in the New World, where, two centuries after "The Masque of Blacknesse," the father of the Declaration of Independence postulated a chain of lust running upward from orangutan to African to colonizer.[4]

The second meaning of the color symbolism, Christian, "washed white" the *Aethiope*, as the blood of the lamb cleansed English sins. The

souls of the damned in medieval mystery plays were often black, a spiritual darkness that, in its rejection of the Christian second birth, allied
blacks with Jews. In a text that foreshadows the American melting pot,
St. Jerome preached, "You are of your father the devil. . . . So it was said
to the Jews. . . . Born in this first instance, of such parentage, we are naturally black. . . . But you will say to me, 'I have left the home of my childhood, I have forgotten my father, I am born anew in Christ.' . . . Your
bridegroom [Christ] . . . has married an Ethiopian woman. He will
miraculously change your complexion so that [you have] . . . been made
white."[5]

Promising regenerative identity, St. Jerome's salvation whitened Jews
much as the king of England whitened blacks. *The Masque of Blacknesse,*
however, was contemporary with the racialization of Jews and Africans
in early modern Europe, the insistence that their sinful souls were imprisoned in sinful bodies from which conversion could not free them.
Reconquered Spain expelled its Jews in 1492, the year Columbus discovered America, and persecuted converted Moriscos in the next century because heresy now resided in blood and not faith. Slaves were un-
dergoing the same racialization, for by the time the slave trade joined
together Africa, Europe, and the New World, it had created the first period in European history in which almost all slaves were black.[6] In dramatizing a royal black conversion to white, Ben Jonson was looking backward to the medieval magus. Whites in blackface in the imperial capitalist
future would play black mimicry of white to expose the fixedness of black
racial inferiority.

Moreover, the power of Jonson's English monarch, in the third meaning of the masques' color symbolism, exemplified not so much medieval
magic as modern sovereignty. Knowledge and salvation were in the
hands of King James, who, standing for art against nature, "can salve the
rude defects of every creature." His orb of illumination, in a locution
that English imperialism would later apply to the natural sun as well,
"neither rises nor sets in Britain." Blackness in Jonson's masques served
the political art of the king.[7]

Even if it were subversively carnivalesque, or else an early instance of
universalizing human sympathy, Queen Anne's desire to play black was
recuperated for political order. Fitting Stephen Greenblatt's model of
the Tudor/Stuart court, *The Masque of Blacknesse* staged subversion in
order to contain it. Queen Anne could descend so long as she ascended.
Blacked-up characters sank into chaos and bestiality in Jonson's play for
the popular theater *The Gypsies Metamorphosed.* Unmasking themselves

to display the difference between their dyed skins and real "tawny faces," they warned against a depravity from which those dark by nature could not escape. Othello is exceptional in the sympathy accorded him in this era, but, with his gentleness instantaneously turned murderous, he does not violate the rule. The only benign Moors on the Tudor and Stuart stage had traded their freedom for singing and dancing on the pastoral plantation. Presented as arcadian denizens cut off from the real world, these slaves were actually at its material base. When blackface took center stage two centuries later in the former English colony that was now the United States, it had traversed the path from Africa to England, from the Stuart court to the popular theater, to be born, in its own myth of origins, on the southern plantation.[8]

Slavery forced Africans to perform for whites; the truth behind the fantasy that blackface accurately represented plantation slaves was that it mimed their expropriation. By domesticating transgressive desire, servitude made blacks safe for white attraction. Neither Africa nor southern slavery actually gave birth to American blackface, however: it emerged in the early nineteenth century from the new cities of the market revolution. Democratized from the court and the plantation, minstrelsy enacted the urban white desire to acquire African American expressive power and supposed emotional freedom without actually freeing the slaves.

If European blackface points to New World colonialism, the forced performance of black laborers on expropriated Indian land, American blackface emerged from the domestic history that formed the United States. The "cry was that we have no NATIVE MUSIC," proclaimed the preface to an antebellum book of "plantation songsters," "until our countrymen found a triumphant vindicating APOLLO in the genius of E. P. Christy, who . . . was the first to catch our *native airs* as they floated wildly, or hummed in the balmy breezes of the sunny south."[9] Among the most popular of the early minstrels, Christy turned black to white (advantage). Democratic descendant of Ben Jonson, he promoted America by advertising himself. Burnt cork, so the minstrel claimed, gave Apollonian form to the Dionysiac African, making art from his nature. The Apollo who turned the sounds of slaves into music supplied the United States with its original national culture.

The move from the Stuart court to the Bowery stage, from high to popular culture, democratized blackface. American minstrelsy, unlike its European antecedents, emerged from intimate contact between blacks and whites, from actual white experience with African American performance. Did popular blackface challenge racial nature in the name of art? Liberated from royal glorification, did it support the proposition that subversion is more likely to be found in popular than in elite forms? Does resistance to elite domination appear when we turn our attention from traditional political arenas and reconceive politics in broader, cultural terms? Although blackface emerged from slavery, did its play with identity undercut the postulate of essential racial difference that justified white supremacy? Or did the beheading of the sovereign instead spread blackface influence, so that it served not the politics of dynastic empire but the culture of an imperial nation? Did the democratization of blackface liberate it from political control, or rather free it to serve new, micropolitical, racist functions in the service of national integration? If theatricality failed to contain subversion and preserve the power of the Stuart court, what was its relation to power in the democratic United States?

II

The slave owner who fathered the Declaration of Independence bequeathed to Americans a double national birth in both slavery and natural right. The Declaration of Independence, demanding freedom from enslavement to England for a new nation built on slavery, is the core product of that *mésalliance* in political theory. Blackface is its central cultural progeny. The Declaration of Independence, speaking for the equality of all men, seemed to promise that black could turn white. Blackface, organic to America's cultural declaration of independence from Europe half a century after the revolution, allowed whites to turn black and back again. From one point of view these forms of emancipation break down racial difference; from another they reinscribe it. However one turns the kaleidoscope, the popular culture form bears on the making of Americans as much as does the political doctrine.

Since politics and culture do not exist in separate, watertight compartments, blackface calls into question both the dominant liberal approach to the contradiction between slavery and freedom and the two perspectives, one focusing on racial oppression and the other on ethnicity, that have come to challenge it. Liberal universalism—from antebellum antislavery to Gunnar Myrdal's *American Dilemma* and Thurgood Marshall's and Earl Warren's *Brown v. Board of Education*—has employed the promise of the Declaration of Independence against the practice of racial inequality. Slavery and segregation violated America's own principles on that view; the answer to racial subordination lay in extending equality to those excluded from it. "In principle the Negro problem was solved long ago; in practice the solution is not yet effectuated," wrote Myrdal, and while he stressed the resistance to matching practice to principle, the redemptive path, as he saw it, lay through the American creed.[10]

But the very recovery of racial inequality as a property of American society rather than of the stigmatized groups—the acknowledgment that produced *Brown*—shattered the liberal consensus along two fault lines. One, subjecting egalitarian theory to the judgment of racial practice, rather than the other way around, subordinated universalism to racism. Racial inequality was no southern exception outside liberalism, from this perspective, but the very ground of American freedom. Indian land and black labor generated the Europe-Africa-Americas trade that laid the foundation for commodity agriculture, industrial production, and state power. Slavery not only financed and undergirded the American revolution, Edmund Morgan showed; by keeping the propertyless proletariat racially stigmatized and in chains, it also permitted the assertion of natural rights for the white population without threatening social revolution. Worse yet, the Declaration of Independence's claim to equality shifted white supremacy onto pseudoscientific grounds. The same man who authored the Declaration, argued Winthrop Jordan, originated scientific racism as the new basis for sustaining racial hierarchy. Faced with southern resistance (including his own) to ending hereditary servitude, Jefferson grounded slavery in an irredeemable defect in black bodies that neither conversion to Christianity nor emancipation could cure. Chattel slavery, the expropriation of Indian and Mexican lands, and the repressive use and exclusion of Chinese and Mexican American labor were the conditions of American freedom rather than exceptions to it.[11]

The second challenge to the liberal position moved in the opposite direction, rejecting the binary racial division to displace race by ethnicity. In one formulation, ethnic pluralism characterized American social relations. The racial was a special instance of the ethnic group, not a contradiction to liberal individualism, and American history was characterized less by racial than by ethnocultural conflict. From the inverse perspective, the melting pot created permeable ethnic and racial boundaries, dissolving Old World, parochial ties to effect a shared American identity. Nathan Glazer and Daniel Patrick Moynihan's *Beyond the Melting Pot* classically stated the first position, Werner Sollors's *Beyond Ethnicity* the second; beneath the argument between these books, however, was their shared turn away from race.[12]

Both the perspective centering on racial inequality and the one decentering race by ethnicity are blinded by their central insights. Racial subordination formed the American nation, giving racist stereotypes an intractable material base resistant to the liberal wish for equality. Thus white predation was inverted and assigned to colored nature, most famously in the attributions to Indians of violence and lack of respect for the property of others, and in the assignment to black men of laziness and sexual desire for white women. The fantasy of racial contamination names, against itself, the contaminated origins of the United States in white supremacy. Nonetheless, a paradox lies at the heart of the racial basis of the formation of the United States. For the development of a distinctive national identity, the emancipation of the United States from colonial dependence on England, derived not only from expropriated Indian land and black labor, but also from a proclaimed intimacy between whites and peoples of color. The society that developed materially from establishing rigid boundaries between the white and dark races developed culturally from transgressing those same boundaries. Hysteria over miscegenation and the mixing of bodily fluids operated alongside racial cross-dressing. The supremacist elevation of the white above the inferior races constituted red and black as points of attraction. White men entered, in sexual and theatrical invasion, the black bodies they had consigned to physicalized inferiority. Minstrelsy practices what James Snead calls " 'exclusionary emulation,' the principle whereby the power and trappings of black culture are imitated while at the same time their black originators are segregated away and kept at a distance." To adapt Milton Gordon's terms, structural segregation of racial minorities engendered white cultural assimilation in the racial interactions that constituted the dominant culture. Racial aversion alone cannot account for the American history of race-based inequality. American identity was formed as well out of destructive racial desire.[13]

The land, the frontier, and Indian war shifted American sacred history from biblical text to New World nature. The captivity narrative was the first American national literature. Together with other tales of Indian warfare, it produced the wilderness hero as the first distinctive American and the frontier myth as the first distinctive meaning of America. Meanwhile, as Daniel Boone and Leatherstocking were becoming national heroes, blackface minstrelsy was emerging as the first and most pervasive form of American mass culture. Both the frontier myth and blackface enacted triumphs over peoples of color. Both also exploited identification, for the Indianization or the blacking up of the white was the crucial step in leaving behind an Old World identity and making a new. Just as frontier violence imitated the imaginary Indian by punishing native Americans for dismembering whites, so blackface symbolically entered the black body, crossing the barrier supposedly erected to protect whites from black desire.[14]

Analogous to the blacked-up E. P. Christy, Natty Bumppo cross-dressed as Indian and yet remained pure because he was "a man without a cross" of Indian blood. But the extermination of Indians as the frontier moved west restricted "the red [race to] our border," in James Madison's formulation, limiting redface largely to metaphor. The actual darkening of skin in popular theater, however, emerged from and regulated relations with "the black race in our bosom."[15] Since race created Americans, the ethnocultural perspective should attend to racial history rather than substitute for it. Racial cross-dressing turned sojourners into pioneers and immigrants into whites. Blackface and the frontier myth, bringing race and ethnicity together, created the distinctive feature of American multiculturalism: racial division and ethnic incorporation.

The rediscovery of the centrality of Indian land and black labor in the creation of the United States has led to claims about the marginalization of peoples of color in this country and the need to make them visible. That reproach may properly be directed to twentieth-century scholarship, particularly the consensus versions of American exceptionalism during the cold war. *The Power of Blackness,* Harry Levin's classic study of the American literary Renaissance, alluded not to African Americans but to gothic, psychological darkness. Levin had forgotten Richard Wright's reminder with regard to *Native Son* that he had not invented horror: rather, as the classic American literature itself insisted, horror had invented him.[16]

Indeed, if cold war scholarship blacked out the power of blackness, the classic literature certainly did not. "The very manner by which American literature distinguishes itself as a coherent entity," writes Toni Morrison, "exists because of this unsettling presence [of first Africans and then African Americans]."[17] Examining texts in which blacks are at the margins, Morrison's *Playing in the Dark* has been accused of falsely making race central to American literature. Although the view from the margins shifts the center, there is nothing marginal in the Indian and black presences that have constituted high and popular American culture from James Fenimore Cooper to William Faulkner to Morrison herself, from Mary Rowlandson to John Ford to Leslie Marmon Silko, from Stephen Foster to Elvis Presley to Otis Redding. Far from ignoring peoples of color, the white gaze renders them invisible, as Ralph Ellison's novel shows—not by averting the eyes but by staring so as not to see. Focusing attention on blackness protects whiteness as the unexamined given, the absence of color, the terrible void at which, Morrison has reminded us, *Moby Dick* tried and failed to make the country look. Blackface, the performance of the white man's African American, opens the door to the meanings of whiteness in the United States.[18]

III

White men portrayed blacks on the American stage before the revolution as bestial figures of low comedy. In the first native musical, *The Disappointment* (1767), a blacked-up white actor plays the vain, greedy, cowardly role that was already the blackface stereotype. But there was no effort to root blackface characters in Afro-American life until the resurgence of American nationalism in the wake of the War of 1812. The Age of Jackson, which began with the slave-owning general's nationalist campaigns against English and native Americans, combined political and cultural democratization. American blackface is a product of that moment.[19]

Westward expansion, the market revolution, and political democratization engendered a national culture in the antebellum United States. Declarations of cultural independence from Europe—including those of Emerson (on nature) and Melville (on Cooper and Hawthorne), as well as F. O. Matthiessen (on the American Renaissance), Richard Chase (on the romance), R. W. B. Lewis (on the American Adam), and Leslie Fiedler (on interracial *Liebestod* along the frontier)—have all located the birth of our canonical high culture in the Jacksonian Age. While the writers of the American Renaissance were striving for national renown, however, the mass public was devouring sensation novels, reform tracts, domestic melodramas, gothic stories, captivity narratives, and frontier tall tales. The canonized writers themselves, writes David Reynolds, drew upon "a raw and vibrant Americanism" in popular literature to combat staid, genteel European imports. But when James Gordon Bennett decided in the 1830s to "blacken his face" to attract an audience for the *New York Herald* with scandal and sensation, his turn of phrase pointed to the most popular and nationalist form of all. For the Jacksonian period was marked by urban as well as westward expansion. It also gave birth—in the cities not the countryside, among the new working class not the pioneers, and in relation to African not native Americans—to blackface minstrelsy. Like the classic American literature of Fielder's description, minstrelsy was an all-male entertainment form, combining racial and gender cross-dressing, male bonding and racial exclusion, misogyny and drag.[20]

When Arthur Schlesinger Jr., in 1946, presented Jacksonian Democracy as an urban, popular, worker-based movement, he failed to make the blackface connection. But the repressed returns in Schlesinger's paean to Jackson's New Deal, where blackface serves this Jewish historian of immigrant descent as the sign of American democratic culture. *The Age of Jackson* begins with crowds, flocking to Washington for Old Hickory's inauguration, who "went to the Amphitheatre to watch George Washington Dixon, . . . first of the great black-face artists." The masses enjoyed blackface, writes Schlesinger, though "the more high-toned preferred [the] bewitching Clara Fisher at the Theatre." Half a century later, Schlesinger, protesting against "the disuniting of America," might do well to remind himself of what he once embraced as the fancy dress of nationalist popular revival.[21]

Yankee, backwoodsman, and blackface minstrel, emerging simultaneously in assertions of American nationalism, were the first voices of the American vernacular to challenge aristocratic Europe. Just as each proclaimed a regional identity—Northeast, West, and South—each also came to signify the new nation as a whole. The Yankee became Uncle Sam, while the backwoodsman metamorphosed into the western hero of the frontier myth. Both these figures, however, were surpassed in national appeal by the minstrel. Edwin Forrest was, in 1820, the first actor on the American stage to impersonate a plantation slave. Three years later, T. D. Rice, claiming to be imitating a crippled black hostler, began to "jump Jim Crow." Coming out of the commercial bustle on the Ohio River, wearing Uncle Sam's red, white, and blue striped trousers and a blue coat beneath his black face, the enormously popular "Daddy" Rice combined Yankee, frontiersman, and minstrel into a single national icon. Dan Emmett introduced the professional blackface minstrel troupe to New York in 1842, and minstrels performed at the White House two years later. For the next half century "our only original American institution," as one minstrel called it, remained the most popular mass spectacle in the United States.[22]

Minstrelsy's successors, vaudeville, Tin Pan Alley, motion pictures, and radio, did not so much displace as incorporate blackface. Ethnic stereotypes performed in blackface were a vaudeville staple. Freeman Gosden and Charles Correll, white men with black voices, invented the serial form that established a distinctive niche for radio. Their *Amos 'n' Andy* became the most popular radio show of the period bridging the end of the Jazz Age and the beginning of the New Deal. Likewise, white Americans created a national popular music by capitalizing on black roots, from Stephen Foster's "Oh! Susanna" and "Old Folks at Home," performed by minstrels in the Age of Jackson; to Irving Berlin's "Alexander's Ragtime Band" and George Gershwin's "Swanee," staples of the blackface revitalization of the early twentieth century; to Elvis Presley and his successors, who found inspiration in black music and performance styles after literal blackface had lost national legitimacy. Movies covered a large territory in American dream life, and playing black was marginal or absent from the normal studio product; but as we have seen, the four transformative moments in motion picture history were founded on blackface. When the eighth edition of *Halliwell's Filmgoer's Companion* used for its cover the blackface poster advertising *The Jazz Singer*, it displayed the links between minstrelsy, vaudeville, and motion pictures.[23]

In 1927—the foundational date for this book—when *Amos 'n' Andy* was on the verge of becoming the most popular radio show in the United States, *The Jazz Singer* opened as both the first talking picture and the first movie musical. *Show Boat*, the first Broadway musical play (in which the story was more than a pro forma excuse for the songs), premiered that same year. *The Jazz Singer* featured Al Jolson in blackface, while in *Show Boat* Tess Gardella, billed as "Aunt Jemima," played Queenie in blackface. *Show Boat*'s subplot featured one of the two major tropes in racial mixing: the tragic mulatta who tries to pass. *The Jazz Singer* took as its subject the other: blacking up. Warner Bros.' first Looney Tunes animation paid homage to Jolson with a black boy named "Bosco." The most ubiquitous cartoon character of all, Walt Disney's white-gloved and black-faced Mickey Mouse, was copied from the *Jazz Singer*.[24]

What does it mean that a structure of exploitation produced a culture of identification? Three interpretations of blackface bear on that question. The most contemporary, by way of its class-based attention to popular culture on the one hand and its gender-based celebration of cross-dressing on the other, approaches blackface as a protest, however com-promised, against rigid, biologized divisions. That perspective is post–new left and postmodern, in that it shifts from radical politics and high culture to subversive moments in a popular culture traditionally considered nonpolitical, turns to the sensationalized body genres of the expressive lower classes, and ransacks history to bring old forms up-to-date.[25]

The postmodern recuperation of blackface as expressive popular cul-ture challenges the censorship of blackface desire in politically oriented, old left, class-based, integrationist condemnations of minstrelsy. Mod-ernist and radical in their suspicion of mass culture, those repudiating minstrelsy favor political transformation to overcome a contaminated past.[26] That view reversed, in turn, traditional celebrations of minstrelsy as the common people's culture, in one form, or, in another, as the pure product of a unified America. I proceed in reverse, from postmodern cul-tural pleasure and danger to modernist political disapproval to patriotic nostalgia. Carrying back the contributions of the more recent histori-ography, I will argue, far from demolishing the original position, sim-ply turns a positive into a negative sign.

IV

Blackface is a form of cross-dressing, in which one puts on the insignias of a sex, class, or race that stands in binary opposition to one's own. Current attention to cross-dressing, however, derives from gender and not racial studies. There are good theoretical reasons to priv-ilege sexual over racial cross-dressing, since the construction of sexual difference is a universal feature of culture. Sexual and racial cross-dress-ing may not do the same work, a possibility that problematizes the use of gender cross-dressing theory to answer questions raised by race. But where the prevailing historical cross-dressing practice has been grounded on race, then the theory must do justice to the resulting sexuoracial sys-tem.[27] I begin by bringing race to theories of gender cross-dressing, and then turn to postmodern accounts of ethnic and racial masquerade.

An early feminist suspicion that cross-dressing gave men license to speak for women has been challenged by the more recent feminist, gay, and lesbian promotion of destabilized gender boundaries. In the first view, the cross-dresser acquires power over the sex from whose position he speaks and reassures himself about his own identity. In the second view, however, the cross-dresser parodies and denaturalizes the binary opposition. The movement from nature to art thereby empowers not Ben Jonson's political sovereign but the role-players, who, performing their own multiple identities, subvert political power.[28]

Supporters and opponents of cross-dressing within gender studies share a common target: the well-defended, rigidly bounded, heterosexual white male. The focus on gender challenges his place as universal subject; it celebrates boundary fluidity, whether in the service of a community of women or of gender transgression. In the United States, however, white males are the historically important cross-dressers, and their transvestitism operates inside their racial masquerade. Cross-dressing came to center stage not as gender play in a period of growing sexual equality, but as racial play in an epoch of racial inequality. Minstrelsy challenged compulsory heterosexuality with blackface female impersonation and straight and gay homoerotic desire, by making race the enabling condition. With occasional exceptions, those most fascinated by whites in blackface, from its theatrical origins to the present moment (and I include myself), have been white men.

Racial integrationists, like gender-benders, wanted to break down a socially constructed binary that was presented as biologically based. But because blackface was the product of slavery and segregation, a defense of cross-dressing did not emerge from the integrationist politics of race. Nor did racial cross-dressing find favor in the shift from a civil rights to a black nationalist perspective. The relative success of middle-class white women compared to blacks, in the wake of the feminist and civil rights movements, may have initially generated boundary-breakdown theories from within the former group and a boundary-maintenance consciousness within the latter. Nationalism, however, risks postulating an essential black subject, thus reinscribing the supposedly overthrown patriarch within the Afrocentric community. Many black intellectuals now insist on historically inscribed, multiple black subject-positions—as hybridity or double consciousness, as individuals or a people (like any other) composed of more than one gender, class, and sexual orientation. Does the rejection of a sealed-off, homogeneous blackness move one closer to supporting the practice of whites speaking as blacks or the theory that rejects fixed identity in favor of performativity?[29]

Cross-dressing allegedly challenges binary categories in two ways: by locating pleasure in the in-between condition (woman dressed as man, white as black) and by parodying the supposedly natural identity. Cross-dressing is said, first, to signify not either/or but both/and, the "both" pointing to the two identities in play, the "and" to the playfulness itself. Because it challenges the either/or, cross-dressing marks what Marjorie Garber calls a "category crisis." Occupying the "space of desire" at the entrance into culture, Garber's transvestite calls into question the repressive division between man and woman, aristocrat and commoner, white and black.[30]

Liminal figures are often border-crossing incendiaries. But marking a category crisis may also provide symbolic reassurance, mastering the anxiety about mobile identities rather than challenging the social order. Garber shows how cultural prohibitions generate the return of what was intended to be repressed. Brilliantly allying her "third sex" with the third term in the Lacanian system of real/imaginary/symbolic, she argues that the transvestite and Lacan's "law of the father" overcome the splitting that characterizes the imaginary, mirror, stage. However, rightly suspicious of those who see transvestitism as simply the refusal to grow up, Garber does not sufficiently acknowledge in theory what her breathtaking proliferation of examples shows in practice: that repressive, narrow, adult identities and play-acting at the excluded alternatives may be mutually reinforcing.[31]

To point to appropriative desire in cross-dressing is not to espouse an essentialism in which, for example, white should remain white, and black, black; rather, it is to investigate whether racial masquerade may be generated and contaminated by the rigid boundary itself. One sign of contamination, in an analogy with an individual's hysterical symptom, is the deauthorization of the cross-dresser, who comes forward as a ridiculous both/and rather than a dignified either/or. Although both/and sounds more radical and inclusive than either/or, its racial history points in quite the other direction. Slaves were both human and property in proslavery thought; the primitive trying to become civilized was made fun of as both man and animal. Blackface played with that doubleness, ridiculing, for example, the alleged misuse of the English language by African Americans. Crossing boundaries to parody those who crossed boundaries, minstrelsy participated in the both/and of racial inequality.[32]

Parody, as the instance of the savage who presumes to speak indicates, implies constraint perhaps more than liberation. Judith Butler is right to argue that "the replication of heterosexual constructs in non-heterosexual frames brings into relief the utterly constructed status of the so-called heterosexual original. Thus gay is to straight *not* as copy is to orig-

inal, but rather as copy is to copy. The parodic repetition of 'the original' . . . reveals the original to be nothing other than a parody of the *idea*
of the natural and the original."[33] But reveals to whom, one wants to
know, for the contemporary critic may decipher a relationship between
the musical imitation and imitated at odds with that intended by performers or perceived by historical audiences. Since stereotypes hold together the centrifugal forces that would otherwise pull believers apart—the difference
denied between human and animal, for example, or the similarity denied
between male and female—the analyst's ability to identify those contra-
dictions should be confused with neither the creator's intention nor the
mass audience's reception.

Moreover, as Butler has also argued, performativity scripts identities.
It defines group members by the roles they are forced to play. Far from
simply escaping power, performance also operates under its sign.[34]
Saidiya Hartman has powerfully applied Butler's notion of performativity to the condition of slaves, who were forced to perform as minstrels
were not. She shows how the master's demand for the production of
pleasure penetrated to the heart of pain, to chattel singing and dancing
on their way to be sold. From the slave-auction coffle to the use of the
fiddle, slaves struggled to seize and subvert their coerced roles. The master's command performances, in Hartman's analysis, compromised and
made vulnerable black efforts to regain and retain self-expression. Slaves
developed masks of entertainment and servitude to protect themselves
from white intrusions.[35]

How do we situate minstrelsy in this field of power? African Americans may have inhabited an expressive culture that whites in blackface
were drawn to copy, and minstrels may have imitated free blacks in the
first instance rather than slaves, but in appropriating African American
virtuosity minstrels presented a masking means of defense as if it issued
forth from the essential black. Turning masking against its originators,
minstrelsy copies of black often mocked black efforts to imitate white.
The genteel version of white supremacy operated according to the same
punishing logic of mimicry. Encouraging blacks to model themselves on
whites, paternalists trapped African Americans into role-playing. Given
that the African "genius was imitative," wrote the plantation historian
U. B. Phillips, slaves learned civilization by copying their masters. Populist whites in burnt cork followed that injunction—just as Butler's theory predicts—to parody the aristocratic pretensions of the planter ruling class. Nonetheless, they denaturalized class only by reducing the
planter to the low human level of the blackface slave.[36]

"Performativity describes [the] relation of being implicated in that which one opposes," writes Butler. That insight should not lead one to confuse black with blackface performances, however, for the racial cross-dressing mode did not oppose the racial hierarchy in which it, like black role-playing, was implicated. If performance makes caricatures, thus essentializing as well as denaturalizing social roles, it is necessary to ask whether, when, and for whom cross-dressing is a "turning of power against itself to produce alternative modalities of power."[37] Blackface, I will argue, loosened up white identities by taking over black ones, by underscoring the line between white and black.

Drag queens who dress as women and whites who black up call attention to the gap between role and ascribed identity by playing what, in the essentialist view, they cannot be. The inverse form of masquerade opens that same gap by acting the ascribed role rather than the forbidden one. Joan Riviere's classic "Womanliness as a Masquerade" reported on independent women who performed as ultrafeminine to cauterize the threat, to both themselves and male co-workers, of their phallic power. This feminine masquerade, Mary Ann Doane suggests, freed Riviere's subjects from woman-as-body—as black was female in *The Masque of Blacknesse* for Ben Jonson's daughters of Niger—and gained them distance from their prescribed identities. Seeking to be subjects rather than objects, they acquired the same sight that the daughters of Niger gained by turning from black to white. Butler notices the other side, however, the price paid by private role-playing, which neither discredits the performed female part for those not in the know (who include Riviere's female masqueraders themselves) nor obtains the bodily pleasure that would come with full embrace of the "masculine" position.[38]

Blacking up is a public rather than a secret border crossing; but unlike the female masquerader, the minstrel passes down. Those with the insignias of power can play at giving them up, suggests Tania Modleski, without putting themselves at risk.[39] Multiple status hierarchies may complicate a single up-and-down directionality, to be sure; how does one classify the drag queen of color? But s/he suggests yet another distinction in performing identities, that between the costume as a way of life and as a part that can be discarded at will. The more freedom there is to try on different genders, ethnicities, and other roles, the more likely the performed identity will have little purchase on the self.[40]

The more performance scripts identity, the more it serves power; the more the freedom to perform any role, the less subversion in the play.

The transvestite seizure and subversion of power relations by mocking them from within is only one cross-dressing modality. It may share a family resemblance with others. Does it share one with minstrelsy?

V

Admiration and ridicule, appropriation and homage, transience and permanence, pathos and play, deception and self-deception, stereotyped and newly invented, passing up and passing down, class, sex, and race—all these elements in contradictory combination can play their role in masquerade. Because cross-dressing contains multiple possibilities in theory, celebratory accounts must enter history. Yet American history seems to stand in the way. One might expect endorsements of masquerade to run aground on their largely repressed past, meeting their match in blackface. In the current excitement over popular culture, however, the direction of influence runs the other way, not disciplining present theory by past practice, but opening the past to contemporary interests.

Some studies, subsuming racial within more permeable ethnic divisions, make blackface one more example of the play with group identity, that is, the supposed use of ethnic stereotypes to break those same stereotypes down. The ideology of pure racial types is discredited, according to these scholars, when Irish blackface performers mock the white man's vanishing Indian, when Eddie Cantor dons Jewface, blackface, and redface in a single show, when Hugh Herbert, playing the Chinese "Chow Chow," breaks into Yiddish before he drops to his knees in an imitation of Jolson's blackface "My Mammy." Other studies turn the minstrel show itself into the center of interracial attraction. Minstrelsy, writes Eric Lott, was "a manifestation of the particular desire to try on the accents of 'blackness' and demonstrate the permeability of the color line." Blackface operated "to facilitate safely an exchange of energies between two otherwise rigidly bounded and policed cultures. . . . Cross-racial desire," as Lott sees it, "coupled a nearly insupportable fascination with a self-protective derision with respect to black people." That explosive combination "made blackface minstrelsy less a sign of absolute white power and control than of panic, anxiety, terror, and pleasure." Or as the headline over a 1993 *New York Times* review put the matter, evincing even more sympathy for minstrelsy than the book under discussion, "Minstrel Tradition: Not Just a Racist Relic."[41]

Love and Theft, Lott's immensely creative, richly textured study, uncovers within blackface what it had to disown: white attraction to African Americans not just as instinct but as authority. Lott's minstrels, far from condescendingly passing down when they masqueraded as members of a stigmatized group, acquire what George Lipsitz (who withheld his term from blackface) calls "prestige from below." The prominent early minstrel Dan Emmett claimed he "always strictly confined [him]self to the habits and crude ideas of the slaves of the South." Minstrelsy was actually born, Lott shows, at more egalitarian sites of interracial mixing, on the docks and in the taverns and theaters of northern and western cities. The people who originated minstrelsy, moreover, also came from below. They may have been straight white males, not women or gay men, but they belonged to the working class.[42]

Blackface, in Lott's view, is an American carnivalesque, allied to rituals of transgression in early modern Europe. It bears a family resemblance to charivaris, where women on top, ritually humiliating men, temporarily reversed the traditional gender order, and to rites of protest, where, for example, male youths in female dress and blackface defended their communal forests from the encroachments of capitalist enterprise. In the American form, young white working-class men challenged the traditional culture of deference and the class hierarchy and self-discipline of the emerging bourgeoisie by speaking in the accents and assuming the bodies of African Americans. Mocking elite hypocrisy and power, expressing an exuberant, democratic culture, minstrelsy, in this view, authorized a black place to stand. Attentive to African American linguistic and performance practices, minstrels, writes William Mahar, "inject[ed] a vital, discordant, and satirical language into popular comedy." Blackface caricature demeaned its subjects, Lott does not forget, but only under the sign of ridicule could minstrels celebrate (the *Love* in Lott's title) "the long-tailed blue," "the rampageous black penis," and appropriate (the *Theft*) black language, labor, and performance styles. Caricature masked "the surreptitious return of desire," in Stuart Hall's phrase, the disowned attraction that retained subversive political potential.[43]

Lott's interracial solidarity points to class; for W. T. Lhamon, blackface mobilized youth revolt as well. Working-class young men were, in Lhamon's analysis, challenging the family structure, sexual self-denial, and adult role-expectations of merchant capitalists and middle-class families. By borrowing black parodies of their masters, rebellious white youths created, against a European-oriented cultural elite, an authentic American vernacular. Blackface "passed well beyond racist travesty," Lhamon insists, because its primary targets were moralizing women and white men with aristocratic pretensions, not African Americans. The self-control and thrift promoted in marketplace and domestic ideology were made fun of in popular culture.[44]

Focusing on class and youth revolt brings postmodern fluidity into productive relationship with bounded social structures. The consequences for interracial solidarity and generational and class conflict, however, are very nearly the opposite of what Lott and Lhamon wish. So anxious are they to find points of identification across racial lines that, protests notwithstanding, they dwell insufficiently both on the exclusion of actual African Americans from their own representations and on the grotesque, demeaning, animalistic blackface mask. Blackface buffoonery varied widely in content but was flawed fundamentally in form, for the color line was permeable in only one direction. Driving free blacks from the stage, burnt cork substituted for African American entertainers. Blackface took hold in the North, where blacks were free, not because it challenged racial subordination but because it replaced African American performance; blacks themselves entertained white masters, on informal as well as formal occasions, where they were safely in chains.[45]

The myth of the American West provides a useful point of comparison. Ralph Waldo Emerson, seeking to liberate American culture from "the sepulchres of the fathers," praised "the exploits of Boone and David Crockett" for injecting "a new and stronger tone in our literature." These Indianized frontier heroes, like Lhamon's minstrels, rebelled against the controls being imposed on middle-class young men. But the rhetorical aggression of Crockett's generational revolt, Carroll Smith-Rosenberg shows, served not social oedipal rebellion but westward expansion. Although as a Whig congressman the real Crockett opposed Jacksonian Indian removal, the mythic Crockett's western violence boasted of the tortures the frontiersman inflicted not on the fathers at home but on women and people of color.[46]

By the same token, blackface was an alternative to interracial political solidarity, not the failed promise of it. Young urban working-class men blacked up to attack African American neighborhoods. Stage blackface followed these blackface riots of the 1820s, and even if the rioters and minstrel audiences were not identical,[47] they came from the same milieu. Whites put on burnt cork to attack blacks onstage as well as off.

Blackface did not engender a single interracial political working-class alliance. On the contrary, as Lott himself writes, the turn to culture in the working class—temperance and religion on the one side, the expansion of blackface on the other—followed the defeat of labor party and trade union militancy after the panic of 1837.[48]

Politically oriented, modernist interpretations also root blackface in class division. But for Alexander Saxton and David Roediger, minstrelsy marks not the "moment when a possible interracial laboring alliance went awry," but rather the point of origin for white worker consciousness in terms simultaneously of class and color. Slavery "stalled the development of a telling critique of hireling labor," writes Roediger, by generating the contrast between degraded, dependent blacks and manly, independent whites. Artisans facing proletarianization, together with day laborers and unskilled workers denied access to mastery of a craft, turned the republican critique of effeminate dependence against blacks.[49]

Minstrelsy constitutes white worker self-consciousness, for Saxton, in straightforward race hatred. But why would white workers assume, perform, and watch an imaginary black body they merely despised? Whereas Saxton sees only racial aversion, Roediger focuses on contaminated racial desire. Attraction did not subvert domination, in his account, but rather required it. The white worker subjected to a new labor discipline turned the African American into (the phrase is George Rawick's) "a pornography of his former life." In Roediger's words, "The white working class, disciplined and made anxious by fear of dependency, began during its formation to construct an image of the Black population as 'other'—as embodying the preindustrial, erotic, careless style of life the white worker hated and longed for." White workers who attacked wage slavery to distinguish themselves from black chattel on the job enjoyed imitations of the imaginary black at play. Enacting "the natural self at odds with the normative self of industrial culture," minstrelsy retained in leisure-time release the pleasure that had to be left behind. Admiring and expropriating what it saw as African American expressive power, minstrelsy split work from play, tied gratification to shiftlessness, and, writes Roediger, deprived black and white workers alike of access to the collective, preindustrial work rhythms of African American labor.[50]

Instead of flirting with interracial solidarity, white workers who crossed racial boundaries turned against public black events. The carnivalesque Negro Election Day festivals, which whites had once joined under the lead of blacks, succumbed both to white urban hostility toward a collective black presence on the streets and to the free black community's concern for public dignity. Negro Election Days were replaced first by blackface riots and then by blackface minstrelsy. Minstrels who played black were the first self-consciously white performers; "blackface literally stepped in as [a] popular entertainment craze at the very moment that genuinely black performers and celebrations were driven out."[51]

Cross-racial identification may or may not have had its transgressive moments; blackface gender cross-dressing expressed only mockery. Far from challenging rigid sexual divisions, minstrel drag ridiculed women who crossed gender boundaries by demanding their rights. The aggressive women of minstrel caricature made grotesque both female bodily desire and the moral authority of domestic ideology. Opened wide enough to swallow "the long-tailed blue," in Lott's account, was the enormous female blackface mouth. White men masked as black women to display and ridicule insatiable female sexual appetite and the weaker sex's pretensions to independence. Minstrelsy's attack on genteel culture paralleled the classic American literature described by D. H. Lawrence and Leslie Fiedler. White youths, both in writing and on the stage, embraced men of color in turning against civilizing female morality. The difference is that there was more sex in working-class blackface than in the boys' books of Fiedler's America.[52]

Minstrelsy did not remain a distinctive class expression for long, however. By the 1840s class conflict was giving way to national unity. Although it had originated in unstructured popular spaces, where performers and spectators changed places, blackface now swept the country as commercial, scripted, mass spectacle, with a separate stratum of celebrated, paid entertainers. Minstrelsy was maturing from popular to mass culture. The young white working-class men who stole black culture rebelliously to create their own class and generational identities were themselves expropriated in turn. Minstrelsy may have staged the sex and violence frowned upon by genteel culture, but like the Baltimore mobs that spurned bankers to attack free black neighborhoods, blackface performed, in Roediger's phrase, the "respectable rowdiness of safe rebellion." The minstrelized black body in lower-class performance spaces did not set class against class but rather released middle-class men from civilized self-restraint. Soon blackface was uniting the sexes as well. Mark Twain may have scandalized his mother and aunt by taking them to a minstrel show, but they ended up laughing as hard as he did: blackface was meeting with family-values approval. Since minstrel pseudopopulism celebrated not worker against boss but America against Europe, and since its masquerades reinforced rather than challenged racial and gender hierarchies, blackface quickly acquired national cultural status.[53]

Blackface did produce a racial politics, but it was a party, not a class, politics, and it allied white workers not with slaves but with masters. The political party that created, against old-family elite deference, the first form of mass democratic politics was also tied, as Alexander Saxton has shown, to the first form of mass culture. Like the early expressions of independent working-class political and economic organization, blackface was co-opted by the Jacksonian Democrats. Most of the leading minstrel performers, as well as the leading minstrel songwriter, Stephen Foster, were proslavery, Democratic unionists; Foster wrote campaign songs for the Democratic Party. Instead of promoting a cross-race political alliance of black and white workers, minstrelsy cemented the cross-class regional alliance between the white-worker and southern-planter wings of Jacksonian Democracy. Far from representing a failed interracial workers' union, minstrelsy realized the Jacksonian dream of allying the northern popular classes with slave labor. Ethnoculturally as well, minstrelsy's sex and violence fit Jacksonian populism better than Whig moral guardianship. In the half century surrounding the Civil War, minstrelsy mostly served the Democratic Party.[54]

The Forty-niners who crossed the country singing "Oh! Susanna" carried Jacksonian expansion westward. They blacked up the third wing of the democracy, the proponents of Manifest Destiny. Blackface spread to California, becoming immediately popular among miners and in the new city of San Francisco. "The national airs of America," Bayard Taylor reported back, "follow the American race in all its migrations, colonizations and conquests." America's national music, "the Ethiopian melodies," were made in the minstrel show.[55]

The nationalization of blackface registered the splintering of the Democratic Party, however, which could no more control blackface than could the white working class. The Forty-niners who sang as slaves freed by the West had no interest in emancipating blacks; they wanted to preserve California for free white men. That free-soil opposition to the expansion of slavery split the Democratic Party.

As longing for a lost home supplemented the ribald sexuality of early working-class blackface, minstrelsy's appeal broadened across class and gender lines. The comforting, emotional slave, an entirely proslavery creation, counterbalanced the sexual aggression enacted by the blackface northern male. In such Foster classics as "Old Black Joe" and "My Old Kentucky Home," slaves were carrying the desire of mobile whites for a stable, ordered, pastoral world. Foster, an antisecessionist Democrat, opposed emancipation even as he wrote Union songs during the Civil War. But he had composed "My Old Kentucky Home" for the stage, blackface Uncle Tom, hero of the novel that had turned plantation nostalgia in an abolitionist direction.[56]

Enacting Harriet Beecher Stowe's insistence that white Americans imagine themselves as suffering slaves, whites in blackface played Tom, Eliza, and Topsy in the theatrical productions of *Uncle Tom's Cabin* that swept the country in the 1850s. Now blackface was not only embracing slaves but also supporting antislavery politics. There was considerable overlap, to be sure, between the proslavery and sentimental abolitionist structures of feeling, for maternalist abolitionism embedded itself in plantation nostalgia. Stowe may speak for freedom, but her heart belongs to the interracial southern home. The fundamental losses required and lamented by *Uncle Tom's Cabin* point backward to the extended black-and-white Shelby family (sans white father) in Kentucky and to the erotic triangle of Tom, St. Clair, and Little Eva (sans white mother). (Stage productions often condensed the novel by having Tom's crucifier, Simon Legree, destroy the Louisiana polymorphous paradise by killing St. Clair.)[57]

Nonetheless, if some stage versions detached carefree and nostalgic slaves from Stowe's antislavery message, others did not. Stowe's romantic racialism celebrated the black race's emotional primitivism and the African's Christian capacity to endure suffering. The novel that, as Abraham Lincoln told Stowe, caused the Civil War realized the sympathetic potential and revolutionary political implications of blackface. But, by taking revenge on the working-class male bonding at blackface's origins, it did so as domestic melodrama, not male youth revolt, with tears and not semen (to invoke Linda Williams's fluid-based classification of low-culture body genres). Although contemporary feminists divide over cross-dressing, it is no surprise that when racial boundary fluidity served antislavery, it took a maternalist form.[58]

Daddy Rice began his blackface career jumping Jim Crow; he ended it playing Uncle Tom.[59] He supplied the two faces of the plantation darky, carefree and ("Old Black Joe") mournful. Antislavery blackface capitalized on the imago of the feminized black male; Jacksonian working-class minstrelsy offered his negative, the oversexed, hypermasculine exhibitionist. Divided between them was the imaginary past self left behind—passive, dependent, and longing for lost nurture on the one hand, grotesque, libidinal, and aggressive on the other.

Working-class audiences cheered for Eliza's escape across the ice and wept for Uncle Tom. Insofar as blackface supported antislavery sentiments, however, it lost both its masculinist and class-specific appeals. Nor did antislavery blackface survive the Civil War. There were significant interracial working-class alliances in the wake of emancipation, as there had not been under slavery. Moments of postbellum labor solidarity across racial lines, however, emerged not from imaginary identifications with a disowned black self in popular culture, but rather from the success of the antislavery political struggle. Blackface served neither interracial labor rebellion nor radical Republican politics, but rather Democratic Party Negrophobia.[60]

Uncle Tom's Cabin remained the most often performed theatrical spectacle in the United States, as touring companies kept Foster's songs alive for half a century. Far from perpetuating antislavery, however, the play mourned a lost antebellum world. Plantation scenes took over the minstrel show after the Civil War. Like other baroque minstrel spectacles, postbellum productions of *Uncle Tom's Cabin* promoted national reconciliation by celebrating the plantation, on the one hand, and intensifying racial division, on the other. Racist caricatures dominated minstrelsy after the Civil War even more pervasively than they had in the Jacksonian period; these were the years, moreover, in which the female impersonator became the most popular blackface type. Although once again tied to the Democratic Party, minstrelsy appealed beyond it, uniting the states after the war more successfully than had the failed unionism promoted by Jacksonian blackface.[61]

With its own version of plantation nostalgia, *Uncle Tom's Cabin* illuminates blackface's southern exposure. If a Puritan mission or a liberal tradition engendered the United States, as the classic studies of Perry Miller, Sacvan Bercovitch, and Louis Hartz maintain, then the slaveholding South is an exception outside the national consensus.[62] Placing blackface, slavery, and race at the center, by contrast, makes the South organic to American national identity. Seen in blackface and from the South, the United States is at once a *Herrenvolk* republic, where racial subordination hides class inequality, and a capitalist society permeated by longing for a lost, preindustrial, feudal home. Agrarian nostalgia from a southern point of view is rooted less in rural innocence—the yeoman farmer myth—than in the racial guilt of slavery. The Civil War may enact the final triumph of liberal capitalism over the slave mode of production, but it also forms the bloodiest chapter in the continuing combination of American freedom with racial inequality.[63]

That blackface reached the peak of its popularity in the years surrounding the Civil War points not to its affinity with abolition but to its role as a register of race relations. Blackface abolition is the exception that proves the rule: burnt cork contaminated every white American political perspective on race. It also spread to the urban nightlife that, at the turn of the twentieth century, drew the respectable working and middle classes out of their homes and into places of public entertainment. Only in "the world of commercial amusements . . . that straddled the social divisions of class and ethnicity," writes David Nasaw, "could [urban dwellers] submerge themselves in a corporate body, an 'American' public."[64] The blacked-up white body unified the body politic and purified it of black physical contamination. Public sites signified their respectability by barring African Americans or segregating them in the audience as "darky shows" and "coon songs" were performed onstage. Occasional African Americans, like Billy Kersands and Ernest Hogan, performed in blackface or wrote coon songs. Hogan's "All Coons Look Alike to Me" swept the country in the 1890s, although his song sheet publisher, Isidore Widmark, claimed to have improved the words and music before putting them into circulation. That same decade, "If the Man in the Moon Were a Coon" sold over three million copies. "The experience of white solidarity inside every performance," Warren Goldstein writes of the vaudeville show, "forge[d] a newly American identity . . . while building and reinforcing . . . the unbreachable wall separating whites from African Americans." That process, as Goldstein observes, climaxed with *The Birth of a Nation*.[65]

Minstrelsy also spread, once African Americans were allowed access to the stage, to postbellum black troupes in blackface, who provided the major commercial entertainment in African American communities. The great classic blues singers Ma Rainey, Ida Cox, and Bessie Smith all got their start in minstrelsy.[66] The occasional African Americans allowed to perform before white audiences also had to don blackface. The greatest of these, Bert Williams, adopted the persona of the "shuffling, inept 'nigger' " and spoke in a stage language that, he explained, "to me was as much a foreign dialect as that of the Italian." Williams, who amused audiences by putting himself in the spectator's place to laugh at his own misfortunes, stated, "It was not until I was able to see myself as another person that my sense of humor developed." Williams masqueraded as a minstrel black, and one need only listen to him sing his signature song, "Nobody," to hear him turn self-denigrating irony against the viewer. Self-torture was, indeed, the condition of Williams's performing genius.[67] Blacks in blackface entertaining African Americans may have operated outside a self-alienating economy of pleasure. Certainly they pushed the form as far in the direction of Afro-American self-expression as it could go, though the spread of burnt cork to cover those it supposedly represented is hardly evidence of progress toward racial equality. Whatever challenge blackface had originally offered to genteel culture, it defined the United States for natives, immigrants, and foreigners, Europeans and African Americans alike, by the turn of the twentieth century.[68]

Slave narratives, the abolitionist Theodore Parker proclaimed, answered the call for an American national literature; blackface was the nightmare realization of Parker's wish, gothic in the specific sense that it enacted the possession of one people by another. Not Negro spirituals but minstrel songs made up the authentic American national music, wrote jazz critic Henry Osgood in 1926; his examples were Stephen Foster's "My Old Kentucky Home" and "Old Folks at Home," and "Dixie," "written by a minstrel, Dan Emmett, for a minstrel show. . . . The property today of all the English-speaking peoples of the world," Osgood continued, blackface numbers like these "were on the song sheets supplied to the crowds that assembled in Pretoria and Johannesburg, South Africa, to welcome the Prince of Wales."[69] Normalized in its own self-understanding, minstrelsy was neither racially nor regionally nor class divided; it served instead as our unifying, national popular culture. The postmodern and modern critiques of blackface disturb the traditional equation between blackface and the United States not by successfully challenging that identification but by defamiliarizing—as contaminated class expression, as political, sexual, and racial domination—our experience of it. Blackface is also made strange when it is set alongside nineteenth-century European nationalism.

CHAPTER 3

Nationalism, Blackface, and the Jewish Question

I

The century and a half running from the American and French revolutions to the dissolution of the Romanov, Hapsburg, and Ottoman Empires saw the replacement of dynasties by territorial nation-states, which formed identity-giving, "imagined communities." Kinship and personal, face-to-face ties unified the dynasties at the top; national churches, royal and aristocratic families, local administrators, and officer corps loosely connected the third estate to the center. Some nations were created within expanding territorial states, on the English, French, and U.S. models; others struggled for independence against one of the dynasties or—in at least one instance, the Irish—against a state becoming a nation and an empire. New nationalisms disintegrated dynasties, strengthened old states, and created new ones. The emergence of a self-consciously national culture in the antebellum United States, from the War of 1812 to the triumph of the North in the Civil War, was part of this process.[1]

In 1812, when the United States was waging a nationalist war on England and Indian tribes, the Grimm brothers published their first collection of German folktales. The effort to establish a national identity by recovering indigenous folk expressions includes minstrelsy as an instance of nineteenth-century nationalism. Blackface, observes Lhamon, illustrates "the Herderian theory of literary growth up from folk culture."[2] Minstrelsy provided the new nation with its "fable of membership," in Lhamon's phrase, just as the recovery of folk culture, from the Celtic revival to the use of traditional music among Slavic and Hungarian composers, served European nationalisms. Music was a central sign and source of distinctive national, popular identities. At the same time, the supposed folk qualities of the popular airs, similar across international borders, gave the aspiring new nations common origins in primordial,

45

premodern bonds. Johann Gottfried Herder originated the idea of a national popular soul from hearing Latvian peasant folk songs. In a programmatic understanding that joins Herder, E. P. Christy, and Friedrich Nietzsche together, nationalism was born from the spirit of music. When, at the end of the century, Antonín Dvořák, influenced by his African American student Harry T. Burleigh, turned to minstrel music and Negro spirituals in the service of Czech nationalism, he was repaying minstrelsy's debt to the Scots ballad and the Irish home song.[3]

Nationalist folk expressions on both sides of the ocean mobilized the masses to overturn old, deferential, hierarchical orders. American nationalism, however, unlike most of its European counterparts, spread within an existing state rather than demanding independence from it (for with the major exceptions of England and France, nation building preceded state formation in Europe). Nonetheless, the newly independent United States was not a strong state, either in terms of administrative apparatus or as a center of ancient loyalties; on the cultural front, moreover, promoters of a distinctive American identity complained of a dependent, colonial relation to Europe for decades after 1789. The difference between the United States and Europe was that whereas European nationalisms were sponsored by educated, middle-class nation builders, American nationalism coincided with the entrance of the masses onto the national political and cultural stage. The incorporation of the popular classes followed state formation and nation building in Europe. Hence, blackface had more genuinely popular origins than early European nationalist expressions. In the absence of a powerful state and traditional political allegiances, the world's first mass political party, Jacksonian Democracy, and the world's first mass culture, the blackface minstrelsy allied to it, cemented national loyalties in the United States.[4]

Black folk, to be sure, did not perform in the national culture that laid claim to them, but that only linked blackface more closely to European folk nationalisms. For, Herderian theories of the upward spread of folk cultures notwithstanding, it was not rural peasants but dislocated, urban, new men who made the primordial folk into the carriers of national identity. In claiming to turn native music into national music, E. P. Christy was in fact participating in an international process. Vernacular protests against traditional elites and hierarchical status orders proclaimed their roots in an organic past. Invented, recovered, or modified traditions bound together the imagined communities that claimed the right to rule themselves. In Benedict Anderson's formulation, modern media encouraged the populace to imagine a complex, highly interactive social world; members of the nation coming into self-consciousness formed a community in secular time by looking back to mythic modes of indigenous oral performance. Modernization produced both the mass-media means for creating new national identities and nostalgia for lost folk worlds, a longing for the country in the city. Liberated among strangers, city dwellers participated in theatrical performances that at once avoided the eyes of the old folks at home and retrieved worlds left behind. Claiming ancient authority, new men capitalized on mass literacy (print capitalism in Anderson's privileging of the novel, song sheets and the penny press for blackface). The spread of mass media (for blackface, the commercial popular theater) nationalized identity; it was in the music halls that the words *jingo* and chauvinism (after M. Chauvin, a character in a play) first appeared.[5]

Nationalisms that claimed to be popular self-expressions, speaking from the position of an idealized, imaginary folk, were actually the vehicles for new urban classes, legitimizing their right to represent a collective consciousness that could not come from aristocratic or church ties. The dispossessed in the cities were the bearers of a national culture, but one that did not necessarily empower those in the countryside for whom they spoke. Nationalist entrepreneurs constituted national identities by denying differences within the national group, or even by teaching the folk a language that they, as speakers of local dialects, did not know was their own.[6]

Blackface minstrelsy, however, began with one subjugated group, the white working class, mimicking the people below them. Blackface, the agent of popular incorporation, penetrated society earlier and more pervasively than its European counterparts, but that only underlines a paradox: in yet another permutation of American exceptionalism, our national culture rooted itself—by way of the captivity narrative and the frontier myth on the one hand, of blackface minstrelsy on the other—in the nationally dispossessed. American national culture created national identity from the subjugation of its folk.

Well before it appeared in Europe, Benedict Anderson shows, the modern nation was born among the elite Creole communities of the New World. At once united by colonial political centers and separated from the distant mother country, Creoles developed a national, revolutionary self-consciousness. Focusing on Latin America, Anderson distinguishes New World political nationalism from later Old World cultural nationalism, on the one hand, and, on the other, finds that the revolutionary Creole communities made national membership racially inclusive. It may be enlightening to reconceive of our founding fathers as Creoles. In the newly independent United States, however, where state weakness increased the importance of cultural nationalism, nationalist culture was not racially inclusive in the sense Anderson intends. National culture in the United States did not embrace the indigenous and imported peoples of color, who mostly lacked any political rights; it appropriated instead the very process of their subordination.[7]

European nationalists normally demanded statehood for their individual group—Irish, Italian, German, Hungarian, Polish, Jewish—even if their own national claims overrode those of other subjugated peoples. Some national revitalizations imagined local cultural or political autonomy within an empire—Welsh in nineteenth-century Britain, Czechs (for Dvořák) in the Hapsburg lands—without demanding independence.[8] There was, however, one European precedent for ethnic nationalism in the service of a conquering empire, and that exception—Scots nationalism—was the major European source for American national culture in both its frontier and blackface forms.

James Fenimore Cooper's Leatherstocking Tales, the first American national literature, are famously derived from Sir Walter Scott. In substituting Indian for Scots tribes, Cooper was following Scott not in siding with vanquished against victor but in elevating the struggle to the epic scale that would glorify the national history. Scott also played a role in the other interracial underpinning of American national culture, for his edition of Scots ballads, *Minstrelsy of the Scottish Border* (1802–3), was an often-invoked source of blackface minstrelsy.[9]

Scott, who promoted national consciousness in the service of union with Great Britain, invented as well as recovered folk traditions. To establish an ancient Scots heroic past independent of Ireland, he endorsed the kilt, differentiated by clan, as the traditional form of Scots dress. As Hugh Trevor-Roper has shown, however, the tartan was no ancient costume revived for nationalist struggle, but rather a modern invention that served the British Empire. Scots regiments wore clan tartans in the imperial army. Textile manufacturers who had originally produced the plaids for (East) Indian consumption now promoted them for the Scottish home market—just as minstrelsy commodified for profit the alleged music of African American primitives.[10]

Like the Scots ballad and the clan tartan, blackface minstrelsy incorporated a subjugated people into an imperial state. In both blackface and Scots dress, the represented folk served the national identity of their conquerors. Minstrelsy, though, took the process a step further. The kilt that romanticized the Highlanders played to a broad, imperial audience, but it in fact originated and had particular appeal among the Lowland Scots. Blackface began with and spread as an entertainment form of whites. Scots folk culture celebrated its bearers, even if, as in Scott's *Old Mortality*, for example, the fanatical turn taken by legitimately aggrieved Scots justified English victory.[11] Blackface, whatever desire lay buried in the form, assaulted the people through whose mouths it claimed to speak.

As with other nationalisms, the blackface recovery of a lost essence was promoted by an elite and taken from a folk. The racial division in the United States, however, split nationalist organicism into a black past and a white future, a black foundation held down by the white success it supported. Other nationalisms proclaimed racial unity to overcome the gap between representative and represented. Blackface placed racial division at its center. It also enacted the feature that, together with racialism, defined the exceptionalist character of American nationality: the power of subjects to make themselves over.

II

In turning white to black and back again, minstrelsy played with the process of identity change that transformed poor into rich, daughters into wives and mothers, and immigrants into Americans. In a nation of former colonials and immigrants, wrote Ralph Ellison, "the Declaration of an American identity meant the taking on of a mask." Because "the discipline of national self-consciousness . . . gave Americans an ironic awareness of the joke that always lies between appearance and reality. . . . The darky act makes brothers of us all."[12]

Ellison was challenging the view of his friend Stanley Edgar Hyman that the minstrel trickster opened a window onto Afro-American rather than American culture. It is evidence for Ellison's position that the first age of self-conscious American self-making coincided with the spread of blackface. As Werner Sollors put it, remarking on the racial barrier to self-creation, "The concepts of the self-made man and of Jim Crow had their origins in the same culture at about the same time." Before Jim Crow came to mean legal racial segregation, however, it identified the blacked-up antics of Daddy Rice. By jumping Jim Crow, Daddy Rice made himself over into a blackface Uncle Sam. The Whigs and Jacksonians both celebrated self-making, for although Andrew Jackson, the orphan who rose from the Carolina backcountry to the White House, came to personify the self-made man in national myth, the term *self-made man* was coined in 1832 by Jackson's opponent in that year's presidential election, Henry Clay. Among foreign observers and Americans, across regions and political parties, the United States offered men the opportunity to overcome the conditions of their birth. Outside the minstrel theater, though, mutability stopped short for exactly the two unalterable identities with which blackface played: race and gender.[13]

Self-making operated in the marketplace, blackface in the theater. Yet for hundreds of years, the theater and the marketplace were conjoined sites of role-playing exchange. Outside the stable boundaries of traditional social structures, carnivalesque presentations of selves and wares defined the market; it was there that appearances took on the magical power to transform people and goods. Buyers purchased performances; hawkers spun a web of illusion, like actors, to create the conviction of value. As the seventeenth-century poet John Hall put it, "Man in business is but a theatrical person, and in a matter but personates himself."[14]

Role-playing emerged in societies of strangers, where one experimented with new identities and sold commodities by marketing a self as well. The costume that constituted the actor's fetish—I am what I am not—was from another angle the commodity fetish, the magical power of the object to gratify need.[15] Capitalism had its sober, family-based, labor-intensive, double-entry bookkeeping side, but it also melted down stable identities and created heretofore unimaginable expectations of possibility.

As it spread, the conjunction of theater and marketplace broke free of defined geographic spaces to permeate the society. In the United States, where the myth of self-making met least resistance from ancient, hereditary identities and established, hierarchical institutions, blackface was the preeminent theatrical vehicle of identity manufacture.

Performing the self created identities on both sides of the naturalized division between men and women. Marketplace self-making contrasted with domestic stability, but the emerging middle-class family had roles to teach women as well. Mothers, wives, and daughters learned from novels, advice books, and schools to project themselves into new identities and experience the feelings of others as if they were their own. Maternal sympathy, however allegedly embedded in female nature, was self-consciously taught by fictional and nonfictional, written and performed, example. For self-presentation in intimate relations, young women turned to role-playing—in parlor games and theatricals, tableaux vivants, shadow pantomimes, and burlesques. The parlor was a stage for social relations, an arena for self-theatricalization, for the construction and sale (into marriage) of the self. Gender limited female mobility, to be sure, including the right to black up, whereas it (mythically) freed white men. The encouragement of sympathetic identification worked together with the limitations on their actual condition to radicalize some women, as female abolitionists crossed the boundary separating them from slaves. In the name of sympathy, middle-class women sometimes also appropriated and regulated the experience of white working-class girls and slaves.[16]

Whether occupying the perspective of others signified shared oppression or imperial advantage for middle-class women, for men empathy has been identified as the engine of capitalist transformation. The modernization theorist Daniel Lerner gave the term *empathy* to the psychological disposition that flourishes in a society of strangers. Psychic mobility, in his view, "the capacity to see oneself in the other fellow's situation," is the condition for geographic and economic mobility. Freeing the self from narrow and unquestioning singularity, empathy allegedly encourages sympathetic attention to how other people feel. It allows development of "the mobile sensibility," in which the "self-system [is rearranged] in response to the needs of the moment." But since Lerner's empathy serves ambition, since role-playing opens a fissure between the role and the calculation beneath it, empathic concern can be difficult to disentangle from exploitation. To put the self in the place of the other may manipulate other for ego's designs. Applying the empathy hypothesis to Iago's interest in Othello, Stephen Greenblatt writes, "Imagined self-loss conceals its opposite: a ruthless displacement and absorption of the other." A mode that seems to express "imaginative generosity" actually instantiates "Western power."[17]

Postmodern performance has an unacknowledged genealogy in the mobile, protean, modernizing self, and in both cases self-effacement can serve self-promotion. There may be all the difference between genuine concern for others and the Iago/Lerner exploitation of it, but the difficulty of distinguishing the parody from the original fed antebellum anxiety. Americans embarked on the self-making project encountered confidence men and painted women. Competition for advantage intensified the worry about being taken; fear of being tricked shadowed the desire for mobility. The opportunity to escape origins fed suspicion about hidden, contaminated origins. The trickster, tall tale teller, and confidence man were American heroes, celebrated in exuberant, democratic humor;

nonetheless, American self-making brought with it a dark underside.[18]

Seeking forms to play with and contain the mistrust of appearances, audiences flocked to spectacles that thematized trickery. Second in popularity only to minstrelsy were the exhibits of P. T. Barnum, who got his start in racial masquerade. Barnum first toured the country with a woman he claimed was George Washington's 161-year-old mammy. He authenticated her age and status with a bill of sale made out to him personally. After the slave died, in 1836, Barnum replaced her with a blackface song-and-dance man. He rigged contests between the blacked-up minstrel and a genuine African American. When the black man tried to tour on his own, Barnum took advantage of his rival's advertising by preceding him on the announced route with his own blackface impostor. Years later during the Civil War, as if to underline the connection between racial cross-dressing and forbidden sexual desire, Barnum celebrated as the biggest hoax ever perpetrated the Democratic Party's issuance under alleged Republican authorship of a pamphlet entitled "In Favor of Miscegenation."[19]

Barnum graduated to nonracial subjects in his American Museum, but the overlap between the showman's origins and minstrelsy is no coincidence. Both Barnum and blackface spoke, to recall Garber, to a multiple category crisis. Both staged anxiety about the confusion between the fake and the real to break down some boundaries and shore up others. As blackface *form* gave permission for role-playing, blackface *content* ridiculed men who tried to fool their fellows and women who disguised their nature. But the form played with changes, across race and gender boundaries, that were forbidden outside the theater and forbidden to women and blacks. In creating a class culture, minstrelsy was the product of the growing inequality of Jacksonian America. In playing with the myth of self-making, it obscured economic hierarchy while it cauterized, by mastering, anxieties over racial and sexual breakdown. Minstrelsy stood against its negatives, the unsexed masculine woman, the miscegenator, and—darkest of all self-made figures of mysterious origins—the racial passer. Iago's possession of Othello[20] established the terms: boundary crossers were punished for crossing boundaries (Othello's miscegenation) through a process by which others crossed boundaries at their expense. Blackface made new identities for white men by fixing the identities of women and African Americans.

Playing with a range of identity crossovers, blackface doubled two potentially racially mixed identities in particular. One, the mulatta victim of race mixing, fashioned tragedy for abolitionists out of what the blackface method introduced as farce. The other, the Americanizing ethnic, crossed the boundary that, racialized, killed the tragic mulatta. It was Americanizing ethnics, first the Irish and then the Jews, who dominated minstrelsy at the antebellum flourishing and early-twentieth-century revitalization of the form. Blacked-up ethnics entered, even as they helped to create, the American melting pot.

III

Theorists distinguish two forms of nationalism, liberal and primordial. Liberal, citizen-based nationalism, derived from the French and American revolutions, demands self-determination for the people of a territory; based on free choice, it puts politics first. Primordial nationalism demands self-rule for an ethnos united by ancient blood ties; here politics emerges from culture, a culture tied to blood. One form is voluntarist, the other organic. Expansionist citizen/state nationalisms incorporate other peoples, whereas primordial nationalisms expand by cleaning them out. The former can metamorphose into the latter, it is recognized, when the state speaks for its citizens to enforce freedom or the national political will becomes identified with a particular national folk. The Jacobin Terror was one form of exclusion; fear of the alien and hysteria over un-American activities is another. Still, the citizenship ideal in both the French and American revolutions was in principle universalistic and not blood-based, it is argued, whatever the coercive implications of actually applying that universalism might have been. Nationalist racism in France, as in the Dreyfus Affair, stood against the republican principles of 1789; efforts to derive U.S. membership from Anglo-Saxon or Teutonic blood violated the Declaration of Independence.[21]

From one perspective American universalism is more thoroughgoing than French. Ethnically homogeneous, the French nation could rely on an inherited, historic identity, however much peasants would have to be made into Frenchmen in the Third Republic. America, by contrast, was a multicultural assemblage of peoples who had left their original homes. Settlers and immigrants embraced a new identity; they did not inherit an old one. The choice of national identity, the constitution of a nation from peoples of diverse origins, was a particular feature of the United States. Thus, at least, various proponents of the melting pot have argued, from Hector St. John Crevecoeur in the late eighteenth century, to Frederick Jackson Turner in the late nineteenth, to Werner Sollors in the late twentieth.[22]

The tension between consent and descent, Sollors suggests in *Beyond Ethnicity,* lay at the very origins of the United States. The Puritans derived their collective identity from conversion, from spiritual and not inherited blood ties. The shift from the chosen to the choosing people did not secularize Americanness so much as sacralize the choice of the United States. But just as the process of choosing a new national identity began with the Puritans, so also did the backward pull of narrow group ties. *Beyond Ethnicity* breaks down the distinction between early settlers in what became the United States, on the one hand, and immigrants, on the other. The colonists were ethnics like their successors, Sollors argues, caught between an inherited, ancestral, Old World, Old Testamant, blood-based, Hebrew particularism and a New World, New Testament, melting-pot, spiritual universalism. Reincarnating the Turner thesis in postmodern, urban form, Sollors stands with "consent," as he labels it, against "descent." But although he sides with the children, preferring their universalism to their parents' particularism, he calls attention to generational conflict, the loss of the old home in making the new, as embodying the pathos of Americanization.[23]

Replacing the Puritan/immigrant opposition with one between consent and descent, however, gives freedom too large a field. The reason is not so much that, as cultural pluralists and ethnoculturalists argue, ethnic boundaries are less permeable and more long-lasting than Sollors believes. Although Sollors reduces arguments for ethnic cultural persistence to the biologically pernicious and sentimentally absurd (in fact, distinctive ethnic life varies as a function of distance from the Old World, regional isolation, and class mobility), the long-term direction for white ethnics is as he suggests. To call that process "consent," however—that is, to identify it with free choice—minimizes nativist and commodity pressures toward homogenization. Sollors complicates "descent." Rightly challenging Horace Kallen's aphorism that one does not choose one's own grandfather, he shows that one chooses (a relation to and between) grandfather(s); but he simplifies "consent," the other master word of his subtitle, to cover all adaptations to the dominant culture.

Nineteenth- and early-twentieth-century American nationalists, although they celebrated consent, also organicized American national bonds. Heirs of revolution, believers in Christian regeneration, and advocates of progress, they rejected Herderian confinement of identity to the recovered past. Language theorists, for instance, believed that American English combined organic discovery with nationalist construction. They celebrated the creative power of national culture, what Kenneth Cmiel calls "the imperial cosmopolitanism of a chosen people."[24]

That process of national incorporation, whose symbol was the melting pot, operated differently for ethnic than for racial groups. Sollors not only softens the pressures on ethnics to Americanize; subsuming race under ethnicity, his happy consciousness too often leaves both racism and nativism behind. To be sure, ethnic groups shared with peoples of color both racially based nativist hostility and the loss of home. But this commonality did not result in a common fate, for ethnic minorities were propelled into the melting pot by the progress that kept racial minorities out. If from one perspective American citizenship was more chosen than French, that chosenness created a mystic national body that insisted on distinctions of blood.

European nationalists, taking the American and French revolutions as their models, advocated inclusive citizenship until the failure of the 1848 revolutions; they did not promote racially based, invidious, biological distinctions until late in the nineteenth century. In one view, traditional elites moved nationalism rightward and onto racist terrain in order to co-opt popular movements. From another perspective, racist nationalism signaled the defeat of liberalizing tendencies in the Hapsburg and Romanov dynasties. Although racism also became more virulent in the United States in the late nineteenth century, there the racist and universalist moments were conjoined at birth, simultaneous in both historical and theoretical conception. The 1790 Naturalization Law denied citizenship to foreign-born peoples of color. Racial Anglo-Saxonism carried westward expansion from early in the nineteenth century, and the alleged biological difference between black and white was used to justify slavery. An instrument of expansionism, incorporating American nationalism, blackface performed not only the possibility of changing identities but also a dark, racially exclusionary side. American nationalism insisted on the racial difference between those to whom it awarded full citizenship rights and those who fronted for its national identity.[25]

The lap of nature turns Old World difference into New World identity in Crevecoeur's *Letters from an American Farmer*. The farmer's celebration becomes a lament when he faces first a caged black slave hung from a tree and then the perils of the Indian wilderness. Marking the melting pot's failure in the face of Indian and black, Crevecoeur's difference between (as we would now put it) ethnicity and race invokes tragic blockage for the ethnic rather than opportunity. Writing before minstrelsy, he wrote too soon.[26]

Because minstrelsy played with ethnic stereotypes, Sollors rightly sees it as an Americanizing stage. In the hands, disproportionately, first of Irish and then of Jewish entertainers, this ethnocultural expression served a melting-pot function.[27] Far from breaking down the distinction between race and ethnicity, however, blackface only reinforced it. Minstrelsy accepted ethnic difference by insisting on racial division. It passed immigrants into Americans by differentiating them from the black Americans through whom they spoke, who were not permitted to speak for themselves. Facing nativist pressure that would assign them to the dark side of the racial divide, immigrants Americanized themselves by crossing and recrossing the racial line. Their discovery of racial inequality propelled the United States beyond ethnicity by transforming ethnic descent into American national identity.

That process began with the first mass postrevolutionary immigration to the United States, that of the Irish. As workers were developing a distinctive class identity in the antebellum period, the working class was becoming distinctively based in the Catholic foreign born. Immigration more than tripled, to 1.7 million, in the 1840s, the decade in which blackface became American national culture; by 1850, the working class was largely born outside the United States. A majority of those workers came from Ireland. Irish American workers and minstrels, combining appropriative imitation of African Americans with political polarization against them, were the major carriers of blackface.[28]

The movement for Irish emancipation under Daniel O'Connell allied the cause of the oppressed Irish with that of American slaves. But although O'Connell, "The Liberator," supported William Lloyd Garrison's *Liberator*, his politics posed a double danger for Irish Americans. First, the focus on Irish independence rather than the American scene raised the specter of the foreignness of the Irish, of their loyalty to Ireland and Rome rather than the United States. Second, in linking two systematically persecuted, disenfranchised, agrarian victims of Anglo-American imperial expansion, Irish opposition to slavery provoked the retaliatory association of Irish with African barbarians. The British conquest, dispossession, and stigmatization of the Irish had proceeded alongside the subjugation of Indians and the enslavement of blacks. Ever since the conquest and colonization of Ireland, the "superstitious," "violent," "lazy," "ignorant" Irish had been identified with American Indians. By the nineteenth century, Thomas Carlyle's "white negroes" were being blackened as well. Assimilation of the Irish to African and New World savages intensified anti-Irish nativism, particularly given what Protestant nativists saw as their savage, cannibalistic, Catholic religious practices. Responding to the mass migration of Irish to London, Liverpool, and the United States, and to the ongoing agitation for Irish freedom, pseudoscientific racism simianized the Irish. Cartoons giving flesh to racist theories of facial structure turned the Irish into black apes. In a final turn of the screw, northern Whigs combined hostility to Irish immigrants at home with sympathy for oppressed slaves far away. Irish immigrants defended themselves against Whigs and Know-Nothings by turning on the objects of their enemies' paternalist sympathy.[29]

Irish Americans traded in antislavery and Irish independence fervor for Americanization through blackface. Politically, blackface fronted for their incorporation into the Democratic Party, a coalition of urban machine constituents and southern Negrophobes. Theatrically, Irish blackface performers drew on the low-comedy traditions of the British stage. Psychologically—in a process I will explore for Jewish entertainers from the next immigrant wave—blackface distanced the Irish from the people they parodied. Demonstrating their mastery of the stereotype, Irish minstrels crossed the cultural border in one direction so they and their audiences could cross it in the other. Blackface brought Irish immigrants into the white working class, freeing them from their guilt by black association. Of course, Irishness did not disappear under burnt cork, and anti-Irish nativism remained powerful for half a century after Irish Americans first donned blackface. Blackface flourished in the transitional period when immigrants and their children were leaving behind Old World identities and trying on new ones. As with the Jews who followed them (I borrow Jeffrey Melnick's insight), blackface helped create New World ethnic identities—Irish American and Jewish American—that were culturally pluralist within the melting pot. Blackface touring companies, popular on the Irish stage, prepared future Irish immigrants for Americanization.[30]

Irish American minstrels continued to welcome immigrants to the United States through the turn of the century. Mickey Rooney, a descendant of those vaudeville, blackface entertainers, paid homage to them in the New Deal motion pictures *Babes in Arms* and *Babes on Broadway* (see chapter 6). Nonetheless, by the early twentieth century Jews had pretty well replaced the Irish on the blackface stage. (Hollywood portrayed the passing of the torch in the 1946 *Jolson Story*.) The two most successful European immigrant groups in the United States,

Irish Catholics and Jews had in common a pattern of stigmatization and legal disabilities in their countries of origin, urban settlement, extremely low rates of return, and a balanced sex ratio;[31] they shared as well, diachronically, predominance in the entertainment business and the use of burnt cork. In the creation of melting-pot culture during the industrial age, it was immigrant Jews and their children—as vaudeville performers, songwriters, and motion picture moguls—who would play the central role.

IV

The 1938 Nazi poster announcing Hitler's show of degenerate music featured a thick-lipped, black saxophone player, straight out of the blackface tradition, with a Jewish star on his lapel (fig. 3.1). The Nazis were discrediting modern music by blaming it on blacks and Jews. Far from inventing the blackface caricature, however, all they did was change the chrysanthemum in the advertisement for Ernst Krenek's "jazz opera" *Jonny spielt auf* into a Jewish star. Krenek was not half Jewish, as the Nazis claimed; even so, the poster displayed the widely held view, in both Europe and the United States, by opponents and supporters of the new music alike, that a special Jewish/black interaction had given birth to jazz.[32]

The same year, 1927, that *Jonny spielt auf* premiered in Berlin, *The Jazz Singer* opened in New York. Ads featured a blackface caricature no less—and no more—visually offensive than the Nazi poster; underneath the burnt cork here, though, in counterpoint to the Jewish star on Jonny's lapel, was the vaudeville Jewish star Al Jolson (fig. 3.2). Although one poster celebrated the Jew behind blackface and the other damned him, the *Jazz Singer* and the Nazi ads looked entirely interchangeable. But they were not. For whereas Hollywood was advertising Jewish assimilation through black association, the Nazis were racializing Jews to smooth the path to their extermination.[33]

Krenek's libretto had counterposed the author's stand-in, an aspiring modern music composer, to the black saxophonist, the amoral, aggressive black icon of American mass culture. Krenek, contrary to the Nazi charge, was no fan of Jonny's. But the popular music so deplored in the story gave the opera its character and mass appeal. By contrast, *The Jazz Singer*'s sound supported its story, in which blackface frees the jazz singer from his ancestral, Old World identity to make music for the

Figure 3.1. *Jonny spielt auf* poster, Nazi version. Courtesy of the Los Angeles County Museum of Art.

American stage. The intended meaning of the Nazi poster was closer to that of *The Jazz Singer* than that of *Jonny spielt auf,* not just because Krenek was a gentile, but also because the poster damned what was celebrated in the American but not the German musical.[34]

Had Krenek been Jewish, one could have drawn another moral from the contrast between the two scripts. In the period when assimilating,

Figure 3.2. *The Jazz Singer* poster, original
version. Courtesy of Dover Publications.
© 1927 by Warner Bros.

vulnerable Central European Jews were transforming high culture, assimilating American Jews were turning to popular culture. The sophisticated urban European Jews and the masses they had left behind became the target of volkish nationalisms. Speaking in the name of the
German volk, and condemning as inferior races not only Jews but also
Africans, Gypsies, and Slavs, the Nazis exterminated European Jewry.
Immigrant Jews in America, by contrast, revitalized popular culture with
white versions of African American folk productions. Mass culture helped
forge political allegiances to the United States, loyalties whose absence
in Europe spurred the collapse first of the Hapsburg monarchy and then
of the Weimar Republic. Entering the melting pot themselves, Americanizing Jews were bringing with them the nationality groups that, in
Central Europe, were turning against both the state and the Jews.

As the Austro-Hungarian Empire disintegrated under the pressure of rival nationalisms, the United States was incorporating those same nationalities into a shared American identity. Whereas the particularist Central European nationalisms extolled primordial blood ties, American nationalism celebrated the spirit. Woodrow Wilson, about to preside over the dissolution of the Hapsburg Empire, explained to a group of newly naturalized immigrants that in other countries loyalty was to the past; Americans, giving up their homes for their ideals, looked to the future. The Hungarian historian Oscar Jaszi, opposing the Magyar suppression of Slavic nationalities, also held up the American alternative, where, as he saw it, old ethnoses were combining to form a new nation. The comparison was in part misplaced, for Jaszi overlooked both the similarity between American nativism and Magyarization, and the difference between population concentrations rooted in a fragmenting dynasty, on the one hand, and smaller, relatively isolated, immigrant communities breaking down in a dynamically growing country, on the other. Setting the United States alongside the Hapsburg Empire, however, throws into relief two other points of comparison between the multinational states: the terms of Jewish assimilation, and the place of the Slavic and ex-slave folk.[35]

Jews in Austrian Galicia and Moravia, the Kingdom of Poland, and the Russian Pale of Settlement occupied a precarious, middleman place, petty traders uneasily situated between backward peasantries and dynastic empires. Lacking a secure social position, Central European Jews identified with the state. Situated among linguistic minorities, they served as intermediaries between local populations and imperial representatives. Small numbers of court and "exception" Jews in the larger cities, working as state financiers, estate managers, and industrializing capitalists, prospered from special privileges granted by the Kingdom of Poland and Lithuania, until its dismemberment, and by the Hapsburg monarchy. Assimilating Jews also looked to the center or dominant state power for security, rather than to their neighbors (the condition to which Kafka's *Castle* was a response); they communicated in German (or, in Budapest, Hungarian), even when surrounded (as in Prague) by Slavic speakers. Within the shtetls and small cities of East-Central Europe, scattered among peasant, linguistic minorities, wealthier, more assimilated Jews served as cultural and economic outposts of the big national cultures, German, Hungarian, and Russian. Jewish journalists and writers were the main exponents of Austro-German culture and a primary cement of the empire. Even after the dual monarchy's liberal period ended in the late nineteenth century, Jews preferred the Hapsburgs to adherents of the anti-Semitic volkish nationalisms. In Russia, although the czarist government persecuted its Jewish minority, and although the Russification movement among assimilating Jews ran up against state anti-Semitism, particularly after the assassination of Alexander II in 1881, nonetheless Russian Jews continued to find their way to the universities and to Russian (rather than Polish or Ukrainian) culture and politics.[36]

Court and "exception" Jews sought protection from the state for themselves as individuals, and often represented traditional Jewish communities as well. Assimilating Jews, though, children of the Enlightenment, repudiated their privileged individual status and communal religious ties; they looked forward to equal citizenship rights and full membership in a liberal state. Jewish emancipation and European liberalism rose together. They fell together, too. The triumph of anti-Semitism and of the forces opposed to liberalism in Europe contrasts sharply with liberal successes and Jewish assimilation in the United States. Jews freed themselves from their shtetl Jewish and anti-Semitic past in the United States, whereas in Europe the past returned in the service of modern anti-Semitism to destroy them. As the target of hate-mongering, primordial nationalisms, Central European Jews were unable to bridge the gap between the state and the volk. Identified with the state but without political power, Jews fell victim to antistate, expansionist racism.[37]

Once the Hapsburg monarchy took an illiberal and (from the Jewish though not the subjugated nationalities perspective) pro-Slavic turn, assimilating Jewish youths, like their counterparts in czarist Russia, turned to Socialism. Jewish Socialists, identified with pariah groups rather than with the dynastic state, united workers of all nationalities. Socialism played a cosmopolitan, integrative role alternative to the dynastic structure of political rule, on the one hand, and the disintegrative nationalisms, on the other. The Socialist and Communist movements of Central and Eastern Europe constituted the major political effort to overcome nationalist xenophobia and incorporate separate peoples into a single political community.[38]

Jews played a disproportionately large role in left-wing movements in both Europe and the United States. Yet although the left was far stronger in Central Europe than in the United States, it fell before the even more powerful anti-Semitic right. National Socialist attacks on Judeobolshevism brought that party to power. The greater strength of American than European liberalism may have disadvantaged the Socialist left, but it also protected the Jews.

Not the sway of American liberalism alone, however, but also two other contrasts between Europe and the United States explain why the citizenship ideal protected American Jews better than their European counterparts. First, in the United States African Americans substituted for Jews as the dominant targets of racial nationalism. The expansion of legal equality, marked by the end of slavery in the United States and Jewish emancipation in Europe, produced a racist reaction on both continents. As legal and historical group distinctions began to dissolve, biological racism took their place. Theories of Caucasian racial supremacy equally stigmatized Jews and blacks, but the extent and salience of the race hatred directed at the two groups divided the New World from the Old.[39]

As mediators in the shtetls and assimilating boundary-crossers in the cities, Jews were targets for those disrupted by the breakdown of segmentary imperial societies, the markers and victims of Garber's category crisis—the role that, as we have seen, was played in the United States by African Americans. To construct a purified volkish nationalism from the urban mob, Hitler hit on Jews. Disgusted initially by the Viennese proletariat, he made an encounter he had with a Jew—"that is no German"—the explanation for the diseased Viennese social body and the point of origin for National Socialism. He could love the German people only once he hated Jews. Anti-Semitism united the disparate nationalities and classes of Central Europe. "When immigrants came to Vienna," writes Steven Beller, "they could hide behind the picture of the Jew as an outsider and thus see themselves on the inside. Although many Viennese might really be 'entnationalisiert' Czechs, they shared with other Viennese the anti-Semitism native to Austrian, Ruthenian, Hungarian, and Polish society where they had originated."[40] That process brought to power not only the anti-Semitic mayor of Vienna, Karl Lueger, but also the anti-Semitic immigrant from the Austrian countryside first to Vienna and then to Germany, Adolf Hitler.

Whereas Jewish outsiders created immigrant insiders in the Hapsburg Empire and the Weimar Republic, in the United States African Americans performed that function. European Jews had lived in legally demarcated ghettos segregated from the surrounding population. If a ghetto is defined as a neighborhood inhabited exclusively by members of a single group and in which virtually all the members of that group live, European immigrant ghettos never truly existed in the United States. The people who came to be ghettoized—who had to be stopped from changing their identities, from passing, integrating, and assimilating—were blacks rather than Jews.[41]

At the turn of the twentieth century, Vienna was the only European capital with an elected anti-Semitic mayor. The United States, by contrast, regularly elected racist mayors, governors, senators and congressmen, and even presidents. But the wish to make America *negerfrei*—a staple of American fantasy even among those opposed to slavery—although comparable to assimilationist and exterminatory solutions to the Jewish question in Europe, ran up against the insider status of black Americans, their necessity in labor and culture. Jewface could front for no nationalism in Europe; even Zionism repudiated diaspora Yiddishkeit. Blackface served nationalism in the United States. Moreover, although Hitler praised the American achievement of *Lebensraum* (by expansion against Indians), the racially exclusionary basis of American citizenship, and the race-based, restrictive 1924 U.S. immigration act, his rejection of what he stigmatized as the Viennese "melting pot" in favor of Aryan racial purity contrasts with the use of blackface in the service of the American melting pot.[42] It was not just that antiblack racism replaced anti-Semitism as the badge of belonging in the United States, but that the badge was worn as blackface, and often by Jews.

That points to the second difference between Central Europe and the United States, namely, the Jewish role in modern culture. Even as their state identification was failing to protect European Jews, in the United States immigrant Jews were Americanizing themselves through their place in popular entertainments. On both continents, Jews proposed cultural and political assimilation, social equality as well as citizenship rights. They worked as cultural and economic middlemen, disproportionately important not only in trade but also in the liberal professions and image-making businesses—newspapers, book publishing, broadcasting, the apparel industry, and motion pictures. (The latter three were the only major American industries in the 1930s that had Jews among the top executives.) As with other diaspora communities in other lands, the occupational structure of American Jews was skewed toward commerce, service, and intellectual exchange—middlemen occupations. But Americanizing Jews were not therefore a sojourner people exploiting those among whom they lived, the charge sometimes leveled against middlemen minorities. With no home to return to, this diaspora people creatively identified its fate with its new homeland.[43]

European Jews were not a sojourner minority either, neither as *ostjuden* in the shtetls nor as assimilating *westjuden* in the cities. It was the duty of Jews to "melt into" the surrounding culture, argued the Viennese Jew Theodore Gomperz. In Israel Zangwill's play *The Melting Pot*, which is set in the United States, a Jewish grandfather and a czarist anti-Semite resist the marriage of their offspring. In *Zwischen Ruinen,* by the Austrian Jew Leo Kumpert, a Catholic priest and a fanatical Hasid oppose intermarriage. Both Zangwill and Kumpert make intermarriage the vehicle of assimilation. But whereas "integration into the full cultural life of the whole populace," to quote Sigmund Mayer, meant in Central Europe not the whole populace at all but only the high-culture elite, in the United States it meant popular culture.[44]

Their turn to dynastic high culture not only cut urban European Jews off from surrounding national minorities, but it isolated them within the center to which they sought access as well. Far from serving as an agent of Jewish assimilation, high culture set Jews apart. Instead of melting into society by means of enlightened culture, Jews in the Hapsburg Empire stood out as distinctively well educated and liberal, committed to the Matthew Arnoldian view of culture as the highest achievement of society. And assimilating Jews who found their path to acceptance blocked by volkish and state anti-Semitism began to create and patronize something new: Viennese modernism. Steven Beller has demonstrated the overwhelming preponderance of Jews in turn-of-the-century Viennese philosophy, psychoanalysis, music, and, as patrons, the modern visual arts. "German high culture" in that city and time, he writes, "was strongly Jewish." Far from acquiring a ticket of admission to enlightened Europe, Viennese Jews were creating the culture of outsiders. Seeking assimilation through the culture attacked as degenerate by Nazism made urban Jews into the isolated targets of volkish and state anti-Semitism, which rejoined them with the *ostjuden* they thought they had left behind. Modern culture provided no safety net for Central European Jews; in the chasm between ethnic nationalities and the state, politically unprotected European Jewry was thrown to its death.[45]

American Jewry filled that gap not with modern high but with melting-pot popular culture. Although tensions between German and East European Jews persisted in the United States, the *ostjuden* who had left the shtetl for the promised land assimilated en masse. They did so by helping to create mass culture for, and participating in it alongside, the same nationality groups that were turning on European Jewry. Israel Zangwill imagined his protagonist melting down separate Old World elements into a New World symphony. Had that music actually appeared in *The Melting Pot* instead of simply organizing it, Zangwill's melodrama would not have been taken, by President Theodore Roosevelt among others, as the defining statement of America. *The Melting Pot* was popular for its intermarriage plot, not its musical synthesis, which remained on too elevated a plane to do its melting-pot work. It reproduced the assimilated German-Jewish elites' effort to bring *Bildung,* cultivation, to the masses, a goal that reflected a fear of mass democracy and hostility to popular culture. In the United States, the creative Jewish cultural role of greatest social significance lay among the more recent *ostjuden* immigrants, and it lay in mass culture. In the garment business, broadcasting, Hollywood, vaudeville, and Tin Pan Alley, the central industries of the culture of mass consumption, assimilating Jewish middlemen and women represented themselves and their American brethren to each other.[46]

Lacking deep roots in the territories it administered and threatened by nationalist and class eruptions from below, the Hapsburg monarchy sustained itself by show. In keeping with the theatrical quality of political life in the empire, the Viennese theater was more important than the parliament. Play-acting was also a mode of behavior for Jews on both continents moving between inherited identities and the gentile society to which they sought admission. The theatrical quality of pre–World War I Viennese life, remembered nostalgically by Stefan Zweig in his memoir *The World of Yesterday,* exposed the fragile place of both the empire and the Jews.[47] In the United States, by contrast, mass-culture performances, self-aware and mesmerizing, engendered deep national loyalties. Blackface colored those transactions.

In U.S. politics as in culture, in the fight for equal rights as in melting-pot entertainment, many Jews forged a special relationship to African Americans. Jews who escaped from European anti-Semitism had a stake in believing both that the United States offered freedom to all and that they themselves were not going to become the central target of American racism, that they were not black. Many Jews treated American freedom not as a given, however, but as something to be achieved in the struggle against all forms of discrimination. Jews opposed racial prejudice in greater numbers, proportionately, than did any other white ethnic group.

Both the struggle for civil rights and the creation of melting-pot culture promoted American inclusion. From one point of view (which we will pursue in the blacked-out subtext of *The Jazz Singer* in chapter 4), politically oriented Jews identified with African Americans as a persecuted, diaspora people, whereas in the cultural realm Jewish parvenus took on black-derived music, along with the plantation myth, as a sign of American belonging. From another perspective, however (one that will also find support in these pages), black-derived popular culture sustained a vitality and variety that liberal homogenizing appeals to abstract equality wiped out. There are, finally, no simple, morally reassuring splits between egalitarian politics and exploitive popular culture, or (from the other point of view) between admiration for distinctive cultural contributions and a falsely universal uniformity. Instead of choosing sides between mass culture and liberal politics in America, it is better to untangle the knot that ties them together.

African Americans endured and resisted an oppression that set them apart in their own country (historically, not essentially), and they created—out of adversity, with African historical resources, and under syncretic influences extending from Scotland through the Caribbean to the frontier—their own forms of cultural expression. Just as no group spins its culture out from a hermetically sealed interior, neither is any culture the exclusive possession of a single group, a pure product that can only be contaminated by borrowing and influence. Racial hierarchy, unequal rewards, and the stereotypes carried by appropriated forms make cultural expropriation a legitimate concern. But to reject all the products of what Zangwill labeled "spiritual miscegenation" is to carry out a cultural revolution of devastating thoroughness. Such ethnic cleansing wipes out the attachments of our parents and grandparents—from the songs of Stephen Foster, with which my mother sang me to sleep, to the music of George Gershwin, to the black jazz created from Gershwin and Cole Porter tunes. And if black-inflected white performance is to be proscribed, what is to be done with the white investment in black artists (the double meaning of investment, tying money to love, only hints at the problem), who themselves vary widely in the influences they felt and in their relations to white promoters and audiences?

Aesthetic and political distinctions might rescue *Show Boat* and *Porgy and Bess* while consigning "My Mammy" to the dustbin of history. We live inside that dustbin, though, and what is beyond the pale for some of us will be a love object for others. Political identification and cultural pleasure vary across the range from admiration to caricature (categories that are themselves often difficult to disentangle); making distinctions is the work of analysis, and distinctions will be made in the pages that follow. Nonetheless, whatever the artistic value one places on Jewish blackface, and however inferior it generally is to the African American music on which it fed, it cannot so easily be either rejected wholesale or disaggregated, retail, into the saved and the damned. The process of cultural conversion must be explored in detail to be grasped whole. For to repudiate the pleasure principle in our ties to the past would also leave behind the African American artists who recovered for themselves, by covering, Jewish blackface productions. From minstrelsy through the Jazz Age, whites claimed to turn black primitivism into art, a justification that, by way of Walter Benjamin, should evoke the inverse of its intended meaning. Instead of seeking political refuge from high culture in popular culture, engaging in contaminated rescue operations, or just saying no to our history, it would be better to apply to both high and popular American forms Benjamin's injunction that our highest cultural achievements are simultaneously monuments to barbarism.[48]

Conversely, the blackface problem, in ways we will be investigating, infected the political struggle for racial equality. Jewish blackface neither signified a distinctive Jewish racism nor produced a distinctive black anti-Semitism. The Jews who inherited the form they made their own were speaking from inside the racial constraints of the promised land. By the same token, far from being the targets of black rural folk, as they were of peasants in Central and Eastern Europe, Jews faced less anti-Semitism from African Americans in the United States than from whites until the late 1960s. But in signifying (in the senses both of standing for and playing with) a Jewish/black alliance, blackface also speaks for the dark side of the American melting pot. The Jewish/black alliance worked better for American Jewish assimilation than did the Jewish/worker alliance for European Jewish cosmopolitanism. If red European Jews fell before right-wing anti-Semitism, blackface American Jews exposed the contrasting situations of Jews and blacks that allowed Jews to rise above the people whose cause and whose music they made their own.[49]

Jews were middlemen not only in their economic and cultural positions but also in their racial and sexual identification: they were positioned between white and black and between men and women. With the spread of scientific racism, social scientists on both continents insisted on the racial inferiority of all non-Teutonic or non-Anglo-Saxon peoples. Could one have predicted in 1900 that, forty years later, racial biology would take over national policy in Germany and not the United States?

Scientific racism, moreover, saw the inferior races as closer to women and children, who, it was said, had developed less vis-à-vis their animal origins;[50] this notion marked a demasculinization of Jewish men with particular relevance for the Jewish question. Racial biology located signs of contamination on black and Jewish bodies; the fantasy of a Jewish world conspiracy discovered hidden power in the Jewish mind. The first mode blackened Jews directly; the other, exemplified in the degenerate music poster, turned Jews into the manipulators of blacks. Both widely shared delusions frame Jewish blackface, but Jewish men themselves were more likely to participate in the former than in the latter.

The Protocols of the Elders of Zion has fueled American anti-Semitism in people ranging from Henry Ford to Khalid Abdul Muhammad; secret Jewish power, although presented in a positive rather than a negative light, also takes over George Arliss's 1929 motion picture *Disraeli*. The Jewish elders of anti-Semitic (and Arliss) fantasy have a feline, spidery, parasitic, sexually ambiguous character. They fold into the masculinized Jewish women of anti-Semitic racial fantasy, for modern anti-Semitism imagines the breakdown of natural sexual difference from both sides of the gender divide. The interpretation of anti-Semitism simply as parricide, from Freud to Norman Cohn, is partly a male Jewish wish for rational authority, a flight from the identification, by assimilating Jews as well as gentile anti-Semites, of the "infected and infecting" Jewish man with the *ostjudisch*, black and female body.[51]

In (the Jewish) Otto Weininger's enormously popular raving, *Sex and Character*, praised by such assimilating Jews as Sigmund Freud, Ludwig Wittgenstein, and Walter Rathenau, Jewish men were "saturated with femininity." "My heart menstruates, a manifestation of the Jewish, feminine principle," writes the Jewish protagonist of (the Yugoslav Jew) Danilo Kis's *Hourglass*. Carl Jung explained, "The Jews have this peculiarity in common with women. Being physically weaker, they have to aim at the chinks in the armour of their adversary." Assimilating Jews were troubled by the charge that Jews manipulated through weakness, a charge to which Freud's own family romances respond—his self-analyzed early wish to be the son of Hannibal's father rather than of his own, and his invention late in life that the Moses with whom he identified was the son of an Egyptian king and not of a lowly slave people. The patriarchal Jew may dominate his children in depictions of the ghetto, but he normally stands, as in *The Jazz Singer*, for defeated, Old World provincialism and not New World power. The hysterical Jewish man, Al Jolson, exposing himself in public performance, negotiates between the two worlds.[52]

Assimilating Jews in Europe and the United States, perfectly aware of their fragile position between contending forces, were more likely to worry about their marginality than their power. The image of Jews as breaking down boundaries and as insidiously protean energized anti-Semitism. Dissolving communal borders, adapting to external forces, and with an ambivalent relation to their own Jewishness, Jewish men between two worlds were seen, and sometimes saw themselves, as between two sexes as well. If the patriarchal Jew of racist fantasy was the superego mirror of the hypermasculine, sexually rampaging, black id, the hysterical or trickster Jewish man blended into the feminized blackface black. Like its nineteenth-century antecedents, Jewish blackface combines racial with sexual cross-dressing. But whereas the earlier Irish working-class blackface fixed upon the long-tailed blue, the imaginary black penis, Jewish movie blackface engendered Crevecoeur's new man, the American, by staging his bond to his—America's—mammy.

Israel Zangwill's protagonist is composing a New World symphony that his audience never hears. Citing it, Werner Sollors observes the role of musical metaphors—symphony, harmony, orchestra—in symbolizing the melting pot. In the songs first of Stephen Foster, E. P. Christy, and Dan Emmett, then of Irving Berlin, Al Jolson, Sophie Tucker, and George Gershwin, music was the melting pot's instrument, not just its symbol. Sound and screen came together in the live musical accompaniment for silent pictures, and the motion picture business employed more musicians, played more music, and paid more money for it than did any other industry. At the conjunction of sight and sound, making Americans by making music, moves Al Jolson. We are entering the plot of *The Jazz Singer*.[53]

PART 2

The Jolson Story

"Oh doctor, put me in your dentist chair. . . .
Lordy, Lordy, what is that up there? . . ."

"I'm going to put my drill in your cavity."
"Oooohh, what is that now, doctor? What is that funny thing I feel getting ready for my cavity? Oh mercy. What is it, doctor? . . . Mmm, doctor. Oh doctor. You're grinding my root too deep.

You keep right on probing, I'm 'bout to lose my head."
"If you can't stand my probing, I'll give you gas instead."

"Oh, Lordy, Lordy, Lordy . . ."

"If you like my treatment, tell the folks in your neighborhood."
"I surely will, 'cause you really done me so good. . . .
Oh doctor, you're rough but you're sooo good."

Hattie McDaniel (with Dentist Jackson),
"Dentist Chair Blues" (1929)

CHAPTER 4

Blackface, White Noise

The Jewish Jazz Singer
Finds His Voice

I

Four race movies—*Uncle Tom's Cabin, The Birth of a Nation, The Jazz Singer,* and *Gone with the Wind*—provide the scaffolding for American film history. From one thematic perspective these motion pictures describe a circle: an abolitionist plantation story is answered by the southern view of Reconstruction, which in turn is answered in the shift from southern racial hierarchy to northern immigrant opportunity. By relocating the struggling immigrants Scarlett O'Hara and her family within plantation nostalgia, *Gone with the Wind* completes the circle. The entire cycle is played out inside white supremacy, however, creating a deep commonality among the films. The full historical development from one movie to the next appears at the juncture of thematic content and film form.

Primitive cinema was embedded in other prefilmic popular entertainments. One-reelers played to live accompaniment by musicians and projectionist/lecturers; short films were exhibited alongside live vaudeville routines. Incorporating within the films and in their mode of presentation their status as shows before live audiences, early one-reelers encouraged audience participation. The artisan-director Edwin Porter came out of this popular theater milieu; his project, however, was far more ambitious. In 1902–3, he shot three brief movies that together lay cinematic claim to the entire American landscape. He filmed successively *The Life of an American Fireman,* a semidocumentary about the modern city; *Uncle Tom's Cabin,* an entirely familiar drama set (as his subtitle announced) "in slavery days"; and *The Great Train Robbery,* the first important movie western and the first blockbuster film. The overwhelming majority of early motion pictures, whether real or staged documentaries or filmed vaudeville routines, did not tell stories. Each segment of Porter's trilogy did. One authority calls *The Great Train*

Robbery the "first dramatically executed American film," for Porter was initiating the shift to the cinematic narratives that would shortly dominate the industry.[1] Porter was not telling just any stories, moreover, but those that composed national mythography. He was bringing into the new century and the new medium the three figures that had long defined American regional identity: the Yankee (modernized as urban dweller), the frontiersman, and the minstrel.[2]

Porter's prefilmic roots show up differently in each of the three movies, for he chose techniques that matched the already-existing regional symbolisms. *Uncle Tom's Cabin,* though the longest and most expensive American film yet made and the first to use intertitles, was formally the least innovative. Nothing that happens in *Uncle Tom's Cabin* (with the possible exception of slaves picking cotton) had not already happened in stage productions of the play. Porter filmed a series of staged tableaux, with minimal action in each scene and no continuity between scenes. He counted on audience familiarity with the plot and the characters to fill in the blanks; the intertitles simply announce which well-known set piece is about to be shown. Angels descend to carry Little Eva away, and Uncle Tom's deathbed visions appear as iris-ins (small inserts spliced in to introduce the tableau), but these are adaptations of stage devices, nothing more. In *Life of an American Fireman,* the camera close-up, a fundamental departure from the stage, shows a hand pulling down the fire alarm; there are no close-ups in *Uncle Tom's Cabin.* The outdoor feel of modern life is made palpable in *Fireman*'s documentary shots of city streets, not on the plantation. A cowboy points his gun at the audience in a *Great Train Robbery* shot that exhibitors were free to place at the beginning or end of the film. Whether that shot scares spectators by pulling them into the screen or simply reminds them that the entertainment is only a film, the direct address contrasts with the end of *Uncle Tom's Cabin.* In that film the new technology, instead of calling attention to itself, draws viewers inside personal and national history to identify with the dying slave.[3]

Set in the past and in the South, *Uncle Tom's Cabin* is static; set in the metropolitan present and on the moving frontier, the other two films are dynamic. Porter interpolated into Stowe's tale a steamboat race between the *Natchez* and the *Robert E. Lee* (where he sets Tom's rescue of the drowning Little Eva), but he was simply filming cardboard cutouts; the spectacle had, in just that form, already found its way into stage productions. For excitement about modern speed and the camera's ability to capture it, one must turn to the speeding train and racing horsemen in the western, the firemen riding to the rescue in the urban drama. Neither the steamboat race nor anything else in the plantation film depicts bodies in motion.

Porter not only filmed motion in the West and the North; he filmed it in a dynamic way as well. Motion pictures had the revolutionary potential to juxtapose events separated in space or time and to bring together different perspectives on a single event. *The Life of an American Fireman* records not just horse-drawn fire trucks racing through the city streets but also the passersby watching them. In his major innovation, Porter showed the rescue of a woman and child first from a point of view inside the burning building and then from the street outside. Whereas later filmmakers used crosscutting to preserve a single, linear temporality, Porter showed the same event from beginning to end twice. The two angles of vision were not point-of-view shots, strictly speaking, since each shows both the character and the event from that character's perspective. But the repetition places the spectator, sequentially, on the inside and the outside positions. Some film historians argue that Porter's pluralization, an alternative to the linear narrative of singular bourgeois subjectivity, was closer to immigrant, working-class experience of space and time. One need not enter the debate over the road not taken in mainstream film history to find Porter's dual perspective appropriate to the heterogeneous, modern metropolis.[4]

Uncle Tom's Cabin has, by contrast, a single point of view, and it is not an abolitionist one. The conflict in the film occurs not between antislavery heroes and proslavery villains but rather between the plantation and the outsiders who threaten it. Those menacing the slaves—slave traders and auctioneers, Simon Legree (he kills St. Clair for defending Uncle Tom in Porter's stage-borrowed version)—intrude into the happy, interracial plantation home. The plantation features emotional, physical contact among Tom, Little Eva ("Tom and Eva in the Garden"), and St. Clair, as well as (in several scenes) merry, dancing slaves. (The combination of the two modes would reach the screen again in the enormously popular 1930s Shirley Temple/Bojangles Robinson southerns.) Whether as entertainers or protagonists, all the blacks are whites in blackface; the prefilmic form of popular entertainment most organically incorporated into *Uncle Tom's Cabin* is minstrelsy.

The two meanings of plantation domesticity—interracial intimacy and blackface entertainment—come together around death. Loyal slaves are gathered about Little Eva as angels carry her away. Tom sees when he is dying visions of his earthly and heavenly home. Porter filmed adventure in the city and on the frontier; his view of love and death on the American plantation dramatizes domestic loss. Firemen rescue a woman and her child, to be sure, and the opening shot of *The Life of an American Fireman* places the fireman on one side of a split screen, the mother and baby on the other. But although the fireman will answer the rescued mother's plea and return to save her child, the entire interest of the scene is in movement and the techniques used to capture it. The core of *Uncle Tom's Cabin*, by contrast, is buried in the historical and personal past—the lost child, Little Eva, and the maternal, sacrificed Uncle Tom. These figures had such a hold on the American imagination—coming as they did from the most popular novel and touring theatricals of the nineteenth century—that seven more silent film versions would follow Porter's in the next quarter century.[5]

Sergei Eisenstein distinguished in the work of D. W. Griffith between modern form and traditional, patriarchal, provincial content.[6] That contrast separates not form from content in Porter but *Fireman* from *Uncle Tom*—with the crucial difference that Porter does not depict the traditional as patriarchal but shows it through a maternal blackface lens. Eisenstein's distinction entirely fails to capture *The Birth of a Nation*, however. Porter filmed three separate regional identities; Griffith combined them into a single national epic. His antebellum plantation may have a more patriarchal inflection than Porter's, but both filmmakers line up the plantation with loss and defeat. Both also make Lincoln sympathetic, one in Uncle Tom's dying vision, the other as a feminized martyr. But whereas Porter's Lincoln redeems the blacked-up, crucified Uncle Tom, the death of Griffith's Lincoln sets the white-sheeted knights of Christ in motion. Griffith's new nation is born not from northern victory in the Civil War but from the ride (derived from *The Battle of Elderbush Gulch*, his own western movie) of the Ku Klux Klan. The Klan, moreover, rides to rescue not a mother and child threatened by fire but a white woman menaced by a black rapist. White men in white sheets smash blacked-up white faces in the climax of *Birth of a Nation*. Griffith's fundamental contribution to full-length motion pictures was to join "the intimate and the epic"; he linked the personal and the historical through racial fantasy. Transcendentalizing the material birth pangs of immigrant, industrial America, Griffith supplied the postbellum United States with its national myth of origins.[7]*

It was not only the Klan that gave birth to the nation, according to Griffith, but also *The Birth of a Nation,* the motion picture itself. By filming speed and cutting between moving targets, Griffith brought modern technology to the Reconstruction Klan. Porter depicted the fireman's rescue from two points of view. Cutting from the Klan to the menaced Elsie Stoneman to the black mob and back again, Griffith showed the Klan's ride to the rescue from a single point of view, that of the director. As with *Uncle Tom's Cabin,* Griffith based his movie on a novel and a play; but whereas Porter presented a familiar story, Griffith created something entirely new. Porter separated his contemporary documentary (*Fireman*) from his staged history (*Uncle Tom's Cabin*). Griffith, claiming historical documentary status for his own fiction, made film the ultimate authority. Fully realizing film's power to seize the audience, Griffith replaced history with the illusionistic, realistic, self-enclosed, cinematic epic.

Just as Griffith emancipated cinema from its dependence on prefilmic entertainment, so he rose above the film audience of which Porter was a participating member. Porter was a working cameraman, editor, projectionist, and bricoleur. There was little division of labor in a Porter production. Griffith, the first director-as-star, attracted mass media attention and presided over massively capitalized projects. Film historians argue over whether films before Griffith actually spoke for their immigrant working-class audiences or just to them. What is certain is that the period in film history that followed Griffith brought immigrants to Hollywood power. By the 1920s men like Porter and Griffith had lost out

---

*The Library of Congress has repressed what J. Hoberman calls our "birth rite" by excluding *The Birth of a Nation* from its collection of "Cinema's First Century" (see Hoberman, "Our Troubling Birth Rite," *Village Voice,* Nov. 3, 1994, 2–4). Not to worry. The 1994 smash box office and Academy Award hit *Forrest Gump* (best picture, director, actor, editing, screenplay adaptation, and visual effects) opens with a Ku Klux Klan scene lifted (or simulated) from *Birth.* Cutting from that movie's hero masking his face to the massed, white-sheeted men on horseback ("they dressed up as ghosts, or something"), the interpolated footage illustrates the work of the founder of the Klan, "the great Civil War hero" Nathan Bedford Forrest, for whom the 1994 Forrest was named. *The Birth of a Nation* thus takes its place alongside the other newsreels from American history—the John Kennedy, Robert Kennedy, and John Lennon assassinations, the Wallace, Reagan, and Ford attempts, Nixon's resignation, and LBJ newsreel—through which Forrest moves (in the award-winning visual effects) and which fail to touch him. *Forrest Gump* passed *Star Wars* in 1995 to move into third place among the top-grossing movies of all time. (See "The Top Money Makers, for Now," *New York Times,* May 14, 1995, H22.)

to immigrant Jews, whose rise to the top of the motion picture business coincided with the development of the Hollywood studio system. Jesse Lasky, Carl Laemmle, Adolph Zukor, William Fox, Samuel Goldwyn, Marcus Loew, Louis B. Mayer, Irving Thalberg, Harry, Al, Jack, and Sam Warner, Harry Cohn, Joe and Nick Schenk, David O. Selznick—of the major powers in the Big Eight Hollywood studios that dominated the industry from the 1920s through the 1940s, only Cecil B. DeMille and Darryl Zanuck were not immigrant Jews.[8]

The men creating mass production studios were rising from their working-class and petty entrepreneur roots to positions as captains of industry. They were transforming local scenes of maker/distributor/audience interaction into centralized hierarchies that revolved around producer power, mass markets, and star fame. As was not the case with the artisanal mode of film production, and with the exception of certain directors and stars, a clear line now separated owners and executives from workers. Given the importance of the immigrant working class as an audience for early cinema, the fact that immigrant Jews should come to dominate Hollywood only once they left the ghetto behind is from one point of view paradoxical. From another it exemplifies the American dream.

Cultural guardians feared early silent cinema as an immigrant menace to the dominant culture. Attending storefront nickelodeons and small-time vaudeville in their own neighborhoods, immigrants watched (in addition to foreign imports) depictions of life around them and comic violence against authority. Some modern film historians, echoing the cultural guardians but reversing their values, believe that nickelodeon cinema united immigrant families across generational lines and resisted American standardization. The enormous variety of short silent films, in the decentralized mélange that was early cinema, included many on immigrant life; *The Jazz Singer* was in the tradition of the immigrant generational-conflict film. But even early cinema reached well beyond urban immigrants, and immigrant Jews rose to Hollywood power as the film audience was becoming predominantly middle class. The Jewish moguls who began as storefront exhibitors and distributors wanted, in Adolph Zukor's words, "to kill the slum tradition in the movies." They saw themselves as transforming motion pictures from sites of class and ethnic division to arenas of modern, mass entertainment, from threats to agents of Americanization. The 1920s motion picture palace, with its narrativized features, live orchestral accompaniment, lavish appurtenances, and mass audiences, silenced and incorporated the participant, immigrant crowds. *The Jazz Singer* depicted popular entertainment as a site of family conflict and an agent of Americanization from the beginning. Faithful to the triumphant tendencies in American Jewish and movie history, *The Jazz Singer,* to borrow Lary May's phrasing, screened out the subversive historical alternatives. It screened them out with blackface.[9]

Blackface also undergirds *The Jazz Singer*'s predecessors, *Uncle Tom's Cabin* and *The Birth of a Nation,* but whereas those films apply burnt cork unselfconsciously, *The Jazz Singer* makes blackface its subject. Thematically, by contrast, *The Jazz Singer* shares *Uncle Tom's Cabin*'s pleasure in blackface entertainment and its identification with suffering blacks, rather than *Birth*'s race hatred. *Birth* and *The Jazz Singer* ostensibly exploit African Americans in opposite ways. *The Birth of a Nation,* climaxing the worst period of violence against blacks in southern history, lynches the black; the jazz singer, ventriloquizing the black, sings through his mouth. *Birth* makes war on blacks in the name of the fathers; *The Jazz Singer*'s protagonist adopts a black mask that kills his father. *Birth,* a product of the progressive movement, has national political purpose. *The Jazz Singer,* marking the retreat from public to private life in the Jazz Age and the perceived pacification of the (fantasized) southern black threat, celebrates not political regeneration but urban entertainment.

These historical contrasts in the use of blackface arise from an underlying identity. Griffith used blacks not to restore plantation patriarchy but to give birth to a new nation. The immigrants absent from his screen were present in his audience; *Birth* used black/white conflict to Americanize them. The jazz singer also escapes his Old World identity through blackface. Moreover, miscegenation as well as assimilation energizes both movies. White identification with (imaginary) black sexual desire, powerfully unconscious in *Birth,* comes to the surface in *The Jazz Singer.* Whereas the white frontier literary hero replaces the white woman with his red brother,[10] *Birth* and *The Jazz Singer* (the former in the psychological subtext of the film, the latter onscreen) use black men for access to forbidden white women. The black desire for white women, enacted in blackface in *Birth,* justifies not only the political and sexual repression of blacks but also the marriage of Civil War enemies, North and South. Blackface promotes interracial marriage in *The Jazz Singer,* by apparent contrast with *Birth.* But anticipating the 1930 Motion Picture Production Code, under which "miscegenation (sex relationship between the white and black races) is forbidden,"[11] *The Jazz Singer* facilitates the union not of white and black but of gentile and Jew.

The Jazz Singer makes its subject what is buried in *Birth*, that the interracial double is not the exotic other but the split self, the white in blackface. Celebrating the blackface identification that *Birth of a Nation* denies, *The Jazz Singer* does no favor to blacks. The blackface jazz singer is neither a jazz singer nor black. Blackface marries ancient rivals in both movies, yet black and white marry in neither. Just as *Birth* offers a regeneration through violence, so the grinning *Jazz Singer* minstrelsy mask kills blacks with kindness.

The Jazz Singer's plot could not be simpler. The desire to be a blackface singer brings young Jakie Rabinowitz into conflict with his cantor father. Returning home a success, and having changed his name to Jack Robin, the son is thrown out of his father's house. Then, when Jack is about to open on Broadway, he learns that the cantor is dying. Torn between his mother and the dancer who got him his break, between Broadway and the synagogue, Jack abandons the show. Replacing his father for the Yom Kippur service, he chants Kol Nidre as the old man dies. In the movie's final scene, however, Jack is back on the Winter Garden stage, singing "My Mammy" in blackface to his gentile girl friend and Jewish mother.

The original reviews of this, the first talking picture, in keeping with the souvenir program issued for *The Jazz Singer*'s premiere, responded as much to Jolson's blackface as to Western Electric's new sound and film projection system, Vitaphone.[12] On the film's fiftieth anniversary, with *The Jazz Singer* now securely established as the first talking picture and blackface an embarrassment, the four film journal commemorative articles barely mentioned blackface.[13] Nonetheless, each publication reprinted movie stills that unavoidably made visible what their texts had repressed: all showed Jolson in blackface. Eighties critics, stimulated in part by Neil Diamond's self-consciously Jewish 1980 remake, downplayed sound in favor of the story, generational conflict, and Jewish assimilation.[14] Yet *The Jazz Singer* actually gives equal weight to all three stories—the conversion to sound, the conversion of the Jews, and the conversion by blackface. Far from being separate but equal, so that one story can be rescued from contamination by the others, the film amalgamates all three. As immigration and technological innovations were creating American mass culture, the film announced Old World, patriarchal defeat to obfuscate New World power. It appropriated an imaginary blackness to Americanize the immigrant son. White masks fail to hide black skin, in Frantz Fanon's analysis, and turn African into European. The beholder's eye alienates the black man from his bodily interior, inflicting an epidermal consciousness on the black masked as white; he is forced to experience himself as he is seen. That same shift from embodiment to eye allows the blackface performer to speak from his own, authentically felt, interior.[15]

II

       Although it is always problematic to identify revolutionary innovations with a single achievement, *The Jazz Singer* can legitimately claim the status of the first talking picture. No feature film before *The Jazz Singer* had lip-synchronized either musical performance or dialogue. None used sound to cut away from and yet retain the previously visible action, and none incorporated words and music into the story.[16] These innovations are still electrifying, because they are preceded within the film by the earlier forms that this movie will destroy: silent, documentary, Lower East Side scenes (fig. 4.1); pantomime gestures; and intertitles. When young Jakie Rabinowitz sings in Muller's café-bar, he announces a cinematic revolution.

       The second sound interval is even more startling. The sound track for Jakie's song was not matched to his lips. When the grown Jack Robin (formerly Jakie Rabinowitz) sings "Dirty Hands, Dirty Face" at Coffee Dan's, for the first time in feature films a voice issues forth from a mouth. Jack then breaks free of both the intertitles that have carried the dialogue and the musical accompaniment that has carried the sound, and speaks his own words: "Wait a minute. Wait a minute. You ain't heard nothing yet," says Al Jolson, repeating the lines he'd already made famous in vaudeville.[17] These first words of feature movie speech, a kind of performative, announce—you ain't heard nothing yet—the birth of sound movies and the death of silent film. The vaudeville performer, Al Jolson, has killed silent movies.

       Jolson paid for his triumph, however, a sacrifice to what Andrew Sarris has called "the cultural guilt of musical movies." Although *The Jazz Singer* and Jolson's next film, *The Singing Fool,* were box office hits, Jolson's career did not prosper in the 1930s. Vaudeville and silent movies complemented each other; talking pictures displaced both. Sarris writes, "Al Jolson became the first scapegoat for the cultural guilt assumed by movie musicals as the slayers of silent cinema."[18]

       The jazz singer may have killed silent movies; within the film, how-

Figure 4.1. The Lower East Side, from *The Jazz Singer*. Courtesy of the Film Stills Archive of the Museum of Modern Art, New York. © 1927 by Warner Bros.

ever, he kills his father. Sarris's extraordinary formalism ignores the connection on which the film insists, between the death of silent movies and the death of the Jewish patriarch. Cantor Rabinowitz expects Jakie to become a cantor, like generations of Rabinowitzes before him. Jakie, however, wants to sing jazz. Familially and musically, Cantor Jake Rabinowitz would lose his own voice. Kol Nidre, the chant on the Day of Atonement for the forgiveness of sins, takes the place of Jakie's singing in the movie's opening scenes. But Jakie does not want to submerge his individual identity in ancient, sacred community. The result is family war. His father beats the young Jakie for singing "raggy-time" songs. He throws the grown Jack Robin out of his house. Jazz was the emblem of generational revolt in the Jazz Age; critics charged it with destroying the family.[19] Jakie's decision to become a jazz singer kills his father. The cultural guilt of the first talking picture is assimilation and parricide.

The Jazz Singer explicitly links its twin killings, of silent movies and the Jewish patriarch, since Vitaphone carries the generational conflict in its three revolutionary scenes—the first, character-embedded, singing voice; the first lip-synchronized singing and first lines of speech; and the first di-

alogue. Together these scenes form an oedipal triangle—antithesis, thesis, synthesis—with the Jewish mother at the center. Cantor Rabinowitz
stops Jakie's singing in the first scene, thus returning the film to silence,
when he drags his son from the stage. Jack talks for the first time in the
second scene, at Coffee Dan's, after the heroine, Mary, admires his song;
his first spoken words introduce the Jewish/gentile romance.

Jewish father stops the voice (antithesis); gentile woman elicits it
(thesis). There is no dialogue at Coffee Dan's, though; Jack only speaks
from the stage to announce his next number. When he returns home,
in the climax at the center of the film, he sings and speaks to his mother.
Sara Rabinowitz frantically caresses her son and murmurs an embarrassed
few words as she and Jack play a love scene. Jack sings "Blue Skies" to
his mother, tells her he'd rather please her than anyone he knows, steals
a kiss from her, promises to buy her a new dress, says he will hug and
kiss her in the dark mill at Coney Island, returns to the piano to play a
"jazzy" version of "Blue Skies," and asks her if she liked "that slappin'
business" on the keyboard. "Slapping" was the jazz term for pizzicato
playing; the sexual origins of the word *jazz*—in copulation—have never
been more spectacularly, or inappropriately, present. A small door opens
in the background, the tiny figure of the patriarch appears, the camera
isolates his menacing head and shoulders, and a voice from the mouth
bellows, "Stop!" (fig. 4.2).[20]

In stopping at the same time the music and the romance between son
and mother, Cantor Rabinowitz ends speech. For the first and only time
in the film there is an extended period of silence, until finally mournful
Eastern European music—replacing "Blue Skies"—returns. Jolson's
singing will as well, but "Stop!" is the last spoken word in the film.
Mother and son try to placate the father, in gestures and intertitles, but
fail. Cantor Rabinowitz sends Jack from the house in silence, but the
damage to silent pictures and the father has been done. "There is one
moment in *The Jazz Singer* that is fraught with tremendous significance," Robert Sherwood recognized in 1927. "Al sits down at the
piano and sings 'Blue Sky' to his mother. . . . His father enters the room,
realizes that his house is being profaned with jazz, and shouts 'Stop!'
At this point the Vitaphone withdraws. . . . Such is the moment . . .
when . . . I for one suddenly realized that the end of the silent drama is
in sight." Jack's father may have the power to stop speech in this film,
but it will cost him and silent movies their lives.[21]

In choosing *The Jazz Singer* as the first talking picture, "the itinerant
peddlers, junk-dealers, and sweatshop entrepreneurs who had parlayed

Figure 4.2. "Stop!" from *The Jazz Singer*. Courtesy of University of Wisconsin Press. © 1927 by Warner Bros.

their slum-located storefront peepshows into" one of the country's major industries were telling their own story.[22] *The Jazz Singer* advertised itself as a Hollywood biopic: "One of the most unique features of *The Jazz Singer*," the souvenir program boasted, "is the fact that it nearly parallels the life of Al Jolson." Like Jakie Rabinowitz, Jolson became a blackface performer against the wishes of his cantor father, and Sampson Raphaelson wrote the short story on which the movie was based after hearing Jolson sing. The jazz singer falls in love with a gentile dancer; Jolson, divorced from one gentile dancer by the time he played the part, was about to marry another.[23]

The Jazz Singer is less Jolson's individual biography, however, than the collective autobiography of the men who made Hollywood. Neal Gabler has shown how the Jewish moguls created Hollywood against their paternal inheritance. Doting on their mothers and in rebellion against their failed *Luftmenschen* fathers, the moguls Americanized themselves by interpreting gentile dreams. They normally hid their "parricide," as Gabler calls it, "against everything their fathers represented," their "war against their own pasts"; but the first talking picture brought that story to the screen. *The Jazz Singer* displays the history of the men who made Hollywood.[24]

Perhaps because its parricidal implications disturbed them, Harry, Al,

Jack, and Sam Warner stressed the harmonious generational cooperation that had produced *The Jazz Singer*. As the souvenir program explained, "The faithful portrayal of Jewish home life is largely due to the unobtrusive assistance of Mr. Benjamin Warner, father of the producers, and ardent admirer of 'The Jazz Singer.' " Paternal approval, as J. Hoberman writes, was enlisted for paternal overthrow.[25] The Warner brothers' patriarch, moreover, was being implicated in a Jewish home life of shouting, beating, exile, and death. In the end, though, the Warner who paid for generational rebellion in *The Jazz Singer* was not Benjamin Warner but his youngest son, Sam.

Benjamin Warner was poor and devout. Sam, however, was antireligious, and after his older brothers married Jewish women uninvolved in show business, Sam chose in 1925 a gentile dancer. As his wife, Lina Basquette, recalls, Sam's brothers were furious at him for marrying "a little eighteen-year-old shiksa." Lina, who had a Jewish grandfather, would shortly be cast as the Jewish daughter in *The Younger Generation*, another tale of filial impiety filmed the year after *The Jazz Singer*. But Sam's attraction to her lay elsewhere; she remembers him asking that she wear her gold cross for his dinner meeting with Western Electric executives in a restaurant that did not serve Jews. When Sam chose for his wife an established member of Ziegfeld's Follies, he was marrying up—in terms of status (stage vs. screen), religion (Christian vs. Jew), and class (her family wealth and salary placed her above him).[26]

Sam Warner had brought his brothers into the motion picture business, was the enthusiast for sound, and was in charge of the Vitaphone project. (His brothers called it "Sam's toy phonograph.") Since the Warner Bros. investment in sound was part of a coordinated strategy to expand the small studio's market share and challenge the preeminence of Hollywood's big three (and not, as was once thought, a desperate attempt to stave off bankruptcy), Jack Robin was enacting Sam Warner's upward mobility through Vitaphone. Sam did not normally make movies, but he came west to supervise *The Jazz Singer*'s production. After Jolson ad-libbed his famous line at Coffee Dan's, Sam reshot Jack Robin's homecoming, added dialogue, and thereby created the love scene with the mother.[27]

Jack faces the crisis of his life after his father forces him to choose between his mother and jazz. In the film's climax, he is torn between replacing his dying father to sing Kol Nidre on Yom Kippur, the holiest night of the Jewish calendar, or going on with the vaudeville show. Kol Nidre is sung on the one evening each year when the skies open and Jews can speak directly to God to ask for forgiveness of sins. Jack's sin would be to choose vaudeville stardom ("Blue Skies") over Kol Nidre. The Warner brothers, also flirting with blasphemy, premiered *The Jazz Singer* on the night before Yom Kippur—the night, in the film, when Jack learns that his father is dying and that he must choose between show business and filial piety. Mixing movie time with worldly time, the studio wanted Cantor Rabinowitz's death and Jack's Kol Nidre to fall as close as possible to the actual Jewish holiday. But this evocation of the Jewish anarchist "Yom Kippur Ball," a satanic night of feasting to blaspheme the holy fast, could not be enjoyed by the Warner brothers. The night before Cantor Rabinowitz was to die in New York, Sam Warner died in Los Angeles. As Jolson's white teeth flashed out from his open black mouth, an infection of the Warner brother's tooth grew inward and poisoned his brain. Sam died of an abscess at the age of thirty-nine. The "screaming and wailing" mother at his deathbed (I'm quoting Lina Basquette) appeared again the next night onscreen at the deathbed of the Jewish patriarch. Sam's dream of bringing together Jewish mother and gentile wife, fulfilled by the dying Cantor Rabinowitz, happened first over his own deathbed. Sam was buried on Yom Kippur eve, and his three brothers, in Los Angeles to arrange the funeral, missed the movie premiere.[28]

Reflection and perhaps agent of generational war to the death, *The Jazz Singer* can hardly be accused of glossing over family conflict. *The Jazz Singer* exemplifies the hysterical text, in recent readings of film melodrama, exposing the familial conflicts buried in the name of realism. Because *The Jazz Singer* depicts the costs of assimilation to family and immigrant community alike, as well as the threat of self-obliteration faced by the son, Hoberman calls it "the bluntest and most resonant movie Hollywood ever produced on the subject of American Jews."[29]

But *The Jazz Singer*'s ending, and its overall family frame, link this hysterical Jewish melodrama not to exposure but to flight. At the film's most hysterical moment, Jack sings first Kol Nidre at the synagogue over his father's dying body and then "My Mammy" to his mother and girl friend at the Winter Garden Theater. The movie was promising that the son could have it all: Jewish past and American future, Jewish mother and gentile wife. That was not what happened in Hollywood. The moguls left their Jewish wives for gentile women in the 1930s and mostly eliminated Jewish life from the screen. They bade farewell to their Jewish pasts with *The Jazz Singer*. Although Americanized Jews ultimately would retain Jewish identities, there was no going back to the Lower East Side.[30]

The Jazz Singer's happy ending is present neither in the original short story nor in the popular Broadway play. A last-minute addition during the filming (like the "Blue Skies" scene), the blackface "My Mammy" hardly wipes away the conflict that dominates the film. Jack is a "cultural schizophrenic," in Peter Rose's phrase; the movie allows no easy, harmonious reconciliation between Jewishness and America.[31] But to weigh the costs displayed within the movie against its happy ending accepts *The Jazz Singer* on its own terms, thus transforming Jewish history in the United States into family melodrama.

The struggle of sons against fathers was an immigrant social fact, but the documents that chronicle that story join generational conflict within the community to hostile, external pressure upon it, a context that is wished away by the first talking picture. All Jack's problems are with his father; none are with the gentiles. Cantor Rabinowitz's hostility to American entertainment is not balanced by any American hostility to Jews. *The Jazz Singer* culminates the tradition of ethnic films that emplotted generational conflict over intermarriage rather than racial prejudice. Jack's *judenfrei*-ing of the Rabinowitz name, so central to the story, as we shall see, responds only to the attractions of Americanization, not to prejudices against Jews.[32]

Also excised from *The Jazz Singer* are the social struggles that united Jews, often across generations, in trade unions, radical movements, businesses, and community organizations. Instead of pitting Jews against nativism, *The Jazz Singer* pits father against son. By domesticating the problem of the Jewish son, as critics of family melodrama would predict, *The Jazz Singer* lets America off the hook and fragments Jewish community. Shifting from ethnocultural to generational conflict, the film celebrates not the Jew as pariah, united with other outcast groups, but the Jew as parvenu.[33]

Two historiographical approaches interpret the 1920s, an older one by way of ethnocultural conflict and a newer one stressing the alliance between youth revolt and the culture of consumption. Provincial, backward-looking nativism triumphs in the former view, which makes the 1920s the last decade of the nineteenth century. Urban, entertainment-centered self-fulfillment triumphs in the latter view, which makes the 1920s the harbinger of the future. *The Jazz Singer,* visible evidence for the more recent historiography, supports the older by what it hides, for its protagonist rises from the defeat not only of his cantor father but of radical, ethnic-based politics as well.[34]

F. Scott Fitzgerald, who "claimed credit for naming" the Jazz Age,

Figure 4.3. Opening page of an Andrew Sarris *Film Comment* article. By permission of *Film Comment*.

understood that it "extended from the suppression of the riots of May Day 1919 to the crash of the stock market in 1929." "The general hysteria of that spring," Fitzgerald wrote in his introduction to the short story "May Day," "inaugurated the Age of Jazz." The story itself follows May Day hysteria from the mob invasion of a Socialist newspaper to a Delmonico's party with its "specially-hired jazz orchestra."[35] The year 1919—that of the great steel and Seattle general strikes, the red scare, race riots, woman's suffrage, and prohibition—gave birth to the nativist politics and the depoliticized youth revolt of the 1920s.[36]

The shift from radical protest to popular culture, enforced by continuing nativism, made possible *The Jazz Singer*. The Jazz Age introduced modern anti-Semitism into American politics, as traditional rivalry between immigrant and old-stock Americans coalesced with ideological racism. (Fitzgerald's mob knocks down a "gesticulating little Jew with long black whiskers.") The anti-Semitic, anti-Catholic Ku Klux Klan (legacy of *Birth of a Nation*) flourished in the 1920s, attacking Jewish control of the motion picture industry. Three years before *The Jazz Singer,* the racist immigration law of 1924 pretty well closed immigration from Southern and Eastern Europe. "By far the largest percentage of immigrants [were] peoples of Jewish extraction," the House Committee on Immigration and Naturalization had warned. Testifying as an expert witness before the committee, Lathrop Stoddard, coauthor of *The Rising Tide of Color Against White Supremacy,* dismissed Franz Boas's denial of racial differences between immigrants and old-stock Americans as "the desperate attempt of a Jew to pass himself off as 'white.' " The Jewish percentage of net migration to the United States, 21.2 percent in 1920, was reduced by the law to close to zero. *The Jazz Singer* premiered six weeks after the judicial murder of Nicola Sacco and Bartolomeo Vanzetti, the final victims of the postwar red scare. (Harvard president A. Lawrence Lowell, who determined that Sacco and Vanzetti had received a fair trial and should be executed, banned African American residents from the college dormitories, and proposed Harvard admission quotas for Jews.)[37]

Nativist pressure created *The Jazz Singer*'s invisible frame. The movie emerged from the moguls' wish to evacuate anti-Semitism from the Jewish question. That wish derived not from Jewish power—Henry Ford's ravings about "Jewish supremacy in the motion picture world" notwithstanding[38]—but from just the context of gentile sufferance that the moguls did not want to acknowledge on film. Wishing away anti-Semitism required leaving Jewishness behind, looking forward to the disappearance of the Jews. Anti-Semitism is *The Jazz Singer*'s structuring absence. The visible cost it leaves behind is borne by Jolson as he plays not a Jew but a black.

A large image of Al Jolson in blackface rises above the title of Andrew Sarris's essay "The Cultural Guilt of Musical Movies" (fig. 4.3). That picture, returning to haunt the text that represses it, insists that one can understand neither the cultural guilt of slaying silents nor the cultural guilt of slaying the father without hearkening to yet a deeper layer, the cultural guilt of exploiting blacks. Riveting sympathetic attention on parents and son, who are united by the movie's affect as they are divided by its plot, *The Jazz Singer* blacks out the non-Jewish group behind the blackface mask. White-painted mouth and white-gloved hands sing and gesture in blackface performance. Black holes in space fragment, stand in for, and render invisible the broken-up, absent black body. The lips that speak Jack's personal voice are caricatured, racist icons. Jack Robin rises through blackface, as vaudeville entertainer, lover, and Jewish son.

Jolson's blackface performance dominates the crisis and resolution of the film. Blackface carries *The Jazz Singer* both backward to the origins of mass entertainment and forward to American acceptance. The sign of what has been left behind appears not in collective Jewish identity but in the instrument of the jazz singer's individual success, the pasteboard mask that points to another American pariah group, African Americans.[39]

III

"This is the turning point represented by Griffith," writes Pascal Bonitzer.

What we have here is a cinematic revolution. With the arrival of montage, the close-up, immobile actors, the look (and its corollary—the banishment of histrionics) an entire facade of the cinema seemed to disappear and be lost forever; in a word, all the excrement of vaudeville. The cinema was "innocent" and "dirty." It was to become obsessional and fetishistic. The obscenity did not disappear, it was interiorized, moralized, and passed into the register of desire. . . . As the body became more or less immobilized and the look was enthroned, morality, perversion, and desire intervened for the first time in the cinema.[40]

Griffith, however, did not banish histrionics forever from film. *The Jazz Singer* revived them, innocent and dirty, with blackface. Blackface was the legacy of vaudeville entertainment and the silent screen; *The Jazz Singer*'s success presided over the beginning of their end. The first talking picture went backward in order to go forward and enter the era of sound. It revived the roots of movies one more time.

Vaudeville, which succeeded blackface minstrelsy as the most popular American entertainment form, was in turn displaced by movies. Each of these spectacles, though, was linked to its predecessor. Vaudeville absorbed minstrelsy, as Jewish vaudeville entertainers like George Burns, Eddie Cantor, George Jessel, and Jolson himself (Heywood Broun called him "the master minstrel of them all")[41] gave blackface a new lease on life. One-reelers, in turn, were originally run in vaudeville shows, and live vaudeville coexisted with silent movies in the 1920s motion picture palace. Silent films complemented vaudeville because they could not reproduce its noise—its musical numbers, sound effects, jokes, and patter. Early sound-movie shorts returned to film origins—newsreel documentaries (mainly Fox) and vaudeville performances (mainly Warner Bros.)—

to show that they could improve on silent pictures. The silent versions of these shorts had exposed the limitations of the stage; the sound versions revealed the shortcomings of the silents.[42]

The Jazz Singer condensed into a single feature film the entire history of American popular entertainment, from minstrelsy through vaudeville and silent films to talking pictures, for the first feature film to bring lip-synched sound into the narrative incorporated vaudeville minstrelsy as well. Warner Bros. did not plan this history lesson; rather, it was responding to audience cues. The studio chose the European costume drama *Don Juan* as its first feature with sound effects and music, and filled the opening "Vitaphone Prelude" of short subjects with prestige opera arias and classical music. The popularity of the single vaudeville skit on the program convinced Warner Bros. to emphasize vaudeville in future filmic undertakings. "Al Jolson in a Plantation Act" was the hit of the second Vitaphone Prelude. The studio built a plantation set featuring corn tassels and watermelons; emerging in blackface from a slave cabin, Jolson sings two songs, "When the Red Red Robin Comes Bob Bob Bobbin' Along" and "Rock-a-Bye My Baby with a Dixie Melody." The red robin supplied Jakie Rabinowitz with his American name, "Dixie Melody" with his mammy. Jolson was preceded by Sam Warner's film of a jazz quartet and followed by George Jessel (who was starring in *The Jazz Singer* on Broadway); by surrounding Jolson with jazz and *The Jazz Singer,* this Vitaphone Prelude set the stage for the first talking picture.[43]

The Jazz Singer is an "interiorized, moralized" oedipal narrative, to recall Pascal Bonitzer's words. But the "desire" that carries it forward is Jack's "innocent and dirty" desire—sung as "Dirty Hands, Dirty Face"—to become a histrionic, vaudeville performer. Classical movies, culminating in sound, may have replaced stock vaudeville caricatures with individuated, interior characters, but Jack develops his character—expresses his interior, finds his own voice—by employing blackface caricature. Blackface reinstated the exaggerated pantomime that restrained filmic gestures had supposedly displaced. "Characterization," to use David Bordwell's oppositions, employed rather than replaced "restless movement." The close-up, montage, and rudimentary shot–reverse shot editing establish the register of desire between Jack and Mary, but reverse shots at Coffee Dan's are subordinated to Jack's performance, and after their first vaudeville encounter he plays all their love scenes in blackface.[44] Blackface supports its antithesis, the film techniques, character development, and triumph of sound that will ultimately take its place. It does so by splitting the protagonist into forward- and backward-looking

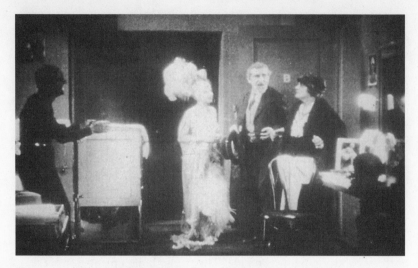

Figure 4.4. The blackface shadow, from *The Jazz Singer*. Courtesy of University of Wisconsin Press. © 1927 by Warner Bros.

halves. The jazz singer rises by putting on the mask of a group that must remain immobile, unassimilable, and fixed at the bottom.

Jack Robin and his black double emerge as split halves of a single self when Jakie Rabinowitz changes his name. "Last time you forgot and addressed me Jakie Rabinowitz," the vaudeville performer writes his mother. "Jack Robin is my name now." Before a last-minute change in production, the next scene was to show him in blackface for the first time, together with the intertitle "Orchard Street would have some difficulty recognizing Jakie Rabinowitz of Beth-El choir under the burnt cork of Jack Robin." The revised scene brings Jack and Mary into intimate contact, however, with the shooting script directing Jack to put a black hand on Mary's white arm as an intertitle speaks the false prophecy of one dancer to another: "He aint got a chance—no Mammy singer for Mary." "Playing a romantic scene in blackface" proved too risky "an experiment," as the scriptwriter, Alfred Cohn, feared it might.[45] Jack in his dressing gown and a black maid in the wings are residues of the original plan, as Jack courts Mary in whiteface; even so, blackface's source in split Jewish identity remains. "It talks like Jakie but it looks like a nigger," says the old Jew, Yudelson, in the shooting script when he first sees Jack in blackface; the intertitle changed "a nigger" to "his shadow" (for Jack's blackface shadow, see fig. 4.4). Two Al Jolson heads dominate *The*

Figure 4.5. *"The Jazz Singer" Souvenir Program* cover. Courtesy of Dover
Publications.

Jazz Singer's souvenir program (fig. 4.5), one in grinning blackface, the
other in white floating slightly above and in front. (Ads for the movie
in the black press also printed that picture.) When blackface Jack looks
in the mirror, his face dissolves into his father standing before the congregation (see fig. 4.9). ("I'm half a cantor and half a bum" is the line

in the play.) Trying to escape the law of the father, Jack refinds it in his split mirror reflection. *The Jazz Singer* is, and knows that it is, a doubles movie.[46]

Other motion pictures that employ the magical doubling device—German expressionist movies and films from the vaudeville comic legacy in particular—also fail to conform to models of the classic narrative film. Silent film's fascination with double exposure, with allowing twin performances by the same actor, coincided with the arrival in the United States of (in its first version) the German expressionist film *The Student from Prague*. Although vaudeville-derived slapstick was the favored fictional genre of early cinema, slapstick, writes Eileen Bowser, "was vulgar, amoral, and anti-establishment, and reformers in the post-1908 period wanted it suppressed."[47] Here I compare *The Jazz Singer* with two doubles films, *The Student from Prague* (1913, 1926; the brief analysis here conflates the two versions) and Charlie Chaplin's vaudeville-derived *The Idle Class* (1921).

Blocked mobility, according to Thomas Elsaesser, generates the double on the German silent screen. These films typically signal a social obstacle in their openings and then shift to the fantastic.[48] *The Student from Prague,* after beginning with a depiction of infantilized student life from which the protagonist is estranged, introduces the old (Jewish-looking) Scapinelli. Scapinelli arranges for the student to rescue a young countess, magically produces gold, and then takes payment by splitting the student in two. Scapinelli seizes the student's mirror image; out of ego's control, it comes between the student and his love. The double interrupts one kiss in the countess's bedroom, another at the Jewish cemetery. Interrupting eros, it enacts forbidden aggression, killing in a duel the aristocratic rival the student has promised not to harm. Liberation of his shadow side finally destroys the student; shooting into the mirror (in the 1926 version), he kills himself. Scapinelli, apparent permission-giving alternative to the countess's father, turns out merely to reproduce him.[49]

Like Jakie Rabinowitz, the student from Prague splits in two to fulfill transgressive desires. But there is no Scapinelli in *The Jazz Singer*. Whereas a black magician controls the student's double, Jack Robin controls his own black double. It does his bidding; it brings him success. Jack is the "master minstrel," in the souvenir program's words; his blackface double is his slave. (Jolson was the credited author of "Me and My Shadow," a routine in which the black tap dancer Eddie Chester copied the movements of the Jewish song-and-dance man Ted Lewis. One-reelers from the 1920s imitated that device by having an African American shadowbox a white.) Instead of W. E. B. Du Bois's "two souls . . . warring . . . in one dark body," in *The Jazz Singer* two bodies, one blacked and one white, heal Jack's single, divided soul.[50]

Contrast the cooperation between the two Jack Robins with the conflict between the tramp and the man of leisure in *The Idle Class,* both played by Charlie Chaplin. Mistaken identity at a fancy dress ball gives the tramp temporary access to the rich man's wife and authorizes slapstick violence by the poor Chaplin against his rich double. This anarchic, rebellious, gestural residue of nickelodeon silent shorts makes fun of the rich, to be sure. Nonetheless, it requires that the classes end where they began, that the tramp return to the road and not displace his double in the family. Otherwise there would be no difference between them, and the film would lose its humor and its social point.

Blackface functions in precisely the opposite way in *The Jazz Singer*. It allows the protagonist to exchange selves rather than fixing him in the one where he began. Blackface is the instrument that transfers identities from immigrant Jew to American. By putting on blackface, the Jewish jazz singer acquires that which is forbidden to the tramp and the student: first his own voice, then assimilation through upward mobility, finally women.

First his voice. Young Jakie Rabinowitz never appears in blackface, to be sure, but he gets the first individual voice in feature films by singing (as the shooting script puts it) "in the most approved darkey manner." As Jakie shuffles on the stage (fig. 4.6), Yudelson reports to Cantor Rabinowitz in an intertitle that he is singing "raggy-time songs"; the original shooting script called them "nigger songs."[51]

Whose sound is it, then, that comes out of the Jewish son's mouth? Jakie finds his voice through black music; Jack will succeed as a blackface singer. The movie insists on the black origins of jazz (I will return to its use of that claim), but it also wants the music to have Jewish roots, and so represents jazz as the link between Jews and America. The texts—original short story, play, movie shooting script, and intertitles—transfer Jewish sacred music to American jazz. The images put blacks into the picture.

"In seeking a symbol of the vital chaos of America's soul, I find no more adequate one than jazz," wrote Sampson Raphaelson in the preface to his published play, reprinted in the souvenir program of the movie. The intertitle that follows the movie credits, "Jazz is prayer," appears to a background of mournful, East European music. "Distorted,

Figure 4.6. Jakie Rabinowitz (Bobby Gordon) sings ragtime, from *The Jazz Singer*. Courtesy of University of Wisconsin Press. © 1927 by Warner Bros.

sick, unconscious of its destination," Raphaelson explained, jazz linked polyglot, New World America to the ancient, wandering Jews. "Carrying on the tradition of plaintive religious melody of his forefathers," as the narrator puts it in "The Day of Atonement," Raphaelson's short story from which *The Jazz Singer* was derived, "Jakie was simply translating the age-old music of the cantors—that vast loneliness of a race wandering 'between two worlds, one dead, the other powerless to be born.' "[52]

Raphaelson's words foreshadow the sacrifice of the short story and Broadway jazz singers on the paternal altar. The movie protagonist, who sings in blackface as his antecedents do not, gives birth to a new identity. "You taught me that music is the voice of God," Jack tells his father in the movie. "My songs mean as much to my audience as yours to your congregation." "He sings like his Poppa, with a tear in his voice," says Sara when she hears him in blackface as the cantor is about to die. "He's not my boy anymore. He belongs to the world." In blessing Jack's movement from cantor's son to jazz singer, Sara sustains his claim that entertainment was the new American religion. When the white-robed and skull-capped Jack replaces his father on Yom Kippur (fig. 4.7; "a jazz singer singing to his God," says the intertitle; the shooting script had "stage's greatest blackface comedian") and then puts on wool cap and burnt cork to sing "My Mammy" (fig. 4.8), he is ex-

Figure 4.7. Kol Nidre, from *The Jazz Singer*. Courtesy of University of Wisconsin Press. © 1927 by Warner Bros.

changing one religious robe of office for another. The "island communities" of traditional America would be homogenized by idols of consumption. If political progressivism had failed to regenerate America, the Jazz Age would bring the younger generation of classes and ethnic groups together around the performer as commodity fetish.[53]

Insisting on the shift from Hebraic particularism to American universalism, neither Raphaelson nor the intertitles acknowledge blackface as the instrument of that transformation. One would never know from Raphaelson—any more than from Henry Ford's accusation that the "Jewish jazz trust makes you sing"[54]—that African Americans and not Jews had created jazz. Blackface gives back to the racial shadow the music taken from its substance.

Much of the early success of Jolson's generation of Jewish entertainers was, as Irving Howe puts it, "gained from acts done in blackface," and Jews had almost entirely taken over blackface entertainment by the early twentieth century. In addition to Jolson, Eddie Cantor, George Burns, George Jessel, Fanny Brice, and Sophie Tucker all got their start in blackface. Jolson's early blackface skit "The Hebrew and the Coon," like the collaborations between Octavius Roy Cohen and Spencer Williams making minstrel films for black audiences, simply recycled

Figure 4.8. "My Mammy!" from *The Jazz Singer*. Courtesy of University of Wisconsin Press. © 1927 by Warner Bros.

stereotypes. But Jewish songwriters and blackface performers also made something new. The shift from minstrelsy to vaudeville, writes Gary Giddins, carried race down to the Lower East Side, and Jewish musicians turned to African American–derived music to create the uniquely American, urban melting-pot sound of the Jazz Age. Irving Berlin (with whose "Blue Skies" Jack Robin seduces his mother) scored his first big success in 1911—and the biggest hit yet for Tin Pan Alley—with the minstrel number "Alexander's Ragtime Band." (Berlin had written "Yiddle on Your Fiddle Play Some Ragtime" two years earlier; he'd gotten his start as a singing waiter at Nigger Mike Salter's saloon and dance hall.) "Originating with the Negroes," as John Tasker Howard expressed the consensus of enthusiasts and detractors alike, "jazz . . . has become a Jewish interpretation of the Negro." "There is one vocation, all known members of which could pass a synagogue door unchallenged," announced *Variety* in 1920, because those who composed "The Syncopated Symphony" were all Jews.[55]

   "We speak of jazz as if it were the product of the Negro alone," wrote Isaac Goldberg the month before *The Jazz Singer* premiered. "True enough, its primary associations, like its rhythms, are black, deriving ultimately from the African Southland. . . . It reaches from the black South to the black North, but in between it has been touched by the commercial wand of the Jew. What we call loosely by the name is thus no longer just black; musical miscegenation set in from the beginning, and today it would be a wise son if it knew its own father." Jews had made more than a commercial impact on jazz, Goldberg continued; although the "Negro ancestry" of Irving Berlin, Jerome Kern, and George Gershwin was "certainly questionable," the "musical amalgamation of the American Negro and the American Jew" is what gave birth to jazz. The *Baltimore Afro-American* excerpted Goldberg's essay under the headline "Jazz Indebted to the Jews."[56]

"Musical miscegenation" was only part of the uniquely cooperative relationship between Jews and African Americans in the first decades of the twentieth century. Nativist coalescence of race and ethnic stereotypes into a single, monstrous alien pushed Jews to think of themselves as allied with other minorities. The Yiddish press, protesting against lynchings and other antiblack violence, likened race riots against blacks to pogroms against Jews. Wealthy German Jews made common cause with "talented tenth" educated members of the black middle class in the struggle for civil rights; Jewish clothing unions organized black workers even as AFL craft organizations excluded them; and Jewish philanthropy and legal services supported black civic institutions and court fights. In fighting for our rights, explained the black writer James Weldon Johnson, Jews also fight for their own.[57]

It is against this background of interracial cooperation that Irving Howe accounts sympathetically for the Jewish attraction to blackface. "Black became a mask for Jewish expressiveness, with one woe speaking through the voice of another," he writes. "Blacking their faces seems to have enabled the Jewish performers to reach a spontaneity and assertiveness in the declaration of their Jewish selves."[58]

Blackface, according to Howe, expressed Jewish solidarity with another pariah group. This filial piety to the blackface Jewish fathers makes Howe himself an easy target for a Jew from the next generation, who risks imitating by reversing *The Jazz Singer*. For to attack blackface may simply be another way of putting it on, as the (gray-bearded) Jewish son writing these lines, like Jolson before him, uses blacks to declare his independence from the patriarch, Irving Howe—and thereby, like the blackface singer, pretends to speak for blacks as well. Still, even at the risk of contaminating the questioner, it is necessary to ask, after Howe, what Jewish "woe" and which "Jewish selves" the jazz singer's blackface ventriloquizes.[59]

Blackface may seem not to express Jewishness at all but to hide it, so that even your own mother wouldn't know you. "Jakie, this ain't you," says Sara when she first sees her son in blackface.[60] But why should the member of one pariah group hide his identity under the mask of another? Where Howe sees only solidarity, I see transfer as well. Switching identities, the jazz singer acquires exchange value at the expense of blacks.

Miscegenation was regression, in racialist theory, because the dark drove out the light. Blackface mimed that process in order to reverse it. Stereotypes located within both pariah groups were exteriorized as black, embraced as regenerative, and left (along with actual blacks) behind. Put Yiddish and black together, wrote Goldberg, "and they spell Al Jolson."[61] Take them apart and their doubling supports the flight of Jack Robin from them both. By giving Jack his own voice, blackface propels him above both his father and African Americans into the American melting pot.

Like the Jewish struggle for racial justice, the black-inspired music of urban Jews was a declaration of war against the racial and ethnic hierarchy of Protestant, genteel culture. Urban entertainment created an alternative, polyglot world, in which the children of Jewish immigrants found new, cosmopolitan identities among Jews, other immigrants, children of old-stock Americans—Randolph Bourne, Hutchins Hapgood, Carl Van Vechten—and African Americans as well. The jazz singer's parricide spreads, from that perspective, out to the paternal cultural guardians of the dominant society. But *The Jazz Singer* refuses that self-interpretation. As Jeffrey Melnick proposes, moreover, far from homogenizing themselves into an undifferentiated whiteness, Jewish entertainers in the early twentieth century were creating new, expressive ways of being Jewish American. But the second-generation ethnic vitality of Tin Pan Alley, Broadway, and the Lower East Side rarely found its way from New York City commercial culture to the Hollywood screen, at least where the depiction of Jews was involved. *The Jazz Singer* divides America between Old World parents and (so far as outward appearances are concerned) a fully assimilated second generation. Screening out the polyglot Americanizing metropolis of the immigrant children, *The Jazz Singer* confines rebellion within the Jewish family. Substituting blackface, which doubled for ethnic and racial variety, the movie points in spite of itself to another truth about the melting pot— not the cooperative creation of something new but assimilation to old inequalities.[62]

Blacks may have seemed the most distinctively American people, the furthest from the Old World identities of Americanizing immigrants, but integral to that distinctiveness was their exclusion from the ethnic in-termixture that defined the melting pot. For Jews and blacks were not moving in the same direction in the 1920s. As nativists attacked ag-gressive Jews and praised black submissiveness, Jewish philanthropists and lawyers believed that a public Jewish presence in the fight for racial equality would only provoke anti-Semitism. Better to litigate and finance civil rights for African Americans, as David Levering Lewis explains their position, "and fight against anti-Semitism by remote control." When Hasia Diner, the historian of Jewish support for racial justice, calls Jews "mouthpieces" for the more powerless blacks, she inadvertently invokes the cultural form, blackface, that spoke for assimilating Jews and si-lenced African Americans.[63]

The 1920 census, eliminating the distinction between "mulatto" and "Negro" and introducing the category "children of foreign-born," was redefining the in-between statuses that threatened Anglo-Saxon purity: mulattoes were nothing but black; children born of European immi-grants in the United States were less than white. The whiteness of Jews was particularly questionable, since a common set of racial stereotypes, which bore fruit in the 1924 immigration restriction bill, bound together Jews, Asians, and blacks under the orientalist umbrella. But orientalism also had a redemptive meaning in the Jazz Age: it signified racially alien, primitivist qualities, embraced by Jewish and black musicians, that would revivify American life. The first Yiddish theater on the Bowery was called "The Oriental." *In Oriental America* premiered in 1896 as the first all-black Broadway show. Twenty years later—about the time the New Or-leans jazz clarinettist Johnny Dodds was recording "Oriental Man"—George and Ira Gershwin wrote a song about four New York violinists from "Darkest Russia," Mischa, Jasha, Tascha, and Sasha: "Sentimental Oriental gentlemen are we." The Oriental sound in jazz, wrote Carl Engel in the *Atlantic Monthly,* owed more to the river Jordan (he was referring not to the Negro spiritual but to its biblical source) than to the Congo.[64]

The conflation of racial minorities into a single, orientalist alien as-sociated Jews with blacks. That identity traps the hero of "The Day of Atonement," who shares "the oriental instinct for undulation" with a Jewish woman in the story; he wants the shiksa. His gentile girl friend admires what she sees as his "careless, happy" dance rhythm; moody and self-doubting, however, he wishes he could "dance standing straight" as she does. As the *Cornell Sun* editorialized in 1924, the same year Raphaelson wrote "The Day of Atonement," "the innate racial characteristics of Jews so conflict with Christian customs and prejudices that happy marriages are impossible." Although the short story ends on an ambiguous note, when the reader takes leave of the protagonist he has been repossessed by his past.[65]

Raphaelson's Jake Rabinowitz, deprived of the magic of burnt cork, is threatened by the fate of Sam Warner; the movie jazz singer enacts Al Jolson's liberation. Blackface plays no role in the short story save for a disparaging reference to "a certain blackface comedian" who, unlike Jack, fails to sing from his soul.[66] Blackface, by penetrating to the movie jazz singer's soul, provides him with the way out of his communal body. Unlike the hero of the short story, Jack Robin plays a person of color instead of being confused for one. By painting himself black, he washes himself white. "The cry of my race" pulls Jack back to his family when he sees his father behind his own blackface reflection in the mirror (fig. 4.9). Blackface, by contrast, liberates the performer from the fixed, "racial" identities of African American and Jew. "The black man should not try to become an imitation white man," warned President Warren Harding (Jolson wrote his campaign theme song), even as Jolson was playing an imitation black man.[67] Freeing Jack from his inner blackness, blackface frees him from his father.

Blackface also gives Jack access to allegedly black qualities—intense emotionality and the musical expression that results from it. In part these were white fantasies, in part black achievements (jazz), and we will be examining *The Jazz Singer*'s relation to both. Whatever their origins, the blackface singer makes those qualities his own. His "musical miscegenation" produces the excitement of racial contact without its sexual dangers, for Jack's child is his music and his own reborn self. As disguise, blackface capitalizes on identity as sameness; under burnt cork, the Jew could be a gentile. As expression, blackface creates individual identity as difference from one's origins. Interiority generated and repressed by the culture of origin finds public form via the blackface mask. Evoking an imagined alternative community identity, blackface frees the performer from the pull of his inherited, Jewish, communal identicalness. The depersonalizing mask reaches a substrate of emotional expression out of which a new selfhood is born. *Variety* explained, "As soon as [Jolson] gets under the cork, the lens picks up that spark of individual personality solely identified with him." Supplying his spontaneity and freeing him to be himself, blackface made Jolson a unique, and therefore representative, American.[68]

Freeing the son from the Jewish father on the one hand, the black

Figure 4.9. The mirror image of Jack Robin, from *The Jazz Singer*. Courtesy of University of Wisconsin Press. © 1927 by Warner Bros.

pariah on the other, Jack's blackface is racial cross-dressing. Just as the white man in classic American literature uses Indians to establish an American identity against the Old World, so the jazz singer uses blacks. If regeneration through violence against Indians won the West, then rebirth through mass entertainment (expropriating black music) won the city. Cross-dressing, says Sandra Gilbert, allows the white man to acquire the envied (fantasized) qualities of the other sex (here race) and yet reassure himself of his own identity: I am not really black; underneath the burnt cork is a white skin. As Elaine Showalter puts it, cross-dressing allows the white man to speak for women (here blacks) instead of to them, and show the actual members of the stigmatized group how best to play themselves.[69]

In *The Jazz Singer*, however, blackface does not simply substitute racial for sexual cross-dressing; rather, the movie's romance unites the two. The blackface shadow points to forbidden women; but whereas the double usually signifies sexual catastrophe, as for the Prague student and the tramp,[70] Jack's double gives him access both to his mother and to her gentile rival. Blackface takes Jack from his mother to Mary, expresses their conflicting demands on him, and finally acquires them both.

Although the rate of intermarriage between Jews and Christians in the early twentieth century, at 1.17 percent, was close to the nearly zero percentage rate of marriages between blacks and whites, popular-culture productions sanctioned the one and forbade the other. The *Bintel Brief* section of the *Jewish Daily Forward,* which responded to urgent readers' requests for help with their daily lives, got its start with advice about intermarriage. The intermarriage melodrama, strongly rooted in the nineteenth century, took on new life in motion pictures and Broadway shows. Intermarriage, first between Orthodox and nonobservant Jews, then between Jews and Christians, encapsulated the problems of Americanization as portrayed in immigrant silent film. *Abie's Irish Rose,* the longest-running Broadway play of the 1920s, followed the dramatic convention of marrying Jewish man to Irish American woman, as did the highly publicized romance between Irving Berlin and Ellin MacKay. (Berlin called the Tin Pan Alley number about his love affair "Society Rose.") May MacAvoy was the stage name of the actress who played the object of Jack Robin's affections.[71]

White immigrants intermarry and blacks do not in ethnic silent film, but that did not deprive blackface of a role in the intermarriage process. The Broadway show second only to *Abie's Irish Rose* in popularity at the end of the Jazz Age was *Green Pastures,* a religious fable in which simple, southern black folk move from being God's chosen people to embracing Christ. "De Lawd" leads "the Hebrews" out of bondage in *Green Pastures,* in the familiar linking of Jewish Egyptian to black American slavery. However (in an allegory that could be read as justifying the end of Reconstruction), God's chosen people fall into dissolute behavior until they take up their "burden" and worship the man who carries the cross. *The Jazz Singer* brings *Green Pastures* together with *Abie's Irish Rose,* for by putting a black face on ethnic intermarriage, it blacks up the conversion of the Jews.[72]

A white bride benefited as did no black from the wedding ceremony; nonetheless, by miming the most tabooed romance in American culture, that between black man and white woman, blackface disempowers both threatening participants. As doubling unifies the immigrant son, fragmentation disassembles not only the blacked-up, emptied-out, African American body but also the female chorus line. The plot diminishes Mary from career woman who gets Jack his break to suppliant and admirer, a member of the audience mesmerized by Jack. She is also assimilated, as the object of the gaze, to the line of showgirls—mechanized, fetishized, assembly-line body parts of what Siegfried Kracauer called in 1927 "The Mass Ornament"—whom the souvenir program shows in Jack's power (see fig. 4.5).[73]

The Jewish star does not triumph by dominating women, however. Blackface is not the instrument of aggression, which is how doubling functions in its comic (tramp) and gothic (student) forms. The student from Prague is passive, gender destabilized—half a man whose double takes charge. The double's aggression blocks access to the higher-status woman, whereas the aggressive tramp temporarily gets her; yet in contrast to both, the aggressive, self-confident Jack Robin (at Coffee Dan's and in the love scene with his mother) is feminized in blackface. He plays not the black sexual menace of Reconstruction, progressive, *Birth of a Nation* fantasy, but the child Negro of the restored 1920s plantation myth. In a decade when Jewish aggression was feared and blacks kept securely in their place, and when white collegians considered blacks less aggressive than Jews, the black mask of deference enforced on one pariah group covered the ambition attributed to the other.[74]

Enacting submission made Jolson, as the souvenir program put it, "the master not only of laughter but of pathos." Prominent teeth and grinning mouth had established the minstrel as a needy, greedy, oral self. Minstrelsy made African Americans into lazy, boastful creatures of physical need, the underside of hardworking, ambitious, white Protestants. Jolson played blackface trickster on Broadway, but not in his movie hits, *The Jazz Singer* and *The Singing Fool*. Drained of the sexuality and aggression that were permitted only as self-ridicule, *The Jazz Singer* left behind a pure figure of longing (fig. 4.10).[75]

Jack appears between Sara and Mary in two scenes—the two in which he wears blackface. The first scene (fig. 4.11), in which the singer displays his divided loyalties, flirts with racial-as-sexual cross-dressing. Neither Jack nor Mary appears in the everyday clothes that signify sexual difference. Jack wears black skin as his costume; in tight-fitting pants and shirt, he is blacking his face and putting on a black wool wig. Mary, undressed in scanty dance costume, is all white. Her visible limbs convey a phallic power that, her availability for the male gaze notwithstanding, accentuates the blackface performer's passivity. To complete the disorientation, Mary wears a giant tiara on her head. In the scene's opening, Mary towers over the seated Jack (fig. 4.12). As one sexual signifier floats from Jack to Mary, another slides from Sara to Jack. When his mother enters, "he starts to kiss her," the published shooting script explains, "then remembers her [*sic*] makeup."[76] Jack actually remembers *his* burnt cork; the editor's *sic* underlines the fact that the makeup is on the wrong sex—and, a souvenir-program production still indicates, it is Mary who first showed Jack how to use it (figs. 4.13, 4.14).

Figure 4.10. Melancholy in blackface, from *"The Jazz Singer" Souvenir Program*. Courtesy of Dover Publications.

Eddie Cantor played *Salome* in blackface and drag. Ike Levisky, the clothing salesman in *Levisky's Holiday* (1913), disguises himself as a bearded lady to enter the circus without a ticket; discovered, he is made the target in a "Hit the Nigger" booth, and his son sells the rotten eggs.[77]

Figure 4.11. Jack Robin (Al Jolson), Mary (May McAvoy), and Sara (Eugenie Besserer) in *The Jazz Singer*. Courtesy of Dover Publications.

Neither menacing nor comic, neither anti-Semitic nor consciously antiblack, Jack's racial cross-dressing has a transvestite component. It masks self-assertiveness in racial as sexual drag. Whether as woman-identified or merely (some viewers may think) as child, Jack gains through blackface the ability to leave home and have it too. Putting on the mask of weakness, the upwardly mobile immigrant acquires the American girl without losing the Jewish mother.

Whiteface imposed a choice on Jack Robin: either Mary ("Toot, Toot, Tootsie") or Sara ("Blue Skies"). The two women come together in blackface, when Jack sings first about the agony of choosing, then about the ecstasy of double possession. As Jack sings "My Mammy" at Jolson's Winter Garden Theater, the camera cuts from the blackface performer onstage to the two adoring women, one in the audience and the other in the wings. Doubles are traditionally fraternal rivals for a single woman,[78] as in *The Student from Prague* and *The Idle Class.* Here, the blackface shadow, by doubling the mother instead, acquires two women for his white substance.

Emblematic of division in both play and shooting script, blackface performs ecstatic synthesis in the movie's finale. The jazz singer moves from Sara to Mary, from the Jewish woman with an earthly husband (called by God to sacrifice his son) to the Christian woman without one.

Figure 4.12. Mary above Jack, from *The Jazz Singer*. Courtesy of the Film Stills Archive of the Museum of Modern Art, New York. © 1927 by Warner Bros.

At the same time, the most powerful erotic bond remains that between mother and son. Maternal hysteria in the "Blue Skies" scene, in Martha Fineman's interpretation, expresses less incestuous desire and more the anxiety of loss; Sara wants to hold her family together.[79] It is hard from the son's point of view not to feel the intermixture of Oedipus and separation anxiety in the maternal home. Camera cuts during the climactic "My Mammy" incorporate Mary, but most fundamentally they bring the performer back home, for the intensified emotion released through burnt cork erupts in the maternal name. The son returns on top, since the editing that concentrates frontally on Jack's performance locates the immigrant spectator above his mother and the rest of the audience in the place of maternal adoration. Jack sings on bended knee at the Winter Garden Theater (see fig. 1.1), but this staged, blackface courtship ritual frees him from the sexualized mother at home to give him back at a safe distance—"I'd walk a million miles for one of your smiles"—the purely nurturing one. The body in motion of "Blue Skies" reduces not to *Birth of a Nation*'s castrated black phallus but to exaggerated white lips that give and ask for nurture.[80]

Blackface allows Jack to play Freud's *fort/da* game, where the child

Figure 4.13. Sara with Jack in blackface, from *The Jazz Singer*. Courtesy of University of Wisconsin Press. © 1927 by Warner Bros.

loses his mother and gets her back,[81] by linking the black mammy to the Jewish mother. Captioning its photograph of *The Jazz Singer*'s last frame with Jolson's final word, "Mammy!," *Photoplay* explained: "Here you behold Al Jolson, piteously imploring the world in general to take him back down South to Georgia, Alabama, or Virginny, to the sunny cotton fields, the little old cabin on Mammy's knees." In accepting that Jolson had a southern mammy, *Photoplay* was counteracting the stereotype of the ambitious, rootless, cosmopolitan Jew, the anti-Semitic turn taken by agrarian nostalgia in the Jazz Age.[82]

Immigrant Jews did share the experience of loss with other mobile Americans, although to conflate it with the slave trade (the conflation that gave mammy her synecdochic power) was egregious. Sophie Tucker (born to Jewish parents in Poland, though Jean-Paul Sartre thought she was black)—who'd begun in New York vaudeville doing blackface in the afternoon and whiteface at night, and who learned her signature song "Some of These Days" from her black maid—introduced "My Yiddishe Momma" in 1925. Singing Yiddish on one side of her record and English on the other, Tucker sold a million copies. Here, too, blackface expresses the "Jewish . . . woe," to recall Howe, of leaving the maternal home.[83]

Figure 4.14. "May McAvoy teaches Jolson the art of movie makeup," from *"The Jazz Singer" Souvenir Program.* Courtesy of Dover Publications.

The mulatta heroine of Nella Larsen's 1927 novel *Quicksand,* counterpoint to the jazz singer, is stopped in her passages between white and black worlds by reduction to a reproductive maternal body. The kneeling jazz singer continues to move back and forth by reducing *his* Jewish mammy to passivity. African American actresses—Ethel Waters, Hattie McDaniel, Louise Beavers—were confined to mammy roles when finally allowed access to the screen. But classic blues performers in African American communities like Ma Rainey, Ida Cox, and Ethel Waters gave mama another meaning, and Tucker, who recorded "Shake That Thing" as well as "Eli, Eli," was a "Red Hot Mamma" indebted to them. "Papa likes the women, mama likes the men," sang Rosa Henderson. Sarah Martin's "Mean Tight Mama" goes "to sleep at break of day." As Bessie Smith put it, "Mama wants some lovin' right now." Edith Wilson sang mammy songs in blackface to whites, ultimately advertising pancakes as Aunt Jemima; prior to that, however, she had performed for African Americans as a blues mama. And Hattie McDaniel, before she was turned into the most famous motion picture mammy of all time, answered back to "My Mammy's" suppliant or grinning open mouth (whose connection to screen mammies will be explored in chapter 6) in her own composition, "Dentist Chair Blues." Displacing the mouth downward—see the epigraph to this chapter—McDaniel and her piano player,"Dentist Jackson," perform the before, during, and after of sexual intercourse. *Contra* Jolson's "mammy" and her own future screen persona, McDaniel gives (musical) pleasure by (miming) taking it in for herself.[84]

Some black women who were left behind sang railroad blues; others, deciding whether to stay or go, refused to submit passively to loss. "There ain't no use to sniffle, whimper, and whine," Hattie McDaniel sang in another of her blues, " 'cause it's your mama going to give you the gate." Ethel Waters—"no man's mama" before she ended her career as a film mammy—gave singing lessons to Sophie Tucker. No response came from Jack Robin's mammy like the one Waters gives a year later to another kneeling man who thinks he can come and go at will: "Stand up when you're making your pleas, no use wearing out your knees; get up off your knees, papa, you can't win me back that way."[85]

The final shot of *The Jazz Singer* fades out on Jolson with his arms outstretched, absolutely perpendicular to his body. The image evokes, in the *Uncle Tom's Cabin* tradition, Christ on the cross. "Don't you think Al Jolson is just like Christ?" remarked Zelda Fitzgerald. She might have been thinking of the Uncle Tom that Edwin Porter brought to the screen, crucified for a flogging with his arms tied to a stick of wood. Blackface Jack's sacrifice, however, empowers the man behind the mask. The title of Hortense Spiller's essay "Mama's Baby, Papa's Maybe" names the denial to slaves of the power and protection of the law of the father, the effort to reduce them to maternal flesh. The blackface inversion—papa's baby, mammy's maybe—uses a surrogate black mammy to escape a real white father. In a sinister version of the psychoanalytic phrase, blackface is a regression in the service of the ego.[86]

As a song of repentance for sins he knows he will repeat, "My Mammy" is a blackface Kol Nidre, but it no longer asks forgiveness from the Jewish Father God. The Lithuanian Jew who's lost his mother (Jolson's died when he was eight) and longs in blackface for a mammy is giving up his Jewish faith for an American dream.[87]

The Jazz Singer's blackface exteriorizes Jewishness, embraces the exteriorized identity as regenerative, and then leaves it behind. The linguistic ambiguity of that "it" has a cultural referent, for however thoroughly blackface relinquishes the Jewish past, it more thoroughly abandons blacks. Yankee, frontiersman, and black, wrote Constance Rourke, were the three humorous masks for establishing a uniquely American identity; urban Jews, racially stigmatized, chose the black.[88] But a sinister paradox inheres in this choice. Assimilation is achieved via the mask of the most segregated; the blackface that offers Jews mobility keeps the blacks fixed in place. By wiping out all difference except black and white, blackface turns Rabinowitz into Robin, but the fundamental binary opposition nevertheless remains. That segregation, imposed on blacks, silences their voices and sings in their name. Replacing the Old World Jew, blackface also replaced the black.

IV

The most obvious feature of *The Jazz Singer,* unmentioned in all the critical commentary, is that it contains no jazz. Al Jolson may have saved minstrelsy from extinction by giving it a syncopated beat, as Hoberman claims, but he did so by blocking out jazz.[89] The "jazz" of the Jazz Age, to be sure, was not the music of Jelly Roll Morton, King Oliver, Louis Armstrong, and Fletcher Henderson. Paul Whiteman, who led the most popular band of the 1920s and sold millions of records, was the acknowledged "King of Jazz." "Mr. Jazz Himself" is a 1917 Irving Berlin song, and Jolson gave "Boston's first jazz recital" in 1919 (the quote is from the Boston *Advertiser*). Gershwin was "King George the First of Jazz." "Jazz," proclaimed Raphaelson, "is Irving Berlin, Al Jolson, George Gershwin, Sophie Tucker"; Tucker's billing changed in the course of her career from "World Renowned

Coon Shouter" to "Queen of Jazz." As Amiri Baraka puts it, "Jazz had rushed into the mainstream without so much as one black face."[90]

Blackface did the work of black faces, standing not for what is now called jazz but for the melting-pot music of the Jazz Age. Almost without exception, popular-culture writing in the 1920s treated Negro primitivism as the raw material out of which whites fashioned jazz. Savage, not polyphonic, rhythm was heard in black music. Jazz was identified with freedom as emotional release rather than as technical prowess. Praise for jazz scores went to white arrangers like Ferde Grofé, as if the sounds made by Duke Ellington, Don Redman, and Jelly Roll Morton came from nature. Improvisational skill, instead of being recognized in African American musicians, was overlooked as being central to jazz, and instead was attributed to such performers as Jolson. It took a decade before a critic linked jazz improvisation to the act of speech; that delayed insight suggests both why the first talking picture wanted to lay claim to jazz—sensing the link between jazz, speech, and individual freedom— and why, in a racially hierarchical society, *The Jazz Singer* assigned freedom to a blackface ventriloquist rather than to an African American jazz musician.[91]

As an "industrialized folk music," jazz allegedly combined the sounds of the jungle and the metropolis.[92] But Jolson's success, contemporaneous with Ulrich B. Phillips's celebratory *Life and Labor in the Old South*, points to the importance of slavery for the new music as well.[93] Blackface began under slavery, when blacks were forbidden access to the stage. *The Jazz Singer* returns them to the plantation. Jakie sings "Waiting for the *Robert E. Lee*" to begin the sound revolution in talking pictures; Jack sings "My Mammy" to end the movie. "Swanee," sung by Jolson in blackface, catapulted George Gershwin to fame. L. Wolf Gilbert, born in Odessa, composed "Way Down Yonder" about Mississippi not the Ukraine; he wrote the lyrics for "Waiting for the *Robert E. Lee*." The Jazz Age rediscovered Foster's "I Dream of Jeannie," making the connection for the first time between Foster's always popular plantation music and his heretofore neglected sentimental home songs. The first usage of *jazz* as a verb noted by the *OED*, from a 1917 New York newspaper, derives the word from "old plantation days."[94]

Jazz, in the dominant Jazz Age myth, began with plantation folk, and white melting-pot musicians made it an artform for modern times. Jazz was indeed a melting-pot music, but it did not have primitive pure racial roots, and its "musical miscegenation" reached fruition inside urban African American communities. Jazz originated not on the plantation but in New Orleans. As Alan Lomax put it, "French opera and popular song and Neopolitan music, African drumming . . . , Haitian rhythm and Cuban melody, native Creole satiric ditties, American spirituals and blues, the ragtime and popular music of the day—all these blended in the rich gumbo of New Orleans music. . . . But the taster, the stirrer, the pot-watcher for this gumbo was the New Orleans colored Creole . . . [and] the black-skinned American musician." If "an interracial marriage was consummated" and "the child of this union was jazz," in Lomax's version of the melting pot, it was a "black and tan wedding," a "musical union" of equals.[95] The music they made did not celebrate or yearn for a lost, innocent paradise. Night spots with African American bands that catered primarily or exclusively to whites had names like New York's "Cotton Club" and the "Plantation Club," but urban sophisticates like Fletcher Henderson and Duke Ellington who played there mostly did not evoke the sunny South. And when blacks in blackface did call up plantation nostalgia, they were usually appealing to whites. While Jolson waited for the *Robert E. Lee,* the African American sitting on the safety valve during the steamboat's race from Natchez to New Orleans (Porter omitted this detail from *Uncle Tom's Cabin*) was in danger of being blown up.[96]

African American jazz was the music of the cosmopolitan New Negro, from New Orleans to Chicago, Kansas City, Harlem, and San Francisco. Blackface minstrelsy in the Jazz Age, by contrast, ventriloquized blacks as rural nostalgia. No longer an exclusive elite institution, as under slavery ("the last of the Cavalier societies" according to *Gone with the Wind*), the plantation supplied a home for the democratic mass. It did so on screen and musical stage rather than in lived communities, not, in Gunther Schuller's words, by providing "a deeply felt musical expression of a certain ethnic group [but as] a rather superficial derived commercial commodity."[97] One should not confuse socially rooted aesthetic judgment of shallowness, however, with lack of psychosocial reach. By domesticating the primitive, in the renderings of Jolson and other songwriters and performers, the plantation supplied the lost and longed for, innocent origins of jazz. In joining a lost southern to a lost Jewish to a lost maternal past, blackface "jazz" restored them all.

The Jazz Singer's blackface facilitated upward mobility in the competitive, urban present by symbolizing the peaceful, rural past. As Raymond Williams has argued for England and T. J. Clark for France, urban parvenus required the myth of the stable countryside.[98] The plantation fulfilled that function in the postbellum, industrializing United States, an American agrarian myth that imprisoned blacks. *The Birth of a Nation* invented black, Reconstruction aggression to unite North and South against it. *The Jazz Singer* watered down revolutionary, black modern music in the name of paying it homage. Like the other doubles movies, *The Jazz Singer* is also about blocked mobility. But whereas the tramp and the student from Prague are defeated by their doubles, blackface blocks mobility for the black double (and the woman) so that his white alter ego can rise.

Jazz may have been the Jazz Age's name for any up-tempo music (Tin Pan Alley was selling most of its product under the heading of "jazz"), but the indiscriminate use of the term no more excuses *The Jazz Singer*'s missing sound than blackface compensates for the absence of blacks. Signifying the omitted referent claims possession of it, for urban mass entertainment let it be known it was capitalizing on its origins. Just as African American performers introduced the cabaret songs that first underlay modern urban nightlife, and then were replaced by whites, so they invented jazz. And just as the first sound picture returned to and domesticated the "slum" origins of movies, so it expropriated jazz. In the thematized, generational, Jewish story, the "white noise" of the title of this chapter is the sacred chant that silences the jazz singer's voice. In the silenced, racial, black story, Jolson's white noise obliterates jazz.[99]*

---

* *The Jazz Singer* returned twice in 1994, in Woody Allen's *Bullets over Broadway*, set in the 1920s, and in Whoopi Goldberg's *Corrina, Corrina*, set in the 1950s. Their variations on the Jewish/black theme mark the distance we have traveled since 1927. Allen's homage to Jolson opens with the version of "Toot, Toot, Tootsie" that Jolson sang in *The Jazz Singer*, modified into real jazz; features a grotesque Mammy; and plots the Allen character's triumph over a show business gangster who could be modeled on Johnny Costello, the man Ruby Keeler left for Jolson. Goldberg plays a black housekeeper in *Corrina, Corrina* who revitalizes a Jewish family (named Singer) after the little girl's mother has died. Corrina restores speech to the silent daughter, Molly. She saves Manny Singer's job in an advertising agency by jazzing up his singing jingles. A "black culture donor," to borrow the phrase Cecil Brown has applied to two other major movies of 1994, *Pulp Fiction* and *Forrest Gump*, Corrina rescues Manny and Molly from suburban sterility by introducing them to black life, faith, and love. Goldberg presides over a sound track that opens with Sarah Vaughn's version of George and Ira Gershwin's "They Can't Take That Away from Me," closes with Stevie Wonder's "We Will Find a Way," and moves between jazz, gospel, and rhythm and blues. We expect Mammy and Uncle Sammy to marry in this contemporary version of musical miscegenation, but the couple must first overcome Manny's emotional rigidity. When Manny Singer and Corrina Washington reconcile and embrace, in the film's penultimate scene, he buries his weeping face in her arms. Cut to Molly teaching "This Little Light of Mine" to her grandmother, who repeats the lines in a heavy Yiddish accent. (Cf. Cecil Brown, "Doing That Ol' Oscar Soft Shoe," *San Francisco Examiner*, *Image Magazine*, Mar. 26, 1995, 25–27, 38–41.)

V

The Jazz Singer retains its magic because, like no picture before or since, it is a liminal movie. It goes back and forth not only between sound and silence, music and intertitles, blackface and white, but also between Kol Nidre and "The Robert E. Lee," Jew and gentile, street and stage, male and female. Jack's putting on and taking off of black-face is synecdochic for the movie's reversibility, its promise that nothing is fixed or lost forever.[100] Going back to the innocent, dirty origins of movies in order to go forward into sound, blackface was talking pictures' transitional object.[101] It gathered together the shift from gesture to look, pleasure to desire, vaudeville to Hollywood, immigrant community to mobile individual, silence to sound—and only then did it become dispensable.

Blackface emancipated the jazz singer from Jews and blacks by linking him to the groups he was leaving behind. The same paradoxical relation applies to speech as well. " 'You ain't heard nothin' yet' was the perfect opening for the new age, a slangy wisecrack that banished the universalized mime of the silent era," writes Robert Ray. But far from replacing the "declamatory, grandiose, and abstract" gestures of silent film with a more "intimate, vernacular, and specific" realism, the more primitive, histrionic blackface technique displaces the more advanced, interiorized one during the course of the movie.[102] Jack never appears in blackface before his father's prohibition stops speech. Blackface, in silent scenes and song, dominates the rest of the film. Jack sings in whiteface before the paternal "Stop!"—in blackface thereafter.

The first talking picture's regression from speech to blackface may seem fortuitous, since the two speaking scenes were ad-libbed, on-the-spot collaborations between Al Jolson and Sam Warner. But no overarching conscious plan was required to give The Jazz Singer its telos. When Jack loses the power of speech, he splits in two. Blocked from overthrowing the father directly, he regresses to blackface's imaginary realm of music, image, and the specular, histrionic self. That step backward prepares a fuller victory. In whiteface speech Jack was first divided, then silenced; hearing a cantor sing "Yahrzeit," the anniversary song for the dead, the jazz singer feels the absence of what he has left behind. Although Jack hallucinates his father's face in Cantor Joseph Rosenblatt as the cantor sings "Yahrzeit" in Yiddish, the mamaloschn was "the mother tongue, . . . the language of women and of the uneducated masses," and of children.[103] Returning home and singing "Blue Skies," Jack recovers through "jazz" music the mother lost in speech. Once he loses her again, he dons blackface. In Marjorie Garber's terms, the musical blackface in between forces no restricted adult identity (either black or white, either male or female, either adult or child) on the racial transvestite. *The Jazz Singer* blackface mimes the torture of being forced to choose.[104]

Language substitutes for the absence of full, unmediated presence, but it can never recover the immediate, sensate, bodily, maternal connection. The power of speech places the subject under the law of the father.[105] That was not the lesson the first talking picture wanted to convey. "No sound, no color," Maxim Gorky had said when he saw his first silent film. "Today I was in the kingdom of shadows."[106] Will Hays, president of the Motion Picture Producer's Association (he had been Warren Harding's postmaster general), introduced the first Vitaphone prelude with the words, "We have advanced from that few seconds of the shadow of a serpentine dancer thirty years ago when the motion picture was born, to this."[107] Shadow stood for soul in European gothic tales, for black in the American imaginary, and for the motion picture image itself. (One reviewer called "Mr. Jolson's shadow" his image onscreen. The racist joke that the "first Negro movie stars" appeared onscreen when Warner Bros. rented a film negative to African American distributors collated these meanings.) Talking pictures aspired to replace shadow with substance.[108]*

That very aspiration opposed speech to blackface in the movies that followed *The Jazz Singer*. The dominant form of nineteenth-century entertainment, blackface slowly withdrew from center stage and finally disappeared from the twentieth-century motion picture. The first talking picture, making blackface its subject and not merely its method, is central to that trajectory. On the one hand, blackface in part succumbed to

---

*René Clair revised the gothic double tale for the age of mechanical reproduction in the first international English-language film, *The Ghost Goes West* (1935). In a spoof of *Nosferatu*, the ghost first haunts his ancestral Scottish castle. There he blocks the romance of his double (played by the same actor) and descendant. When a supermarket magnate buys the castle and reconstructs it in Florida, the castle turns from ancestral burden into tourist attraction and moneymaker. Advertised like a P. T. Barnum exhibit, the ghost now promotes romantic as well as capitalist freedom. To mark the shift from uncanny doubling to commodified, mass-produced entertainment, Clair brings on a kilt-wearing marching band. The first four members are African Americans; the rest of the long line (shades of Sir Walter Scott) are whites in blackface. (See Gerald F. Noxon, "The European Influence on American Film," in *Sound and the Cinema: The Coming of Sound to American Film*, ed. Evan William Cameron [Pleasantville, N.Y., 1980], 145.)

the cinematic demands for realism, which were intensified by the coming of sound. Speech gave voice to complex inner emotions that pantomime and intertitles were unable to represent, and it devalued techniques that distracted from diegetic self-sufficiency. Just as sound fostered cinema's aspiration accurately to reproduce reality—to replace shadow with substance—so it did away with blackface as speech. If blackface was the victim of the technological revolution for which it had fronted, then Sarris's cultural guilt of movie musicals returns, pointing not only to the slaying of silent pictures in general but to the specific destruction of blackface.[109]

On the other hand, the talkies did not kill blackface immediately, and the terms of its death and continued life explain how cultural guilt can attach to the destruction of the vicious blacking-up practice. For sound entered into an already-existing bifurcation in classic Hollywood between spectacle and story. Musicals and comedies had vaudeville roots, and though they brought performance together with plot, they often subordinated narrative to display.[110] Talking pictures in other genres intensified the aspiration to verisimilitude that had defined movies since Griffith. *The Jazz Singer,* however, rescued blackface as pleasure principle while undercutting it as realism. The first movie musical, *The Jazz Singer* was also the first movie to work musical numbers into its plot.[111] This conjunction of narrative and spectacle ultimately vindicated not verisimilitude but a utopian plenitude of feeling. "My Mammy" set the precedent for production numbers in talking-pictures Hollywood. Without encompassing *The Jazz Singer*'s social and technological spread, minstrels under cork (as we shall see in chapter 6) sang and danced the emotional intensity that blackface performance enabled. The classic Hollywood musical would locate itself squarely within the blackface melting-pot tradition.[112]

But if *The Jazz Singer* initiated the movie musical—Hollywood poetry—it did undermine the use of burnt cork in Hollywood prose. And cultural guilt inheres in that disappearing act as well. For blackface condensed two social meanings: heightened authenticity and American acceptance for the (Jewish) individual, subordination for the anonymous (black) mass. *The Jazz Singer*'s self-awareness about the former called attention to the role of performance in creating individuality. And while this self-understanding anticipated postmodern celebrations of performance, when read against the grain the movie in fact exposes the imprisoning structure of the performative. Although white actors performed under cork in musicals and comedies, to play blackface dramatic roles violated cinematic conventions of realism. Since sound increased film's ability convincingly to counterfeit reality, blackface-as-realism only got in the way. Calling attention to the figure behind the mask, it exposed the illusion that the individual was in charge of his or her voice, that it issued forth from an authentic interior. Better to bequeath spoken blackface to actual black people who, most importantly in the southern genre (its centrality to talking-pictures Hollywood is addressed in chapter 6), played the parts minstrelsy had prepared.

Blackface was not just left behind, however—for production numbers, nostalgia, or African Americans; it was universalized as well. During the period when it was perfecting Vitaphone, Western Electric was also conducting an experiment at the site of production. The "Hawthorne experiment" is as germinal in industrial sociology as *The Jazz Singer* is in the history of film, and the two have speaking in common. Getting workers to talk and feel listened to, the company discovered, increased productivity more than did the effort to create silent, efficient human machines.[113] Talk, encouraged as inner self-expression, functioned as social control. In production as in consumption, in work as at play, the company stood behind the workers' words, Jolson to their blackface. "Master Minstrel" Al Jolson models the dreams of his fans, dreams produced socially for private consumption and ventriloquized as one's own. Freed from traditional cultural and communal restraints, the jazz singer becomes a component part of standardized organizations and standardized dreams. To cover up that mode of production, blackface realism had to go. For it exposed the illusion that the individual was speaking and not being spoken for—whether by language, capital, the mass consumption industries, or by the locus of all three for thirty years after *The Jazz Singer* (returning to capture the White House in the 1980s), talking-pictures Hollywood.

That, at least, is the conclusion suggested by an extraordinary picture published in a film magazine as part of the fiftieth-anniversary celebration of *The Jazz Singer* (fig. 4.15).[114] The picture is captioned with the magazine's version of the first words of speech in a feature movie, Jolson's "Wait a minute, I tell ya. You ain't heard nothing. You want'a hear 'Toot Toot Tootsie'?" The photo shows a white man sitting on a throne-like chair, with rows of identical-looking blackface drummers seated around and behind him. One figure in blackface stands front and center, his arms outstretched in song. A blowup reveals the singer to be Jolson himself. But Jolson sang "Toot, Toot, Tootsie" alone in whiteface in *The Jazz Singer;* this image reabsorbs him back into a minstrel troupe.

Figure 4.15. The blackface minstrel troupe, reprint from *Take One;* from *Mammy.*
© 1930 by Warner Bros.

He represents the rows of blackface automatons, themselves synecdochic
for the reproduction of identical identities in film technology and mass
society. The image thus undercuts the caption that misidentifies its picture. Unmentioned—like blackface itself—in the article that prints it, the
photograph makes visible the link between blackface and sound that is
repressed in the text. For this silent picture assigns control over speech
not to democratic, individual, or collective voices, but to the unidentified king of blackface, his authority sustained by the interchangeable
identities of those who sing his song. This unmarked man sitting on his
throne does not appear in *The Jazz Singer*. He runs the minstrel show
in *Mammy,* the Jolson film that actually contains this scene.[115] Call him
Uncle Sam.

CHAPTER 5

Racial Masquerade and Ethnic Assimilation in the Transition to Talking Pictures

I

In 1890, when Philip Krantz and Abraham Cahan were starting a Yiddish-language socialist newspaper (the *Arbeiter Zeitung*), Cahan proposed launching the venture with an article on cannibalism in Africa. Krantz, wholly focused on promoting socialist doctrine on New York's Lower East Side, objected. Cahan was also a socialist and went on to edit the *Jewish Daily Forward* for half a century. But just as he had moved from Russian to Yiddish to reach Jewish immigrants in their own language, so he believed that African cannibalism would attract an audience for Krantz's doctrinal statement, "Our Program."[1]

Cahan had read the article he proposed to translate and publish, "Life Among the Congo Savages," in *Scribner's*. This popular journal offered its readers a mixture of fiction by such writers as Henry James, Sarah Orne Jewett, and Robert Louis Stevenson; political articles—Theodore Roosevelt's account of leading his white and colored troops up San Juan Hill appeared within the decade; and displays of exotic peoples. The newspaperman turned explorer Henry M. Stanley was often featured. Closer to home, Jacob Riis's "How the Other Half Lives," his tour through the urban jungle, appeared four months before the article on Congo savages. The documentary, classificatory impulse that attended imperial expansion was taking in not only exotic non-Europeans but urban immigrants as well. Cahan himself, "discovered by [the] . . . renowned . . . literary Columbus" William Dean Howells, as Theodore Dreiser put it, was soon publishing stories in English about the Lower East Side. The genteel readers of *Scribner's* could make the connection between the "benighted savages in the heart of Africa" and Riis's "street Arabs"; between the "cannibal orgies" on the Dark Continent and the "dark hallways and filthy cellars" at home, "crowded, as is every foot of the street, with half-naked children"; between the savage "craving for . . . human flesh" and cries of "Nyana! Nyana! (Meat, meat)" and the "pigmarket" in the Jewish quarter where "crowds . . . pushing, struggling, screaming, and shouting in foreign tongues, a veritable Babel of confusion," buy everything except the forbidden flesh that gave the market its name. Just as nineteenth-century cartoons and racial doctrines were turning Irish into Africans, so the multiethnic New York slums brought savagery to the heart of civilization.[2]

Jews, to be sure, were more the object of sympathy in *Scribner's*, and cannibals the object of horror, but reform impulse jostled exotic display both in the article about Cahan's prospective readers and the one he translated for them. After all, as Stanley told readers of *Scribner's*, pygmies, who ate everything in sight, human flesh included, "were the intellectual equals of about fifty per cent of the modern inhabitants of any great American city of today." Although Stanley was reducing immigrants to pygmies, he was also elevating African savages, for, he insisted, "I see no difference between the civilized and the pygmy! . . ." Let light shine upon the trackless region," Stanley concluded. "Some will survive the great change and . . . prove themselves to be very much like the rest of humanity."[3]

The progress Stanley imagined from savagery to civilization would catch up Riis's other half as well. The *Arbeiter Zeitung*'s "Cannibalism in Africa"—for Cahan won his dispute with Krantz—was a step toward "the more rapid Americanization" Cahan favored, but it neither brought "the Jewish workers to socialism" nor promoted Stanley's universal civilization.[4] Just as the *Forward*'s famous *Bintel Briefs,* letters from readers sharing their concerns, introduced immigrant Jews to daily life in America, so "Life Among the Congo Savages" introduced them to American culture. In discovering savages, they were discovering America. Thanks to Cahan, they began to move from being the objects of exotic interest to being the reading subjects interested in exotic places, from what they shared with cannibals to what they shared with readers of *Scribner's*.

Far from discovering something new in the period of mass immigration, Cahan had hit upon the oldest American story. He was creating a line of descent from the first self-styled children of Israel in the New World to the Jewish immigrants who followed them. Variants of "Cannibalism in Africa" were performed in the Yiddish theater—*Among the Indians,* for example, where the "swindler" clothing salesman, "Willie the peddler," afraid of being lynched by savages, learns that it pays to offer the best cloth to "black field hands" and Native Americans on the Kansas frontier. There were many ways in which, to quote James Barrett, "immigrant workers discovered the importance of race in American life," just as there were modes of acculturation that did not involve racialization.[5]

Race and ethnicity were, however, at the core of one creation of the United States as an imagined community: the shared experience of loss of home. Cahan himself imagined a fictional protagonist who succeeds in the garment business through "convincing personation," that is, by playing a role, but whose prosperity leaves him with "a brooding sense of emptiness." Cahan's hero laments in the novel's last words, "I cannot escape from my old self. My past and my present do not comport well. David the poor lad swinging over a Talmud volume at the Preacher's Synagogue seems to have more in common with my inner identity than David Levinsky, the well-known cloak manufacturer." The Jewish socialist was making lost community and inner division the price of individual success. By the last decades of his editorship, the *Forward* was consumed by nostalgia.[6]

Sampson Raphaelson had begun with loss. He made his protagonists suffer for fleeing their roots, first in the short story and Broadway production of *The Jazz Singer* and then in the passing play, *White Man,* that he wrote after the success of its twin.[7] Raphaelson's Jew is punished by guilt (abandoned mother and dying father), his African American by sex and violence (child tainted in its white mother's eyes by black blood, the pull of Harlem for the male racial passer). The Jew's fate is uncertain at the end of one play, the imitation white man is dead at the end of the other. But the fact that the playwright gives the same name, Mary, to both men's forbidden object of desire indicates that the difference in racial stereotypes coexists alongside the similarity in racial condition. As with David Levinsky, a gap opens between the false front of each play-acting parvenu and the repudiated community residing in his interior. Both the Jew fleeing his past and the African American passing as white lead a "sham existence," pretending to be what they are not. They are divided within, as Hannah Arendt describes the German Jewess Rahel Varnhagen, who "masquerades" before the society to which she seeks admission in order to "separate herself from the dark mass of her people."[8]

Raphaelson's heroes anticipate the protagonist of Fannie Hurst's Jewish generational-conflict film *Symphony of Six Million* (1932). "When Felix lost the ghetto, he lost himself," says the woman he left behind. "He lost his soul." Keeping company with Raphaelson, the popular Jewish novelist and screenwriter, who herself passed as gentile, doubled her Jewish family drama with a book and movie about black passing, *Im-*

itation of Life (1934).[9] In their use of the Jewish/African American parallel, Raphaelson and Hurst turned the American family romance (as the wish through passing to replace the parents of one's birth) into melodrama.

Raphaelson, however, escaped from racial melodrama into theatrical comedy. In his long-running Broadway hit *Accent on Youth,* life imitates the scripts of the playwright-within-the-play to break down the sexual barriers of age and (covertly) gender. While he was imagining metamorphosis through role-playing in *Accent on Youth,* Raphaelson was also writing the screenplays for Ernst Lubitsch's early sound comedies. Their first collaboration, *Trouble in Paradise* (1932), celebrated a confidence man and a confidence woman—thieves masquerading as aristocrats.[10]

Even as Raphaelson was leaving ethnic and racial passing behind for pure theater, Hollywood was combining the two. The movie jazz singer, as we saw, unified Raphaelson's failed ethnic and successful theatrical halves. The jazz singer might have been, as Al Jolson, "the Russian Jew" with whom David Levinsky would "readily change places, . . . who holds the foremost place among American song-writers and whose soulful compositions are sung in almost every English-speaking house in the world."[11] The difference between Raphaelson's and Jolson's jazz singer is the difference between passing and blackface. Passing, a secret, shameful deception in the cultural trope, put the actor always in danger of exposure. The audience was dupe, authority, and enemy all at the same time. Blackface performed deception to create a bond between actor and spectator. The audience was in on the open secret, and the love affair with the audience—mass culture—replaced the abandoned ethnos. Whereas passing trapped immigrants in the unalterable identities fixed on blacks, racial masquerade freed them from their communities of origin. Some Jewish performers, like the movie jazz singer, moved into an entirely gentile present; others—more typically in earlier vaudeville and sheet music communities—forged new, shared, American Jewish identities for the children and grandchildren of immigrants.[12]

Passing was the cultural trope assigned sympathetically to African American daughters, as in *Imitation of Life;* Jewish sons like the jazz singer put on blackface. Unprecedented in Hollywood for showing the racism that drove "Aunt Delilah's" daughter to pass, the domestic labor (making pancakes) from which her mistress profited, and the suffering soul beneath mammy's cheerful, fixed smile, *Imitation of Life* nonetheless redeemed mammy through maternal self-sacrifice alone. Delilah's death, moreover, called the punished prodigal daughter permanently back home. Twinned with the sympathetic racial passer by the mother left behind, the blackface son played happy ending to the passing daughter's tragedy.[13] The emphasis on performance—in vaudeville-turned-Hollywood comedy and music, in ethnic shtick, and in camera address—far from being detached from narrative, served the Americanization plot. At least that was the story *The Jazz Singer* told. By the time Louis B. Mayer, Arthur Freed, and Busby Berkeley brought *Babes in Arms* to the screen, on the eve of World War II, they were summing up a century-old tradition.

In *Babes in Arms*, as in *The Jazz Singer*, minstrelsy mobilizes the entire history of American entertainment in the service of making Americans. The babes in arms—children of retired vaudevillians—are putting on "Babes in Arms" to revive the family fortunes killed by talking pictures. The modern entertainment form has destroyed its predecessor, creating a rift between the children putting on the show and their disapproving parents. In addition, ethnocultural conflict exacerbates the generational divide. The town busybody and moral guardian, who speaks for traditional, Protestant America against the urban, vaguely Irish, vaudevillians, wants to take their children away from them.

Blackface comes to the rescue. The young performers get their chance on Broadway through a minstrel number, which heals the divisions along generational, ethnic, moral, and entertainment-form lines. "My daddy was a minstrel man," Judy Garland begins her song. "I'd like to black my face," she sings in blackface, "and go again down memory lane with an old-fashioned minstrel show." This, the central spectacle in *Babes in Arms*, offers all the pleasures of the traditional minstrel spectacle, with Tambo and Bones comic blackface routines, Mickey Rooney's dialect imitations, and a mass blackface production number. The talking picture, descended from vaudeville and entertaining genteel America, pays homage to the blackface origins of American mass entertainment.

Spectacle has a higher purpose than mere pleasure, however. "High there, Yankee, give me a thankee, you're in God's Country now," sings Mickey in the movie's finale. "We've got no Duce, got no Fuehrer, we've got Garbo and Norma Shearer," celebrates Hollywood as the patriotic alternative to authoritarian, European politics. Mentioning the acquisition of Garbo, the song alludes to the melting pot that transformed even *Ziegfeld Follies.* Germans and Italians from supporters of dictatorship into democratic moviegoers. The myth is enacted by national couples (one man wears a yarmulke) whom Rooney welcomes as Yankees and invites to dance. In this production number called "God's Country," racially based nationalisms of descent confront a spiritually based, inclusive, American national identity. But there were no African Americans among Mickey Rooney's minstrels, and no Latino or Asian immigrants appear among the dancing couples in the movie's melting-pot conclusion.

Babes in Arms inherited a film tradition that had begun in *The Fights of Nations* (1907), where every ethnicity but one relinquishes its distinctive weapon—knives for Latins, swords for Scots, razors for blacks, "guile or gesture" for Jews—to march together under a proscenium arch festooned with American flags. The group missing from the parades, in a replay of the exclusion of "Dahomeyans" from the parade of all other ethnic villages at the closing of the 1893 Chicago World's Fair, was African American.[14] American nationalism may be spiritual, not racial, from a European perspective, but from an American one race is the instrument of spirit.

Babes in Arms speaks for a motion picture industry that, as agent of Americanization, replaced—or rather incorporated—both the frontier myth and the minstrel show. Like the Yiddish press and the original forms of antebellum, urban blackface, early one-reelers were often sites of immigrant, working-class self-presentation. But as we saw in chapter 4, the Jewish moguls who came to dominate Hollywood repudiated "the slum tradition in the movies." In dissolving divergent class, regional, and ethnic histories into a single, unifying American dream, the moguls propelled their own move from Hebraic particularism to American universalism.[15]

Released the same year as *Gone with the Wind*, *Babes in Arms* exemplifies the New Deal blackface musical (to which the next chapter will turn). Summing up *The Jazz Singer*'s ethnic Americanization, the film also points backward to other movies made during the transition to sound, when the technological revolution that ended silent pictures coalesced with the end of mass immigration, when nativist prejudice against ethnic urbanity confronted the new morals and forms of entertainment of the Jazz Age. The jazz singer's racial cross-dressing, as we saw, enacts the pleasures and dangers surrounding not only race and ethnicity, but domestic and technological change as well. The first talking picture, celebrating its technological breakthrough and allying talking pictures with parricide, built a potentially explosive foundation for the American family. The jazz singer must make technology serve the home because its promise of freedom—in car and radio as well as motion picture—invaded traditional American family life. Further, his lost and then found domestic haven defuses any threat from the career-oriented, sexually available New Woman by transforming her from danger to support for domesticity.

A transformational movie, *The Jazz Singer* does not stand alone. Hollywood followed the success of the first talking picture with a brief flurry of blackface entertainments—at least seven in 1928 alone.[16] Many of them were filmed minstrel shows; I leave those aside, however, to examine the blackface plot of four motion pictures made between 1927 and 1930, in which racial cross-dressing promotes an American home. That function does not encompass all filmic blackface, but it does spread across genres and from blackface to other instances of racial masquerade. The four films are an urban melodrama, *Old San Francisco* (1927); a musical review, *The King of Jazz* (1930); a musical family melodrama, *The Singing Fool* (1928); and a musical comedy set in the West, *Whoopee!* (1930).

Old San Francisco was one of the five movies Warner Bros. released before *The Jazz Singer* that had occasional sound effects and a synchronized musical score. A minor box office success that attracted little notice at the time, *Old San Francisco* is important for its normality. Directed by Alan Crosland (who later shot *The Jazz Singer*), its racial cross-dressing extends the European immigrant/white/black triangle of eastern cities (and of *The Jazz Singer*) to the Chinese, Irish, and Old California Spanish of the West. *The King of Jazz,* an all-color musical and vaudeville review advertised as the most expensive film ever made, starred Paul Whiteman, the most popular band leader of the Jazz Age. In this film, jazz is a white man's music with black roots that turns immigrants into Americans. *The Singing Fool* was Warner Bros.' part-silent, part-talking, part-singing blackface sequel to *The Jazz Singer*. Shifting the focus of Jolson's first movie from crossing ethnic boundaries to crossing gender boundaries, *The Singing Fool* was the top box office hit of the 1920s. Finally, *Whoopee!* returns Indians to the ethnic intermarriage story by way of blackface, redface, and gender destabilization. Starring Eddie Cantor, and based on his top-grossing Broadway musical of 1928–29 (Whiteman's orchestra was in the pit), it was among the most successful movies of 1931. Five movies (including *The Jazz Singer*), however significant and widely seen, do not of course establish the dominance of a pattern even for the end of the Jazz Age. They do, however, provide evidence for the pattern's existence and—the primary purpose of the analysis that follows—elucidate its character.[17]

Romantic triangles in each of these movies do not identify fixed points of rivalry in the traditional Freudian pattern. Whereas in some anxious

American texts the process of negative identification fixes and unfixes the identity of the white middle-class male,[18] the circuits of desire in Americanization films deliberately mobilize identity exchange—between colored and white, man and woman, ethnic and American.

Making visible the significance of race in the continuing creation of American identity, racial masquerade points to white privilege. In addition, since the sources of white advantage in the slaughter of Indians, the enslavement of African Americans, and the exploitation and exclusion of Asians were too terrible to acknowledge directly, racial masquerade released the tension. Narratives about Jazz Age music emancipated it from its African American roots. Sentimentality confused the question of whose grievances merited redress. Humor exploited racial stereotypes, but it also played with the hypocrisy of racial divisions, sometimes stopping short of full disclosure, sometimes going all the way.

Repudiating 1920s nativism, these films celebrate the melting pot. Unlike other racially stigmatized groups, white immigrants can put on and take off their mark of difference. But the freedom promised immigrants to make themselves over points to the vacancy, the violence, the deception, and the melancholy at the core of American self-fashioning. These films make us wonder: Do cross-dressing immigrants buy freedom at the expense of the imprisonment of peoples of color? Or does that freedom itself look less like consent and more like the evasion of crimes, less like making a new self and more like endless disguise?

II

Old San Francisco brings together two staples of early-twentieth-century popular fiction and film, the ethnic intermarriage plot and the yellow peril melodrama. Dolores Vasquez, granddaughter of a "Spanish Californian" rancher, and Terrance O'Shaughnessy, nephew of a San Francisco Irish-American politician, fall in love. Terrance's uncle works for the villain, Chris Buckwell, who endangers Dolores's property and her virtue, only to be exposed later in the film as a Eurasian passing as white. After he is unmasked, Buckwell kidnaps Dolores. What saves her from the traffic in women, and destroys him, is the San Francisco earthquake.

Old San Francisco may seem like straightforward propaganda for Oriental exclusion, following the Supreme Court decision of 1922 making "Orientals" ineligible for American citizenship. But that view, adopted in occasional recent attention to the movie, fails to account both for the sympathy shown the Chinese at the beginning of the film and for the orientalist ambience that permeated 1920s Hollywood: movie palaces (like Grauman's Chinese Theater in Hollywood itself), narrative themes, set decor, costumes, and other objects of eroticized consumption and exotic display. Hollywood orientalism could bring once-forbidden pleasures to the mass movie audience as long as actual Asian Americans were kept out. Instead of illustrating a "social contradiction" between Oriental exclusion and Hollywood's Oriental turn, *Old San Francisco* shows how the one was the enabling condition for the other. Redistributing its initial sympathy for both the exploited Asians and Spanish, *Old San Francisco* condemns the Asian racial passer and blesses mobility across ethnic lines. It thereby appropriates orientalism not for miscegenation, prostitution, and dangerous drugs, but for the libidinized American home.[19]

As *Old San Francisco* begins, the urban Chinese and rural Spanish are equally victims of Anglo enterprise, greed, real estate speculation, and political corruption. Masquerade and sexual desire across group lines turn the opening upside down. Buckwell (who the film audience thinks is an Anglo) confines the Chinese to Chinatown and threatens Old California Spanish property—the latter threat being a stand-in for the American taking of Mexican and Indian lands. The 1913 California Alien Land Law forbade aliens ineligible for citizenship—meaning Asians—from owning land. *Old San Francisco* separated Asian Americans and Mexicans from their land by sympathizing with expropriated Old Californians (who had lost title irretrievably long ago), transforming brown-skinned Mexican agricultural laborers into lighter, exotic, Old Californians, and blaming an Asian for confining his own people to the slums. For the man playing an Anglo capitalist turns out to be an Oriental white slaver. Masquerading as a pious Christian to enter the Vasquez ranch, Buckwell seizes, not the ranch, but Dolores (fig. 5.1). Sexual violation allows the girl to "penetrate his secret," for when he raises and lowers the cloak over his face in a second rape scene, an intertitle announces: "The heathen soul of a Mongol stood revealed."

In turning the Chinese from victims to agents of greed, *Old San Francisco* joins the Oriental exclusionist politics of the California labor and progressive movements.[20] Just as the attack on Chinese labor slid from the capitalists who employed Chinese to the Chinese themselves,

Figure 5.1. Chris Buckwell (Warner Oland) seizes Dolores (Dolores Costello) in *Old San Francisco*. Courtesy of the Film Stills Archive of the Museum of Modern Art, New York. © 1927 by Warner Bros.

so the movie reveals the apparent Anglo capitalist as an Oriental. The surveyors who invade the Vasquez ranch are Buckwell's agents, revenging his failed invasion of the Vasquez woman. When the source of the threat shifts from white to Asian, the target shifts from property in land to property in women. Putting yellow faces on what it had earlier depicted as an Anglo menace, *Old San Francisco* endorses what it had first bemoaned: the passing (in both senses) of the California Spanish. Grandfather Vasquez's prophecy that "the city will bury us and our traditions beneath an alien civilization" is at once fulfilled and reversed: the movie transfers alienness from Anglos who endanger Spanish to Orientals who menace whites. Instead of threatening the independent freehold and traditional culture, the "alien civilization" threatens white female virtue. Instead of burying Spanish California, the alien civilization will itself be buried in the film's climax, the San Francisco earthquake.

Hollywood movies of the 1920s and 1930s typically portrayed Latins as "lazy peasants and wily señoritas." *Old San Francisco* and *The Jazz Singer*, by contrast, repudiate nativist prejudice against (white) Latins and

Jews. Setting Terrance's love for Dolores against Buckwell's lust, *Old San Francisco* blesses attraction across ethnic lines. Racial cross-dressing in both *The Jazz Singer* and *Old San Francisco* creates generational conflict, and, as in other ethnic intermarriage movies of Hollywood's early years, sympathy is distributed between the older generation's resistance and the younger generation's desire. Whichever side they ultimately choose, generational-conflict movies acknowledge the pull of Old World ties.[21]

Old San Francisco scores its victory for love when the force keeping the lovers apart is no longer the parental victim (who dies failing to protect his granddaughter) but the racial villain. The Oriental passing as white takes the place of the Spanish grandfather in the triangle with daughter and Irish lover. Once illegitimate desire moves from property to sex and is exposed as racial passing, the Spanish girl can marry the Irish boy and embrace American enterprise. Grandfather Vasquez's insistence that "blood will tell" and that his daughter should marry her Spanish suitor, Terrance's rival, falls to the younger Spaniard's cowardly inability to defend granddaughter and ranch. "Was it a Spaniard, then, who wrote, 'Home Sweet Home?' " Terrance asks Dolores, encouraging her to believe that domestic happiness does not require ethnic exclusiveness. But far from repudiating blood for love—or Werner Sollors's descent for consent—*Old San Francisco* illustrates the process Michel Foucault has described that substitutes one exclusion for another, as feudally based blood exclusiveness is replaced with democratically based exclusion of Chinese blood.[22] *Yellow* may be a term of character in the West, distinguishing some Spaniards, like some Anglos, from others, but the term also denotes an Oriental racial trait that cross-dressing cannot hide.

Warner Oland, cast as the cantor father in *The Jazz Singer,* plays the Oriental villain in *Old San Francisco. The Jazz Singer*'s souvenir program featured two pictures of Oland (the only actor besides Jolson so honored), one as evil Oriental and the other as patriarchal Jew (fig. 5.2). The double casting points to traits united in the Jewish patriarch that are split between Buckwell and Grandfather Vasquez. Oland's two roles suggest the orientalist connections between the stereotyped races—between Oland as Mongol and the Jewish moguls, for example. But *The Jazz Singer*'s blackface links Jews and blacks in order to separate them; *Old San Francisco* rejoins the Chinese passing as white to his own people.[23]

As in *The Jazz Singer,* racial masquerade transfers value from the traditional, patriarchal family to melting-pot America. *The Jazz Singer* blesses Jewish blackface, whereas *Old San Francisco* condemns racial

Figure 5.2. Warner Oland as Jewish patriarch and Mongol villain, from *"The Jazz Singer" Souvenir Program*. Courtesy of Dover Publications.

passing. But the cross-dressing Chinese villain hides the movie's own racial transfer between Spanish and Asian. Asian masquerades as white in the story, moreover, but the actor playing the Asian passing as white is himself white passing as Asian. Buckwell's "unknown origins" are the shadow underside of the humble beginnings of the Jacksonian self-made man and of the typical movie mogul. Just as the moguls wished to separate themselves from the immigrant Jewish slums, so the old Spanish

aristocracy hides the Mexican workers in the fields. Buckwell, now a plu-
tocrat, has a black servant; compounding the confusions of racial masquerade, the servant is played by a white in blackface.

The specter of miscegenation, defused when the racially ambiguous
jazz singer dons blackface and thereby moves from the "Oriental" to the
white category, takes over *Old San Francisco*. The California law pro-
hibiting miscegenation defined it as intermarriage between the white race
and the "negro, mulatto, or Mongolian."[24] Racial cross-dressing facilitates intermarriage, not between whites and peoples of color, but between whites divided by ethnic lines. Put more exactly, racial masquerade moves ethnics from a racially liminal position to a white identity.
Racial cross-dressing in both films collapses the division separating Anglos from some other Americans, but it allows Spaniard and Jew in by
keeping Asian and black out. Buckwell's passing is criminal (as the jazz
singer's is not) because of the threat to white womanhood contained in
his yellow blood.

The first time Buckwell dons an Oriental robe, the camera reveals his
"Mongolian brother" with him in their underground room. Racial im-
purity joins moral to physical deformity, for the brother is a dwarf whom
Buckwell keeps imprisoned in a cage. In Cecil B. DeMille's *Ten Commandments* (1923), a historical spectacular that moves between two
stories, the biblical saga and a modern domestic melodrama, the Eurasian
seductress of the contemporary tale has leprosy. Her biblical model is
Miriam, who defies God by "worship[ping] the golden calf of pleasure"
and is disfigured by that same disease for her erotic writhings beneath
the golden statue. Buckwell hides behind the name Chris; secretly he
worships a bejeweled Buddhist idol. Sex, disease, and pagan religion all
flow from degenerate blood. Dolores saves Terrance from (Irish) drink-
ing and consorting with prostitutes; Buckwell is condemned by his contaminated bodily fluids.

Buckwell's Chinese concubine, revealed when his identity is exposed,
marks the shift from Asian victims to Asian villains, inheriting the sexual menace of the Eurasian femme fatale. The dark, sultry Dolores is
whitened by contrast with Buckwell's concubine, who helps kidnap her;
sympathy for Dolores as Spanish granddaughter is replaced by sympathy for her as victim of Asian desire. As sexual melodrama covers over
the dispossession of Mexican land, so materialism as menace shifts from
Anglo commercial speculation to Chinese opium, jeweled opulence,
idol worship, and sexual depravity.

When he is exposed as Oriental, Buckwell carries Dolores to a Chi-

Figure 5.3. Dolores menaced by the yellow peril (Buckwell on far left) in *Old San Francisco*. Courtesy of the Film Stills Archive of the Museum of Modern Art, New York. © 1927 by Warner Bros.

natown opium den and house of prostitution. Dolores is stripped of the mourning black she had put on for her grandfather, dressed in bridal white, and displayed for sale (fig. 5.3). Spun about before Oriental eyes, touched by Oriental hands, Dolores four times tries to escape from the locked room. The camera follows her in four different directions, each time only to find an Asian blocking the door.

New York's Chinatown, wrote Jacob Riis, was "honey-combed with scores of the conventional households of the Chinese quarter: the men worshippers of Joss, the women all white, girls nearly always of tender age, worshipping nothing save the pipe that has enslaved them body and soul."[25] That is to be Dolores's fate. In actuality, Chinese girls were the victims of the Chinatown traffic in women, owing to the grossly unbalanced sex ratio perpetuated by the Chinese exclusion law. *Old San Francisco*, like the yellow-peril pulp novels from which it derived, turned the victimized woman white.[26]

Victimization Americanizes and thus whitens Dolores when the movie discovers that whites are the true victims. Ancestors are either impotent, if Spanish, or monstrous, if Chinese. But just as her grandfather could not preserve her Spanish blood, so her lover cannot protect her white blood. Terrance's Irish brogue, intrusive in the early titles, disappears as he "becomes acclimated," in the words of *Variety*.[27] Nonetheless, even as an American, he is powerless against the mass of Asians. Dolores prays to God, and He sends the San Francisco earthquake. A mad, Old Testament–quoting derelict had earlier called God's curses down on Buckwell and mammon; as Buckwell is being crushed, he sees the prophet again. The jeremiad directed against Buckwell as agent of modern materialism is ultimately fulfilled against the Asian as white slaver.

Prayer and divine intervention also save DeMille's heroines, one (in *The Ten Commandments*) endangered by the leprosy passed from the Eurasian seductress through her husband, another (in *The Godless Girl*, 1928) imprisoned and physically branded as a result of her atheism.[28] Sign that the individual male subject is helpless on his own, these *dei ex machina* revise melodrama's traditional rescue formula. For the power of the hero, however, they substitute Hollywood rather than God. *Old San Francisco* introduced Vitaphone as a threat to family continuity: the very first sound effect, a gunshot in the prologue, kills the founder of the Vasquez line. His sword, helpless against the Anglo gun, transubstantiates into the sword of Dolores's religious vision, the sword that brings on the earthquake. But in the climax, both the report of the gun and the sight of the holy sword are reduced to insignificance. The overwhelming sound effects of earthquake and fire constitute the major use of Vitaphone in the film. Orchestrated crowd scenes of panic and the sight and sound of crashing, burning buildings testify to the authority of Hollywood special effects. Profane technological progress threatened the Vasquez ranch; the miracles of modern technology rescue the Vasquez woman.*

Earthquake and fire destroy Chinatown, the modern Sodom and Gomorrah. Chinatown is a melting pot, the crucible in whose burning interior a new American identity forms. Although this Christian meaning is not intended by the film, the redemptive sacrifice of Chinatown gives birth to the American family. Having shown Chinatown's destruction from inside and within, the camera pulls back for an aerial view of "the

---

* *The First Auto*, another silent feature with Vitaphone sound effects, anticipated *The Jazz Singer* in emplotting as generational war-to-the-death the technological revolution in film. The father owns a livery stable in *The First Auto*. Accusing his son of betrayal for becoming an auto mechanic and race car driver, he nearly causes the young man to be killed. *Old San Francisco* lined up technological progress on the side of the family by shifting the opposition to progress from Spanish grandfather to Asian racial passer.

cleansed streets of the Oriental quarter," the modern ethnically cleansed neighborhood built on Chinese American ruins. The aerial perspective becomes the point of view of Dolores and Terrence as they look out over the city. Removed from the urban carnage, they constitute the American family, for the camera cuts from their distant vantage point to their baby on a rocking horse.

Spanish and Chinese no longer share pariah status as the victims of American progress. Although civilization has confiscated the productive property of Chinese and Old California Spanish, the Spanish granddaughter has gained a compensatory domestic space. With rocking horse replacing vaquero's horse, she enjoys orientalist property like other Americans—jazz records and motion pictures, for example—in consumption and display. As the teeming crowds of immigrants are destroyed, the individualist, rural Spanish move into the American home. As observers of the reformed urban scene, the melting-pot couple are no longer interactive members of it.[29] They stand for the movie's spectators, whose position they have achieved. The medium is the message, for just as the special effects of Hollywood prove more powerful than Buckwell's makeup, and his masquerade hides Hollywood's own, so the sign of achieved Americanization is passively to observe the spectacle of Americans being made. The Warner brothers were preparing to move that story closer to their home, in *The Jazz Singer*. The proceeds of *Old San Francisco*'s opening night in New York went to benefit the Hebrew Orphans' Asylum.[30]

III

Old San Francisco expels one alien to incorporate another. *The King of Jazz* appropriates African American music to Americanize immigrants and exclude blacks. The link between the Dark Continent and the melting pot, to which Abraham Cahan's translation of the *Scribner's* article about cannibalism pointed, becomes explicit in *The King of Jazz*. Part of the tradition that runs from blackface minstrelsy through *The Jazz Singer* and *Babes in Arms*, *The King of Jazz* makes Americans out of American entertainment. Since that entertainment is American thanks to its African American origins, "the melting pot of music" in *The King of Jazz* digests and expels its own beginnings. Asian Americans are a visible presence in *Old San Francisco;* indeed, their elimination comprises the plot. African Americans, in contrast, are an absent presence in *The King of Jazz* because their exclusion sets the movie in motion. Nonetheless, closeness is the prior condition for separation in both movies, the method by which the properties of one group are expropriated for another. The property in *Old San Francisco* is orientalist exoticism and Old California/Mexican/Indian/Asian American land; in *The King of Jazz*, it is African American skilled labor and emotional expression.

Antebellum blackface minstrelsy grounded American popular culture in expropriated black production. In insisting on the authenticity of blackface imitations, myths of minstrelsy's origins revealed what Eric Lott has labeled the reciprocal problems of "love and theft."[31] Black and white closeness (the precondition for the authenticity of blackface) raised, on the one hand, the specter of interracial love, whose material basis was the sexual exploitation of slave women but whose transgressive feature in minstrelsy was homoeroticism. The creation of distance by excluding actual blacks from performance, on the other hand, raised the specter of theft; the material basis here was slave labor.

The popular music of the Jazz Age, deriving from ragtime, New Orleans jazz, and other black performance styles, inherited minstrelsy's obsession with roots. An obligatory black man who made rudimentary noises, in the jazz myth of origins, gave the music its name; for Paul Whiteman, he was "that jazzy darky player, named James Brown and called Jas." Minstrelsy had begun as a ribald, vulgar popular cultural form, and that is how opponents saw the melting-pot music of the Jazz Age. Rather than rejecting the genealogy, defenders stressed the distance jazz had traveled from its primitive, African, slave roots.[32]

Advocates of Jazz Age music argued that whites transformed black raw material into art. "Our whole present music is derived from the negro," the popular-culture critic Gilbert Seldes insisted in 1924. Negroes could not help but be their primitive music, writers in the mass circulation magazines and newspapers explained. Whites did the skilled labor of musical arrangement and intelligent performance. "The negro side" of jazz, as Seldes put it, "expresses something which underlies a great deal of America—our independence, our carelessness, our frankness, and gaiety. In each of these the negro is more intense than we are, and we surpass him when we combine a more varied and more intelligent life with his instinctive qualities. . . . The greatest art is likely to be that in which an uncorrupted sensibility is *worked* by a creative intelligence." Having resolved the problem of theft by assigning labor to whites, Seldes gave an illustration: "Nowhere is the failure of the negro to exploit his gifts more obvious than in the use he has made of the jazz orchestra. . . . No negro band has yet come up to the level of the best white ones, and the leader of the best of all, by a little joke, is called Whiteman."[33]

Paul Whiteman was the acknowledged king of jazz, and, like "King Jazz" himself, all the "Jazz Kings" celebrated in a 1926 *Literary Digest* article of that title were white. Just as did Seldes, so Whiteman insisted on the African origins of jazz: "Jazz came to America three hundred years ago in chains," he began his autobiography; but although the "joyful noise" came from Africa, "Negroes themselves knew no more of jazz than their masters." In Whiteman's autobiography and in music critic Henry Osgood's book on jazz, mostly anonymous African Americans (none are named by Osgood) supply the prehistory of the music, replaced by named, white performers when the author reaches what he calls "jazz."[34]

"Jazz is the spirit of a new country, . . . the essence of America," the music "of the common people," Whiteman proclaimed. Standing against an imitative, "high-brow," European-oriented culture, it inherited the American nationalism of Walt Whitman, Nathaniel Hawthorne, and Edgar Allan Poe. "Americans—and the term included Slavs, Teutons, Latins, Orientals, [were] welded into one great mass as if by the giant machines they tended," wrote Whiteman. Jazz, removed from its origins in African American labor and community, gave these machine-age workers their leisure-time release. Since only Americans could express the national music, "the most important item in the jazz equipment is that each player shall be American"; yet although Whiteman included "nationalized citizens" of foreign ancestry in his band, he, like all other white band leaders of the 1920s, excluded African Americans.[35]

Whiteman performed that exclusion twice, first in his 1924 concert at Aeolian Hall in New York City (an event, according to one historian, second only to talking pictures in importance for 1920s popular music)[36] and then in *The King of Jazz*. The concert, scheduled for Lincoln's birthday, February 12, was an "Emancipation Proclamation, in which slavery to European formalism was signed away." Whiteman was emancipating jazz from enslavement not just to Europeans but to black Americans. He took his orchestra, as the movie reviewer Creighton Peet put it, "into the sacred precincts of Aeolian Hall in an attempt to make an honest woman of Jazz, at that time a cheap and notorious wench." The orchestra played "The Livery Stable Blues," complete with imitation barnyard noises, to show how far the music had traveled, in Whiteman's account, "from the day of discordant early jazz to the melodious form of the present." This "crude jazz of the past" was counterposed to *Rhapsody in Blue,* played by its composer, George Gershwin, as the high point of the concert.[37]

Exclusion reinforced expropriation. "The Livery Stable Blues" came, Whiteman acknowledged, from "an old Negro melody." But he endorsed a judge's dismissal of a copyright infringement suit against the Original Dixieland Jazz Band, the mendaciously named white group whose hit record of that song had launched the Jazz Age. "As to the moral aspects of the theft, there aren't any," Whiteman concluded; the Original Dixieland Jazz Band served not only to deflect the problem of theft away from Whiteman but also to move his band one safe step further from the African American original.[38]

Advanced technique plays a similar distancing function in *The King of Jazz.* Just as the prologue to *Old San Francisco* announces the Anglo displacement of the Spanish, so Whiteman's prologue introduces the white appropriation of Africa. The band leader himself introduces the first-ever cartoon animation in color;[39] it will show how he became king of jazz. The scene opens on the rotund, immaculately dressed band leader "big game hunting in darkest Africa." When a lion chases Whiteman and is about to devour him, the white hunter takes out a violin and plays. The lion begins to dance; instead of swallowing Whiteman, its wide-open mouth (which would become the symbol for MGM) speaks the word Al Jolson had made famous, "Mammy." Africans and snakes dance as Whiteman continues to play. Far from being their own product, music calms the primitives. It turns them into plantation, blackface mammies. A soothing, nurturing mouth, naming the black nurse of white boys and men, replaces the lion's devouring orifice. Jazz, which here domesticates Africans into creatures on which white men feed, is the trophy the white hunter brings back from Africa.

Warner Bros. paid homage to Jolson with its first cartoon character, a black boy named Bosco, who was featured in "With Bosco in Africa." Another Warner Bros. variant on *The King of Jazz* cartoon, "Porky in Whackyland" (1938), transports Porky Pig to "darkest Africa." Hunting the dodo, Porky encounters a jazz band. As figures with strangely shaped bodies and limbs dance, a large-lipped creature mouths, "Mammy, mammy, mammy, mammy."[40] The rawer version of jazz, that of Looney Tunes, puts "mammy" into the African mouth. The cooked version, Whiteman's, acknowledges that the white man has elicited "mammy" from out of Africa's mouth. The former allows African creation, animalistic and grotesque. The latter makes Africans passive recipients of their own, distorted music.

Having served their originary function, African Americans are, with two exceptions, excluded from the musical numbers and vaudeville sketches that make up *The King of Jazz*. One appearance presents a genteel version of the opening cartoon. Jazz, intones a voice-over, combines the most primitive and the most modern elements, "for jazz was born from the African jungle to the beating of voodoo drums." First an "all blacked up" (in skin-tight, India rubber costume) white man does a "voodoo dance" "on top of a huge tom-tom";[41] then female ballroom dancers glide across the floor; finally George Gershwin plays *Rhapsody in Blue*. The primitive male dancer is segregated from the women whose pleasure he inspires, for the libidinal character of jazz flirted with transgression along not just gender lines (sexual pleasure for respectable women) but also racial ones.

Jazz, the product, in Isaac Goldberg's phrase, of "musical miscegenation,"[42] could not be seen as promoting interracial sex. The "mammy" aspect of jazz spilled over into sexual excitement, and the only scene in *The King of Jazz* where an actual black person appears flirts with the sexual risk, only to neutralize it. Whiteman, filmed from behind and apparently alone, conducts from a park bench as white couples dance; the number is called "Public Park." Each band member sings and dances with a woman on his arm. Whiteman turns around in the middle of the scene to reveal a little black girl on his lap. Repeating the paternalist racial relation established in the opening cartoon, the interracial couple is safely set off, as white father and black child, from the adult, dancing partners. Peet had wondered what sort of child Whiteman's "honest woman" jazz would give birth. Paternalist miscegenation produces a musical baby that is not the offspring of interracial, sexual exploitation but the catalyst of romance between whites.[43]

The representation of African Americans in *The King of Jazz*, culturally routine, provoked little comment. Reviewers attended instead to the film's trick photography, which one praised as emancipating the film musical from the "ghostly past" of the stage. Critics divided on whether the photographic effects (Whiteman's band emerges, for example, from his briefcase) enhanced or detracted from the music. But all praised the opening cartoon and the "Melting Pot" finale, for the new technology and the new music joined together in the film's climax to make Americans.[44]

Figure 5.4. The Paul Whiteman band in redface. Courtesy of Williams College Archives.

In this culminating scene—perhaps borrowed from the Americanization graduation ceremony at the Ford Motor Company's Highland
Park Model T assembly plant, or modified from the 1915 film of Zangwill's, *The Melting Pot*, where Old World "flotsam and jetsam" dropped
into "a giant crucible . . . [are] convert[ed] from all races and countries
into American citizens as the hero plays his violin"—Whiteman stirs an
enormous, steaming pot. A voice-over declaims, "America is a melting
pot of music, where the melodies of all nations are fused into one great
new rhythm." Suitably costumed singers and dancers perform their national music, one group after another. Ethnic insignias identify English,
Italians, Spaniards, Scots, Germans, Irish, Mexicans, Russians, and Poles.
As Whiteman wrote in his autobiography, "The incredible pressure was
bound to blow off the lid" of machine-tending, ethnically diverse, industrial America, "and it might conceivably plunge a whole nation into
nervous prostration or insanity." Instead of the lid blowing off the melting pot of music after the nine different ethnic performances, however,
out from its enormous base dances a chorus line of American cowgirls.
(Figure 5.4, another version of Americanization, shows Whiteman and
his band dressed as Indians.) "For sheer spectacle, the Melting Pot finale can't be beat," enthused *Photoplay*. The movie ends with couples

from the different nations (one man wears a yarmulke) dancing to American music.[45]

Israel Zangwill's caldron melted down Old World metals to produce a stronger alloy. But Whiteman's "restorative," "brewing in New Orleans . . . to the national nerve complaint," invokes a cooking pot as well as a crucible. The cooking pot, instead of being a caldron in which cannibalism devours civilization, harks back to the maternal origins of melting-pot imagery. The breasts and lap of New World nature, in eighteenth-century visual and linguistic depictions, gave birth to a new American man. Viewed from that perspective the finale of *The King of Jazz* inverts its prologue, for jazz turns the devouring lion's mouth into the vehicle for cooking up a new, American stew, making Americans out of the separate ingredients of the old.[46]

African Americans, like the Asians of *Old San Francisco*, are the melting-pot medium; neither group is included in the final message. No African or Caribbean nation enters the melting pot of music; no dark skins (in *Old San Francisco*, recall, all the Mexicans are white) dance as representatives of their own nations or in the American melting pot. By the compensatory cultural logic of the Jazz Age, Whiteman's music has nothing to do with jazz.

IV

All the movies discussed in this chapter played variations on themes in *The Jazz Singer*. The central subject of *The Singing Fool* was gender. *The Jazz Singer*, I argued, feminized its protagonist. Singing in blackface about the price of success, about the loss of home that joined immigrant to native-born, mobile American, the jazz singer crossed the border not only between white and black, but also between desire for and identification with the woman. If *Old San Francisco* foreshadowed the first talking picture's ethnic example, *The Singing Fool* followed its gender example. Perhaps because blackface domestic tragedy drained of its ethnic particularism had a wider appeal, *The Singing Fool* was the top box office success of its time. Although Jolson's Jewishness, *The Jazz Singer*'s subject, is barely acknowledged, it is the condition of the gender cross-dressing.[47]

In minstrel ideology, blackface wildness invoked Africa, while blackface nostalgia conjured up the lost plantation. Minstrel consciousness not only repressed the savagery experienced by slaves on plantations; it also appropriated for voluntary immigrants and migrants to the New World the homesickness of the single group of Americans who were actually stolen from their Old World homes, and whose children were stolen from them under slavery. Jolson sings about loss in his first movie, moreover, to facilitate gain. Blackface spectacle looking backward, to Jewish mother and Russian/plantation home, projects narrative progress forward for the immigrant son. The balance shifts from gain to loss in *The Singing Fool.* The entertainer who had used blackface to move from Jew to American and to sing "My Mammy," now uses it to become Mammy and mourn the loss of his child.

Jolson plays a singing waiter, Al Stone, in *The Singing Fool,* who rises to show business stardom and marries the show girl he loves. When she leaves him for another man, taking their child with him, Al falls into the gutter, and he resumes his career only to discover that Sonny Boy is dying. Once again the performer goes on stage from a deathbed (this time of son rather than father) to sing out his blackface soul in the climax of the film.

The Singing Fool's opening shots invite us into Blackie Joe's, the cabaret where Al Stone performs. The peephole through which prospective guests are inspected marks the speakeasy as illicit; the mobile camera is the film audience's peephole, moving up to, in, and around the hidden room. It reveals dancers first through the window, then on the dance floor. Traveling into their dressing room, the camera presents two show girls from the back raising their naked legs. The first image of Molly, shot from below, shows her lying on a dressing-room bed with one long, thin, bare leg crossed over the other. The intrusive, voyeuristic camera fetishizes the showgirl leg as the sign of female sexuality. Sexual aggression is assigned to the woman, not simply employed to display her: Molly's foot will crush the sheet on which Al has written her a song.

Silent for its opening, *The Singing Fool* switches to sound for Al to sing that song. As in *The Jazz Singer,* Jolson introduces his first song in *The Singing Fool*'s initial, lip-synched, talking sequence. Both scenes display the famous voice and patter at once to celebrate talking pictures and to make Jolson's sound the instrument of his success. Song raises the Jolson character to stardom in both movies and wins him his girl. Louis Marcus, a producer in Blackie Joe's audience, gives Al his chance. Identifying the fatherly producer Jewish moves ethnicity from the jazz singer

Figure 5.5. Molly (Josephine Dunn) between Al Stone (Jolson) and Marcus (Edward Martindel) in *The Singing Fool*. Courtesy of the Academy of Motion Picture Arts and Sciences. © 1928 by Warner Bros.

and his family to a show business impresario. On the one hand, that shift acknowledges the Jewish role in the entertainment business, but on the other it eliminates the jazz singer's conflict between Jewish and American worlds.

Unlike the jazz singer, the singing fool is never a rebel. "I hope you'll like me," he pleads with the audience. "Well, anyway, my mother likes me." Instead of challenging a real father, the singing fool is aided by a surrogate, the Jewish producer. But paternal permission—removing the barrier between the son and his object of desire—proves a deeper obstacle to romance than patriarchal prohibition. The exchange of looks between Molly and Al that registers their desire follows Molly's interception of an approving look from Marcus to Al. She kisses Al after he sings "It All Depends on You," the song she had originally rejected; the kiss is a performance for the producer. Molly brings Al to Marcus; the three form a triangle, Molly between the two men. Marcus looms above the young couple; in a tight head-and-shoulders shot, he is the proud father (fig. 5.5). Cinematographers used "bust shots" to focus on facial expressions, but such disembodiment often signifies castration.[48] Marcus is cut off above the waist, but the image that places Al under the sign of the father points forward to the singer's emasculation at Molly's hands. Audience and producer approval have created desire in Molly, but it is triangulated desire.

Molly only marries Al because Marcus has come between them. Her lover replaces the producer in the next section of the film. While a montage reviews real-life Jolson hits, a voice-over announces, "In the following four years, Al wore out eight pianos, rhymed 'Mammy' with 'Alabammy' 981 times—and did more for Dixie than Robert E. Lee." But the arm that reaches out to a close-up of Molly's face, pinches her cheek, and pulls her offscreen is revealed to belong to another man. His sexualized, fetishized body part echoes Molly's leg. Cut to Al, eager to please, entertaining his audience. Instead of phallic body parts, the camera shows his singing mouth and entire body. Trotting up to his younger wife and her lover at their table, Al hovers over them; he has replaced the castrated father in the earlier triangle with Marcus. Al may deserve sympathy as eager son and cuckolded husband, but he borders on the ridiculous.

The triangle introduced in the next scene, Al, Molly, and their child, makes him the vehicle for pathos. Al, at home, embraces and caresses Sonny Boy; cut to Molly alone in bed (fig. 5.6). Al sings "Sonny Boy" to the toddler, sending him to sleep; Molly primps alone before her mirror. Molly refuses Al's kisses and expressions of endearment; the child enters the bedroom to interrupt their fight. Sonny Boy goes to his father; Al, carrying the child back to his bedroom, sings "Sonny Boy" again. Cut to Molly alone in bed, back to Al rocking Sonny Boy. In the next scene, Al calls home from the cabaret to discover that Molly has taken Sonny Boy and left him.[49]

The most successful film of the jazz age inverts the stereotypical sex roles. Wife wants sex; husband wants affection. Wife has lover; husband has child. Wife looks nonmaternal, with exposed legs and no breasts; husband rocks baby. Wife leaves home for lover and career; husband mourns the loss of his child.

When Al returns to his empty house, *The Singing Fool* reverts to silence for the first time since his opening song. A paternal "Stop!" silenced the jazz singer, interrupting the romance between mother and son. In *The Singing Fool* a transgressive maternal relationship is also punished, but this one features Al, not as son who wants mother, but as mother who wants son. Success entails loss in both the plots and the lost sound of these films. But whereas the jazz singer wanted both Jewish mother

Figure 5.6. Al, Molly, and Sonny Boy (David Lee) in *The Singing Fool.* Courtesy of the Academy of Motion Picture Arts and Sciences. © 1928 by Warner Bros.

and son, the singing fool (like many working women) wants both career and child.

More elaborately than *The Jazz Singer, The Singing Fool* brings the new technology into its plot. The movie reverts to silence to show Al's penultimate farewell to his son and the decline of his singing career; silence, as in *The Jazz Singer,* stands for loss. Losing the food that goes into his mouth as well as the sound that comes out of it, a starving Al slips into skid row. When he is finally rescued and restored to vaudeville stardom, he also gets back his voice.

The movie goes backward into silence for the last time in a vaudeville-derived routine featuring Al and his black dresser. Evoking the dual forms of vaudeville and silent pictures that the talkies would displace, this silent scene also plays a role in the narrative. In the film's single reference to his Jewishness, Al gives the dresser a turkey leg for his cat, with the intertitle reassuring, "It's all right, it's kosher." After the black man falls asleep, Al wakes him by tickling him with a straw. The half-awake dresser reaches out for an imaginary woman. A reminder of what is missing behind Al's bantering, the child's voice he has not heard again, the silent scene between Jew and black foreshadows the blackface climax of the movie.

The Singing Fool returns to sound when the dresser tells Al to call the hospital and he learns that Sonny Boy is dying. Al, reaching out for his son in the hospital bed, repeats the dresser's gesture, but the boy's "Take me, daddy" speaks parent/child *Liebestod,* not sexual possession. Al, the nursing father, holds the child to his breast; he sings "Sonny Boy" and rocks him to sleep. Carrying the dying child in his arms, Al is Uncle Tom in Porter's *Uncle Tom's Cabin,* carrying the dead Little Eva. Cut to Molly, slim and alone, all in white. When the doctor tells her Sonny Boy is dead, she collapses on the bed. The camera, repeating the shot that introduced her, exposes her legs from behind. One hangs from the bed; it is bare above the knee. The jazz singer killed his father by becoming a blackface singer rather than a cantor. The singing fool, by contrast, is an innocent; an abandoning mother has destroyed his home and is to blame for the death of their son.

The jazz singer Americanized himself through blackface, not just by choosing New World entertainment over Old World ritual, but also by providing the emotional form to mourn the loss of the old. Blackface, I have argued, was the transitional object whose emotional linkage to a world left behind facilitated movement forward and away. Blackface provided the emotional climax, the catharsis, of *The Jazz Singer. The Singing Fool* opens with a "My Mammy" shot, the blackface performer on his knees with his arms outstretched (see fig. 1.1); thereafter, however—to the same purpose of climax—it withholds blackface until the film's final scene.

"I'll feel better if I try to work," says Al, and he begins to apply burnt cork. He puts it on slowly, covering neck, nose, cheeks, top of head. As the catatonic Al, paralyzed by grief, disappears under the cork, a close-up shows his expressive, sad, blacked face, lips exaggerated, holding back tears. A hit of the first Vitaphone Prelude, preceding *Don Juan,* was Giovanni Martinelli performing "Vesti la giubba," and the great tenor's clown-costumed, whiteface rendition of Pagliaccci's grief may well have encouraged Warner Bros. to make *The Jazz Singer* and *The Singing Fool.* In celebrating performance as vehicle for emotional intensity, Hollywood was celebrating itself, with a self-consciousness about losing self-consciousness that complicates descriptions of classic Hollywood's illusionistic, narrative realism. Blackface gives full expression to the feelings that would otherwise lock Al in frozen melancholia. Faking cheerfulness when he relinquishes Sonny Boy and nonchalance when he is rescued from starvation, catatonic when Sonny Boy dies, Al cries real tears for the first time in his blackface performance of "Sonny Boy." The recording was the first single to sell a million copies.[50]

The jazz singer's acting, the vehicle for changing identities in order to Americanize, also recovered the feelings of abandonment concomitant to progress. The blackface singing fool performs loss at its most fundamental. Representation, wrote the film critic André Bazin, originated in the effort to bring back the dead; as Will Hays told the first Vitaphone audience, thanks to talking pictures "neither the artist nor his art will ever wholly die." The line "I still have you, Sonny Boy," anticipating the theft of the child by his mother, now holds on to a son who is present only in the ability of talking pictures to make absence present and thereby memorialize death.[51]

Al collapses after his performance; in the penultimate shot of the film, echoing the earlier triangles with Molly and Marcus, Molly and her lover, Molly and Sonny Boy, Al is supported between the stage manager and his new, loyal girl friend, Grace (fig. 5.7). In the final frame he rests his blackface head on Grace's shoulder. Blackface has carried Al from man and father, to woman and mother, to child.

The singing fool's performance facilitates authenticity, but at the expense of those supposed to have closer access to feeling: women and African Americans. *The Singing Fool* was probably a woman's film, like the 1930s weepies that followed it. Women dominated the film audience in the 1920s, and they were passionate about certain male stars. Rudolph Valentino became the missing phallus of his female audience, Miriam Hansen suggests, through his orientalist sexual and ethnic ambiguity. If Valentino was the object of women moviegoers' sexualized, maternal gaze, the singing fool offered maternal mouth and breast. Just as the Valentino cult disturbed traditional defenders of male sexual privilege, so *The Singing Fool*, challenging film theorists' stereotypes of the male gaze, reproached the sexually aggressive, dominating man. But *The Singing Fool*'s target was less the traditional man than the New Woman. The feminized man wins sympathy at the expense of the sexual, abandoning woman. The threat to traditional family values comes neither from new technologies (like the car and talking pictures) nor from Americanization, but from the New Woman. *The Singing Fool*, as an early version of male feminism, is a precursor of *Kramer vs. Kramer*.[52]

Blackface is the method of Al's maternalization. The portrayal of the black man as mother not only (as with Little Eva's mother in *Uncle Tom's Cabin*) reproaches the white woman who refuses to play that role; it also makes the black man nurture whites. Blackface operates as vehicle for sexual as for ethnic mobility by offering freedom for whites at the price of fixedness for blacks. The white man plays with a nurturing, emotional

Figure 5.7. Al supported by Grace (Betty Bronson) and the stage manager (Robert Emmett O'Connor) in *The Singing Fool*. Courtesy of the Academy of Motion Picture Arts and Sciences. © 1928 by Warner Bros.

identity that fixes black man, like white woman, as mother and child. The forbidden liaison between black man and white woman is realized in the black man as mammy. Cross-dressing, as *Old San Francisco* also testifies, is not reversible across race and gender lines.

The Jolson figure escapes ethnic imprisonment in *The Jazz Singer*. Cantor Rabinowitz, fixed in a traditional identity, sings Kol Nidre as ritual. His grown son, ethnic only in performing the sacred number, can take or leave his ethnicity; in *The Singing Fool*, he may seem to leave it behind. The feminization of the black man, however, also leaves its mark on Jolson's singing fool. As if to take back the jazz singer's triumph, the singing fool (like the protagonist in most Jolson films to follow) remains a supplicant. Jewishness placed a limit on the gentile dreams Jolson could interpret to his mass audience. A liminal figure, he was not permitted full, patriarchal authority. For the Jew to perform his transitional functions in classic Hollywood, linking immigrant to American and man to woman, he had to know his place. That is the message of the comedy that brings together ethnic and sexual cross-dressing, blackface and the myth of the West—Eddie Cantor's *Whoopee!*

V

Whoopee! begins where *The King of Jazz* ends, with a western production number. Instead of dancing out of a melting pot, here cowgirls join with cowboys to form the spokes of a human wheel. But Busby Berkeley's wagon wheel explicitly performs the function the melting pot pretends not to do: like drawn-up covered wagons, the wheel excludes those outside its circle. The first outsider is Henry (Eddie Cantor), a hypochondriacal Jewish weakling out of place in the West. The second is Wanenis, the Indian in love with Sally, the white girl whose marriage to Sheriff Bob the wagon wheel number celebrates. Indian and Jew come together, like Asian and Spaniard in *Old San Francisco*, as those threatened by American progress.

Unlike *Old San Francisco*, however, *Whoopee!* dwells on the relationship between the excluded rather than substituting one group for the other. The comic tie between Indian and Jew places *Whoopee!* in a tradition of Jewish/Indian spoofs, from Yiddish theater and vaudeville to Mel Brooks's *Blazing Saddles* (1974), productions that typically mock the white man's tragic, noble savage, intermarriage story. The first movie in which Cantor starred, *Whoopee!* may also derive from Cantor's friendship with the part-Cherokee "cowboy," Will Rogers, who wrote the introduction to Cantor's autobiography. The jazz singer, first successful in San Francisco, exemplifies the Turner thesis, for Jack Robin loses his ethnic particularism on the frontier. When the Jew goes west as vaudeville Jew— as Eddie Cantor—he at once facilitates and subverts the melting pot.[53]

Whoopee! disturbs not just ethnic and racial boundaries but, like *The Singing Fool*, sexual ones as well. Cantor's stereotypical Jew is a timid neurasthenic. If the high intermarriage plot brings together white girl and noble savage, the low one makes Henry the target of sexually aggressive ("I like weak men") Nurse Custer.

Whoopee! makes humor from the outsider status of Indians and Jews. Indian burlesque was a vaudeville standard; Fanny Brice sang "I'm an Indian" in Yiddish, and Cantor's first job was in a review called "Indian Maidens." "I'm only a small part Indian," Wanenis tells Henry. "How small?" "My grandfather married a white girl." "So did mine," responds Henry. He is speaking as a white man, but since Jews were "Oriental," racially stigmatized, and themselves the protagonists of intermarriage plots, the joke has a double edge. Is or is not this "half-breed," as Henry calls himself, a member of the group into which Wanenis wants to marry? "I've gone to your schools," Wanenis explains to Henry. "An Indian in a Hebrew school?"[54]

Whoopee! also makes fun of the opposite crossover, the Indianization of whites, by making its Dances with Wolves a Jew. After a captivity narrative spoof places Henry and Sally among the Indians, Wanenis's father ("Old Black Eagle, not old man Siegel," sings Cantor to the tune of Jerome Kern's recent *Show Boat* hit, "Old Man River") invites Henry to join his tribe. Disguised as an Indian ("Me big chief Izzy Horowitz"), Henry adopts a Yiddish accent to haggle over the price of an Indian blanket and doll he is selling to a rich white man. The message is that Jews would have gotten a better price for their land. Ads for *Whoopee!* show Cantor wearing Indian feathers (fig. 5.8), but, as in the movie, redface does not disguise but rather calls attention to the Jew under the costume. Claiming to be an Indian fire chief, Henry holds a Pueblo wall scaler and his nose: "Here's my hook and ladder."[55]

Degrading physical humor and violations of bodily integrity spread from ethnic jokes to sexual relations. Henry takes pills and receives injections from Nurse Custer. He and the rich white man roll around on the ground examining each other's operation scars. When the half-naked Wanenis appears in Indian feathers, Henry subjects him to a minute, intimate, physical inspection. These plays with the grotesque body, borrowed from blackface minstrelsy and Cantor's vaudeville shows, mock genteel romance. But male body contact is made respectable by being mobilized for intermarriage. "Making Whoopee," the song whose ridiculous pun joins Indian war dances to sexual play, comes down on the side of marriage. Conjugal fidelity disciplines indiscriminate heterosexual pleasure in the song's lyrics, and polymorphous, homoerotic perversity in the movie's subtext.[56]

In response to Black Eagle's invitation to join the tribe, Henry rein-

Figure 5.8. Henry (Eddie Cantor) in redface in *Whoopee!* Drawing from the *New Yorker*, Oct. 4, 1930.

states the intermarriage plot by bringing up Pocahontas. "Pocahontas saved John Smith," responds Black Eagle. Henry asks, "Why didn't he do something for his brother Al?" New York governor Al Smith, dubbed by Franklin Roosevelt "the happy warrior," was Cantor's boyhood hero—"as if the lady of the Statue of Liberty had sent her own son to receive these poor, bewildered immigrants," the actor wrote in his autobiography. Before viewers have time to reflect on Henry's joke—the failure of Pocahontas (and, by extension, the melting pot) to save Al Smith from anti-Catholicism in the 1928 presidential election—Henry goes on: "And I don't mean Al Jolson." Cantor, like Jolson, achieved stardom through blackface, so the reference to the two Als brings ethnic prejudice alongside racial masquerade.[57]

Blackface is the fulcrum at the center of Cantor's multiple cross-dressings. "I brought my negro friend up north," Cantor wrote of his blackface persona, by "add[ing] an intellectual touch to the old-fashioned darkey of the minstrel shows." Cantor's trademark character was "the cultured, pansy-like negro with spectacles"; Cantor and the "whitest black man I ever knew," the African American blackface vaude-villian Bert Williams, appeared as "Sonny and Papsy." As a blackface per-former Cantor was ambiguously male/female and black/white; he played Salome in drag and moved from man to woman to black eunuch in a slave harem in the movie *Roman Scandals*.[58]

As it facilitates intermarriage in *The Jazz Singer*, so blackface brings *Whoopee!*'s Indian and white lovers together. Henry, helping Sally escape her wedding to Sheriff Bob, hides in an oven. When the stove is lit, he explodes out in blackface. Like Whiteman's lion, Jolson's mammy, and the prototypical exaggerated blackface mouth, the oven associates black-face with primitive orality. The disguise fools Sheriff Bob and encour-ages Sally to confess her love for Wanenis. Promoting anarchic violence against the forces of law and order, blackface also facilitates intermar-riage in the low plot. Cantor sings "My Baby Just Cares for Me" in black-face, and sings it again sans cork to Nurse Custer to end the film. Trans-forming Jew from frightened melancholic into violent trickster, blackface shifts the meaning of "cares for" from nursing to sex. When Sheriff Bob tries to wipe Henry clean, he leaves him with what look like Orthodox Jewish earlocks and beard.

Racial cross-dressing promotes ethnic intermarriage in *The Jazz Singer* and *Old San Francisco; Whoopee!* may seem to bless racial intermarriage as well. Indians, to be sure, were not universally the targets of inter-marriage taboos. As the John Smith–Pocahontas story attests, Indian-white intermarriage was one way to provide the white presence in the New World with a native ground. Nonetheless, racist hostility certainly extended to Indians. "My one drop of Indian blood makes your people hate me," Wanenis explains to Sally. *Whoopee!*'s spoof of the one-drop theories of racial contamination that flourished in the Jazz Age ac-knowledges the racial prejudice buried in *The Jazz Singer* and dominant in *Old San Francisco* and *The King of Jazz*.

When, parodying the intermarriage melodramas, Black Eagle wants Wanenis to return to the ways of his people, the combination of tradi-tional loyalty and white prejudice seems to doom the romance. But faced with the love between Wanenis and Sally, Black Eagle reveals that Wanenis has not even a drop of Indian blood; a parodic descendant of James Fenimore Cooper's Oliver Effingham, he is a foundling the chief raised as his own child.[59] Wanenis may not know it, but, like Henry, he has been masquerading as an Indian. As in the plot of Rudolph Valentino's *Sheik,* the dark object of female desire turns out to be white beneath his mask. *Whoopee!,* like *The Jazz Singer,* celebrates racial cross-dressing, not miscegenation. The amalgamation that gives birth to a distinctively American culture substitutes for the mixing of blood.

Nineteenth-century melodramas pitted Indian fathers against those chosen for marriage by their children. These plays, antecedents for *The Jazz Singer* and *Old San Francisco,* were transferring legitimacy from descent to consent, in Werner Sollors's terms—from parental tribalism to the melting pot. That permission giving was done in bad faith, however, since the victors who wrote the dramas were the ones who conferred the Indians' blessing on those who took their place. *Whoopee!* spoofed the entire tradition.[60]

Turning Wanenis white is parodic; unlike *Old San Francisco* or *King of Jazz, Whoopee!* does not eliminate the racial in favor of the ethnic group. The Indian/Jewish confusion proleptically ridicules Hollywood for eliminating Jewish characters from movies—for Sam Goldwyn explaining, "A Jew can't play a Jew. It wouldn't look right on the screen"— such that the only Jews in front of the camera at Harry Cohn's Columbia Pictures were said to be playing Indians. Nor does *Whoopee!,* like the other movies discussed here, put technological innovation in the service of new identities. Even the dance numbers, Busby Berkeley's first Hollywood productions, are, like the movie as a whole, self-mocking. *Whoopee!,* with its blackface and redface masquerades, remains in the technologically more primitive, anti-illusionistic, vaudeville and early silent movie tradition.[61]

Even so, *Whoopee!* participates in the tradition it ridicules. By making savages noble and confining the Jew to slapstick, *Whoopee!*'s plot privileges the racial over the ethnic minority, but its method has the opposite effect. Although Cantor's stereotyping may edge into anti-Semitism, it is the vehicle for Jewish self-expression. Like the vaudeville routines and Vitaphone shorts of Lou Holtz, George Burns, Gregory Ratoff, and George Jessel, Cantor's performance helped shape a recognizable, authentically Jewish-American milieu. No Indians, by contrast, will recognize themselves in the cardboard straight men and women for Jewish humor. Wanenis has not a drop of Indian blood, and the other actors playing Indians are palefaces too.

Cantor's blackface does not even pretend to depict real blacks. *Whoopee!*'s blackface is Jewish, its redface (Cantor aside) is goyish—to

borrow Lenny Bruce's distinction between mocking, physicalized signifiers and pious, disembodied ones—for the film privileges an urban-
minority voice over the racially based, homogenizing, melting-pot myth
of the West in *The King of Jazz* and *Old San Francisco*. Race is the assimilating vehicle for ethnic disappearance in the other movies; in this
one it supports Americanizing ethnic self-assertion.[62]

Cantor gains power over his ethnicity by performing it. Signifying on
his Jewishness, however, playing with the stereotype rather than challenging it, is also a sign of the narrow constraints within which he was
able to assert his ethnic identity. Jews remain tarred by the masks (Cantor's comic or Jolson's tragic) that win them acceptance in the promised
land. The sexual cross-dressing implied in Jewish neurasthenia and male
horseplay may point either to polyphony or, as in *The Singing Fool*, to
the limits of Jewish liminality. But however one evaluates the transgressions in *Whoopee!*'s ethnic and sexual carnivalesque, the movie, it is necessary to say, provides no vehicle for nonwhite self-expression.[63] Bad taste
is its virtue, but *Whoopee!* plays with, mocks, and operates wholly inside
the ethnic, sexual, and racial hierarchies of Jazz Age America.

Blackface carried Cantor from the slum to the stars. It had, however,
"become an inseparable part of my stage presence," Cantor wrote in his
autobiography, titled *My Life Is in Your Hands*, "and I feared that the
day might come when I could never take it off. I would always be Eddie
Cantor, the blackface comedian, but if I ever tore the mask off I'd be
nobody at all." Resolving that "I was not going to be a slave to a piece
of burnt cork for the rest of my acting days," Cantor convinced Florenz
Ziegfeld to let him appear in whiteface. Unlike African Americans, inadvertently invoked by Cantor's refusal to be a slave, the white man in
blackface could change the color of his skin. "It was the first time I felt
revealed to the audience and in personal contact with it," Cantor confessed. In Cantor's initial whiteface skit, which stole the show at the 1919
Ziegfeld Follies, a doctor subjected him to an invasive physical exam. The
comedian connected that exposure to a later routine, "in essence" the
same as the initial one, that turned on his Jewish identity. Cantor's free
association moves him from the stage doctor's into the audience's hands.
The Jazz Singer escapes his Jewish past in blackface. Cantor, thanks to
blackface, can finally reveal himself to the mass audience as a Jew.[64]

Like the jazz singer, however, the urban Jew finds a southern home.
Cantor's autobiography ends with "the slum boy of the tenements"
preparing to embark on the stage production of *Whoopee!* and, "a modern pioneer," buying a house in Great Neck, Long Island. Cantor's

neighbor is Nathan S. Jonas, "an imposing gentleman with a trace of Southern aristocracy" who has planted a "boxwood garden reminiscent of Southern estates" and developed "one of the most beautiful and exclusive country clubs in America." "Space and time are the slaves that tremble under the wand of wealth," writes Cantor, and these modern slaves allow the financier to "return to the simple and primitive" pastoral life. Cantor is incorporated into the family homecoming, for the boy who at the age of two had "floundered in the streets of New York, fatherless and motherless," writes that he is "now sitting in a flower-laden bower with my parents. Mr. and Mrs. Nathan S. Jonas have become father and mother to me."[65]

If Cantor's autobiography lacked the comic courage of *Whoopee!*'s convictions, the Marx Brothers supplied it. Cantor's plantation refuge could well have been the Long Island estate the polyglot immigrants invade in *Animal Crackers* (1930), where the socialite, Roscoe W. Chandler, is really "Abie the peddler," and where Groucho, taking off on Henry M. Stanley, plays Geoffrey T. Spalding, "the noted explorer returning from Africa." ("Hurray for Captain Spalding, the African explorer; did someone call me *schnorrer?*") "I wish I was back in the jungle, where men are monkeys," says Groucho. Africa has elephant tusks; "Of course, in Alabama there's the Tuscaloosa." Then, in a "program . . . coming to you from the House of David," the barbershop quartet of Groucho, Chico, Harpo, and Zeppo lament and replace their lost home. They mangle, not the version of "Swanee River" that helped launch the Jazz Age, written by one East European Jew and performed in blackface by another—not Gershwin and Jolson's "Swanee"—but the original Stephen Foster minstrel ballad, "Old Folks at Home."[66]

PART 3

"Democracy and Burnt Cork": The End of Blackface, the Beginning of Civil Rights

I have assumed that the slaves were merely human beings, that innately Negroes are, after all, only white men with black skins, nothing more, nothing less.

Kenneth Stampp, *The Peculiar Institution: Slavery in the Antebellum South* (1956)

You can't defend practices that are based on group preferences as opposed to individual opportunities, which is what America has always been about. . . . [Affirmative action is] an un-American argument . . . because . . . America's about individuals, not about averages or groups.

Senator Joseph Lieberman (1995)

CHAPTER 6

New Deal Blackface

I

In 1942 Veit Harlan, having directed the notorious anti-Semitic propaganda movie *Jud Süss* for Hitler, was permitted to make a technicolor spectacular. *Die goldene Stadt* was Germany's first technically successful color film; like *Jud Süss*, it met with an enthusiastic reception.[1] Whereas *Jud Süss* imitated *Birth of a Nation*, *Die goldene Stadt* was the Third Reich's *Gone with the Wind;* indeed, a comparison between the Harlan and Selznick productions exposes the contrasting places of Jews and African Americans in Nazi and New Deal cinema. That contrast will set the stage for the blackface musical—whose neglected significance for talking pictures is the subject of this chapter—and for the emergence after the Nazi defeat of the first Hollywood movies to address racism and anti-Semitism. Both the blackface musical and the racial-problem film, I will suggest, are progenies of *The Jazz Singer*. This chapter and the next investigate the unacknowledged indebtedness of civil rights films to the blackface tradition they were trying to leave behind.

That *Die goldene Stadt,* the golden city, is free of Jews is no evidence that Veit Harlan was having second thoughts about his collaboration with the Nazis. The lure of gold is breathtaking in *The Golden City,* which appears first as a magical, glimmering, postcard of Prague, and then as the city in the flesh. But the eroticized precious metal is as dangerous in its beautiful as in its Jewish guise; whereas the Nazi propaganda film *The Rothschilds* (1940) shows "devilish fumes rising from the witches' cauldron of the Jewish quest for gold," the golden city also conceals poisonous cosmopolitan plotters, and its glitter draws Harlan's heroine to her death.[2]

Anna, a Sudetenland German who inhabits the lush, picturesque Central European countryside, is in rebellion against the constricted patriarchal world and the fiancé who would lock her into it. Taking the reins of her carriage into her own hands, and whipping her horse and herself into a frenzy, she wildly embraces the engineering surveyor from Prague. The surveyor, removed from the village by Anna's father, sends the postcard that entices her to the golden city. Although he means Anna no harm, the engineer cannot save her from her aunt and the aunt's illegitimate son. A set of scenes of gross physicality, which establish the aunt's erotic involvement with both her son and her niece, climax when the young man takes his resistant but excited virgin cousin to bed.

Jud Süss, with its sinister Jewish financier/rapist and the "dirty, fat, hook-nosed, and physically repellent" horde of Jews he admits into Stuttgart, was preparing the ground for genocide. Shown in towns throughout Germany as Jews were being taken away, and to concentration camp guards and soldiers to prepare them for mass murder, the film ends with the expulsion of the Jews from the city (an homage to the end of *Birth of a Nation*, in which African Americans are herded onto ships to be returned to Africa). In *Die goldene Stadt*, Anna's aunt and her bastard replace the Jews of *Jud Süss*. The son is a parasite who lives off women; there are neither paternal authorities nor productive workers in Prague. An instance of Nazi ideology, *Die goldene Stadt* separates labor from gold, production from consumption, the healthy countryside from the corrupt metropolis.[3]

But traditional peasant life is also in need of modernization. Pregnant, unmarried, and abandoned, Anna returns home to paternal rejection. She drowns herself and her unborn baby in the swamp on the edge of the Moldau. As the raped victim of Jewish "race defilement," Kristina Soederbaum (Harlan's wife and the actress who played Anna) had already drowned herself onscreen in *Jud Süss*. "The phantom of the swamp" had also claimed Anna's mother before *Die goldene Stadt* begins. Superstitious villagers mistrusted the engineer and opposed draining the swamp, but Anna's father accepts progress after her suicide. The snake that had made its home in the swamp is replaced in the final frames of the film by productive acres of wheat. In the middle of these fields is Anna's tombstone. Bringing technology to the countryside, against the seductive, parasitic city of gold, Harlan's swamp draining prefigures the words that would welcome inmates to Auschwitz: "Arbeit macht frei."[4]

The final image of *Die goldene Stadt* echoes the opening shot of the Hollywood blockbuster released only three years before, whose credits roll across a breathtaking panorama of cotton fields. Just as *Jud Süss* had roots in Hitler's favorite film, *The Birth of a Nation*, so *Die goldene Stadt* derived from *Gone with the Wind*.[5] But whereas Harlan's wheat fields are empty of human life, in the American film choreographed masses of slaves hoe cotton to the sound of plantation music. Although censored from the souvenir program,[6] African Americans are featured in *Gone with the Wind*'s opening close-ups. Providing the backdrop for "the last of the cavalier societies," with its "knights and ladies, masters and slaves," blacks also undergird the movie's plot. Their presence in the American movie, together with the elimination of Jews from *Die goldene Stadt,* sums up a central difference between the National Socialism for which Veit Harlan made movies and the political movement that David O. Selznick supported, Franklin D. Roosevelt's New Deal.

Scarlett O'Hara, like Anna, is a rebellious young woman unsatisfied by her socially appropriate marriage partner. Force stimulates her sexual pleasure in the marital rape scene with Rhett Butler, a precursor of Anna's seduction. Scarlett, however, is less a sexual initiator than Anna, her sexual pleasure is less graphic, she is already married when she is taken to bed, and her child is legitimate. Both women are punished for their independence, but although Scarlett's child dies, like Anna's unborn baby, the American woman heroically perseveres. From one perspective Anna is punished more severely than Scarlett because she is more sexual. From another, Scarlett is allowed more freedom because the old order has broken down in civil war; there is no longer, unlike in Harlan's Central European countryside, any legitimate patriarchal authority.

These alternative explanations share a common social ground, in whose absence *Gone with the Wind* would be another *Birth of a Nation.* What saves the New Woman from the dangers of freedom in Selznick's American South is the support of African Americans. Whereas Anna is betrayed by the family servant, Marushka, who is plotting to marry her father, black slaves and servants protect Scarlett for the entire three-and-a-half-hour/twenty-year length of the film. Unlike Veit Harlan's Jews, African Americans are part of the O'Hara "love of the land." (Whereas Selznick could "smell the magnolias" when Hattie McDaniel appeared for her screen test dressed "as a typical Old Southern Mammy," Louise Beavers hurt her chance for the part by showing up in furs.)[7] Scarlett, like Anna, seizes the reins of a horse carriage. But when she rides recklessly into danger, a black man rescues her from rape. Prissy (Butterfly McQueen) may not be able, as she pretends, to act as a midwife, but McDaniel is never anything less than solid wisdom and competence. Scarlett can be rebellious because her slaves are not. Since there is no question of revolution, she and her African Americans safely exchange roles. It is Scarlett who delivers the baby, having learned to work from those who work for her. Gentlemen bid for dances with ladies at a wartime "slave auction"; when Scarlett is reduced to laboring in the fields after the southern defeat, her freed black servants hoe and plant alongside her.[8] Although McDaniel was excluded from the segregated Atlanta premiere of *Gone with the Wind,* where she would have been mixing with the other guests rather than serving them, her place was taken by Mrs. Martin Luther King Sr.'s Ebenezer Church choir.[9] We are not quite finished with explicit attention to *Gone with the Wind.* But instead of taking as our central object the most popular motion picture in Hollywood history, let us look at depression-era film through its lens.

II

The New Deal, no historian would disagree, brought the immigrant to the center of American politics. Shifting the orientation of the majority party from the hinterland to the metropolis, Roosevelt's victories were foreshadowed in their urban, ethnic underpinnings by the Catholic Al Smith's 1928 run for the presidency. The 1930s and 1940s were also, with the coming of talking pictures, the golden age of the Hollywood studio system. In the standard film history accounts, urban, Americanizing immigrants joined the rest of the country in watching mass-produced studio genre films that purveyed the quintessential national narratives—gangster pictures, musicals, screwball comedies, domestic melodramas, westerns. The 1930s left its mark on the genre mix, from this point of view, by bringing the urban ethnic milieu of gangster films together with screwball comedy's class reconciliation—by combining Frank Capra's populist politics, on the one hand, with the cinema of escapist entertainment that allowed moviegoers to flee the depression, on the other.

Some of the most important and popular films of the period are missing from this picture, films grounded on race. As the Jazz Age came to an end, *The Jazz Singer* and *The Singing Fool* broke all existing box office records. At the same time that Jolson was the top Hollywood box office star, *Amos 'n' Andy* was the most popular radio show.[10] (By the middle of the depression decade, Fletcher Henderson's arrangements were making Benny Goodman the "King of Swing," as "the Swing Era," in Gunther Schuller's words, was "spicing up familiar commercial, popular material with a Harlem oriented musical seasoning and selling it via a white band for a white/musical/consumer audience.")[11] The Motion Picture Exhibitors' coveted top-ten list of stars was headed in 1934 by Will Rogers, who put on Stepin Fetchit's black voice in the southern-genre film *Judge Priest* (1934); from 1935 through 1938 by Shirley Temple, who starred in four films with Bojangles Robinson (including the Civil War southerns *The Little Colonel* and *The Littlest Rebel* [both 1935], where she puts on blackface; and in 1939 by Mickey Rooney, who led a blackface minstrel show that year in *Babes in Arms.* Margaret Mitchell dined at the White House after the success of the Selznick production of her novel. Far from being a blockbuster exception to New Deal culture, *Gone with the Wind* proves the rule.[12]

Transformative films in American motion picture history, *The Jazz Singer* and *Gone with the Wind* use documentary effects and social range to lay claim to film as history. As with *The Birth of a Nation* and Edwin Porter's trilogy, however, representational aspirations point less to historical accuracy than to the politics that produced these movies, their worldviews as ideology. Whereas Porter and Griffith belonged to the origins, success, and decline of progressivism, *The Jazz Singer* and *Gone with the Wind* are the harbinger and triumph, respectively, of the New Deal coalition. *Birth of a Nation* represents the Hitlerian moment in America, national integration on racialist terms, where the defeat of the fathers (southern in the Civil War, German in World War I) is blamed on the central group around which each country's racist political fantasies are organized, Jews in Germany and African Americans in the United States. As in *Jud Süss,* rape organizes *Birth of a Nation,* although the victim in *Birth* leaps to her death to avoid racial defilement rather than as its consequence. (Here *Jud Süss* is faithful to *The Clansman,* the novel on which *Birth of a Nation* was based.)[13]

The black rapists that *Birth* put on the screen continued to hold sway in southern politics during the Jazz Age and the New Deal, as evidenced by lynchings in the former Confederacy, the trial of the Scottsboro Boys (young black men convicted with no credible evidence of raping two white women on a train), and opposition to a federal antilynching bill (including FDR's failure to support it as his devil's pact with the South). A black man also attacks Scarlett O'Hara in the novel *Gone with the Wind.* Responding to NAACP objections during the filming of the movie, however, Selznick insisted that he had "left no stone unturned in our

efforts to eliminate from our picture any possible objections which the
Negroes of America may have had to portions of the novel. . . . I feel so
keenly about what is happening to the Jews of the world that I cannot
help but sympathize with the Negroes and their fears," Selznick explained, and he promised to portray the black characters as "loveable,
faithful, high-minded people [who] . . . would leave no impression but
a very nice one."[14]

Selznick spoke at the level of national consensus—as seen in *The Jazz
Singer* and *Gone with the Wind*—for although the producer compared
the political attacks on *Gone with the Wind* to the earlier campaign
against Griffith's *Birth of a Nation,* he insisted that he had "cleaned up"
Margaret Mitchell's Pulitzer Prize–winning novel. *Birth's* Reconstruction and progressive black beast literally turned white when Mitchell's
rapist moved from the book to the movie. The black men who assault
Scarlett O'Hara in the novel metamorphose in the film not into *Birth's*
sexual assaulters in blackface—for whom they could easily be mistaken
(and were by Carleton Moss in his *Daily Worker* attack on the movie)—
but into dirty, lower-class, white trash, and the large black man in motion in the motion picture turns out to be running not to rape Scarlett
but to rescue her. The black woman at *Birth's* center is a mulatto seductress, mistress of the northern abolitionist, and the prototype for
Anna's aunt in *Die goldene Stadt.* She is reborn as the jazz singer's and
Scarlett's mammy. Instead of promoting black emancipation, mammy
sustains white freedom, not by menacing it, like the rapist, but rather,
as the Motion Picture Academy recognized in presenting its Oscar award
to Hattie McDaniel, by performing the best supporting actress role.[15]

"Two entertainers in the twentieth century rose to fame on one word,
'Mammy,'" writes Carleton Jackson. "The first was Al Jolson, whose
Mammy endeared him to generations of theatre goers. The other was
Hattie McDaniel."[16] McDaniel had begun her career as a blues mama
in minstrel shows playing before black audiences. After her triumph in
Gone with the Wind she sexed up her tour as the film's mammy by
singing "Mammy . . . wants to have a good time." In the course of her
act she would shift back and forth from Jolson's "I'd walk a million miles
for one of your smiles, my Mammy" ("I want my children that I nestled
to my breast, black and white, with so much zest") to "The moment
when you danced by I felt a thrill, that's what mammy wants." That was
not what Selznick wanted, however. Combining the roles of pro-
ducer/patriarch and Jewish son, he opposed McDaniel "stooping to
things that might be offensive." Although she eliminated her most rib-

ald lines, McDaniel's mammy/mama crossover did not prove popular with white audiences. Returning to her film mammy persona during the war, McDaniel would go on to play a maid in *Beulah*, the most popular radio show in American history. (The role she took over was originated, going *Amos 'n' Andy* one better, by a white man.)[17]

Gone with the Wind, David O. Selznick, and Hattie McDaniel, heirs to the jazz singer and his mammy, anchor classic talking-pictures Hollywood. The Jewish role has now moved offscreen, but far from excluding ethnicity in its concern with race, the two films that frame New Deal cinema makes visible the relationship between the two. The New Deal coalition, an alliance of northern ethnics and southern whites, appears onscreen with the former Jakie Rabinowitz singing "My Mammy" in blackface in New York and with the Irish O'Haras making, losing, and struggling to revive a southern plantation. Race Americanizes white immigrants in both films. African Americans ground the O'Haras in the great American historical epic of slavery, the Civil War, and Reconstruction. Blackface moved Jakie Rabinowitz in *The Jazz Singer*, and Jolson in life, from immigrant Jew to American, as it had earlier done for Irish immigrants on the cultural border between black and white. Their status as migrants from the countryside (South) to the city (North) also provided a point of identification for immigrant and black fans of *Amos 'n' Andy*.[18]

American politics was organized around antiblack racism rather than anti-Semitism. That fact was hardly without consequence, as we have seen, either for European immigrants in general, facing nativist pressure as they made themselves into white Americans, or for Jewish moguls, blackface entertainers, and songwriters in particular, putting their American dream on the screen during Hollywood's golden age. Jewish immigrants and their children inherited and often struggled against the racial representations that signified American belonging. But they also— witness Selznick in *Gone with the Wind*—made those representations their own. Jews were the most black-identified immigrant group, and one form of that identification, blackface, defamiliarizes the other, the Jewish/black civil rights alliance, as we will see it made visible on the Hollywood screen. The shared and divergent situation of immigrant Jews and native African Americans brings together the two New Deal genres that are the subject of this chapter and the next: the blackface musical and the racial social-problem, or civil rights, film.

Transformative motion pictures, in their claims to total cinema, cannot be subsumed under standard genre categories. Instead, *Gone with the Wind* and *The Jazz Singer* synthesize genres that separate before and after them. Moving back and forth between silence and sound, black-face and whiteface, Jew and gentile, street and stage, *The Jazz Singer*'s genre liminality is part of its generic liminality. The first talking picture unites the subgenre of the social-problem film that it climaxed, the generational-conflict/intermarriage/passing motion picture, with the genre it originated, the musical, more particularly, the self-reflexive movie musical about making musicals or making music, which encompasses at its foundation the blackface musical.[19]

As Jim Kitzes insists about the western, even within established genres, with their own formal rules, building blocks, and symbolic structures, film presents itself as history.[20] The social-problem and musical genres may seem to offer opposed historical visions—heavy and light, tragedy and comedy, realism and escape, narrative and spectacle. "Black-face became a trademark of the professional entertainer," explained the former editor of the Hollywood *Reporter* in 1977. "There is nothing social or political about blackface."[21] But where escapist entertainment puts on the mask of the oppressed, it exposes, in itself, the social problem. Moreover, the mixture of the two genres in the first talking picture— the use of musical blackface to encapsulate and solve the social, generational problem by Americanizing the immigrant son—supports Robin Wood's and Vivian Sobchack's suggestion that placing apparently opposed genres together illuminates ideological work that remains less apparent in a single genre.[22] From one perspective the racially inflected social-problem film supplies the reality escaped from in blackface musical utopia. Not only do blackface stereotypes carry over into race-relations movies, however; the blackface celebration of performance infects them as well, since role-playing and identity transformation organize both genres. Both use the Hollywood method to cross the racial/ethnic divide.[23]

The two genres separated again after *The Jazz Singer*, as the generational-conflict social-problem film went into decline and was supplanted by the blackface musical. The Jewish novelist and screenwriter Fannie Hurst supplied the major examples of the generational-conflict film, *The Younger Generation* (1928) and *Symphony of Six Million* (1932), about the Jewish "lower east side—a melting pot where the younger generation struggles to free itself from the order of the fathers"[24]—and *Imitation of Life* (1934), on black passing. Blackface had replaced black actors onscreen in social-problem silent films and other genres of narrative cinema. Although talking pictures, a large step toward narrative realism, ended the era in which whites played black in dramatic roles, sound's ability to capture the singing voice revived blackface minstrelsy. Serving music in the Vitaphone shorts and *The Jazz Singer,* synchronized sound originally called attention to performance rather than supporting illusionistic, realist cinema. Musicals continued the spectacle side of sound. If *The Jazz Singer* ended the use of blackface as unselfconscious method of impersonating African Americans (as in *Birth of a Nation*), it introduced to feature films blackface as conscious film subject. White performers put on burnt cork in self-reflexive celebration of American entertainment itself. Beginning with *The Jazz Singer,* blackface musicals established Hollywood's roots in the first American mass entertainment form.[25]

There were some roles for blacks as entertainers in the 1930s—usually variations on the narrativized minstrel roles of mammy, tom, and coon, particularly in the genre that *Gone with the Wind* climaxes, the southern (exemplified by the Shirley Temple/Bojangles Robinson films, John Ford's *Judge Priest,* and *Jezebel* [1938]). Blackface musicals, nonetheless, sustained the tradition of whites playing black as spectacle. In the classic period of Hollywood narrative realism, with its claims to verisimilitude and its focus on individual, interiorized character development, the musical in general and the blackface musical in particular retained the gestural, playing-to-audience, theatrical, self-reflexive, non-realistic, utopian qualities of silent film.[26]

As a family melodrama, *The Jazz Singer* used music to evoke conflict and loss, and in the first years of talking pictures other musicals followed its example. The early-depression-era musical comedies *Gold Diggers of 1933* (starring Jolson's wife, Ruby Keeler) and *42nd Street* (1933) made music out of social problems; the former, a deliberate New Deal parable, ended with a production number, "My Forgotten Man," that evoked in name an FDR campaign speech and in sound and image the bonus marchers on Washington. "Forgotten Man's" foreboding concludes the show on a disjunctive note, however, and by the mid-1930s the musical genre had transformed itself, according to Rick Altman, by associating music with pleasure rather than pain.[27]

The blackface musical is an instance. Most musicals using blackface in the 1930s and 1940s fall into two subcategories, both derived from *The Jazz Singer:* they are either backstage musicals about putting on a show or biographies of the central figures in the history of American popular music. The first group includes such unsuccessful Jolson vehicles as *Mammy* (1930) and *The Singing Kid* (1936), Fred Astaire's *Swingtime* (1936), Mickey Rooney and Judy Garland's *Babes in Arms* (1939) and

Babes on Broadway (1941), Fred Astaire and Bing Crosby's *Holiday Inn* (1942, the film that introduced the best-selling record of all time, Irving Berlin's "White Christmas"), and *This Is the Army* (1943, starring Ronald Reagan, the only film made before the end of World War II, aside from *Gone with the Wind* and *Bambi,* to remain half a century later among the all-time top one hundred Hollywood box office hits). The second group comprises retrospective, nostalgic films that, from 1939 to 1949, took blackface from its antebellum origins to post–World War II America, recounting the lives of Stephen Foster (*Swanee River* [1939]; the movie also features the blackface minstrel E. P. Christy, played by Jolson); Dan Emmett, who, together with Christy, was the most popular early minstrel (*Dixie* [1943]); George Gershwin (*Rhapsody in Blue* [1945]; Jolson repeats his blackface rendition of "Swanee" in this film); and Jolson (*The Jolson Story* [1946] and *Jolson Sings Again* [1949]). (*I Dream of Jeannie* [1952], a low-budget Foster biopic, *The Eddie Cantor Story* [1953], and the Danny Thomas *Jazz Singer* remake [1952], all critical and box office failures, bring the subgenre to an end, though it came back from the dead in Neil Diamond's *Jazz Singer* [1980].)[28]*

As grounded in *The Jazz Singer* and *Gone with the Wind,* and culminating in the immense postwar popularity of *The Jolson Story* and *Jolson Sings Again,* the blackface musical was among the most important genres of New Deal cinema. In 1946, the most profitable year for Hollywood since the beginning of film, when the average audience each week reached nearly 75 percent of potential moviegoers, *The Jolson Story* was one of three films to monopolize the Academy Award nominations and one of three to follow *Birth* and *Gone with the Wind* in setting box of-

---

*Although Neil Diamond's *Jazz Singer* could not center on blackface in 1980, the remake is egregiously faithful to the racial politics of the original. Jess Rabinowitch (a.k.a. Jess Robin) gets his musical start with a black group. Their first performance together allows Diamond to black up his face and Afro his hair, supposedly not to entertain whites but to pass before an all-black audience. Jess leaves the black group behind when he achieves stardom. The member who got him his chance, Bubba, reappears only when Jess is torn between his music and his Jewish father and wife (she replaces Jakie Rabinowitz's mother), and as the instrument of reconciliation between Jess and his new gentile wife, and between Jess and his father. Black people exist to take care of Jess; he does nothing for them. Diamond opens and closes the movie by singing, behind footage of almost entirely nonblack immigrant crowds on the streets of New York, "Every time that flag's unfurled, they're coming to America" (adopted by Michael Dukakis for the 1988 Democratic national convention). The song ends with the last shot of the film, a freeze frame on the star with a single arm raised in a gesture of triumph (rather than the two arms outstretched in the original *Jazz Singer*'s gesture of pathos). That same image had dissolved in the opening sequence into the Statue of Liberty.

fice records. *Jolson Sings Again* led all films in 1949 in box office receipts. Significantly, the other 1946 movie that combined Academy Awards with box office success, apparently at the opposite pole from *The Jolson Story*, was *Best Years of Our Lives*, a social-problem film about returning World War II veterans. The film second to *Jolson Sings Again* in 1949 box office receipts was a racial social-problem film, *Pinky*. *Home of the Brave*, which combined *Best Years of Our Lives*'s war subject with *Pinky*'s racial theme, was also among the top thirty grossers of the year—re-markable for a low-budget, independent production. The racial/ethnic social-problem film, both in its original generational-conflict and later antidiscrimination forms, thus appears as the underside of the blackface musical.[29]

That the social-problem and musical genres are split halves of a sin-gle Ur-film is suggested not only by their common *Jazz Singer* roots but also by the simultaneous success of *Jolson Story* and *Best Years*, *Jolson Sings Again* and *Pinky*. The link between the two genres, and the omnipres-ence of race in the immediate aftermath of World War II, are also evi-denced by the other of the three top box office hits of 1946, David O. Selznick's *Duel in the Sun*. Hoping that this blockbuster western melo-drama would rival *Gone with the Wind*, Selznick brought Lillian Gish (from *Birth of a Nation*) and Butterfly McQueen (from *Gone with the Wind*) together with Gregory Peck, Joseph Cotten, Lionel Barrymore, and Walter Huston. He cast Jennifer Jones as Pearl Chavez, a Jekyll-and-Hyde "half-breed" ancestrally divided between her respectable English paternal and her sexually dissolute Indian maternal blood, romantically torn between the upright, considerate Jesse McCanless (Cotten) and his abusive, magnetic brother, Lewt (Peck). The film opens with Pearl's fa-ther killing his wife and one of her johns, then welcoming his own exe-cution. It closes with the dying Pearl, having stalked and shot Lewt to stop him from killing Jesse and been fatally wounded in return, locked with her lover in an embrace to the death. Although *Duel in the Sun* con-demns the racial slurs of Lewt and his rancher father (Barrymore), Pearl Chavez's writhings and her humiliating sexual passion illustrate her fail-ure to be "a good girl"—the truth of what the racists say. Bringing *The Jazz Singer* up-to-date, moreover, Selznick put brownface on the gen-tile girl, Jones, for whom he was leaving his Jewish wife (and thereby trumping his father-in-law, Louis B. Mayer, who had also left *his* Jew-ish wife).[30]

Combining racialized sexual hysteria with liberal political attitudes, *Duel in the Sun* is the illegitimate parent of the civil rights movies that

followed it. Between 1947 and 1949, when the Popular Front over-
lapped with early civil rights cold war liberalism, Hollywood produced
six more films exposing racial prejudice. The industry's first two movies
on anti-Semitism, *Crossfire* (1947) and *Gentleman's Agreement* (1947),
were followed in 1949, in a literal transfer, by four movies on antiblack
racism: *Pinky, Lost Boundaries, Home of the Brave,* and *Intruder in the
Dust.*[31]

These civil rights movies are the stepchildren of the generational-
conflict films of the silent and early-sound screens. Unwilling to show
nativist hostility to immigrants, the earlier motion pictures displaced anti-
Semitism in the wider society onto generational conflict within the Jewish family: in *The Jazz Singer,* for example, resistance to Jew becoming
American comes from the Jewish father, not from gentiles. The end of
mass immigration to the United States and the destruction of European
Jewry produced nostalgia for a lost Jewish world instead of the fear of
Old World figures blocking the path to Americanization. This shift takes
place visibly in the blackface musical, where the *Jazz Singer* patriarch
metamorphoses into the adorable, supportive old-people dolls—"Stepin
Fetchits," a later critic would call them—of the Jolson biopics.[32] Outside Hollywood as well, the portrayals of family conflict and crisis in Yiddish cinema and Jewish publications of the first part of the century would
be buried by retrospective celebrations of the Jewish family as the source
of Jewish American success. Nathan Glazer and Daniel Patrick Moynihan in *Beyond the Melting Pot,* for example, juxtapose Jewish family co-
hesion to black family pathology to explain Jewish success and black failure.[33]

However sentimentalized the postwar depiction of Jews, the genocide nonetheless turned Hollywood attention to anti-Semitism. It also
called attention to the racial oppression of African Americans. Racism
and anti-Semitism, the unacknowledged condition for blackface musicals and generational-conflict films from *The Jazz Singer* to *Jolson Sings
Again,* are made visible on the screen in the civil rights movies. But these
films also expose the underside of Jewish/black identification in their use
of blackface stereotypes and their portrayal of relative Jewish privilege.[34]

The doubled postwar genre films—Jolson biopics and racial social-
problem pictures—straddle the fissures surrounding race and war that
would ultimately shatter the New Deal coalition. Looking backward
from that political coming-apart, one could identify the Jolson films as
"Dixiecrat" for their southern nostalgia, social-problem films such as
Crossfire (whose director, producer, and writers would soon fall victim

to the House Un-American Activities Committee) as (Henry) Wallaceite. Not only do the Jolson biopics hold together the southern/Jewish alliance, however, but the social-problem films are defined by it as well. The continuation of the New Deal coalition for two decades after the war, in spite of pressures from white supremacists on the right, civil rights and anti–cold war activists on the left, shows up in the way the two genres in the late 1940s, rather than being polarized, interpenetrated. The racial social-problem film, although it poses itself against the blackface musical, is actually an inheritance from it.

III

Ella May flees to the kitchen, in John Ford's *Judge Priest* (1934), to avoid Flem Talley's indecent advances. As Ella May is making lemonade, Flem overhears Jeff Poindexter (Stepin Fetchit) in conversation with the Judge (Will Rogers). Ella May's father is looking for Flem with a rifle, says Jeff, in the excruciating, nearly incomprehensible stutter and drawl that was the trademark of the highest-paid African American actor in Hollywood. The Judge responds that he can do nothing until Flem is shot; with that Flem abandons Ella May's front porch in a hurry. The camera pans to the bushes, revealing Judge Priest hiding alone; he has been doing blackvoice.

Will Rogers ventriloquizes Stepin Fetchit because the two men are joined together (fig. 6.1). The film opens, as it will close, with a trial scene. The Judge who admonishes Jeff, "Hey, boy. Wake up," is himself allowing his mind to wander to Civil War reminiscences. Laziness acquits Jeff; he convinces the Judge that he is innocent of chicken stealing because he was fishing. The scene's final shot shows the two men from the back, walking down a country road side by side, fishing poles in their hands. After the Judge appropriates Jeff's voice, he catches Jeff trying on his coon coat. With cross-dressing as with chicken stealing, the Judge does not respond by reinstating the law-and-order line between judge and criminal, coon coat owner and "coon," white and black. Instead, to get Jeff to play "Dixie" in the trial that closes the movie, the Judge will promise that he can keep the coat.

Speaking Jeff's voice to invoke paternal prerogative, the Judge and Stepin Fetchit together stand in for Ella May's absent father. Their sol-

Figure 6.1. Judge Priest (Will Rogers) with Jeff Poindexter (Stepin Fetchit), in *Judge Priest*. Courtesy of the Film Stills Archive of the Museum of Modern Art, New York. © 1937 by Twentieth Century–Fox Film Corp.

idarity weaves through a plot in which the Judge's great-nephew courts Ella May over the opposition of his snooty mother, and in which the Judge defends in court a man accused of assaulting Flem Talley. Although his identity is not revealed until the movie's climax, that man is Ella May's returned father, and he has indeed assaulted Flem. He is put on trial because Flem and his friends deny that they attacked him first. To enlist sympathy for the stranger, the Judge has arranged for the story of his Civil War bravery to be interrupted by the sounds of "Dixie" from outside the courtroom. Initiated by a ragtag group of black men playing tambourine, harmonica, and banjo, and led by Stepin Fetchit in the Judge's coon coat (fig. 6.2), the march with Confederate flags to the southern national anthem will be joined by whites erupting out of the courtroom; they have found the veteran innocent.

As Civil War hero, Henry Walthall in Klan robes led the ride to rescue *Birth of a Nation*'s heroine from a black rapist; Walthall also plays the minister in *Judge Priest* who recounts the exploits of Ella May's father. A generation after *Birth*, the sexual aggressor is a poor white (Flem), not a white in blackface. Released the year of the (white) southern tex-

Figure 6.2. The acquittal in *Judge Priest*. Courtesy of the Film Stills Archive of the Museum of Modern Art, New York. © 1937 by Twentieth Century–Fox Film Corp.

tile workers' general strike and general strikes in San Francisco and Minneapolis, *Judge Priest* turned racial menace into class threat.[35] New Deal southerns, climaxing with the whitened rapist in the film of *Gone with the Wind*, followed that lead. The defeat of the fathers opened the South and its women to black assault in *Birth*. Conjuring up Ella May's father in *Judge Priest*'s blackvoice scene, the twinned white grandfather and black servant have brought him back to life.

The Shirley Temple/Bojangles Robinson films also feature an interracial couple that, generated out of an absent or disabled father, heals white family disruption. In *Just Around the Corner* (1938), for example, Bojangles and Shirley pick cotton in a musical benefit for "Uncle Sam," instead of pulling him apart like the selfish interest groups in the cartoon that the little girl sees. Shirley also cooks and cleans house wearing the mammy bandanna she first donned in blackface in *The Littlest Rebel*. As James Snead points out, the black man restores the white family instead of getting a family of his own.[36]

Just as Shirley Temple and Will Rogers play black in this world, so the black soul in *Judge Priest* aspires to being washed white in the next one. "Massa Jesus wrote me a note," Aunt Dilsey (Hattie McDaniel) sings, leading a black church choir. "Say he gonna wash me white as snow, though I be black as tar."[37] The Judge joins in the spirituals with his washerwoman/cook and a black female chorus. As the heads of Aunt Dilsey and the Judge replace one another in the picture frame, they sing, "Yes Judge," "Yes Dilsey," then together, "Saving Daniel from the Lion's Den." Daniel turns out not to be an African American redeemed from slavery (as in the spiritual "Didn't My Lord Deliver Daniel"), but rather Ella May's father, the southern veteran of the Civil War. He is rescued by the interracial alliance between—to give the characters the names by which audiences knew them—Will Rogers and Stepin Fetchit.

Not technically a blackface film, since the part-Indian Will Rogers changes his voice, not the color of his skin, *Judge Priest*'s use of sound displays the message and the method of the blackface musical film. Opening to the sound of "My Old Kentucky Home," Ford's movie counterposes the class pretension and vulgarity of the New South (the greed and status consciousness of the upper class, the violence and sexual aggression of the lower) to the interracial solidarity of the Old South. *Intolerance*, the film title by which D. W. Griffith transmuted *Birth*'s racial prejudice into intolerance of his Ku Klux Klan movie, resurfaces as a word in *Judge Priest* to condemn the family exclusiveness that blocks Ella May's marriage to the Judge's great-nephew, not the racial exclusiveness the film takes for granted. The chain gang shown in flashback at the film's climax is the one from which Ella May's father and other white men were released to fight the Yankees. Their "battalion from hell" displaces the actual postbellum southern hell of black chain gangs. (The chained-together convicts who work in Scarlett O'Hara's paper mill are also white.) The gesture to lynching in the screenplay, which proposed showing a mob with dogs chasing Stepin Fetchit in mistake of another black man, survives in the film only as the Judge's joke that he won't save Jeff from a lynching "this time" if the black man plays "Marching Through Georgia" outside the courtroom. The black minstrel troupes who marched to and from their performances singing "Dixie" to protect themselves against white southern violence are here enlisted for racial harmony.[38]

Released in the middle of the fight to save the Scottsboro Boys, in a year of mob mutilation of black victims and the campaign for a federal antilynching bill, *Judge Priest* offered the nation another South, where interracial imitation stands against ambition and enterprise. Set in the past, "among the familiar ghosts of my own boyhood," *Judge Priest* displays the role of the South in the regionally and racially united dream life of the United States.

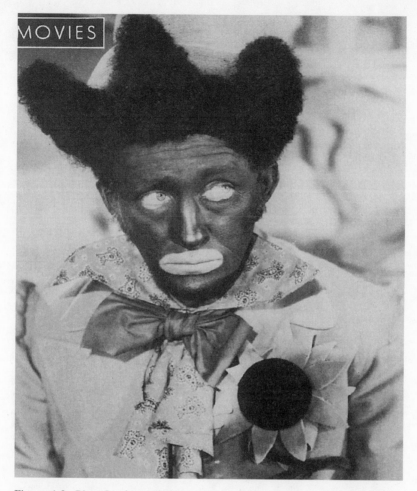

Figure 6.3. Bing Crosby as Dan Emmett in *Dixie*. Courtesy of the Film Stills Archive of the Museum of Modern Art, New York. © 1943 by Paramount Pictures, Inc.

Judge Priest introduces us to the genre of blackface musical: to the ideology of its content—organic nationalism—and the ideology of its form—self-making, performance, artifice. In content, the blackface musical offers regression as national integration. Mammy is at the childhood and southern root, supporting the ease of transfer from white to black and back again—whether as Judge Priest doing Stepin Fetchit's black voice, as Dan Emmett performing a blackface "Dixie" (for Bing Crosby as Emmett in blackface, see fig. 6.3), or as Crosby and Marjorie Reynolds

Figure 6.4. Al Jolson publicity photo. Courtesy of Movie Star News. © by Warner Bros.

celebrating Lincoln's birthday in blackface in *Holiday Inn* (see fig. 6.7). The wide-open, maternal or infantile blackface mouth—Jolson's in publicity photos (fig. 6.4) or singing "My Mammy," Larry Parks's in extreme closeups in the Jolson biopics, the teeth-filled "African" masks behind Marlene Dietrich when, aided by blacked-up native women, she does her "Hot Voodoo" gorilla striptease in *Blonde Venus*—is, as in *Dixie*, the stage entrance from which blacks make everything available to whites (fig. 6.5). The open blackface mouth was everywhere, wrote Bernard Wolfe in 1949: "Aunt Jemima, Beulah, the Gold Dust Twins, 'George' the Pullman-ad porter, Uncle Remus—we like to picture the Negroes grin-

Figure 6.5. The open blackface mouth in *Dixie*. *Life,* June 15, 1943, 80.
© 1943 by Paramount Pictures, Inc.

ning at us. . . . At Mammy's Shack, the Seattle roadside inn built in the
shape of a minstrel's head, you walk into the neon grin to get your ham-
burger. And always the image of the Negro—as we create it—signifies some
bounty—for us. Eternally the Negro gives . . . grinning from ear to ear."[39]

Nostalgic longing for an imaginary southern past served contemporary political integration in depression and wartime America. "Let me
sing of Dixie's charms, of cotton fields and mammy's arms" is how "the
uncrowned king of minstrelsy" opens and closes the Al Jolson/Irving
Berlin musical, *Mammy* (1930). (The number would become *The Jolson Story*'s theme song. Compare the *Mammy* production number, fig.
6.6, with the celebrating blacks at the end of *Judge Priest*, fig. 6.2). At
Mammy's end the Jolson character, wrongly accused of attempted murder (his rival loaded the gun for the blackface stage routine), rides the
rails home to his mother. Enveloping her in hugs, kisses, and tears, Jolson sings, "Whatever comes my way, I'm everything to my mammy."
As he sings about mammy in the minstrel parade that ends the film, the
camera isolates on a black mammy in the crowd.

Minstrelsy also appropriated Abe Lincoln. When Bing Crosby and
Marjorie Reynolds celebrate Lincoln's birthday in blackface, in *Holiday*

Figure 6.6. Al Jolson in a *Mammy* plantation production number. Courtesy of the Film Stills Archive of the Museum of Modern Art, New York. © 1930 by Warner Bros.

Inn's march through the national holidays, they are backed by two segregated bands. One is in whiteface, one in blackface (fig. 6.7). Mamie (Louise Beavers) and her pickaninny children join in for the chorus: "Who was it set the darkies free? Abraham." (Beavers had to force feed herself and put on a southern accent for her mammy roles,[40] rendering Kafkaesque her reassurance to her prospective employer at the beginning of *Imitation of Life*, "I don't eat like I look.") Judy Garland calls Mickey Rooney her "Abe Lincoln" in *Babes on Broadway* because the production he is putting on to send settlement house children to camp will free her from "slavery" to her job. Mickey and Judy lead the extended minstrel number that saves the show, ends the film, and mobilizes minstrelsy for the war effort, "Black Up for That Blackout on Broadway" (fig. 6.8). *The Jolson Story* ends with a medley of plantation songs: "Waiting for the *Robert E. Lee*," "Rock-a-Bye My Baby with a Dixie Melody," "Old Black Joe," "My Mammy." Jolson sings again, to initiate the music in the sequel, "If it's true what they say about Dixie, . . . if it's true that's where I belong."

Figure 6.7. Bing Crosby celebrates Lincoln's birthday in *Holiday Inn*.
Courtesy of the Film Stills Archive of the Museum of Modern Art, New York.
© 1942 by Paramount Pictures, Inc.

To hide minstrelsy's roots in northern, proslavery idealizations of the
South, which it was repeating, Paramount moved Dan Emmett from
New York to New Orleans for *Dixie*. Blackface female impersonation and
homoerotic physical play, cleansed of their ribaldry, are fun for the whole
family. In the vision of interracial harmony to which these nostalgic films
return, the Civil War, not race relations, is the source of division in American life. Blackface heals that division in allowing whites playfully to ex-
propriate black. Southern domestic repose supports northern acquisitive
self-making, the southern parvenu and redneck replace the black beast,
and Warm Springs, Georgia (location of the "Little White House" and
home of the "Southern Negro . . . [who lifted FDR] into his bed" each
night) joins with Tammany Hall to perpetuate the Democratic Party politics out of which blackface had originally sprung, namely, Martin Van
Buren's alliance between the planters of the South and the "plain republicans" of the North.[41]

The innocent national childhood in *Dixie* and *Swanee River* was
also—as in the *Babes in Arms* minstrel number performed by the children of retired vaudevillians—the point of origin for Hollywood. The

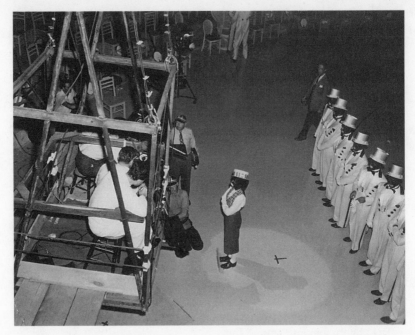

Figure 6.8. Judy Garland in blackface in *Babes on Broadway*. Courtesy of the Film Stills Archive of the Museum of Modern Art, New York. © 1941 by Metro Goldwyn Mayer.

line from minstrelsy to motion pictures not only rooted the present in the past; it also made the entertainment business the vehicle for national integration. The New World religion of *The Jazz Singer*, blackface makes America "God's country" in *Babes in Arms*. As method and signifier of American patriotism, the minstrel number has pride of place in the military musical narrated by and starring Ronald Reagan, *This Is the Army*. Promoting army minstrel shows during the war, the USO called minstrelsy "the one form of American entertainment which is purely our own." When the *New Yorker* placed *Dixie* alongside the war movie *Pilot Number 5*, the "Democracy and Burnt Cork" title of the review implied blackface's contribution to the war effort.[42]

Blackface also served the war effort in Jolson's comeback to entertain the troops and help the Jews in *Jolson Sings Again*'s version of World War II (fig. 6.9). Thanks to *The Jolson Story* and *Jolson Sings Again*, when Jolson performed for Korean War soldiers he was once again a national icon. Lt. Gen. Walton Walker regretfully declined viewing the show, he

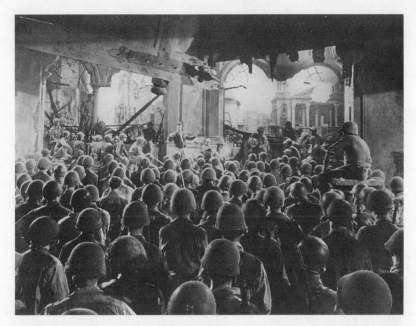

Figure 6.9. Larry Parks as Jolson entertains the troops in *Jolson Sings Again*. Courtesy of the Film Stills Archive of the Museum of Modern Art, New York. © 1949 by Columbia Pictures.

wrote Jolson, because "I have a show of my own." If war was theater, theater was mobilized for war. Named 1949 Personality of the Year by the Washington, D.C., Variety Club, Jolson received the award from the under secretary of defense. He visited the White House, where President Truman remembered seeing him in minstrel shows in his youth. Author of Warren Harding's 1920 presidential campaign song, Jolson was moving along with other Jews from the pre–New Deal GOP to the cold war Democracy. The performer "died in action," as Columbia Pictures' Harry Cohn put it, suffering a heart attack after his trip to Korea. Eulogized by Eddie Cantor as "a casualty of war just as much as any soldier who died on the battlefield," he received, posthumously, the Pentagon Order of Merit. Obituaries marked Jolson's ascent from "part of a mob scene in a Yiddish play" (Israel Zangwill's *Children of the Ghetto*), through blackface, to inauguration by the mass audience as "king," "the greatest single entertainer of our time."[43]

In defining Americanness as entertainment, however, blackface musicals slid from content to form, presenting American identity in terms

Figure 6.10. Eddie Cantor blacking up. Courtesy of Movie Star News.

of performance and self-making. Calling attention to their nostalgia, blackface musicals are self-reflexive at their core. They make themselves as performances, and not the world they represent, the basis for American patriotism. The blackface performative proleptically subverts the wish for subversion in its postmodern copy (see chapter 2) by the power of the cross-dressing original. Synecdochic for Hollywood, blackface gives America its meaning—self-making through role-playing—in films like *Holiday Inn, Swanee River,* and *Dixie.*

There is a primal scene in every blackface musical: it shows the performer blacking up. (For a publicity still of Eddie Cantor applying burnt cork, see fig. 6.10.) The scene lets viewers in on the secret of the fetish: I know I'm not, but all the same . . . The fetish condenses the unanalyzed magical significance assigned to blacks, functioning like the substitute phallus in Freud's analysis and like the commodity in Marx's. Signifying transvestite masquerade and the expropriation of black labor, burnt cork fetishized not only blackness but sexual difference and the commodity form as well. But although blackface is detachable and reattachable—like Freud's fetish—making visible the pleasure of putting on and taking off burnt cork may seem to violate the Marxian/Freudian rule that demystifying the fetish interferes with its work. If the fetish is a story masquerading as an object, then bringing the story into consciousness should deprive the fetish of its magic. What remain hidden, however, are the historical crimes embedded in the fetish's invidious distinction; here white over black parallels man over woman (if we revise Freud to make the phallus itself a fetish) and capitalist over worker. In a culture that mythicizes self-making, moreover, the blackface fetish acquires power by being shown to be put on; blackface joins white power over black to personal mobility and self-expression. But what looks like uncovering origins, exposing how the magic works, is the deepest mystification of all, for it attributes the ability to change identity to individual construction of the self.[44]

"Fifteen nights a year Cinderella steps into a coach and becomes queen of Holiday Inn," says Marjorie Reynolds as she applies burnt cork to her face. The cinders transform her into royalty. Although blackface was often justified as disguise, as in the *Holiday Inn* scene, that was itself a ruse, for the audience was always in on the secret. Dirt was the magical, transforming substance in blackface carnivalesque (particularly transgressive for the blackface Jew, since the term ham actor originated from the use of ham fat to wipe off burnt cork). On the one hand, the filthy mask ("Dirty hands, dirty face," sings young Jakie Rabinowitz) brought the performer down to the earthy substrate, the ape he aped; but on the other, the masquerade identified him not with the mammy but with the trickster. Orality in its performed form was less the sucking mouth of nurture and more the signifying mouth of changing identity.* Black mimicry, black performance, the black mask, the technique by which the subjugated group kept its distance from and mocked its oppressor, was itself expropriated and made into a blackface performance for whites.[45]

The mammy singer asks for unconditional love by pretending to be what he is not. Like mammifying, signifying evokes childhood, the protean playfulness of unfixed racial and sexual identity. Having starred in four domestic melodramas of parent-child devotion (as son in *The Jazz Singer* and *Mammy,* as father in *The Singing Fool* and *Say It with Songs* [1929]), Jolson reverted to playing Gus, the vaudeville trickster of his wildly successful Broadway shows—one of which, *Big Boy* (1930), he brought to the screen. The double and successor to *Mammy, Big Boy*

---

* "Al Jolson made a million bucks looking like that," Richard Pryor says to Gene Wilder, convincing him to put shoe polish on his face and act the trickster. Pryor and a blacked-up Wilder together elude the law in *Silver Streak* (1976).

displays Jolson in blackface not just for musical numbers but for the entire film, not as a minstrel who longs for his mother but as a jockey in love with his horse.

Blackface comedy sanctioned sexual aggression; the minstrel mouth has teeth, and, as Bernard Wolfe put it, underneath the "magnanimous caress" was "the malevolent blow."[46] After blacked-out mayhem in *Big Boy,* for example (the restaurant lights go off), Gus emerges holding a brassiere. *Swingtime*'s adult, phallic version, "Bojangles of Harlem," opens on a large hat and head with white lips that turn into shoe soles. A blackface Fred Astaire appears at the crotch of the giant black legs formed when chorus girls pry apart the shoes. Separated from Astaire and taken off by the chorus girls, the legs dance behind him as if they were his shadows. Blackface dresses up the trickster Astaire, whom we have seen black up and who remains under burnt cork in the cardsharp scene that follows the dance. An homage to the African American tap dancer Bojangles Robinson, the number also quotes *The Jazz Singer,* for Astaire's blacking up seduces both women (here financial backer and ingenue rather than mother and girl friend) between whom he is torn.[47]

Since mammy nurtured whites, maternal longing brought white and black into intimate bodily contact. Sexual conquest, by contrast, insisted on the racial boundary. Minstrel nurture, sex, and trickster aggression nonetheless had in common their self-proclaimed black roots, and the blackface musical used two methods to separate the blackface performer from African Americans and justify white theft. One, adumbrated in *The King of Jazz*'s opening cartoon, juxtaposed the creative white in blackface to the primitive black. The other, the comedy technique of *Whoopee!,* wiped off the burnt cork to celebrate the virtuoso underneath the mask. The former rooted performance in organic nationalism; the latter trod a line between self-aggrandizement and self-exposure.

Show business biopics invoke black music as the raw material for the American national sound. Brief scenes in *Swanee River, Dixie,* and *The Jolson Story,* featuring work songs, spirituals, or jazz, establish African Americans as the source of the music made by white men. (Lou Silver, the orchestra leader in *The Jazz Singer,* was musical director for the Foster biopic.) Foster hears a black work song at the beginning of *Swanee River;* it inspires "Oh! Susanna." His girl friend can finish the tune properly because she was "brought up on Negro music." Foster envies her, though at least he "had a colored nurse." "They have something all their own. It's music from the heart, the beat of a simple people, . . . and by jingo, it's the only real American contribution to music." Repaying his debt to African Americans, Foster composes "Old Black Joe" for his wife's faithful slave. African Americans sing "Swing Low, Sweet Chariot" on a Mississippi riverboat near the beginning of *Dixie;* Dan Emmett (Bing Crosby) joins in, reducing the black singers to a supporting chorus. When Jolson comes upon a New Orleans jazz band in *The Jolson Story*—"They call it jazz. . . . There are no words, but you could make words for it"—he breaks with the old-timey music of Dockstadter's minstrel show. "Why can't I pick my own [songs]?" he pleads with Dockstadter. "Well, not exactly my own. I mean, it's stuff I picked up. They just need to be polished up by somebody good in New York."*

For some listeners the gap between the briefly heard Afro-American music and the eviscerated tunes that dominate the films would not only fail to establish a genealogy but would also endanger the intended aesthetic hierarchy. (The breakthrough Jolson popular song attributed to the influence of jazz is "My Mammy.") The movies themselves, unconscious of that self-subversion, reveal their theft anxiety by displacing robbery from the hero to a blackface trickster who robs him. Mr. Bones steals Emmett's money and then becomes his collaborator; E. P. Christy steals Foster's song and then becomes *his* collaborator. In *Rhapsody in Blue,* the tricksters are Oscar Levant, who does blackvoice, and Jolson, who sings "Swanee" in blackface. (For Jolson as Christy in *Swanee River* and as himself singing "Swanee" in *Rhapsody in Blue,* see figs. 6.11 and 6.12.) Emmett and Foster, rather than black Americans, are the victims of theft, and these innocents, forgiving their confidence men, legitimate their own blackface robbery. Juxtaposing the authentic, supportive black to the blackface trickster, the films sanitize the trickery that the form, blacking up itself, proclaims.

With the appearance of African Americans onscreen in talking pictures, a blackface Jolson sometimes performed among them (fig. 6.13). Such juxtapositions, as in *Life*'s placement of Bing Crosby alongside Bo-

---

* *Rhapsody in Blue* (1945) inverts the pattern, showing a sophisticated Hazel Scott in Paris performing Gershwin's "I Got Rhythm." *The Story of Vernon and Irene Castle* (1937) takes the opposite tack. Although the couple (Fred Astaire and Ginger Rogers) audition for their first show to the music of "Down by the Levee," the film entirely eliminates James Reese Europe, whose band backed the Castle dance craze and laid the foundation for New York jazz. Europe returns split in two, in white as the Castle factotum (Walter Brennan) and in black as the servant of Irene's snooty rival. (See Thomas R. Cripps, *Slow Fade to Black: The Negro in American Film, 1900–1942* [New York, 1977], 252.)

Figure 6.11. Al Jolson as E. P. Christy in *Swanee River* (1939). Courtesy of the Film Stills Archive of the Museum of Modern Art, New York.

jangles Robinson (fig. 6.14), by demonstrating how well white played black, answered back to the advertised claim of Bert Williams and George Walker that blacks in blackface were the real thing. The climax of black-face as virtuoso performance, of course, came when the players removed their masks. Necessary also to establish the difference between black and white, wiping off the burnt cork entailed its own dangers, however. Gus turns to the audience at the end of *Big Boy*, surprising it with his un-covered white face. The self-revelation reassured southern audiences that no black man was engaging in verbal and physical abuse of whites.[48] But Jolson goes further. Reverting to minstrel reminiscence, he breaks character again to discredit his nostalgia. The old black Joe grandfather he's been invoking was named Moishe Pippick. As for the old Kentucky home, with mammy cooking ham on the stove—"That's not my house," says the Jewish comedian.

Jolson turned black disavowal into immigrant Jewish self-assertion in other movies as well. As part of an elaborate blackface *Wonder Bar* (1934) production number, "Going to Heaven on a Mule," Jolson reads a Yiddish newspaper in blackface. When his radio sponsor proposes another mammy number in *Say It with Songs,* the Jolson character re-

Figure 6.12. Al Jolson sings "Swanee" in *Rhapsody in Blue*. Courtesy of the Film Stills Archive of the Museum of Modern Art, New York. © 1945 by Warner Bros.

jects "I'll smother my mother with kisses when I get back to Tennessee" in favor of "I'll smother my father with bedushkas when I get back to Odessa." In the family reunion at that film's end, Jolson orders "ham and eggs. No, I was wrong. Just the eggs."

Jolson's most elaborate deconstruction of his mammy persona appeared before his film career began, in "Maaaaaam-my! Maaaaam-my! The Famous Mammy-Singer Explores His Native(?) Sunny Southland," published in the magazine for urban sophisticates, *Vanity Fair*. No one, according to the editor's note, was "more identified with the sunny Southland, . . . more irrevocably linked with cotton fields," than Jolson. The Jazz Age magazine was presenting the performer's account of his first trip south. According to Jolson, "Having spent the greater part of my life singing about my mammy in the sunny Sout', I had begun to believe that such a person really existed. The fact that I was born in St. Petersburg, Russia (not Florida!) had long since slipped my mind." But instead of "the Dixie of my dreams," the mammy singer found "thousands of tumble down shacks"; instead of the banjo-strumming "southern darkey, . . . famous wherever minstrel shows have played," he encountered a "northern negro" who told him he came to Florida in the

Figure 6.13. Al Jolson and his black chorus in *Big Boy*. Courtesy of Movie Star News. © 1930 by Warner Bros.

winter because "the northern tourists is such easy pickings." "You are probably as eager as I am to get back to your mammy and the scenes of your childhood," insisted the blackface performer. "Boss," responded the allegedly real African American, "you can't be from down yonder or you wouldn't feel that-a-way." "Don't you miss the darkies humming . . . , your mammy's chicken frying in the pan?" "Boss, . . . it wasn't until I came north that I knew a chicken had anything but a neck." The only "southern drawl" Jolson hears at Palm Beach is from south Delancey Street, and belongs to Marcus Loew; it as if he is warning readers that Hollywood's Jewish moguls would soon be capitalizing on the blackface persona that another Jewish immigrant, Jolson, had invented. In claiming that theater owner Sam Schubert let him go south only after his loss of voice was diagnosed as a "suppressed desire" to see his mammy, Jolson was proleptically ridiculing the plots of two of his movies, *The Singing Fool* and *The Singing Kid*, in which the broken and restored parent-child bond explains the loss and recovery of his voice.[49]

The mammy role threatened to infantilize Jolson, and the spoof made

Figure 6.14. *Life* compares Bing Crosby in blackface (in *Dixie*) to Bill Robinson (with Lena Horne in *Cabin in the Sky*). *Life*, July 5, 1943, 9. © 1943 by Paramount Pictures, Inc., and © 1943 by Metro Goldwyn Mayer.

it clear he was not the needy innocent he was portraying. Jolson's disavowal of the mammy singer was designed to remasculinize the performer. When he and his bride, Ruby Keeler, returned from their honeymoon and Jolson began filming *Mammy*, he was asked if his new wife was his mammy. "Don't call her mammy. She is my mama," said the forty-two-year-old blackface star about the dancer less than half his age. "It's a dark outlook that faces me in my mirror."[50] Jolson wanted audiences to be aware that he knew exactly what he was doing. In its *Vanity Fair* version, reclaiming the immigrant Jewish American self as the maker of blackface also made room, unusually, for black signifying. Comic Jewish self-assertion was more likely to create Jewish/black solidarity when it was also a reminder that the immigrant Jew could never really wipe himself clean.

Self-assertive, ethnic self-mockery played well to Jolson's immigrant Jewish and cosmopolitan urban audiences. Robert Benchley and Gilbert Seldes, far from distinguishing Jolson's sentimentality from his irony, praised the performer's "supernatural," "demonic" presence. According to Seldes, Jolson was "so great that he cannot be put in any company." "John the Baptist was the last man to possess such a power," wrote Benchley. "It is as if an electric current had been run along under the seats."[51] The biblical John the Baptist began the conversion of the Jews; ethnic shtick showed Americanizing Jewish audiences that the mass entertainment idol was still one of them. But Jewish jokes reduced the popularity of the movies Jolson made after *The Singing Fool*. Instead of progressing forward to the deracinated American identity promised in *The Jazz Singer* and realized in "Sonny Boy," the later movies reverted to Jewish vaudeville. Eddie Cantor, who had also moved from vaudeville to Hollywood, became one of Universal's top moneymakers while Jolson released flop after flop. Cantor sustained his popularity in the 1930s by no longer playing the Jew.[52]

Jolson's Jewish self-exposure went too far not because of its method but because of its particularistic content. Audiences were turning away from the focus on ethnic conflict, not from masquerade itself. With the end of mass Jewish immigration, the dramatization of Jews becoming American was losing its appeal. In *Babes in Arms*, on the eve of World War II, blackface still Americanized ethnics; but generational conflict between Old World and New, like Americanizing campaigns against ethnic disloyalty, more and more belonged to the past. Blackface no longer negotiated immigrant rites of passage; that function of the form would move, as we shall see, to the racial-problem film.

Losing ground as ethnic self-assertion in depression and wartime Hollywood, blackface incorporated Jewish nostalgia after the war. The ethnic-family situation comedy was also featured on radio and early TV. The nostalgically remembered ethnic family not only tied the generations together; ethnic solidarity also dressed up class hierarchy and placed it in the past.[53]

The Jewish family carried a special significance. Although the extermination of the Jews made barely a dent in American political consciousness during the war, it became a subject of lament once the war was over. Not only decimated in Europe, Old World Jews were also disappearing from America. They returned to the screen not as the powerful, menacing patriarchs of the generational-conflict movies (even if sympathetic, even if ultimately defeated) but as subjects of affection. Jolson's and Gershwin's film parents are quaint old-people dolls, cute, caricatured, and deprived of authority. Instead of marking generational conflict, as in *The Jazz Singer*, blackface in *The Jolson Story* incorporates Jews of all generations. Jolson's obituaries, following the lead of the biopics, made "the mammy singer" good for all the Jews.[54]

The Jazz Singer joined romantic to generational conflict; the Jolson and Gershwin biopics displace the latter with the former. The jazz singer's postcard home, giving the immigrant son a new identity, announced his name change from Rabinowitz to Robin; the *Jolson Story* postcard, linked to the change in the boy's voice, announces his sexual coming of age. (Larry Parks, who plays the grown Jolson, enters the film immediately after the postcard.) The first postcard split the family; the second elicits parental pride in filial success. Jolson's parents initially resist his desire to sing in vaudeville, but they are won over so quickly that for most of *The Jolson Story* they are as caught up in his career as he is. "For me it's not necessary," says the father when Al remembers to put on a yarmulke at the homecoming meal—and with that the religious issue exits the movie. Far from opposing intermarriage, Jolson's father acts as his go-between in *Jolson Sings Again*. Blackface killed the jazz singer's father. In the Jolson biopics, it not only has parental support, but it also turns out to be good for Old World Jews. Jolson gives up show business for his wife, not his father, in *The Jolson Story*; in *Jolson Sings Again*, his father reminds him of Nazi atrocities to convince him to perform for American troops.

Enlisted in the service of the family, motion picture blackface was repeating the movement of nineteenth-century minstrelsy into the American home. Originally an all-male transvestite form, blackface had continued to play with gender in *The Singing Fool* and *Whoopee!* Burnt cork's homoerotic, ribald origins leave their traces in *Dixie*'s minstrel routines, where blackface men, some in drag, roll around the stage together. Emmett's marriage proposals, to two different women, ignite fires (as suggested by camera cuts from the proposals to actual conflagrations). But Emmett marries the genteel, crippled woman, not the innkeeper's show business daughter, and his blackface rendition of "Dixie" at the end of the film calms the audience so that a third conflagration can be extinguished. This World War II movie washes out sexual and political conflict to make the Civil War serve domestic unity.

The minstrel motion pictures of the 1930s and 1940s, however, far from abandoning mutability and public performance for a naturalized private space, turned blackface into domestic artifice. Grounding romance on impersonation, these films bring performance into the most intimate, familial settings.

IV

Jim (Bing Crosby) quits show business at the beginning of *Holiday Inn* (1942). He creates a country hotel that, in celebration of the national holidays, will open only fifteen days a year. Jim, who wants to settle down, falls in love with Linda (Marjorie Reynolds). He worries that when Ted (Fred Astaire) sees her dance, Ted will use the lure of Hollywood glamour to seduce her away. This Hollywood movie makes Hollywood its target, attacking show business with song and dance routines. When Jim puts blackface on Linda to hide her from Ted, and he and Linda celebrate Lincoln's birthday under burnt cork (see fig. 6.7), the freedom they celebrate in the name of "darkies" is their own freedom to costume themselves for fancy-dress balls. Lincoln's birthday explodes any opposition that might exist between domesticity and make-believe.

Blackface cannot hide Linda from Ted and a show business career forever; angered that Jim did not tell her of the movie offer, she leaves him for Hollywood. In having Ted and Linda (or is it Astaire and Reynolds?) make a movie called "Holiday Inn," *Holiday Inn* resurrects the show business/domesticity opposition in the diegesis even as it undercuts it by being itself a film called *Holiday Inn*. A menacing camera with long lens introduces the film-set-within-the-film, "one of the most authentic reproduction jobs we've ever done," says the director. As Ted and Linda dance to a reprise of the *Holiday Inn* sound track, Jim eats Thanksgiving dinner alone at the real Holiday Inn. "Your Hollywood success was empty; you've lost the one you love"—the director explains her role to Linda on the set. "You know. All that hokum."

By counterposing "Holiday Inn," the film-within-the-film, to Jim's Holiday Inn, *Holiday Inn* may seem to be defending the romance that "Holiday Inn"'s director calls hokum. It is not so easy, however, to distinguish "Holiday Inn" from *Holiday Inn*. When the director-within-the-film presents show business doubling as a mockery of the real thing, his opposite number is neither *Holiday Inn*'s director nor Jim but rather Mamie (Louis Beavers). For Jim isn't entirely alone on Thanksgiving; he is comforted by his cook and her children. "I knows Miss Linda like I knows my own kids," Mamie tells him. Trickery won't work with her; he can only win her back with love. Love, simplicity, and truth telling characterize Hollywood's African American mammies, who support their white families without having personalities or making demands of their own. Hattie McDaniel's favorite poet may have been Paul Lawrence Dunbar, author of "We Wear the Mask," but it was whites in blackface, not mammies, who were allowed to perform the separation of self from role onscreen.[55]

Having hidden Linda behind burnt cork, Jim has already shown he is no Mamie, and fortunately he does not follow her advice. Traveling to Hollywood, the trickster turns the tables on his former partner. Locking Ted in his hotel room, isolating him in a private space away from the scene of the action, Jim invades the movie set. Linda is sadly singing "White Christmas" in the film-within-the-film, and as she imitates Jim's motion of picking up his pipe and hitting the Christmas tree bells, he takes up the tune. The director-within-the-scene stops the music, but not before the director *of* the scene has used it for his happy ending.

Incorporating artifice into its love story, *Holiday Inn* at once celebrates Crosby's Holiday Inn as a retreat from show business fakery and makes his tricksterdom—genetically blackface—the technique for making a home. Marrying blackface to "White Christmas," the method within the diegesis undercuts the manifest message of the film to instantiate a deeper lesson. *Holiday Inn* belongs to the growing sense, captured in Martha Wolfenstein's term "fun morality," that spontaneity took work, that the natural had to be made. The need to perform emotions to bring them into being, what Arlie Hochschild calls "emotion work," was always intrinsic both to blackface and to domestic advice books. But World War II created a special problem. The absence of men at war, followed by the need to orchestrate the traditional family's restoration, denaturalized the domestic just as its naturalness was being proclaimed.[56]

Marjorie Reynolds moved after the war from Hollywood musical star (in *Dixie* and *Holiday Inn*) to television housewife. The actress playing Mrs. Chester Riley in *The Life of Riley* explained to *TV Guide*, "I've done just about everything in films from westerns to no-voice musicals, and now with the Riley show I'm back in the kitchen were every wife belongs." No-voice musicals referred to the Hollywood lip-synch masquerade, in which Reynolds opened her mouth for another woman's voice. But the musical comedy star had not relinquished pretending to sing in order to prepare real food. Cooking up the mass-produced turn from class and ethnic conflict to immigrant nostalgia, Reynolds's kitchen was in the television studio.[57]

If *Holiday Inn*, *Dixie*, and other blackface musicals made burnt cork work *for* love, the Foster, Gershwin, and Jolson biopics counterposed work onstage *to* love. Restoring the traditional opposition between blackface and domesticity, they allied burnt cork not with carnivalesque sexuality but with the creative vocation. Biopics replaced the oedipal drama of *The Jazz Singer* with a conflict that would come to organize cultural life in the 1950s: that between wife and husband, love and career.

Three of Jolson's four wives were young enough to be his daughters, Stephen Foster was an alcoholic with a failed marriage, and George Gershwin was gay. The three musical miscegenators hardly embodied traditional family values. Cultural salience rather than historical accuracy nonetheless lay behind the conflict in their biopics between blackface and domesticity, as is illustrated in the move of the Jolson-Keeler marriage to the screen. Jolson and Ruby Keeler had come into conflict as her career flourished and his declined. The Warner Bros. effort to revive Jolson's box office status by casting him with Keeler in *Go into Your Dance* (1935) was a failure. *The Jolson Story* reverses that trajectory. Julie Benson (Keeler refused the use of her name) wants to retire from show business to the country, and the marriage ends when she realizes Jolson can't give up his work.[58]

Career pressures and male ambivalence about the family were the postwar issues to which this movie spoke. The independent woman served as scapegoat for male discontent with domesticity, particularly in the context of the drive to return working women to the home. The shift in postwar films from the upper-class lady and urban working girl to the suburban housewife would also make mammy dispensable. In the 1948 film *Mr. Blandings Builds His Dream House,* Gussie (Louise Beavers) helps move the Blandings family from New York City to their dream house in the suburbs. The movie closes with the grinning mouth of the mammy who, while serving up breakfast, has blurted out the jingle "If you ain't eaten Wham, you ain't eaten ham." Unlike earlier Jolson movies, this "Selznick Release" (the film's opening title) makes ham an issue for Madison Avenue rather than Jews. Gussie has inadvertently supplied Mr. Blandings (Cary Grant) with the advertising slogan that saves his job, but she has done so (looking forward to the suburban domestic comedies of the 1950s) at the expense of her own.[59]

The Jolson Story version of the domestic drama, by contrast with *Mr. Blandings,* redeemed the man who chose against family as living the tragedy of devotion to work. Keeler was a successful Broadway dancer and movie star. By positioning Jolson's wife against her own career, making her suffer as a homebody whose husband prefers the stage, *The Jolson Story,* with its focus on men's conflict between work and family, hid the other family issue: the enforced movement of women from paid work to the home. Housebound female moviegoers could suffer vicariously from the Foster/Gershwin/Jolson renunciation of domestic happiness for art.

To give up the stage is to relinquish burnt cork. Blackface organizes the first half of *The Jolson Story,* from the moment the young performer, in counterpoint to his lack of interest in girls, blacks up. Blackface offers a tour through Jolson's classics and grotesque close-ups of Larry Parks's wide-open, singing mouth. Once Julie Benson enters the picture, Jolson never blacks up again. *The Jolson Story* inherits early minstrelsy's opposition to love and marriage, but the fire put out by Julie is neither homoerotic solidarity nor career ambition; rather, it is the performer's love affair with himself.

Heterosexual romance, whether it climaxed in marriage (*Dixie*) or renunciation (*The Jolson Story*), never gave blackface the weight ethnic Americanization had once supplied. Audiences flocked to the Jolson biopics to bathe in blackface nostalgia and in the spectacle of entertainment. But instead of producing the blackface synthesis of content and form, nostalgia and self-fashioning, that had flourished for a century, *Jolson Sings Again* placed these two attractions at cross-purposes. Blackface self-awareness, the instrument of identity transfer, had always defined minstrelsy; but the extreme self-consciousness of *Jolson Sings Again* indicated that the form was in trouble. When the film restored the retired performer to the blackface stage, it was bringing blackface as national culture to its end.

V

Putting blackface into history reveals the pressure being placed on both the ideology of the content and the ideology of the form. In insisting on the blackface roots of American entertainment, the blackface musical wanted to create a seamless tie to the past. Attempts to incorporate the past, however, opened up a fissure between the gone-with-the-wind plantation and the present of racial conflict, between domestic service and military service, between the plantation darky and the urban, self-assertive New Negro of the war. The African American presence in factories, in the army, and on the street produced white race riots around southern military bases and inside northern cities. *Life*'s photographs authenticating *Dixie*'s historical accuracy may have used surface imitation to hide historical lies, but history took its revenge in the pictures of the Detroit race riot of 1943 that appeared in the same issue;[60] indeed, there would have been a smaller gap between an accurate account of antebellum America and contemporary race conflicts. *Swanee River* and *Dixie* conclude with the Civil War, but their exercises in national reconciliation through blackface undermined blackface as racially reconciliatory during World War II.

The modern civil rights movement, of black militance and mass protests, was born during the war. Since it was African American self-representation from which blackface nostalgia sought escape, blackface came under growing criticism in those years. The context remained one of compliance among blacks and almost universal endorsement among whites. Some middle-class blacks who praised African American minstrels had spoken out against whites in blackface. The *New York Age*, for example, advertised black-in-blackface minstrel shows; Lester Walton reviewed them favorably in its pages while attacking "the disgraceful antics . . . of white actors under burnt cork."[61] There had been a failed effort to drive *Amos 'n' Andy* from the air. Although the middle-class blacks who led the boycott campaign in part objected to the caricatured portrayal of African Americans, they often accepted the *Amos 'n' Andy* conflation of minstrelsy with actual black practice. Many opponents of *Amos 'n' Andy* wanted to distance themselves from black popular culture and adopt genteel white standards of behavior; the masses of blacks who listened to the show, however, opposed the boycott.[62]

Jolson himself was never an African American target. Unlike some of his contemporaries, he avoided performing the most grotesque caricatures (although African Americans playing buffoons do recur in his pictures). Audiences at Harlem's Lafayette Theater cried during *The Jazz Singer*, and the black press greeted that film with enthusiasm. The *Amsterdam News* called it "one of the greatest pictures ever produced" and wrote of Jolson, "Every colored performer is proud of him." Blackface, the paper knew, was the vehicle by which black performers had gained access to the stage. The *Pittsburgh Courier* hoped that the Jolson role would open film opportunities for African Americans. The Urban League welcomed Hollywood's opening of a Jim Crow casting office with the coming of talking pictures.[63] The Duke Ellington Band, playing in Amos and Andy's blackface comedy *Check and Double Check* (1930), was the first credited black band in an otherwise all-white movie; the two lightest-skinned musicians were forced to black up. The *Amsterdam News* called Ellington's movie appearance the high point of his career. His band played the *Amos 'n' Andy* theme song—it came from *Birth of a Nation*—at a *Chicago Defender* ghetto parade honoring Amos and Andy when the NAACP was trying to drive their radio show from the air.[64]

Blackface was the African American ticket of admission to the entertainment business, and any subversion had to operate within severe limits. The Lafayette Theater floor show during *The Jazz Singer* run, for example, introduced a "novelty": it redistributed Jolson's parts so that Cantor Silverbush sang the Hebrew holy chants Eli, Eli and Kol Nidre, and the black singer Willie Jackson performed Jolson's "jazz." Although the *Amsterdam News* praised the film, it gave four times as much space to the floor show. "It is hard to tell which is the greater attraction," the newspaper proclaimed. Given the constraints under which black popular culture operated, the covert disassemblage of blackface at the Lafayette Theater was the limit of resistance. A decade later the *Amsterdam News* praised the blackface climax of *A Day at the Races* (1937), where the Marx Brothers don blackface to escape the sheriff and then lead a festive, interracial parade.[65] The finale's democratic chaos does look good alongside Jolson's blackface antics among plantation blacks in such films as *Mammy* and *Big Boy* (see figs. 6.6 and 6.13). The Marx Brothers ridicule everything they touch, including racism and anti-Semitism: in *Monkey Business* (1931), Groucho, Harpo, and Chico escape "immigration restriction" by smuggling themselves into the United States in barrels labeled "kippered herrings."

It was not the Marx Brothers' burnt cork that accommodated African Americans to the form, however, but the fact that, outside the NAACP, almost no whites questioned it. White liberals mostly assumed that blackface was another instance of cross-racial sympathy. Eleanor Roosevelt and the cosmopolitan journalist and Socialist Heywood Broun loved *Amos 'n' Andy. Rhapsody in Blue,* with its left-wing screenwriters Elliot Paul and Howard Koch, brought back the blackface Jolson. Larry Parks, who played him in the Jolson biopics, was the Communist leader of the left wing of the Screen Actors Guild (which opposed "discrimination against Negroes in the motion picture industry" and the stereotyping of African Americans). When Parks recanted before the House Un-American Activities Committee (see chapter 7), it was for communism, not blackface.[66]

Leftists and race liberals did attack the way blacks were depicted on the wartime Hollywood screen. The NAACP mounted what Carleton

Jackson calls a "crusade against 'mammyism.' " Dalton Trumbo, screenwriter and future member of the Hollywood Ten, published his "Blackface, Hollywood Style" in the NAACP journal, *Crisis*. Yet Trumbo's attack on stereotypes that were enforced on black actors (he ignored whites in blackface) ran up against the uncomfortable fact that black entertainers—many of whom had performed in blackface—were among the few prominent African Americans whom the civil rights organization could celebrate. John Lovell Jr. illustrated his sympathetic retrospective of the "Negro minstrel show" in *Crisis* with a picture of Bert Williams and George Walker performing in blackface. *Crisis,* moreover, mounted no campaign against minstrelsy in the 1940s. In his scathing exposé of racism in the entertainment business, written during the war, L. D. Reddick (the black historian and curator of Harlem's Schomburg Collection) had only kind words for Jolson.[67]

Growing black militance, however, combined with Truman's cold war embrace of civil rights, opened a social space for African American protests against minstrelsy. *Crisis* illustrated Louis Armstrong "doing the kind of 'mugging' for the camera that is becoming very unpopular with Negro movie-goers."[68] Although *Song of the South,* Disney's 1946 version of the Uncle Remus stories, was one of the most popular movies of the year, winning awards from the Motion Picture Academy and *Parents* magazine, its stereotyped black primitives came under widespread attack. Mammy was on her way out of Hollywood, and so, finally, was blackface. By 1949 the form was in serious trouble.[69]

VI

Blackface perfectly captured the Hollywood paradox that spontaneity required construction, but burnt cork could no longer hold that contradiction together. There were reports that opposition to blackface caused its use to be limited in *Jolson Sings Again;*[70] indeed, the infinite regress of self-referentiality in that film has a distinctly mannerist feel. Blackface, made too self-conscious by civil rights scrutiny, is reaching the end of its line.

There is no blackface in *Jolson Sings Again* until the film is almost over; withholding the blackface for which audiences longed and that they knew was coming was a technique that had helped Jolson's most popular film,

The Singing Fool, reach its climax. It is used to the same effect in *Jolson Sings Again,* but with a difference. *Jolson Sings Again* made blackface method the subject as had no film before it, generalized it to Hollywood special effects, and left it behind. No longer the carrier for a Jewish self divided between parental past and American future, and increasingly suspect from a civil rights perspective as the insulting doubling of blacks, blackface in its film apotheosis moves entirely off the street and onto the stage, out of society and into entertainment. Self-consciousness, going too far, has turned back on itself instead of venturing out into the world. *Jolson Sings Again* introduced the postwar Hollywood paradise of consumption and special effects, the increasingly self-enclosed world of 1950s musicals that separate art from life. But the film's self-reflexivity cuts the present off from the past, something that most 1950s musicals avoided doing. Appropriated black music and performance styles would energize 1950s popular culture, taking the musical forms both of rock and roll and of nostalgia: the year, 1956, that Elvis Presley recorded "Heartbreak Hotel," Jerry Lewis (born Joseph Levitch) had a top-ten hit with the song that had been number one for Jolson in 1918 (with which, on his Vitaphone short, he in fact entered talking pictures, and with which, as we shall see, Larry Parks ended *Jolson Sings Again*), "Rock-a-Bye My Baby with a Dixie Melody." Yet 1950s minstrelsy could no longer root itself in open blackface display.[71]

Jolson Sings Again climaxes with the making of *The Jolson Story,* and the introduction of Larry Parks as the actor who will play Jolson has two unsettling features. The first is that the Parks who appears as himself has already been playing Jolson for most of two movies, so that the Jolson who watches Parks play Jolson (fig. 6.15) *is* Parks playing Jolson. The second is that Jolson's agreement to put his songs through his impersonator's mouth, by displaying Hollywood's lip-synch technique, separates the singing voice from the image that is producing that voice as if it were its own. When Larry Parks as Larry Parks mouths the words of "Toot, Toot, Tootsie," he is presenting the song that, the first to join voice to lips in a feature film, introduced talking pictures. But whereas *The Jazz Singer*'s "Toot, Toot, Tootsie" expressed spontaneity and integration, echoed (in blackface) in *Jolson Sings Again* it only introduces splitting and self-consciousness. Hollywood normally employed lip-synch to create the illusion of unity between image and sound. By showing off lip-synch in *Jolson Sings Again,* the motion picture industry was exposing not only Larry Parks but also itself.[72]

A further irony is hidden in this scene, of which Jolson followers

Figure 6.15. Larry Parks as Jolson in *Jolson Sings Again* watches Parks play Jolson in *The Jolson Story. Life*, Sept. 12, 1949, 94. © 1949 by Columbia Pictures.

would be aware, for it was on lip-synching that his career foundered. Primitive sound techniques restricted the use of voice in Jolson's first two, immensely successful part-talkies, and they required that he be filmed while he actually sang. He did not lip-synch "Toot, Toot, Tootsie." When prerecording of songs developed, and sound took over the entire set, Jolson mouthed his own previously recorded voice. Since he never did a song the same way twice, however, lip-synching inhibited his spontaneity. Talking-pictures technique, which gave Jolson his apotheosis, thus brought about his decline. The blackface mass idol would return only as the voice behind someone else's face.[73]

That was poetic justice, as the movie was perfectly aware, for he had achieved stardom as the voice behind another's (black)face. We get our first view of blackface in the lip-synch scene, through the eyes of Parks as Jolson watching a screen test of Parks under burnt cork (fig. 6.15).[74] Looking at Parks, we hear Jolson sing the revolutionary song in which sound first came out of the singer's mouth in a feature film. Jolson had not sung "Toot, Toot, Tootsie" in blackface in *The Jazz Singer*, however. *Jolson Sings Again* made the link between blackface and speaking one's own words only to undercut it. Blackface, which creates visual doubleness, is introduced in the context of calling attention to the separation of voice from body. Burnt cork, self-consciously using doubling to create spontaneity, had freed the jazz singer from his Jewish father. It gave him his self, his individual identity as opposed to a communal, patriarchal one. Lip-synching redivides that self in two, producing identical doubles of the singer that created consciousness of self rather than providing access to difference. Instead of being heard through blackface, and so acquiring an interior, the lip-syncher was silenced when he was seen. Burnt cork gave Jolson the voice he lost with lip-synching. Now lip-synching gives him back his motion picture voice at the price of his visual absence from the screen. It enlists this more universalized and technologized I-am-what-I-am-not in the service of what is exposed as the authenticity effect.

Far from hiding the triple doubling—cork and skin, voice and body, Jolson and Parks—the film makes the most of it, for after displaying lip-synch and blackface for Parks's-as-Jolson's eyes, it has Jolson meet the actor who will play him. Two identical images of Larry Parks shake hands (fig. 6.16); there is little effort to make one look older or otherwise different from the other.[75] Parks-as-Jolson begins the story of his life as he wants it to appear on film. The camera cuts to Parks-as-Jolson before a mirror, showing Parks-as-Parks—the actor who will play Jolson—the classic Jolson moves. The mirror effect puts four images of Larry Parks on the screen; cut to Parks-as-Parks moving his lips in blackface, back to Parks-as-Jolson watching his blackface double sing. The whiteface Parks-as-Jolson throws himself silently into the song, rooting on and applauding the blackface Parks-as-Parks. (To those who knew that the real Jolson had never accepted not playing himself and, for interfering with the production, had finally been thrown off the set of *Jolson Sings Again*,[76] the Parks foursome, which excluded the real Jolson as it multiplied images of him, would have been particularly ironic.)

Jolson Sings Again has two more doublings to come: Jolson's with the spectator and its own with *The Jolson Story*. Parks-as-Jolson watches the premiere of *The Jolson Story;* an enthusiastic member of the motion picture audience—just like the rest of us—he offers popcorn to the lady sitting next to him. Parks sings "My Mammy," the song that ended *The Jazz Singer,* and when the actor playing Jolson in blackface interrupts his number with the apparently spontaneous but completely familiar line "It's my mammy I'm talking about," it takes no postmodern critic to grasp that it's doubly not his mammy. The mammy isn't Jolson's, and Parks is no Jolson. The power of the scene comes from the magic by which the performer has made his not-mammy, for the space of the performance, his own.

After a long medley of Jolson classics, some in blackface, some not,

Figure 6.16. Parks as Jolson meets Parks as Parks in *Jolson Sings Again*. *Life*, Sept. 12, 1949, 94. © 1949 by Columbia Pictures.

Jolson Sings Again ends. Twice. When "The End" fills the screen the first time, it turns out to announce the end of *The Jolson Story*. (The reprise of Jolson's post–*Jolson Story* return to fame includes one more disorienting doubling, a radio scene in which Parks as Jolson moves his lips inside a soundproof radio booth. But the film audience now knows it is watching film lip-synch and not radio technology, and that it cannot hear Parks not because he is in a soundproof booth but because he is not making a sound.) The film comes to its second and final end with Parks playing Parks-as-Jolson reenacting the benefit that we earlier saw (with Parks playing Jolson) as being the inspiration for *The Jolson Story*. This time Parks-as-Jolson goes out with "Rock-a-Bye My Baby with a Dixie Melody," the tune that incorporates musical homages to "Old Black Joe," "Swanee River," and other signifiers of the American southern plantation that is the ancestral home not of the North, not of most of the South, not of post–World War II America, not of the immigrant Jew;

it is the plantation transformed from the nightmare home of black Americans to the cornucopia of whites in blackface—and thus, retrospectively, through history as fantasy, transsubstantiated by cinders into the home of all those who did not come from there, the home that may be gone with the wind but that Jolson, or rather Parks-as-Jolson, can bring back to life.

But the return of the South after the mirror stage produces an alienation effect that confirms Jacques Lacan's analysis: the child (here, the son) who sees himself in the mirror experiences separation of his bodily self not only from his ideal self but also from his mother.[77] The mirror in *Jolson Sings Again* marks the absence not just of Jolson but of his mammy. When the movie brings them back—after the film-within-the-film has called attention to the medium—the ideology of the form has undermined the ideology of the content, for mammy organic nationalism is now solely in the past and on the stage.

As a self-destroying artifact, the top box office hit in 1949 sheds light on two film genres from which it is normally sundered. Just as the blackface musical exposes the imaginary core of the racial social-problem film (see chapter 7), so *Jolson Sings Again* brings back down to earth the utopian musical of the post–World War II decade.

Backstage musicals like *Jolson Sings Again* were on their way out in the late 1940s, displaced by self-enclosed worlds that fully integrated music and life. Backstage musical realism, which motivated the song-and-dance routines and displayed the lives of working actors, inhibited the sweep of musical fantasy. Blackface itself, once it came under suspicion, was a reality principle that only complicated pleasure; to leave the backstage subgenre behind effaced the musical's roots in minstrelsy. *Jolson Sings Again* climaxed and made strange the musical's blackface myth of origins.*

---

*The legacy of *Jolson Sings Again* surfaces at the climactic center of the Warner Bros. 1954 extravaganza *A Star is Born*. With Judy Garland (as Vicky Lester, formerly Esther Blodgett) and James Mason (as Norman Mayne) in the audience for the film in which Garland's star is born, the first thing we see through their eyes is Garland singing "Swanee." "Swanee" introduces *A Star is Born*'s major production number, "I Was Born in a Trunk," whose song-and-dance tells the story of Garland/Blodgett/Lester's rise to stardom (in the film-within-the-film). After many song-and-dance routines and costume changes, Garland sings the song that gets her her chance, "Swanee," complete with the line "Mammy, Mammy, how I love the old folks at home." Although *A Star is Born*'s "Swanee" must dispense with blackface, its compensatory self-referentiality is monumental. The number ("Swanee") is within the number ("Born in a Trunk") that is within the number ("Swanee") within the film-within-the-film. "Swanee" links George Gershwin to his brother,

We can follow the apotheosis and subsequent effacement of black-face in the career of the most important producer of musicals from 1939 to 1953, MGM's Arthur Freed.[78] Freed began his career as a musical producer by taking over the Mickey Rooney/Judy Garland vehicles. Returning to the origins of American entertainment, he blacked up his young stars. His first musical was *Babes in Arms,* which advertised the minstrel roots of Hollywood, and he projected blackface forward into the World War II present ("Black Up for That Blackout on Broadway") to conclude *Babes on Broadway.*[79] The producer then shifted from black-face to the all-black *Cabin in the Sky* (1943), where (with a nod to the enormously popular Broadway and Hollywood musical *Green Pastures*) a religious frame does the backstage work of motivating the action. In moving from blackface to religion, Freed was reversing the direction of the first blackface musical, *The Jazz Singer,* which had replaced Jewish communal faith with blackface as the New World religion. Freed was going underneath blackface to give African Americans access to the screen.

But not for long. Instead, *Cabin in the Sky,* by combining the older view of African American folk authenticity with appreciation for urban black sophistication,[80] began to make the musical itself the unselfreflexive object of worship. Freed followed *Cabin in the Sky* with the first of his self-enclosed musical utopias, the breakthrough *Meet Me in St. Louis* (1944). Until his last successful production, *Band Wagon* (1953), he never looked back to blackface again. *Band Wagon* shows why. In it, an aging Astaire returns to his song-and-dance roots, so the film opens with an homage to black tap. What it shows, however, is acknowledgment as domination, for Astaire dances on a platform above the African American shoe shine boy, an old man who flips his rag, dances, and blacks (up) Astaire's shoes.

Before coming full circle and to a dead end with *Band Wagon,* Freed completed in 1951 three classic musicals that together encapsulate, by suppressing, the history of their genre. One, *Show Boat,* thematized racial passing as tragedy (when the direction was black into white). The second, *An American in Paris,* removed Gershwin from his blackface mi-

Ira, the lyricist of "Born in a Trunk." Garland singing "Swanee" condenses into a single figure the history of American entertainment in burnt cork from Stephen Foster ("Old Folks at Home") through Al Jolson ("Swanee" and "Mammy") to Garland's own black-face reprise of American entertainment, "My Daddy Was a Minstrel Man," in *Babes in Arms,* fifteen years before *A Star is Born.*

lieu. With Gene Kelly as Gershwin's stand-in, the film turned the artist's Paris failure (shown in *Rhapsody in Blue*) into a triumph. The third, *Singin' in the Rain,* by critical consensus the greatest musical ever made,[81] combines backstage self-referentiality with utopian self-enclosure. It successfully achieves that synthesis, avoiding *Jolson Sings Again*'s alienation effect, by burying—save for two revelatory moments—its own blackface origins. Blackface momentarily erupts in the shift of names for the film within the film, and again in the shift from speech to motion.

At the beginning of *Singin' in the Rain,* Don Lockwood (Gene Kelly) and Lina Lamont (Jean Hagen) are making a silent costume drama, "The Duelling Cavalier." The success of *The Jazz Singer,* however, forces the studio to switch to sound, and Lina Lamont's vulgar ethnic voice is impossible for talking pictures. Kathy Selden (Debby Reynolds) lip-synchs Lina's voice for the remade film-within-the-film. Don and Kathy fall in love, their true romance contrasting with the publicity-seeking, studio-staged liaison between Don and Lina. Revealed in the film's climax as the authentic voice appropriated by the established star, Kathy will replace her humiliated rival in the next film with Don.

Singin' in the Rain, as the plot summary reveals, is the double of *Jolson Sings Again.* Progenies of *The Jazz Singer,* the films divide Jakie Rabinowitz's Americanization through blackface in two. *Jolson Sings Again* exposes blackface with its ethnic function removed; *Singin' in the Rain* replaces blackface with the conflict between ethnic and American. The Jolson biopics play down the coming of the talkies (perhaps because Columbia Pictures did not want to advertise Warner Bros.); their climax brings lip-synch into the present. But the lip-synch that dominates the last part of *Jolson Sings Again* retrospectively makes strange, by exposing the workings of, both Jolson biopics. Lip-synch organizes the entire plot of *Singin' in the Rain,* but it works diegetically rather than self-consciously, since the film is set at the moment of the transition to sound. The thematization of lip-synch in *Jolson Sings Again* undid *The Jazz Singer*'s unity of voice and image. *Singin' in the Rain,* in contrast, reunites image to voice by freeing the all-American girl from the older ethnic woman whose voice she has been ventriloquizing.

Hagen plays Lina Lamont as a self-worshipping Cantor Rabinowitz; both older figures block the younger generation's access to show business success and romantic love. Similarly, in both *The Jazz Singer* and *Singin' in the Rain* technological progress is made to serve youth. Talking pictures covered ethnic Americanization with burnt cork in *The Jazz Singer;* in *Singin' in the Rain,* the talkies expose the crude voice of the silent-picture star. Reynolds as Kathy Selden makes visible the Jolson-as-Jolson role in *Jolson Sings Again,* supplying the voice for the actress onscreen. In so doing she advances to the Jolson role in *The Jazz Singer,* for her happy ending is to replace the star in front of the camera. When Don pulls back the curtain to reveal Kathy backstage behind the microphone, he reduces Lina Lamont to grotesque pantomime. Opening the curtain brings together voice and image, life and art, man and (appropriate) woman.[82]

By presenting Lina Lamont as stealing Kathy's voice, *Singin' in the Rain* hides its own theft, as Carol Clover has discovered.[83] Just as *The Jazz Singer* appropriated African American music, so *Singin' in the Rain* steals African American dance. Thematizing voice, the narrative distracts attention from the actual source of the film's greatness, its black-inflected dance spectacles. The voice theme pays homage to *The Jazz Singer,* but ultimately the false trail through voice that leads away from blackface returns to the scene of the crime.[84]

Singin' in the Rain deflects its anxiety of black influence onto "The Duelling Cavalier," which is being made under the shadow of the first talking picture. Don, having just read about *The Jazz Singer* in *Variety,* crosses the set of a jungle movie and greets one of the savages with "Hiya Maxie." The cannibal turns out to be a blackface Jew. At a film party where a voice onscreen (the reference is to Will Hays's appearance in the first Vitaphone Prelude) announces the coming of *The Jazz Singer,* Kathy hits Lina with a cake intended for Don and leaves her covered in whiteface. The film people within the movie expect *The Jazz Singer* to fail, but Cosmo's (Donald O'Connor) piano-playing parody of "My Mammy," including mimicry of Jolson intoning the sacred word, is interrupted by the producer: he is shutting down his silent picture to convert the studio to sound. The talking "Duelling Cavalier" reduces its premiere audience to laughter. ("Give me a picture like *The Jazz Singer,*" shouts one man.) Inspired to remake the film as a musical, and casting about for a new title, Don and Cosmo patter from "The Duelling Cavalier" to "The Duelling Mammy" to "The Dancing Cavalier." "The Duelling Cavalier," of course, spoofs *Don Juan,* the first Vitaphone feature with sound effects. So long as Don Lockwood is making the costume drama, Gene Kelly plays him as an imitation John Barrymore, the star of *Don Juan.* And just as Warner Bros. shifted from European history to American popular culture for their revolutionary talking picture, so do Don and Cosmo in *Singin' in the Rain.* But whereas *The Jazz Singer* displayed the black face of popular culture, *Singin' in the Rain* buries it.

In the Don/Cosmo set of free associations, cavalier produces mammy (perhaps aided by Hattie McDaniel as mammy in "the cavalier society" that was gone with the wind), and dueling leads to dancing. But, as Carol Clover observes, there are two missing titles between "The Duelling Mammy" and *Singin' in the Rain*. The obvious one, "The Singing Mammy," would recall Jolson's triumph. *Singin' in the Rain* is no mere copy of *The Jazz Singer,* however; except for the Jolson references, mammy plays no role in Gene Kelly's film. The missing title that names its theft is the one that is omitted between "The Duelling Mammy" and "The Dancing Cavalier," namely, "The Dancing Mammy."

The blackface irruptions in *Singin' in the Rain* display its anxiety about black dance influence. The film makes diegetic not its blackface but its talking-pictures debt to *The Jazz Singer,* as we see when "The Du-elling Cavalier"'s failed synchronization between the Vitaphone sound system and the film reel suggests to Cosmo that Kathy could lip-synch Lina's voice. In its emphasis on speech, however, *Singin' in the Rain* also exposes, as a return of the repressed, its roots in black performance. Re-belling against the faux-aristocratic elocutionist who is teaching them proper diction, Don and Cosmo turn his tongue-twister into the black-inflected tap dance routine "Moses Supposes." Catching up the stiff, be-wildered speech teacher, they loosen him up too. The birth of the talkies is utopian, in *Singin' in the Rain* as in *The Jazz Singer,* because sound frees the performers to imitate black. Preceding the failed premiere of "The Duelling Cavalier," "Moses Supposes" supplies the song-and-dance that will replace "The Duelling Cavalier" with "The Dancing Cavalier." After Kathy gets the idea to turn "The Duelling Cavalier" into a musical, she, Don, and Cosmo dance out of their depression with "Good Mornin'."

Following but covering up *The Jazz Singer*'s path, blackface liberates the filmmakers-within-the-film. It moves them from silence to sound, from pantomime to song-and-dance, from black to white, from black-and-white ("The Duelling Cavalier") to technicolor ("The Dancing Cavalier" production numbers and *Singin' in the Rain*). Surfacing for the briefest of moments before she is buried for good, mammy allows the cast of *Singin' in the Rain* to make "Singin' in the Rain." For at the film's end, the tiny figures of Kathy and Don stand before a giant poster of themselves advertising "Singin' in the Rain," the film they are star-ring in together after the success of "The Dancing Cavalier." United ro-mantically, they get top billing in the film we have just seen. The self-referentiality that opened a gap between *Jolson Sings Again* and history, between the stage and the world, here encloses viewer and cast in musical paradise.[85]

Mammy's burial leaves one more onscreen effect behind: the trashing of Lina Lamont. Rejecting mammy instead of longing for her, *Singin' in the Rain* declares another difference besides blackface from *The Jazz Singer*. Patriarchy stood in the jazz singer's way. What blocks Kathy's romance with Don is a vulgar harridan who may not actually be old enough to be the ingenue's mother but is stupid enough ("I was calling him Don before you were born") to announce she is. In the shift from ethnic to domestic conflict during and after the war, older career women like Lina Lamont were the scapegoats. Kathy replaces her as star onscreen. In contrast to the jazz singer, however, Reynolds owes her triumph to no sound of her own. For the singing voice that comes out of her mouth belongs to an invisible third party. In a final turn of the screw, although Kathy sings for Lina onscreen, it is Jean Hagen who sings for Reynolds offscreen.[86] Like Lina Lamont, Reynolds is the beneficiary of lip-synch.

Kathy takes the place of Lina because, Pygmalion-like, the ingenue is a male creation. Kathy has Lina's hysterical, high screech in her first scene with Don, where she accuses the silent-picture star of being "nothing but a shadow onscreen." Her gestures imitate Lina's at the end, when the open curtain reveals her to the audience. These doublings, intended to underline Kathy's progress from shrew to devotee, unconsciously expose the bonds of womanhood. Suppression of the female voice, which links Kathy to Lina, undercuts the message of the movie.[87] Nonetheless, the focus on female rivalry makes visible the fear of female power; what the diegesis suppresses but the spectacle reveals is that 1950s popular culture was built on black foundations. *Jolson Sings Again*, in contrast, deliberately called attention to the work of (false) integration that burnt cork could no longer do. *Singin' in the Rain* buried blackface to build a stairway to paradise. *Jolson Sings Again* consigned blackface to history and theater. In the present was the social-problem film.

CHAPTER 7

"We Could Cross
These Racial Lines"

Hollywood Discovers Civil Rights

I

Hitler's rise brought to an end Hollywood's cycle of Jewish generational-conflict films. Responding to the Nazi seizure of power, and to the fascist sympathies of the Hays/Breen Production Code Administration (the industry group with the power to censor films), the Jewish moguls evaded anti-Semitism by simply eliminating Jews from the screen. Warner Bros. won its first best picture Academy Award in 1937 with *The Emile Zola Story*. Although the studio depicted the Dreyfus Affair, it cast the Jewish actor Paul Muni as Zola rather than Dreyfus, and allowed no one to speak the word *Jew*.[1] That same year, in *They Won't Forget*, the studio fictionalized the notorious 1915 lynching of Leo Frank by turning the Jewish pencil factory manager into a "Yankee professor."[2] The moguls did not stop with making Jews disappear, moreover. Earlier in the depression decade, to defeat the socialist Upton Sinclair for California governor after he won the Democratic primary, they faked newsreels in which solid citizens opposed Sinclair and a bearded Jewish anarchist supported him.[3]

As the Jewish movies were fading away, Hollywood did produce the generational-conflict film about black passing *Imitation of Life* (1934). Thanks largely to the performance of Fredi Washington as the light-skinned African American, *Imitation of Life* opened a window on the issue of racism. Two years later, *Show Boat* commented critically on the process of "musical miscegenation" even as it exemplified it, for Magnolia, who has learned to sing from Julie's "colored folks' " music, gets her starring chance when the "one-drop" rule that labels Julie black drives her from the stage. These passing films were the only talking pictures before World War II to disturb racial harmony. Jews and African Americans played small, sympathetic, nondemeaning roles in movies made during (and about) the war. Charlie Chaplin's *The Great Dictator*

(1940) and Ernst Lubitsch's *To Be or Not to Be* (1942) supplied brilliant satires on Nazi anti-Semitism, but no Hollywood movie during the early years of World War II faced up to prejudice against Jews within the United States. Finally, in 1944, the screenwriters Philip and Julius Epstein, who had written scripts for Frank Capra's "Why We Fight" series explaining war aims to military personnel, produced their Broadway play *Mr. Skeffington* for Hollywood.[4]

To allay fears of Jewish influence, the Epstein brothers placed their leading man under a twofold constraint. At that time in Hollywood, Jews could play blacks, but in serious, dramatic roles they could not play themselves. Expanding on the tradition of whites in blackface acting for African Americans, therefore, a gentile actor, Claude Rains, plays the Jewish businessman. Mr. Skeffington's punishment—the second constraint—is the condition for audience sympathy. When the social problem film a few years later crossed over from Jew to black, the genre would liberate Jews from suffering African Americans.

Before the movie begins, Job Skeffington (born Skevinskaya) has fought his way up and out of the Lower East Side. The businessman's change of name, a leftover from the generational-conflict genre, spoke to the fact that 80 percent of the fifty thousand Americans who filed name change petitions in the 1940s were Jews.[5] Significantly, however, the protagonist's original family name contains two mistakes. One, the substitution of a Russian for a Jewish patronymic, indicates nervousness about ethnic Jewish origins even when they have been left behind. The other, the female form, *-skaya*, foreshadows the movie's replacement of ghetto aggression with Jewish male feminization.

Shown briefly as the target of racial prejudice on the eve of World War I, Mr. Skeffington is released from a concentration camp on the eve of World War II. These two exposures of anti-Semitism frame an intermarriage story; closer to *The Singing Fool* than to *The Jazz Singer*, its subject is sexual politics, not religious conflict. Like the hero of Fannie Hurst's *Symphony of Six Million*, the Jew who has left his roots behind must learn to serve.

Job's conflict is not with his parents (as in the classic intermarriage film) but with his wife. *Mr. Skeffington* was a Bette Davis vehicle, another of the films—like *Jezebel* (1938), *Dark Victory* (1939), and *Now Voyager* (1942)—that punish her for having a will of her own. Having married the businessman for his money, Mrs. Skeffington carries on with other men. Although Job refuses to show his vulnerability, he is not without feelings. Wedded to a woman who does not love him, like Jolson in *The Singing Fool*, the cuckolded husband turns for comfort to his child. (As a sign of his affection, he presents her with "a little Sambo doll.") When the Skeffingtons divorce, the child wants to stay with her father; unlike Sonny Boy, she does.

The singing fool's wife is punished by the death of her son; Bette Davis, as she ages, by the loss of her looks. Job, who has gone to live in Berlin, is also the target of retribution. The Nazis put him in a concentration camp, take his wealth, and put out his eyes. But Job's unconditional love releases the equally broken-down woman from her "life in front of the mirror." The film's final scene reunites the old couple in a pietà: blind Job rests his head on the breast of the woman, still beautiful in his memory, whose grotesque, lined, over-made-up face he cannot see. Having saved Bette Davis by his suffering and devotion, the Jewish Job ends as Christ.

Unprecedented in linking anti-Semitism in the United States and Nazi Germany, *Mr. Skeffington*—or rather Job Skeffington—pays the price. Doing the blackface Jewish Christ as Uncle Tom, Jolson had played suffering—as mammy in *The Singing Fool*'s pietà, ending "My Mammy" with his arms outstretched in *The Jazz Singer*'s finale. Crucified in burnt cork, the jazz singer rose again as himself. In the postwar racial problem films, blacks would also replace Jews on the cross and in the pietà.

The first film to make that transfer, the swan song of Jewish generational-conflict movies after the hiatus of the Hitler decade, was the Robert Rossen/Abraham Polonsky collaboration *Body and Soul* (1947). Hollywood produced three Jewish generational-conflict films in 1946–47 in addition to *The Jolson Story*. Two were remakes, one of *Abie's Irish Rose*, the other of Fannie Hurst's *Humoresque*. The former, like *The Jolson Story*, eliminated all intergenerational and ethnic conflict; the latter, as *Variety* put it in its congratulatory review, was "virtually a new story, stripped of any racial connotations as was the case originally."[6]* The third film, which like *The Jazz Singer* linked Jewish intergenerational conflict to the Jewish/black bond, was *Body and Soul*.

Now a film noir classic, *Body and Soul* was made at the apogee of Communist influence in the motion picture business. If any film gives

---

*Clifford Odets co-authored the screenplay for the remake of *Humoresque*, in which John Garfield (soon to be the protagonist of *Body and Soul*) starred opposite Joan Crawford. The original *Humoresque* had placed an extraordinarily intense mother-son bond in the social context of the Jewish question; as with other Americanization films (the *Jazz Singer/Jolson Story* pair, for example), the remake moved family romance from ethnicity to sex. Doubling only the mother instead of (like *The Jazz Singer*) the musician as well, Garfield's *Humoresque* pitted against each other the two older women who support the credence to the hallucinatory charge that a Communist conspiracy was seizing control of Hollywood—the charge that revived the House Un-American Activities Committee and propelled President Ronald Reagan of the Screen Actors Guild onto the national political stage—this is the one. With its mixture of urban poetry and left-wing propaganda, *Body and Soul* was a creature of the Popular Front, the Communist/liberal alliance that joined reform politics to popular culture in the name of recovering a usable American past. HUAC targeted both *Body and Soul* and *Crossfire,* the film noir on anti-Semitism made the same year. *Body and Soul*'s director, Robert Rossen, and screenwriter, Abraham Polonsky, like *Crossfire*'s producer, Adrian Scott, and director, Edward Dmytryk, had been members of the Communist Party. Like the stars of *Body and Soul,* Canada Lee, John Garfield, and Anne Revere, they were all about to fall victim to HUAC. The political persecution of Garfield and Lee contributed to their early deaths during the Hollywood inquisition.[7]

If the shared fate of the two male stars, martyrs to the House Un-American Activities Committee, ironically consummated the bond the film wanted to forge between African Americans and Jews, the problem within the movie itself lay less in the obviousness of the conscious message than in the buried, unconscious, one. Although *Body and Soul* may seem to sacrifice art to politics, its political unconscious actually resurrects the cultural myth from which Rossen and Polonsky were trying to escape.

Just as *The Jazz Singer* was the first movie to make Jewish blackface its subject and not just its method, so *Body and Soul* was the first Hollywood film to place at its center the relationship between an African American and a Jew. Black serves as intergenerational transitional object in both films. Yet *Body and Soul* repudiated the Jewish exploitation of black embedded in the first talking picture. Despite trying to take back *The Jazz Singer, Body and Soul* ends by falling under its sway.

On both the black and Jewish fronts, *Body and Soul* marked a new departure for the motion picture business. Hitler's rise to power and the

---

hero's passion for the violin, his mother and his benefactress and lover. The mother appears first as a supportive figure of devotion, especially by comparison to the desperate, alcoholic, passionate Crawford character. But since ethnic conflict does not separate mother and son, the incest taboo alone must do the trick. It turns out to be as fatal as *The Jazz Singer*'s blackface, for the mother helps drive her son's lover (and her own double) to suicide.

Americanizing moguls' wish for invisibility had driven Jews from in front of the camera. Rossen himself had co-authored the screenplay for *They Won't Forget,* the film that converted Leo Frank into a WASP. Since the cycle of generational-conflict films had come to an end in the mid-1930s, gentile actors—Claude Rains as Job Skeffington, Larry Parks as Al Jolson (Gregory Peck would shortly follow them in *Gentleman's Agreement*)—starred as Jews in the rare movie on a Jewish theme. John Garfield was the first Jew allowed to play a Jewish leading man in over a decade.[8]

Even more revolutionary was the African American presence in the film. As we shall see, the first postwar films to center on racial prejudice, *Crossfire* and *Gentleman's Agreement,* confronted anti-Semitism rather than antiblack racism. *Body and Soul,* whose bond between Jew and African American prepared the ground for the five subsequent motion picture treatments of discrimination against blacks,[9] created one of the first substantial, ungrotesque African American film roles. Canada Lee, who played the part, felt liberated from Hollywood racism; he rejoiced that the word *Negro* was never used in the film.[10] But just as blackface in *The Jazz Singer* grounds white freedom in black servitude by standing in for actual blacks, so omitting the racial word in *Body and Soul* fails to free the African American actor from inheriting the sacrificial role. It is now time to look at the movie.

John Garfield (a.k.a. Julie Garfinkle) wakes from a nightmare in the first scene of the film. Close-ups of a sweating face and the screaming sound of "Ben! Ben!" introduce the agitated, claustrophobic aura of the former Group Theater and Warner Bros. star. Who is Ben? All the audience knows from the overheated first few minutes of the film is that Ben's death has sent the Garfield character back to his mother. Garfield gets a diegetic name, Charley, and an occupation, boxer, but we learn nothing more about Ben. Although he "couldn't find a place to lie down . . . after they took Ben away," and although he is defending his title that night, Charley's mother tells him to leave her house.

"You thinking about Ben, Charley? Everybody dies. Ben. Shorty. Even you." The scene has shifted to the pre-bout dressing room. Charley is in his trunks, but the speaker and the meaning of his menacing words are a mystery. The rest of the film—until it returns to the championship fight—is the flashback that motivates this opening.

Ben, we will learn, is a black boxer (Canada Lee), for whose death Charley feels responsible. Desperate for money and with a blood clot in his brain, Ben had thrown his own championship match to Charley, receiving the promise that his head would be spared. Because "the crowd likes a killer," however, the gangster who fixed the fight did not tell Charley that Ben had been paid to lose. Charley thinks he knocked Ben out fairly; shocked when he hears the truth, he takes on the damaged ex-champ as his trainer.

Ben replaces Shorty, the boyhood friend who has been Charley's caretaker and conscience up to now but who was killed by the mob. Gangsters, we already know, had also killed Charley's father when they bombed a speakeasy next to his candy store. Charley's desire not to end up poor like Pop had propelled him into the fight game over his mother's objections. To her wish that her son could have grown up in a better neighborhood "so he wouldn't make a living hitting people," Pop had answered, "You think I picked the east side like Columbus picked America?" The rhetorical question locates immigrants on the side not of Columbus and pioneer freedom, but of Native Americans and slaves. Underscoring the limited choices faced by the immigrant poor, Mom is forced to ask for charity after Pop is killed (fig. 7.1). Her responses to the visiting social worker's questionnaire name for the first time what we already know: "Race: White. Religion: Jewish."

Standing with the immigrant Jewish working class, *Body and Soul* attacks the parvenu who rises, like the jazz singer, by leaving his community behind. Boxing is a "business." Charley is "not just a kid who can fight. He's money." (In an inside joke at the expense of the studio system, Roberts, the gangster to whom Charley sold his "body and soul," shares his name with Bob Roberts, the producer of this [also named with tongue in cheek] Enterprise Studio film.)[11] Once Charley is champ, his agreement to throw his title defense and bet against himself is an "investment." This way of making money is opposed by both his mother (Anne Revere) and Peg (Lili Palmer), the artist he wants to marry. Jewish girl and Jewish mother join in repudiating Charley for choosing the path of gangster/capitalism.

"I can't marry you. It'd just mean marrying [Roberts]," explains Peg. *Body and Soul* opposes that intermarriage, which also entails Charley's liaison with a torch singer. The show girl with whom the jazz singer falls in love, rewarding his move from cantor's son to mass culture, becomes the temptress in *Body and Soul*. The Garfield film chooses against intermarriage and for interracial solidarity between black man and Jew.

"The neighborhood," which does not know that Charley has chosen capitalism against it, has put its money on the champ. "Everybody's betting on you," a local named Shimin tells Charley. The only character

Figure 7.1. Charley's mother (Ann Revere) asks for charity in *Body and Soul*. Courtesy of the Film Stills Archive of the Museum of Modern Art, New York. © 1947 by United Artists Corp.

marked by name and accent as distinctively Jewish, Shimin appears in this scene (and no other) to remind Charley, "Over in Europe the Nazis are killing people like us. Just because of their religion. But here Charley Davis is champeen."[12] Ben echoes the message: "It always felt so good after the fight. Walk down Lenox Avenue. Kids all crazy for you. And proud." Not only is Charley following Ben in selling out his own people; he has also risen on Ben's back, as the graphic shots of the Jewish fighter knocking down the African American make all too literal. Peg cringes during the pummeling; the torch singer shouts, "Kill him, Charley! Kill him!" *Body and Soul* insists on what *The Jazz Singer* shows in spite of itself: that the black face represents the sacrificed immigrant Jewish community. The left-wing film takes the pariah side against the upwardly mobile Jewish son.

"You fixed the fight, didn't you?" Ben demands of the champ after his invocation of Harlem. The thought agitates the trainer, who punches Charley's exercise bag to show him how to win. Roberts enters and orders Ben out of the training camp. "You don't tell me how to live." "No, but I'll tell you how to die." The distraught black man collapses backward, gets up, starts swinging wildly ("I can take it; I'm the champ."), and falls face down. The scene replays the end of Ben's fight with Charley, only this time the ex-champ is dead. He has left behind Charley's nightmare. The next night the Jewish fighter rises four times from the canvas, finally knocking out his (Irish) challenger in the last round.

Polonksy had resisted an early effort to eliminate the black fighter from his film. As he put it half a century later, "There is an obvious deep relationship between people held not so much in contempt but in a deep antipathy by society. Garfield [was Polonsky referring to the actor who stood up for the script or the character who stood up for Ben?] refused to be part of the betrayal."[13]

The Garfield/Polonsky Jewish/black identification gave *Body and Soul* its innovative power; still, the movie could not escape its past. In finishing off Ben and elevating Charley, *Body and Soul* tells the truth (embedded in *The Jazz Singer*) about the contrasting prospects in the United States for African Americans and Jews. Faithfully mirroring the greater obstacles to black than to Jewish success, *Body and Soul* conditions Jewish/black solidarity on Jew knocking out black. But although it insists on the contaminated character of Charley's victory, the result is to turn boxing history inside out. The first version of the *Body and Soul* screenplay based Charley on Barney Ross, a Jewish boxer from the ghetto whose father owned a candy store, who had won the lightweight and welterweight world boxing championships and a silver star at Guadalcanal. When Polonsky added the black prize fighter to the plot, he reversed the actual relations between Jewish and black boxers in the period. During the 1930s and 1940s, African Americans were taking over boxing from Jews and other white ethnics: Joe Louis knocked out Maxie Baer, Henry Armstrong knocked out Barney Ross. Baer disparaged Louis before their fight; Louis punished him in the ring. Film censorship had originated to stop audiences from seeing documentary footage of Jack Johnson defeating Jim Jeffries. Charley may not be a great white hope (Jack London's term for Jeffries); even so, no black man knocks him down. Unlike Jeffries, Baer, and Ross, Charley Davis beats his black opponent.[14]

Black boxers did throw fights in this mob-controlled sport, but it was Jake La Motta who lay down for Billy Fox (the African American) the year *Body and Soul* was made. Although *Body and Soul* exposed the fix that undergirds white ethnic success, it participated in spite of itself in the cultural ritual that forged white manhood in racial conflict in the ring. When the white fighter became Jewish, he inherited the culture's wish for a victory of white over black. *Body and Soul* wanted to repudiate that wish, but it could not film black victory.[15]

Body and Soul remade Clifford Odets's generational-conflict boxing drama, *Golden Boy*. (Denied the starring role in the 1937 Group Theater production of the play, Garfield had accepted a Warner Bros. offer and left New York for Hollywood. He was too ethnic for the 1939 movie, however, which starred William Holden, and so produced *Body and Soul* himself to have another shot at the part.)[16] Odets's golden boy, Joe Bonaparte, gives up the ring and returns to his Italian father after he kills a black boxer. As will Charley, so a worried Joe visits the black boxer's dressing room following the knockout (fig. 7.2). The refusal of forgiveness by the boxer's brothers—the first time in Hollywood that blacks did not give whites what they wanted (and the last time for another quarter century)—is overcome by their father. To an orchestral, Negro spiritual background (in the movie), the father tells Joe that we all carry burdens, and his son's death is Joe's. Like the shot of "The Chocolate Drop" facedown in the ring—which is repeated when Charley knocks out Ben—the message of ethnic reparation moves from one boxing film to the other. Just as it ends *Golden Boy*, so aggression against the black boxer introduces Charley's bond with Ben.[17]

Knowing his victory was contaminated, Charley promises to "look after Ben"; Charley may have something to atone for, but also, as he puts it, "I need someone I can trust." It is Ben who looks after Charley. He and the torch singer enter Charley's life together as replacement for the Jewish mother and Peg. The black man not only takes care of the fighter after (since the movie is in flashback) his mother turns him out; he also replaces her as Charley's conscience. But whereas his Jewish mother is judgmental and unforgiving (she resembles Cantor Rabinowitz; as part of the larger change in representations of family dynamics, in the twenty years between *The Jazz Singer* and *Body and Soul* the parents have switched roles), Ben offers basic trust. Supporting Charley as his mother does not, saving him from destructive self-interest, Ben succeeds where Mom fails. Leslie Fiedler's American *Liebestod*, in which white men escape the demands of women into doomed interracial male solidarity, was moving from the Protestant frontier to the urban ghetto. A year before Fiedler published his "Come Back to the Raft Ag'in, Huck Honey!" Ben played Nigger Jim. Both the jazz singer and the champ look forward to marriage. But the transformative bond for both (here Canada Lee succeeds Jolson himself in blackface) is with a black man.[18]

"What're ya gonna do, kill me?" Charley challenges Roberts once he

Figure 7.2. Charley (John Garfield) visits the injured Ben (Canada Lee) in *Body and Soul.* Courtesy of the Film Stills Archive of the Museum of Modern Art, New York. © 1947 by United Artists Corp.

has won the fight he was paid to throw. "Everybody dies." The speech inverts Roberts's death sentence on Ben, for the words Charley hears before entering the ring and now throws back at the gangster were first spoken by Roberts to Charley's manager when they set up the black champion. "Everybody dies" establishes Ben's legacy to Charley, the bond between black and Jew. Only one body is resurrected, however; in this film's spiritual miscegenation, Ben has died to save Charley's soul.

   In the barely lit, arresting opening shot of *Body and Soul*—set at night and undecipherable until the end of the film—Charley's exercise bag swings slowly above an empty canvas. We will come to learn that punching the bag set off Ben's fatal attack just a few hours before, and as the camera pans from the swaying object to Charley's nightmare, the exercise bag evokes the body of a lynched black man. "Black body swinging in the southern breeze, / Strange fruit hanging from the poplar trees"— the shot pays homage to Billie Holiday's signature song, "Strange Fruit." Written for her by the Jewish Communist songwriter Lewis Allan,

"Strange Fruit" was originally recorded at Café Society, Barney Joseph-son's integrated Greenwich Village nightclub frequented by such artists as Canada Lee, Paul Robeson, Benny Goodman, and Polonsky himself. If the filmmakers had attended Billie Holiday's 1946 Los Angeles concert at the Embassy Theater, they would have heard her sing "Strange Fruit" when they were beginning work on the picture.[19]

"It is the tragic heroic fate of the black American to bring humbly forth grand humanity from a social oppression that thoroughly contradicts the possibility of humanity itself," writes Gerald Early in *The Culture of Bruising,* his essay on black boxers. "It is the same urge, the same spirit, that motivates Uncle Tom."[20] *Uncle Tom's Cabin,* with Tom played in blackface, was the most popular touring theatrical in the years following the Civil War. Although the word *Negro* is never uttered in *Body and Soul,* Canada Lee plays the black Christ.

Jolson had performed Uncle Tom's suffering—ending "My Mammy" with his arms outstretched in *The Jazz Singer,* playing mammy in *The Singing Fool.* Black sacrifice also restores Charley (on *The Jazz Singer* model) to his championship, his mother, and his love. *Mr. Skeffington* redeemed Job as the suffering maternal Jew; Charley leaves that role behind for Ben to play. The Jewish boxer has succeeded the African American as mob-sponsored champion paid to throw away his crown. Peg warned Charley that he would end up like Ben; thanks to Ben, he does not. Taking up the blackface jazz singer's cross, Ben dies for Charley's sins.

If *The Jazz Singer* was one doubles movie behind the Garfield/Lee collaboration, Oscar Micheaux's 1924 *Body and Soul* was another. Paul Robeson played in that all-black film both a rapist masquerading as a minister and his virtuous brother—"two souls . . . warring . . . in one black body," to recall Du Bois. When Rossen and Polonsky redistributed the parts into black soul and white body, they enabled the one to save the other.[21]

Was a different relation imaginable in 1947 between African American and Jew? Taken from an earlier movie, the title *Body and Soul* in turn suggested as sound track for the film the jazz standard "Body and Soul." Originally written by the Jewish songwriter Johnny Green, the Coleman Hawkins 1939 version of the tune was an artistic and popular success, still heard on jukeboxes when *Body and Soul* was released. If Hawkins's interpretation was insufficiently thematic and melodic for the film, Rossen and Polonsky could have turned to the 1935 Benny Goodman/Teddy Wilson/Gene Krupa performance. Goodman, one of the original investors in Café Society, had broken the Jim Crow barrier in musical ensembles when he hired Teddy Wilson for the tour on which they recorded "Body and Soul." Both the Goodman/Wilson and the Hawkins recordings were instances of "musical amalgamation" in which African Americans had leading, independent roles. Closer to home, Rossen and Polonsky could have used Billie Holiday's own version, with which she had followed "Strange Fruit" at the same 1946 Los Angeles concert. They knew this music; Polonsky remembers dancing with his wife to Benny Goodman's "Body and Soul" at the Hotel Pennsylvania in New York. In the end, though, whether forced by the Musicians Union or by his own sense of Hollywood requirements, Rossen incorporated Green's tune into a brooding, melodramatic, orchestral background noise credited to composer Hugo Friedhofer and conductor Emil Newman. That European high-culture choice, repeated in making Charley's girl friend an artist, came at black expense. Jazz Age white popular music replaces the sound of black jazz in *The Jazz Singer*. But whether Euro- or American-centric, the result is the same. Like the absence of jazz in *The Jazz Singer,* the missing jazz in *Body and Soul* points to the African American sacrifice that both movies register—mammy singer on the cross, Ben on the canvas—even as they enact it.[22]

Body and Soul introduces the race relations cycle of late-1940s Hollywood, the set of films that explicitly address racial prejudice. *Gentleman's Agreement* (1947, costarring Garfield and Revere) and *Pinky* (1949) together sunder Jewish from black upward mobility. *Home of the Brave* (1945 [Broadway play] and 1949 [film]) brings racism, anti-Semitism, and interracial solidarity problematically together. Like *Mr. Skeffington* and *Body and Soul,* these films and others resembling them were made by Hollywood liberals and radicals, Communists and NAACP allies. The civil rights films "cross these racial lines," to quote Michael Roemer once again,[23] with the intention of repudiating minstrelsy. The confusions of identity with which they play, however, repeat the Jewish blackface of *Body and Soul,* where Charley tries on, to free himself from, Ben's role.

II

As *Body and Soul* shows, the racial problem film is not the binary opposite of the blackface musical. The two most popular civil rights movies, *Gentleman's Agreement* and *Pinky,* and *Lost Boundaries* as well, concern putting on an identity that is not one's own. All three are passing films. *Gentleman's Agreement* took as its subject the *Mr. Skef-fington* technique of gentile playing Jew, just as *The Jazz Singer* had the-matized the blackface method a generation earlier. Phil (Gregory Peck) in *Gentlemen's Agreement* is an old-family Protestant passing down. Pinky (Jeanne Crain) plays a light-skinned African American who has gone north and passed up. But because the actress playing Pinky is her-self white, her skin privilege allows white viewers to share the suffering she endures as black.[24] Moreover, Pinky is not passing as white in the North but suffering as black in the South for the entire film. Both pass-ing movies, like the blackface musical, are vehicles for passing down. Blackface plays off of essential racial difference, whereas the sympathetic racial passer suffers for a stigmatized difference that is not real—though that distinction, as we shall see, will break down too.

No one passes in *Home of the Brave,* where a Jewish doctor treats a black soldier for partial amnesia and hysterical paralysis. At crucial mo-ments, however, the doctor plays the roles of significant figures in the soldier's wartime mission. As with blackface and passing, Hollywood cel-ebrates itself in *Home of the Brave* by making acting redemptive. Jewish assimilation and upward mobility were transferring ethnic performance, the putting of oneself in another's place, the empathic trying on of mul-tiple identities, from blackface and vaudeville to journalism (in *Gentle-man's Agreement*) and the helping professions (a nursing school in *Pinky,* the psychiatrist's office in *Home*). Instead of teaching immigrants to be Americans through blackface, *Home*'s role-playing is the method by which the immigrant son, the doctor, heals his patient's divided self. Middle-class professionals—journalist, doctor, and nurse—substitute for theatrical performers in the racial problem film. Hollywood, inheriting and universalizing blackface in the blackface musical, celebrated itself as the institutional locus of American identity. In the social problem film it allied itself with the therapeutic society. Generic overlap suggests in-stitutional overlap; Hollywood was not just Hortense Powdermaker's dream factory, but also the American interpreter of dreams, employing role-playing as national mass therapy.[25]

Both the blackface musical and the social problem film change iden-tities through masquerade. Binary opposition, therefore, resides not so much between the two genres as between the two most popular racial problem films, *Gentleman's Agreement* and *Pinky*. Their opposition, moreover, goes back to the split upon which the original mixed-genre film, *The Jazz Singer,* depends: that between the Jew who can change his identity and the African American who cannot change hers.

Figure 7.3. Pinky (Jeanne Crain) and Dicey (Ethel Waters) do Miss Em's laundry in *Pinky*. Courtesy of the Film Stills Archive of the Museum of Modern Art, New York. © 1949 by Twentieth Century Fox Film Corp.

Darryl Zanuck and Elia Kazan, NAACP allies from the single major studio, Twentieth Century Fox, without a dominant Jewish presence at the top, established Hollywood's terms for Jewish/black mobility. Zanuck, author of the *Old San Francisco* screenplay, had differentiated early in his career between legitimate and illegitimate racial passing. He and Kazan, filming *Pinky* after their success with *Gentleman's Agreement* (Oscars for best picture and best director), shifted from a Protestant journalist masquerading as Jew to a light-skinned southern Negro who has passed as white. That identical structure creates a stunning difference. At the moment in *Gentleman's Agreement* when Phil's fiancée can no longer endure the trouble his passing has brought to her life, Cathy (Dorothy McGuire) blurts out, "It's no use Phil. . . . You're doing an impossible thing. You are what you *are* for the one life you have. You can't help it if you were born Christian instead of Jewish." The movie, and the favorable review in *Commentary*, the organ of the American Jew-

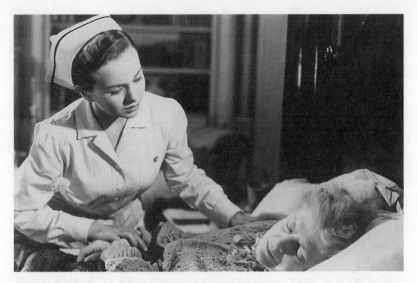

Figure 7.4. Pinky nurses Miss Em (Ethel Barrymore) in *Pinky*. Courtesy of the Film Stills Archive of the Museum of Modern Art, New York. © 1949 by Twentieth Century Fox Film Corp.

ish Committee, reject that insistence on unalterable identity, which would not only prevent gentiles from understanding how Jews feel but also deprive Jews of the freedom to assimilate. *Pinky*'s Miss Em, the southern aristocrat who shares an old-family, upper-class background with Phil's Darien, Connecticut, fiancée, makes a similar speech to Pinky; this time, though, the movie takes the side of aristocratic, fixed identity. Submitting to her grandmother's (Ethel Waters) emotional blackmail, Pinky has agreed to nurse the dying matriarch, whose laundry her grandmother, now herself too old to serve, has done for years (figs. 7.3 and 7.4).

At this point Pinky still plans to return north and marry the white doctor to whom she is engaged. By the end of the film, however, she has followed Miss Em's admonition, "Be yourself," and, with a black doctor, has opened a training school for black nurses in the mansion Miss Em has bequeathed her. She sends her fiancé away with the words, "I'm a Negro and I don't want to be anything else." As a white actress playing a light-skinned African American, Jeanne Crain can, like Gregory Peck, pass down. As a Jew, Phil can pass up; Pinky, as a black, cannot.[26]

Showing Pinky as the victim of southern racism nonetheless broke a Hollywood taboo, especially since passing raised questions about the racial purity of anyone claiming to be white. *Imitation of Life* and *Show Boat* were the only Hollywood precedents for *Pinky,* and several southern cities banned Kazan's film. The Supreme Court ruling overturning that censorship extended first amendment protection to movies for the first time.[27] Still, the speech freed by the court came down against passing and for segregation.

"Says they ain't white enough," says one nurse to another in the closing scene of the film. She is repeating Pinky's grandmother's comment on the sheets, not on her granddaughter. Black women in starched white uniforms change bed sheets under a sign that says, "Miss Em's nurses training school"; embracing her black roots, Pinky is returning to white laundry. Director Kazan and screenwriters Philip Dunne and Dudley Nichols were on the left; Dunne would soon be blacklisted, and Nichols had written the screenplay in which Judge Priest's washerwoman leads the chorus of black women thanking Jesus for his promise to wash them "white as snow." To this viewer there is irony in the final scene, whether intended or not. However, no contemporary reviewer saw the last words, pointing to Pinky by way of the sheets, as undercutting the film's resolution. As Ralph Ellison pointed out in the review of the four 1949 race movies that gave its title to his classic essay collection, *Shadow and Act,* what Pinky is not is a segregation-accepting, southern Negro; to return to southern segregation she has had to reject what she has become, and that is the choice that, in the name of the givenness of identity, the film endorses. Going beyond Roland Barthes's "principle of myth" that "transforms history into nature," *Pinky* attacks history as unnatural, reversing Pinky's historical change in the name of racial nature.[28]

That choice may have a different political valence now than it did in 1949; the light-skinned black-nationalist student with whom I saw the film was far more sympathetic to it than was her integrationist Jewish professor. Like Pinky, she did not want to stand with the fiancé, the white professional man who insisted that the southern blacks were "not your people" and told Pinky "there'd be no Pinky Johnson after [she] was married." But in counterposing loyalty to one's people to integration, *Pinky* accepts the dichotomy of the passing and generational-conflict films—now overcome, as the Jolson films and *Gentlemen's Agreement* would have it, for Jews. The postwar Jewish films, whether with Parks as Jolson or Peck as a Jew, flee any possible conflict between group distinctiveness and loyalty, on the one hand, and integration, on the other. *Pinky* insists on that conflict to justify segregation.

Movie endings cannot erase what has come before, and it is clear that

Pinky and *Gentleman's Agreement* are both troubled by race discrimination. The contrasting endings also fail to hide what these films share with blackface: a fascination with racial masquerade. Nonetheless, the opposed endings are decisive. As in blackface, Jews rise and blacks serve. Since the condition of white ethnic mobility is that blacks be kept in place, mobility cannot extend from blackface to black passing.

Racial fixity is allied with class hierarchy in the South, assimilation with class permeability in the North. If the exclusive northern upper class was the target of *Gentleman's Agreement*, the southern upper class protects its Negroes from upwardly mobile parvenus like Miss Em's niece, who attempts to break the matriarch's will, and from the white trash who try to rape Pinky. Assaulted by whites, physically in the graphic attempted rape and legally in the fight over the will, the light-skinned African American is also the victim of dark-skinned blacks. Their stereotypical violence and thievery infuriated James Baldwin in his review of the novel from which the movie was made. (Hostility from blacks, not whites, also drives the black doctor to pass in *Lost Boundaries*.) As Baldwin pointed out, Pinky's light skin promoted white viewer identification with victimization not just of but also by African Americans.[29]

Pinky decides to uplift her race. She opts for southern segregation, the fixed black identity on which white play with identity depends, whereas *Gentleman's Agreement*, in the name of mobility, attacks the idea that Jews are any different from other people. That contrast, realized in the endings, also works throughout the films. There is a black milieu in *Pinky*, but only a few isolated Jews in *Gentleman's Agreement*. This departure from the original generational-conflict films, which embedded ethnics in Old World communities, redistributes black fixity and Jewish transfer into two separate movies. And that is a sign that blackface is in trouble, for neither film can hold together, play with, and simultaneously reinforce and dissolve racial difference.

Both films ground themselves in racial masquerade's play with identity, the ability to move back and forth, but both reject mutability in their climaxes. When Phil's son is subjected to anti-Semitic insults, Cathy reassures the boy: "It's not true. You're no more Jewish than I am." Phil is furious at this distinction—central to blackface—between those who can and those who cannot stop being members of the stigmatized group. Cathy wants Phil's Jewface to be nothing more than a magazine assignment, a game. For Phil, the conditions that gave rise to that game must end. Pinky's choice of segregation leaves the same message—not to dissolve the difference between Jew and gentile but to insist on the difference between white and black. Unlike musical blackface, these movies, to use the title of Chester Himes's fictional exposé of racial passing, are proposing "to end all stories," to abolish the conditions that enable their own storytelling.[30]*

Gentleman's Agreement stands for the northern, Jewish solution to the race problem, *Pinky* for the southern one imposed on blacks, but the contrast between the movies is also underlined by a third term, *gender*. As in both versions of *Imitation of Life* (1934, 1959), the African American daughter who wants to pass is drawn back into the body of her mammy.[31] Women are what they are; men are what they do. Women, especially black women, are embodied; men transcend. Just as white ethnic mobility requires black fixity, so men need women. Mammy allows the blackface Jew, the jazz singer, to move forward; she pulls the white-face African American back to her maternal roots.**

Men, both Phil and his Jewish friend, move forward in *Gentleman's Agreement* to marriage, integrated housing, and middle-class careers. The woman moves backward, in *Pinky*, to gender and racial solidarity. Allying community with segregation, *Pinky* was reflecting social reality

---

*Martin Ritt's *Paris Blues* (1961) plays another variation on the end of blackface and the beginning of civil rights, one that suggests that Leslie Fielder was the uncredited screenwriter. Ram Bowen ("Rimbaud," played by Paul Newman) gives up Joanne Woodward to remain in Paris and compose jazz, whereas his best friend, Eddie (Sidney Poitier), gives up jazz and their friendship to go back home with Diahann Carroll. The two men first meet the two women under a poster—wide open, smiling mouth and raised trumpet—of Wild Man Moore (Louis Armstrong—the Moor come to Paris, as Glenn Ligon pointed out to me). After Ram says good-bye to Woodward under that same poster, workers cover it over with an ad for the Larousse Encyclopedia. End of Armstrong presiding over interracial, male jazz. Poitier is returning to the United States for love, family, and "the cause." Ram Bowen, whose music has been dismissed as frivolous by an elitist French composer, is relinquishing libido (is it Joanne Woodward or Sidney Poitier?) for his art. The actual jazz art in the film, what the audience hears when Ram Bowen's band plays, is the music of Duke Ellington. (Moreover, the Paul Newman character who takes center stage in the movie is derived from a Jewish band member whose role in the 1957 novel by Harold Flender is subordinated to that of the black tenor sax player—the Poitier role in the film.) (On *Paris Blues*, see Krin Grabbard, *Jamming at the Margins* [forthcoming from University of Chicago Press], chap. 5.)

** Douglas Sirk's remake of *Imitation of Life* (1959) changed the white heroine from a pancake-producing businesswoman to an actress who neglects her daughter. Since the black girl passing as white takes the actress as her model, Sirk may have intended to extend the film's attack on black impersonation to the Hollywood method itself. However, the result is to punish the racial passer as bad daughter and the career woman as bad mother. Only the mammy—mother of one role-player and servant to the other—remains above (or is it below?) reproach.

through a distorting mirror. Blocked in its efforts to win white social and political acceptance in the decades after the Civil War, the mulatto elite did ally itself with the people it might otherwise have left behind. But that alliance produced, in the years surrounding *Pinky,* not the acceptance of segregation but the fight for integration.[32]

Under the sign of mammy, *Pinky* stands for female community as well as segregation, as does *Imitation of Life. Pinky* was the first Hollywood film to show an interracial romance (although both actress and actor were in fact white); but instead of the traditional, two-parent family that propels exogamy (as in *The Jazz Singer*), Miss Em and Granny together pull Pinky away from heterosexual and interracial relations into a community of women (figs. 7.4 and 7.14). They do what Miss Bea and her mammy, Delilah, had done to Delilah's daughter, Peola, in *Imitation of Life.* But the more rebellious Peola requires a dead mother to pull her back. In the claustrophobic final shot of Douglas Sirk's remake, white mother and daughter embrace the returning prodigal in the car at her own mother's funeral.* This love that feels like death and confinement deprives the reformed racial passer of the social space of Miss Em's nursing home; psychological melodrama, here as elsewhere, may convey a deeper truth than social realism.[33]

The nursing home's light-filled hospital room tells its own truth, to be sure, about the institutions that black professionals, significantly women, built under the constraints of segregation. Nonetheless, to employ mammy to signal female community as submission was no favor to black women. Making history, the combination of Pinky and Granny produced a figure opposite to the black nurses changing white bed linen

---

*As Lora Berlant points out, *Imitation of Life*'s interracial female community supplies white women with their (black) bodies. Just as that reconnection blocks black passing, so the white daughter is deprived of the object of her desire, her mother's fiancé, by the incest taboo. The result—echoing the proslavery Henry Hughes's "Mulattos are monsters. Amalgamation is incest"—is to make racial change a crime against nature. Sirk's remake puts the white man in the funeral car, but, the law of the father having done its work (against passing and incest and in favor of a restrictive female community), he is not in the final frame. Sirk's elaborate marching-band funeral shows that the mammy figure had her own community, of which the white mother and daughter were unaware. But her own daughter (the Jewish actress Susan Kohner, passing as African American) is reproached for having had no connection to it either. (See Loren Berlant, "National Brands/National Body: *Imitation of Life,*" in *Comparative American Identities: Race, Sex, and Nationality in the Modern Text,* ed. Hortense J. Spillers [New York, 1991], 110–41; Donald Bogle, *Toms, Coons, Mulattoes, Mammies, and Bucks: An Interpretive History of Blacks in American Films* [New York, 1973], 57–60, 150, 191–92; Henry Hughes, *Treatise on Sociology, Theoretical and Practical* [New York, (1854) 1968], 239–40.)

in *Pinky*'s segregated finale—a figure who harked back not to the Ethel Waters who played mammy, but to the one who sang "Get Up Off Your Knees." Six years after *Pinky,* Rosa Parks's refusal to move to the back of the bus initiated the most significant American mass protest movement of the second half of the twentieth century.

III

Do gender and regional differences explain the divergence of *Pinky* from *Gentleman's Agreement,* or is the black/Jewish contrast more fundamental? A thought experiment would imagine changing the black protagonist from woman to man, moving him north instead of returning her south, and transforming the gentile as Jew into a Jew as black. Stanley Kramer and Carl Foreman carried out that experiment as *Pinky* was being filmed when, turning black the Jewish protagonist of Arthur Laurents's Broadway play, they made *Home of the Brave* into a film.[34]

Why did Kramer and Foreman black up Laurents's Peter Coen? For one thing, it looked like better box office, after two films on anti-Semitism, to shift from Jews to blacks. In addition, to "daringly substitute a Negro" for a Jew, in the prose of *Time* magazine, was, so the *Saturday Review* thought, to make a more radical choice.[35] However vicious, American anti-Semitism was not the racism that organized the society. While the United States was defeating Nazism with a Jim Crow army, there was growing recognition that American Negrophobia was the counterpart of European anti-Semitism. The NAACP journal, *Crisis,* warning against the "kernel of fascism" in the South, exposed "Southern Schrecklichkeit." "These are not wrecked Jewish establishments in Nazi Germany, but Negro businesses in democratic America," ran the caption under pictures of a "Kristallnacht" in Columbia, Tennessee (fig. 7.5). *Crisis* exposed antiblack and anti-Semitic appeals in the successful 1946 reelection campaign of Detroit mayor Edward Jeffries. The *Jewish Frontier* showed that the Cicero, Illinois, race riot a few years later was fed by rumors that "Jews were planning to move Negroes into Cicero." Both *Crisis* and *Commentary* campaigned against discriminatory college admissions policies and restrictive covenants that excluded Jews and blacks from white Christian neighborhoods, the plot device on which *Gentlemen's Agreement* turns.[36]

Figure 7.5. *Kristallnacht* in Tennessee. *Crisis* 53 (Apr. 1946): 110. Courtesy of *Crisis*. Photos by Wiles-Hood and Acme.

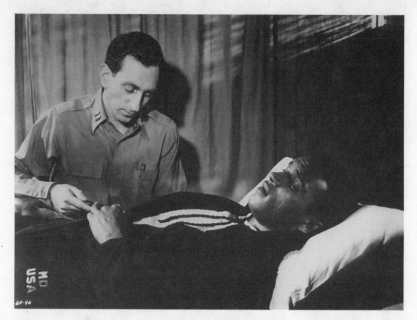

Figure 7.6. *Home of the Brave*'s doctor (Jeff Corey) injects Mossie (James Edwards). Courtesy of the Film Stills Archive of the Museum of Modern Art, New York. © 1949 by United Artists Corp.

These parallels served the black/Jewish civil rights alliance. The most virulent racists were also anti-Semites, *Crisis* reminded its readers. Racists blamed Jewish judges for tolerating black criminals. Reporting a Klan revival in the South and an increase in southern anti-Semitism, *Crisis* quoted Tennessee kleagle Jesse M. Stoner's pronouncement, "Anti-Semitism and white supremacy go hand in hand." *Commentary,* founded by the American Jewish Committee after the destruction of European Jewry, made the fight for civil rights in the United States a central concern of the magazine's first five years. Kenneth Clark, the African American social psychologist on whose research the Supreme Court would rely in *Brown v. Board of Education,* wrote for *Commentary.* James Baldwin's first two published short stories, the only *Commentary* fiction of the period not to center on Jewish experience, appeared in the AJC organ.[37]

But although shared opposition to racism generated the civil rights alliance of the two diaspora peoples driven from their homelands, African Americans and Jews, that alliance also exposed the more privileged position of Jews, both in society and in the civil rights organizations them-

Figure 7.7. The doctor forces tears from Mossie's eyes in *Home of the Brave*.
Courtesy of the Film Stills Archive of the Museum of Modern Art, New York.
© 1949 by United Artists Corp.

selves, where most of the money, legal resources, and social scientific ex-
pertise (though, crucially, not all) was in the hands of Jews, and where
integrationist goals and legal means would work better for Jews than for
blacks.[38] Kramer's film marked that difference when, in painting its Jewish soldier black, it turned its doctor into a Jew—not explicitly, but by
replacing his gentile name with no name at all, giving him a Jewish nose
and appearance, photographing him from angles and in close-ups that
emphasized his facial look (figs. 7.6–7.9), and, unlike the play, hinting
at his own experience of racial prejudice.

One massive social fact, however, ought to have made impossible the
transformation of victim from Jew to black, even in Hollywood—and
yet not a single reviewer named it, not even those most critical of the
film for avoiding the real character of racial oppression in the United
States. In the Jim Crow American army of World War II, no black soldier could have been in the company of whites. The American armed
forces were entirely segregated during the war, and the postwar debate
over integration could not have been missed by anyone concerned about
civil rights. A 1946 army report proposing that an occasional Negro tech-

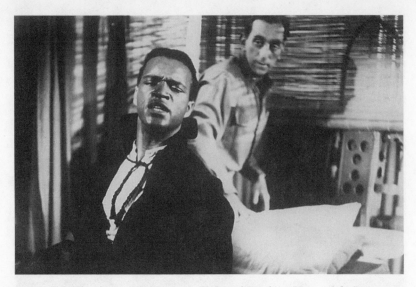

Figure 7.8. The doctor impersonates T. J. and Finch in *Home of the Brave.*
Courtesy of the Film Stills Archive of the Museum of Modern Art, New York.
© 1949 by United Artists Corp.

nician enter white units "where Negro personnel with special skills can
be utilized to advantage as individuals" might have explained the black
soldier's presence among whites, since he is brought in as the only available surveyor. That report not only postdated the war, however; it was
also never implemented. Civil rights forces pressed for military integration in the year before *Home* was filmed, and A. Philip Randolph and
the NAACP threatened black draft resistance if the army remained Jim
Crow. When, under pressure from black militance and the Henry Wallace threat, Truman finally issued his executive order in 1948 looking
forward to military integration, the army dragged its feet. It did not place
black and white troops together until the Korean War.[39]

By blocking out Jim Crow, instead of endorsing it as *Pinky* had done,
Home took its lone black man out of a black milieu. Textually the African
American alone is vulnerable to racial hate, subtextually, as with blackface, to racial love. In the film's plot, Peter Moss (Peter Coen in the play,
played in the movie by James Edwards) has suffered partial amnesia and
a hysterical paralysis after his best friend, white, is killed on a mission to
map a Japanese-held island. Through drug-induced narcosynthesis and
flashback, the doctor elicits the story of racial tension among the five soldiers on the island. *Home* thereby does what the Office of War Infor-

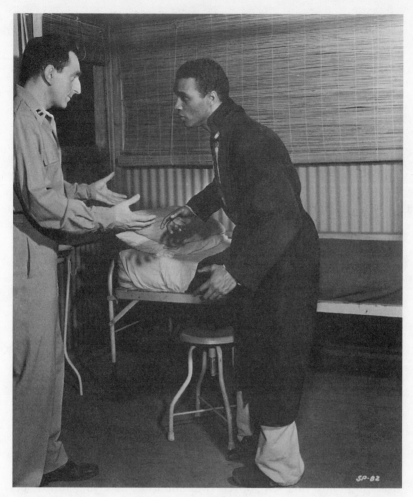

Figure 7.9. The doctor gets Mossie to walk in *Home of the Brave*. Courtesy of the Film Stills Archive of the Museum of Modern Art, New York. © 1949 by United Artists Corp.

mation wanted and most war films failed to do: unite combat to the larger issue of why we fight. How can America be the home of the brave, the film asks, if it is not the land of the free?[40]

A government official had proclaimed during World War II, "By making this a people's war for freedom, we can help clear up the alien problem, the negro problem, the anti-Semitic problem."[41] This New Dealer's guilt by association aligned African Americans and aliens, not white supremacists and nativists, alongside anti-Semites. *Home of the*

Brave also inadvertently makes visible the political unconscious that infected even those supporting civil rights.

Stanley Kramer named his black soldier for Carleton Moss, the Hollywood journalist who, having attacked *Gone with the Wind* in the *Daily Worker,* had then written and starred in the World War II army film *The Negro Soldier.* Acknowledging the "evils which still hinder complete integration," Moss nonetheless urged black troops to resist Japanese propaganda about American Jim Crow. Once the war ended Moss had served his purpose, and the army dropped him, as he put it, for "my un-American past." Three years later Moss promoted the film on race prejudice in the war against Japan made by his leftist friends.[42]

To accomplish Carleton Moss's goal of promoting democracy, however, the film cripples Peter Moss; it humiliates him in extended and visually intrusive ways. Although the announcement that Moss cannot walk is made at the beginning of the film, the camera first shows him, in flashback, as arguably the first dignified, erect, nonstereotyped, intelligent black leading man to appear on the Hollywood screen. Moss, unlike the white soldiers, has already volunteered for the mission in the scene where he meets them. As the white men hunch over, fearful and vacillating, not wanting to join the mission but afraid to refuse, he towers above them.

That opening scene projects the painfulness of Moss's fall. Most of the movie analyzes him as a man brought down by racism. But the film does not show what it tells, for Moss can close himself off to racial insults. Made abject by the Jewish doctor's interventions, he becomes abject again, in flashback, through his love for and loss of his white friend. The doctor injects him (fig. 7.6), forces tears from his eyes and words from his mouth (fig. 7.7), hovers over him while he's lying in bed, lectures him, berates him, sneaks behind his back (fig. 7.8) to scare him with the voices of members of his mission (T. J., his persecutor, and Finch, his dead friend), holds him, cures him, and is finally the recipient of his devotion. The film puts blackvoice imitations and racist stereotypes, including a reference to Finch and Moss as Amos and Andy, into T. J.'s mouth. That method of distancing itself from blackface allows *Home* to do its own blackface on a far more powerful, because loving, level.

A fundamental contradiction runs through this film. Its ideology is "Jewish" on the *Gentleman's Agreement* model: northern, male, and integrationist, the film insists there is no difference between black and white. But its spectacle, its affect, enforces black difference as bodily excess. Assimilated to Jew at the high level of mind, Moss is made emotion-ridden and female at the low level of body. As hysterical body, Moss (né Coen) blackened an anti-Semitic stereotype that troubled the assimilating Jew. Was it integrationist identification with the victim of racial oppression that made the film so powerful a viewing experience for two white male adolescents, one Jewish, one not, watching the film a continent and a decade apart?[43] Was it aspiration to the position of power in which Jew/white helps black? Or was it male adolescent anxiety about tears, the open body, and gender confusion—brought again into play when these now grown men watched the film together with a leading (and female) film authority on cross-gender identification?

In forcing words and tears from the black face, the Jewish doctor, imitating the jazz singer before him, is effectively putting on blackface. He is making the black face and body perform emotions forbidden to his (male, Jewish) self. In turning Moss into an infant and mammy, he also joins the doctors who invade women in innumerable postwar psychological films, doctors who heal women's divided identities, as this doctor heals Moss. As a doctor film, *Home* participates in the postwar turn to psychology and the faith in the professional expert to solve the country's postwar maladjustment.[44]

Like *Home*'s doctor, *Gentleman's Agreement*'s journalist also responds to a victim of racial discrimination. John Garfield, the Jewish boxer in *Body and Soul,* plays Dave, a returning World War II veteran, in *Gentleman's Agreement.* "How must a fellow like Dave feel?" Phil wonders when he is looking for an angle for his series on anti-Semitism. Maybe he should ask Dave what happens to him inside "when you hear about Jewish kids getting their teeth kicked in by Jew-haters in New York City." But, Phil decides, "There isn't any way you can tear open the secret heart of another human being," so he takes on a Jewish identity himself. *Home*'s Jewish doctor, opening up the black soldier's heart, makes the other choice. Even so, the privileged subject position within the film will turn out, as in the women's films, to reside not with the doctor but with the patient.

The move from stage to hospital, from blackface musical and *Jolson Sings Again* to postwar psychological film, may seem extreme; in fact, by way of Phil's Jewface (fig. 7.10) and Jolson's army entertainment (fig. 6.9), it is doubly mediated. *Gentleman's Agreement* aligns passing with illness. Phil's mother's heart attack generates his decision to put on the mask of a Jew. Phil "was scared. I was a kid again. My mom was sick"—and that propels him to realize that he'll "know the answer [to

Figure 7.10. Phil (Gregory Peck) decides to pass as a Jew in *Gentleman's Agreement*. Courtesy of the Film Stills Archive of the Museum of Modern Art, New York. © 1947 by Twentieth Century Fox Film Corp.

anti-Semitism] only when I feel it myself." Phil has to be scared before he can understand. Then, like Jolson in *The Jazz Singer* and *Jolson Sings Again*, he stares at himself in the mirror. The blackface Jolson saw the mirror reflection of his father; Parks-as-Jolson saw himself. The gentile Peck sees in himself a face that could be Jewish. He describes to his mother his resemblance to Dave—dark hair, dark eyes, no accent, no mannerisms—as she lies in her bed. Camera cuts and Phil's agitated movements break down the distance between mother and son as Phil wins his mother's approval for Jewface. She calls his masquerade "the best medicine I could have had." (The same actress, Anne Revere, who supports Phil's identification with the Garfield character, Dave, played Garfield's Jewish mother in *Body and Soul*. For Revere with the two men to whom she played mother, see fig. 7.11.) The boundary breakdown of blackface and passing, derived historically from slavery and mammy, originates psychologically in the mother/son symbiosis, the time before a stable, self-enclosed, white male identity is in place. Mammy supports mutable identity in the blackface musical; the ill mother blesses Jewface in one social problem film; *Home* takes the next step and makes the victim of racial prejudice sick.

Figure 7.11. Phil, his mother (Ann Revere), and his Jewish friend (John Garfield) in *Gentleman's Agreement*. Courtesy of the Film Stills Archive of the Museum of Modern Art, New York. © 1947 by Twentieth Century Fox Film Corp.

Home belongs with the postwar focus on psychology in advertising, industrial relations, and child rearing, when the production of private desire motivated consumption and served regulatory functions for corporate, state, and professional institutions. The turn to psychology, to reestablish the home-front division of labor interrupted by depression and war, targeted women in particular. But damage repair began with the soldiers themselves. Soldiers are ubiquitous in post–World War II films, and they typically have home-front adjustment problems. Jolson ends up in a hospital bed in *Jolson Sings Again,* victim of a lung collapse while entertaining World War II troops (fig. 6.9). The entertainer-as-war-casualty reminds us that *Home* is a combat film. The war film's effort to intensify immediate experience, through combat semantics and the documentary effect, moves into the social problem film by way of passing and psychological invasion. The combat wounds of returning veterans, in such films as *Best Years of Our Lives* and *The Guilt of Janet Ames* (1947), signified internal disturbance. They were read both through the psychological tests administered to soldiers during the war and through the pervasive wartime discourse about the psychological disabilities that made so many soldiers unable to fight. Old-fashioned, moralistic condemnations of cowardice were displaced during and after World War II by attention to psychosomatic disorder. The poetic line that is *Home*'s leitmotif, "Coward take my coward's hand," asks what it means when, in the home of the brave, soldiers are rendered unfit for combat.[45]

But if psychological disablement is a universal problem of the World War II fighting man, what does race—the land of the free—have to do with it? It is in the space between the specificity of racial disablement and the universality of male lack (exhibited, for example, by the armless veteran in *Best Years*) that *Home* locates itself. The doctor's psychological detective work makes Moss and the audience experience how race prejudice has turned the black soldier into "half a man" (the title of NAACP leader Mary Ovington's book on the Negro problem). In the claustrophobic mis-en-scène of jungle and hospital room, camera angles crowd and decenter the frame, cut off body parts, and merge the Japanese menace with the pervasive racialized surround. Racial slurs, by T. J. in the Pacific and from Moss's memories of his prewar past, are brought home when Finch, having left behind the maps, starts to call Moss a "yellow-bellied nigger" for arguing against Finch's return for them. The film seems to be saying that, unable to respond aggressively to racial intimidation, Moss unconsciously wanted his best friend to be hit. When Finch dies, the analysis would go, Moss turns his racial anger inward. This psychology of the oppressed, anticipating Frantz Fanon's *Wretched of the Earth* by a decade, seems confirmed when the doctor finally gets Moss to walk by calling him a yellow-bellied nigger. Moss, exemplifying the Fanonian solution, moves forward in anger.[46]

Fanon's goal, however, is rebellion, race-conscious and violent, a direction in which *Home* can hardly go, both for political reasons and because it would acknowledge the legitimate anger blacks feel toward sympathetic whites.[47] Finch wants Moss's reassurance that he is not like all the others; it turns out that he is. Having exposed black rage, *Home* must dissolve it. On the one hand, not Moss but the invisible Japanese enact the violence of people of color. On the other hand, between the diagnosis and the walking cure intervenes the rejection of the analysis on which the film depends. The doctor has told Moss he was glad when Finch was shot, not because of the racial slur, but because all soldiers are relieved when the man next to them takes the bullet. As with *Pinky*, the ending cannot undo the film, but as in *Pinky* the ending that seems to undercut the film is also its telos. Only the Jewish father—not gentile hostility—structured the jazz singer's divided feelings about assimilation. *Home*'s psychology, which begins by exposing white supremacy, ends up reproducing *The Jazz Singer*'s evasion.

Home consciously shifts to survivor guilt so that Moss can share with white soldiers a common humanity; the unconscious desire is to evacuate the divisive racial ground. Washing Moss white is insufficient to wipe away white guilt for his suffering, however, and when the film elicits African American forgiveness, racial stereotyping returns. The first part of *Home* deprives Moss of his black milieu as racial specificity, on the *Gentleman's Agreement* model (there are no other blacks either in the neighborhood where Moss grows up or in his army), but insists on the racial specificity of the wound to his psyche. By the film's end this distribution has been reversed. As the message deprives Moss of his difference as caused by racial prejudice, by a compensatory logic the story restores his racial difference as less than whole. The racist source of his disability is denied only after the movie turns Moss into the racially abject.

Home subjects Moss to three primal scenes of abjection. The first brings Finch and Moss together after Finch has been tortured by the Japanese. In the first shot the camera closes in on Moss alone, as Dmitri Tiomkin's mysterious, menacing wartime music mixes with the strains of "Sometimes I Feel Like a Motherless Child." Moss falls on the ground and cries, "Nigger, nigger, nigger, nigger." Supposedly a sign that he has been broken by racist slurs, the incantation announces the racist stereotype that, however sympathetic, is about to take Moss over. The dying Finch crawls through the mud to Moss, who gathers his mutilated white friend into his arms (fig. 7.12). An extended series of close-ups shows Moss babbling to Finch and listening for signs of life. His head on Finch's chest, Finch's head on his chest, hysterically rocking and cradling his friend's dead body, Moss is enacting a black and white pietà. (Stanley Kramer loved the image so much that he used it again a decade later at the climax of *The Defiant Ones;* compare figs. 7.12 and 7.13.)* Moss is thereby, as is evident from comparing Moss with Finch to Pinky with her granny (figs. 7.12 and 7.14), playing mammy. The abject is gendered feminine, writes Carol Clover;[48] Moss has united on his own body the mammy and Mary (name of Jack Robin's gentile girl friend) to whom Jolson sang in The Jazz Singer's climax. (The identical scene from the play, where Peter Coen shouts, "Jew, Jew Jew, Jew," only enters the

---

*In *The Defiant Ones,* Sidney Poitier and (the Jewish actor) Tony Curtis play convicts who escape from a prison chained together. By the time they sever the physical chain, a psychological one has replaced it. The film ends with the black convict jumping off a train that the white man is unable to catch. The two await capture, and in the final shot (fig. 7.13) Poitier cradles Curtis in his arms.

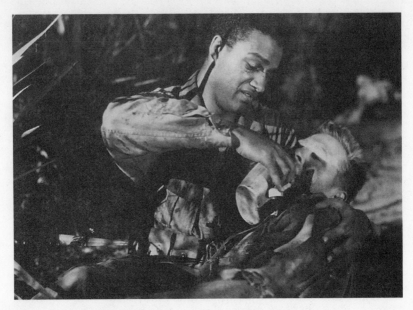

Figure 7.12. James Edwards plays mammy to Lloyd Bridges in *Home of the Brave*. Courtesy of the Film Stills Archive of the Museum of Modern Art, New York. © 1949 by United Artists Corp.

American racial mythography when the filmmakers color Coen black.) Having become a mammy, as the succession of *Life* stills from the film shows (figs. 7.15 and 7.16), Moss will lose the use of his legs.

The second scene, consummating the cure through tough love, shows the doctor supporting Moss and calling him Peter after his racial insult has finally provoked the paralyzed soldier to walk (see fig. 7.9). No one in the army has ever called him Peter, Moss gratefully tells the doctor, but the first name that the doctor now incessantly repeats is no advance over "Mossie," the name given the African American in dialogue and on the cast list; no white soldier, after all, is ever called by his given name.

Moss's final abjection ends the movie, as he goes off to open a bar and restaurant with Mingo, the white soldier who, doubly castrated in the film's symbol system, has lost both his arm and his wife (fig. 7.17).*

---

*Half a century after *Home of the Brave,* in the Academy Award–winning *Forrest Gump* (1994), it is the black soldier with ideas for a food business who is killed in the (Vietnam) war, and it is his white best friend (Forrest) who, failing to rescue his buddy from an invisible Asian enemy and having him die in his arms, takes as his partner an amputee. Falling back on minstrelsy, *Forrest Gump* makes fun of the black soldier's protruding lower lip;

Figure 7.13. Sidney Poitier plays mammy to Tony Curtis in *The Defiant Ones.*
Courtesy of the Film Stills Archive of the Museum of Modern Art, New York.
© 1958 by United Artists Corp.

Moss knows in his head that the doctor is right, that his survivor guilt
makes him like other soldiers, but he only believes it in his heart when
Mingo describes a similar feeling of relief. By reaching Moss's racial
anger, the doctor has gotten him to walk; only interracial camaraderie,
though, can lift his depression.

In bleeding black man into white, against the traditional model of
closed-off and invulnerable manhood, *Home* provoked nervousness
about homoeroticism among white male reviewers. *Crossfire* had replaced the murdered homosexual of the book from which the movie was
made with a vaguely effeminate Jew. *Home,* completing the circle, turned
its Jew into an African American homoerotically bonded with a white.
The movie and Leslie Fiedler's essay "Come Back to the Raft Ag'in,
Huck Honey!" appeared at the same time. As Ellison responded to
Fiedler, however, the scandal lay not in interracial male love but in its
route through black humiliation, not in cross-gender liminality but in
the need to color black the bearer of the identificatory wound. The ma-

the film's idea of fellowship is to bond its feeble-minded hero with a Stepin Fetchit and
to deprive the crippled veteran of both legs.

Figure 7.14. Pinky (Jeanne Crain) and her granny (Ethel Waters) in *Pinky*. *Life*, Oct. 17, 1949, 112. © 1949 by Twentieth Century Fox Film Corp.

ternal black man would offer a less contaminated healing were he not invented to care for whites. Tying Moss to the disabled veteran, the movie intends to dissolve the stigmas attaching to racial difference and amputation (and, subliminally, homosexual love), but in proclaiming that two damaged men could make a postwar life together, the movie was allying the black man with the cripple.[49]*

*Kaja Silverman shows how, in *The Guilt of Janet Ames* (1947), a war widow is cured of her hysterical paralysis: disavowing her recognition that the returning veterans from her dead husband's platoon, like him, lived failed lives, she makes herself responsible for his (and by implication, their) lack. Although Janet Ames (like the roles Bette Davis played in *Mr. Skeffington* and other films) is blamed for emasculation, as Peter Moss is not, the two postwar hysterical-paralysis films share a close family resemblance. The woman in one

Figure 7.15. Mossie cradles Finch in *Home of the Brave*. *Life,* May 23, 1949, 144. © 1949 by United Artists Corp.

IV

In making Moss abject, *Home* was blacking up social-problems Hollywood. It was completing the movement of exposed emotionality from the Jews—publicly displaying their hysterical excess in generational-conflict films like *The Jazz Singer*—to the blacks. *Home*'s Jewish doctor orchestrates abjection rather than being subject to it, but Jews in motion pictures had not escaped the danger of self-exposure once and for all. In the House Un-American Activities Committee investigation of Communist influence in Hollywood, which began two years before *Home*'s filming, they were a major target. Half of the Hollywood Nine-

movie, the black man in the other, both take on white male trouble. (See Silverman, *Male Subjectivity at the Margins* [New York, 1992], 106–19.)

Figure 7.16. Mossie loses the use of his legs. *Life*, May 23, 1949, 144.
© 1949 by United Artists Corp.

teen originally named as Communists by HUAC were Jewish; so were
half of the Hollywood Ten actually called to testify. The Hollywood Ten
refused to participate in HUAC's degradation ceremony. Their anger
protected them from psychological invasion; they went to jail instead.
Larry Parks, the gentile Communist who'd risen to stardom playing a
blackface Jew, was also scheduled to appear before the committee; his
reprieve enabled him to make *Jolson Sings Again*. When the committee
reopened its investigation in 1951, its first "cooperative witness" was the
now repentant Parks. In a way far worse than he had anticipated, HUAC
fulfilled Parks's fear that he had "entered so completely into the part [of
Jolson that he would] never have a recognizable personality of his own
again." Parks's testimony—Eric Bentley calls it "perhaps the most pa-
thetic in all the annals of the Committee"—is the fourth scene of abjection surrounding *Home* for, like the movie, HUAC was turning
social-problems Hollywood into blackface.[50]

Figure 7.17. The amputee (Frank Lovejoy) and the healed black man (James Edwards) in *Home of the Brave*. Courtesy of the Film Stills Archive of the Museum of Modern Art, New York. © 1949 by United Artists Corp.

Parks "opened himself as wide as possible to" the committee—a phrase he repeated seven times—in the hope that HUAC would not make him inform. The actor defended his Communist Party member-ship during the war as the product of youthful idealism and sympathy for the underdog. "If a man doesn't feel that way about certain things, he is not a man," Parks explained as his manhood was being taken away. The Jolson movies, by raising Parks to stardom, had made him a com-mittee target. "My career has been ruined because of this," Parks said, begging the committee (and here Gregory Peck's words from *Gentle-man's Agreement* echo in the mind) not to "tear open the secret heart of another human being." "I'm asking you as a man, having opened myself as wide as I know how," Parks pleaded; "forcing me to name names . . . is like taking a pot shot at a wounded animal. . . . Don't pre-sent me with the choice of . . . going to jail or forcing me to really crawl through the mud." "He feels so bad about what he has to do," Parks's lawyer, Louis Mandel, explained. If the committee forced him to name names, Mandel implied, Parks would go along, although "what he is going to give you will only eat up his insides. . . . He may have to sacrifice the arm with gangrene in order to save the body. Even though he doesn't like it, he will walk around the rest of his life without an arm." *Home,* whose protagonist was hysterically crippled because he thought he had betrayed his friend, redeemed the condition of the one-armed man; Parks spoke the cost of amputation.[51]

And then, from out of the wide-open mouth of "the most completely ruined man you have ever seen," the names poured out. "Morris Carnovsky. Joe—" "Will you spell that name," interrupted committee counsel Frank Tavenner, who knew perfectly well how to spell Carnovsky but wanted to call attention to the alien ethnicity. Parks pushed on. "I couldn't possibly spell it. Carnovsky, Joe Bromberg, Sam Rossen, Anne Revere, Lee Cobb"—four Jewish men and a gentile woman—and more and more. "Gregory Peck?" asked Tavenner. "I have no remembrance of ever attending a meeting with Gregory Peck." Peck, never a convincing Jew, was no subversive either. Even as the star of *Gentleman's Agreement* escaped exposure, however, the open blackface mouth of the Jolson biopics took over Parks's whole body.[52] Forced to repeat his Jewish blackface routine, Parks was singing once again before HUAC.*

The committee bludgeoned Parks into opening himself up; love produces that effect and affect in *Home. Home,* on the blackface model, placed a role-playing Jew in charge of a hysterical black; HUAC, mocking *Home's* aspiration to universality, abased the American from Kansas to the level of blackface Jew. *Home's* ending announced a victory, as if sending Moss and his one-armed white friend out into an unchanged society was not setting them up to be knocked down again. Parks knew

---

*I discovered to my amazement as I was completing this book that Arthur Laurents, author of the Broadway *Home of the Brave* and himself a victim of the blacklist, had written a play half a century later called *Jolson Sings Again.* The punning title refers to Larry Parks's HUAC testimony, but although the play is about the Hollywood blacklist, and the title and play link (as I have) *Home of the Brave,* HUAC, and *Jolson Sings Again,* the action takes place in Laurents's circle, not Parks's. Laurents's stand-in first appears onstage as the author of a Broadway play whose Jewish protagonist has, without his knowledge, been turned black for the movie version. The Jewish/black crossover (of *Home of the Brave*) then dissolves into the play's major twinned themes: the exposure of Communists and of homosexuals. For the playwright is secretly gay, and as his friends are faced with naming names, he is writing a play about homosexuality. (He hopes to get John Garfield for the lead.) When that play finally appears on Broadway a decade later, however, the gay protagonist has turned straight. Alerted to Laurents's play by Frank Rich ("West Coast Story," *New York Times,* Feb. 16, 1995, A15) too late for the Seattle Repertory Theater production, I am grateful to Peter Franklin of the William Morris agency for making available a copy of the script.

he had suffered defeat. James Edwards, the actor who played Moss, joined in the successful NAACP campaign to remove *Amos 'n' Andy* from television. But in rejecting the path of abjection that Parks shared with Moss, Edwards entered not Moss's rosy future but Parks's unhappy Hollywood ending. Victim of the cold war witch hunt that would set back racial progress and drive Hollywood even from the ground staked out in *Home,* Edwards refused to name names before HUAC and was blacklisted.[53]

Home's final scene was meant to be redemptive, creating a new community out of the breakdown of racial barriers following the loss of the old. Melodrama more convincingly restores lost innocence than makes something new, however,[54] a difficulty underlined by the historical obstacles in 1949 to Moss and Mingo's interracial community. A solution plausible in the play, given Jewish assimilation, discredited the movie, which replaced the Jew with the African American. The wish structured by the film—that internal damage externally implanted allies Jews with blacks and can be resolved in interracial friendship—renders *Home* powerful fantasy and dangerous history. Can blacks trust their Jewish friends, James Baldwin was asking in *Commentary* fiction and essays? Intending to answer that question affirmatively, *Home* makes visible the reasons for Baldwin's suspicions.

Retaining black difference, *Home* creates an African American man who nurtures and forgives whites. The repressed social position of blacks in the Jim Crow army, who were largely confined to supply, medical aid, and cleanup tasks, returns in the black-man-as-mammy.[55] But racial polarization encourages the white male adolescent viewer to cross over from black difference to black identification—out of the longing to give up, by crossing the racial divide, both the self-enclosed, closed-off, invulnerable male identity and the guilt toward those who are sacrificed to construct it.

In turning the problem of racism into that of its psychological effect on the victim, *Home* was a creature of its period, for it was via the psychological-damage route that support for civil rights reentered American politics after the three-quarters of a century silence following the end of Reconstruction. The Supreme Court declared segregated schools unconstitutional five years after *Home* because of their harm to black children's self-esteem. The classic 1950s treatments of the race problem in social psychology and history, Abram Kardiner and Lionel Ovesey's *Mark of Oppression* (before *Brown v. Board of Education*) and Stanley Elkins's *Slavery* (after it), both presenting African Americans as victims without agency, indicted racial oppression as engendering a psychological wound. (Elkins, as if paying homage to *Home,* not only made Jewish concentration camp inmates his model for slaves but also drew upon his own experience in the wartime army to formulate the debilitating effects of total institutions.) The damage hypothesis, as Elkins called it, would shortly produce the Moynihan Report, entitled "The Negro Family: The Case for National Action" (1965), as well as subsequent treatments of ghetto pathology that consign racism to history. Looking for past trauma rather than present injustice for the effects of racism, the psychological turn may seem to have taken race relations in the wrong direction.[56]

From another perspective, however, it was not so much the use of psychology that made Peter Moss vulnerable to whites as it was his isolation from other African Americans, on the one hand, and, on the other, the film's refusal to face the actual source of his material and psychological vulnerability, the structure of authority itself. In part a flight from army racism, that evasion was also in keeping with the condition under which World War II movies of the 1940s could convey immediate experience: they not call into question the army chain of command.[57] That constraint took on new meaning, however, when *Home* turned its Jewish soldier black, for the film thereby entered a discourse that had cast its shadow over African Americans in the military since the Civil War: the debate over whether black soldiers had the ability and courage to endure combat.

"Our fellow pale-face Americans would have us and the world believe that we make poor soldiers," wrote a *Crisis* book reviewer shortly after the end of World War II.[58] By assaulting black men in authority, placing black soldiers under white officers, and striving to keep them from combat, the army made African Americans responsible for the weakness it forced upon them. The NAACP condemned the army's wartime claims, endorsed by Secretary of War Henry Stimson, that black soldiers lacked the capacity to master modern military weapons. *Crisis* also rejected accusations that blacks lacked the will to fight. Competence was one thing, however, and psychology another; instead of simply rejecting the psychological discourse, *Crisis,* like *Home,* turned that discourse against discrimination. To deny that African Americans faced a motivational problem in the Jim Crow army only played into the stereotype of the happy, submissive darky. If there was psychological recalcitrance, in the NAACP view, racism, not racial cowardice, was to blame. *Home* created a psychologically incapacitated black soldier but, except at the end, attributed his weakness to racism. Militant African Americans had their own version of that analysis, whose similarity to the movie exposes the chasm between the two.[59]

As *Crisis* presented it, racism was not a diffuse set of attitudes concentrated in one discontented soldier, but rather a property of the army structure of command. *Home*'s racist is a single private, and its colonel is more enlightened than its major. Army hierarchy was the problem for *Crisis*. With its high concentration of southern officers, the army was "running a plantation as far as Negroes are concerned," one soldier told black former army chaplain Grant Reynolds. Reynolds "discovered the South more vigorously engaged in fighting the Civil War than in training soldiers to resist Hitler." Black soldiers were subject to daily racial insults and humiliations. That did not make them less willing to fight, but, Reynolds concluded, it would be understandable if they turned their resentments against the army rather than the army's enemy. Black militants wanted to hold out that threat for the future, if army racism did not change, without having it used against black soldiers in the present.[60]

Could psychological insight be brought into play when collective black soldiering in the Jim Crow army broke down? Just as *Home* inserts itself between *Gentleman's Agreement* and *Pinky*, so it bears comparison with a movie that was not made, a soldier's story of the 1944 Mare Island mutiny and court martial of African American navy stevedores. The fifty black men of the Port Chicago San Francisco Bay naval yard who were court-martialed for refusing to load munitions were, like Peter Moss, responding to military death. Already resentful of their place in the military and their treatment by the southern-dominated chain of command, many of the mutineers were survivors of the worst homefront disaster of the war, the Port Chicago tragedy, in which more than "200 Negroes were blown to bits" loading high explosives. In Reynolds's words, "they had gathered up the mutilated bodies of their former buddies. The psychological strain produced thereby, aggravated by the general resentment they have built up against the navy for the way they have been treated, must be considered in passing judgment against such men."[61]

The Mare Island soldiers, like Moss, broke down. Mare Island, like *Home,* generated accusations of cowardice and questions about whether black soldiers had the capacity to serve. But for Reynolds, service was already their condition, under the auspices that "the traditional beast of burden has no right to complain." The Mare Island mutineers, moreover, recovered the remains of many black comrades; Moss cradled the mutilated body of a single, white friend. The mutineers chose to resist; they did not develop hysterical symptoms. If they were "rendered psychologically unfit to give their best service to the country," wrote Reynolds, it was by army racism, not survivor guilt. Their "mass court-martial" contrasted with Moss's individual narcosynthesis, and Reynolds proposed substituting for the law not therapy but "justice"; he advocated turning the tables and court-martialing "those responsible for the miserable plight of the Mare Island mutineers." Half a decade later, when *Home* was going into production, Reynolds and A. Philip Randolph were planning their own mutiny, mobilizing the threat of draft resistance to force army integration. In a period of growing black collective militancy, *Home* generated sympathy for its African American soldier by making him an isolated victim. Unseen, menacing, interchangeable Japanese fill the anxious space of *Home*'s community of color. The price for gaining white sympathy for the lone, unthreatening African American was the elision of the actual conditions of black military service: the bonds among black soldiers, the collective life, communal resistance—and the punishment of African Americans in uniform.[62]

The army punished African American solidarity on Mare Island; *Home* advocates solidarity across racial lines. For the phallic display of traditional minstrel transvestitism, where white men in blackface, some in drag, made much of black male sexual power, *Home* substitutes tenderness. Because the condition of that tenderness was black emasculation (in the racial imaginary's phallic economy), the repressed was going to return. *Home* wants to take the integrationist, *Gentleman's Agreement* path against *Pinky*. But with its nurturing black soldier and its disabled-male solidarity, *Home* is closer to the *Pinky* matrix than the integration/segregation, North/South, male/female oppositions suggest. The commonality between *Home* and *Pinky*, by the law of the return of the repressed, turned the opposition between them—integration vs. segregation—in a direction neither film desired, foreshadowing the split between Jews and militant blacks that would bring the civil rights period to an end. Presiding over that rupture was neither the Jewish professional man nor the black working woman but the figure repressed not only in those films but in all of Hollywood since his demonic appearance in *Birth*. Did that figure finally overthrow blackface, or was he only performing it one more time—the aggressive black man, the Black Panther, Malcolm X?

CHAPTER 8

Conclusion:
Abington Township

Jewish blackface and civil rights spoke from the shared position of Jews and African Americans. Both practices emerged under white supremacist conditions, however, in which Jews could represent blacks but not the other way around. Support for civil rights, in the words of Harry Fleischmann of the postwar American Jewish Committee, ran the danger of "paternalism," of being something Jews did "for Negroes rather than with them."[1] Burnt cork, though it was hardly put on "for Negroes," also operated inside paternalism—as signified by Uncle Sam. Like the black presence in postwar civil rights films, blackface was maternalist as well, since mammy represented the things blacks did, among other white Americans, for Jews. The relationship between blacks and Jews was not timeless, however, and the year 1949, we can now see, marks a turning point.

At the simplest level, that turning point separates the first and second top-grossing movies during 1949, *Jolson Sings Again*, which looked backward through the long history of burnt cork, and *Pinky*, which looked forward to the civil rights era. From that perspective, the emergence of a civil rights movement during World War II brought literal blackface at the level of national consensus to an end. But the shared worlds of the blackface musical and the civil rights film—racial masquerade in form, mammy in content—erode any rigid boundary between them. From that perspective, blackface made visible the deep structure of American history, that discrediting literal burnt cork has still not dismantled, in which the black role must serve the white.

By the irony of American history, the same material conditions in Jewish life—an immigrant Jewish working class facing anti-Semitism—had produced both Jewish blackface and the Jewish/black civil rights alliance.

Liberal politics stressed equality of individual opportunity, whereas mass culture capitalized on black group difference. In the space between, civil rights and blackface bled into each other. The end of blackface left intact a civil rights alliance that did not come apart until the end of the 1960s. But just as the civil rights stirrings in the wake of World War II discredited literal blackface, so the continuation of metaphorical blackface contributed to the fragmentation of the 1960s movement. The end of literal blackface foreshadows, therefore, both the victories of the civil rights movement and its troubles.

The year 1949 marked the temporary apogee of civil rights in both Hollywood and Washington. The last year before the motion picture blacklist was also the year in which the first Democratic presidential candidate ever to run on a civil rights platform was elected to office. Truman issued his executive order integrating the army during the 1948 campaign; the next year he put a Fair Employment Practices bill before Congress. Cold war anti-Communism and the hot war in Korea ended that initial civil rights period, but the forces set in motion, continuing through *Brown* and the Montgomery bus boycott, would bear fruit in the movement of mass protest that began in 1960 at the Woolworth lunch counter in Greensboro, North Carolina.

The resistance to civil rights after 1949, and the movement's focus on the South, kept alive the Jewish/black alliance for two more decades. That alliance, in spite of widely publicized instances of black anti-Semitism and of Jewish recriminations against affirmative action and the ghetto "culture of pathology," still operates—in Washington politics, across a range of activist organizations and issue areas, and in the disproportionate support Jews (compared to other white groups) give to black and black-supported liberal white political candidates. Nonetheless, the conditions that fundamentally separated Jews from blacks reached fruition in the years immediately after World War II.

By the early postwar period, American Jews had achieved a position still denied today to American blacks: as Laurence Thomas puts it, they were "generally regarded by others not belonging to the group as the foremost interpreters of their own historical-cultural traditions."[2] In significant measure, recognition of Jewish authority was compensation for genocide. The slave trade and slavery had produced the opposite consequence for African Americans, however, so one must compare the African American situation to the fate not only of European but also of American Jews.

A racialized class boundary had come fundamentally by 1949 to separate the everyday life experiences of Jews and blacks. While the children of immigrant Jewish workers moved into the professional middle class, the vast majority of African Americans remained, at best, low-paid agricultural, service, and manual workers. Movement up the class ladder also entailed horizontal movement from the city to the suburbs. And Jolson's "My Mammy" points to that other fundamental, collective, identity-forming institution: not the workplace, but the home. As both material dwelling and imagined community, in conflicts over residential segregation and traditional family values, the home became the site of a Jewish/black divide that neither blackface nor civil rights could bridge. Black and white were more likely to work together on the job than (unlike Christian and Jew) to inhabit the same neighborhood. It was no accident, therefore, that whereas *Gentleman's Agreement* looked forward to housing integration, *Home of the Brave* envisioned no more than workplace solidarity; interracial living space remained the greatest taboo.[3] Even so, *Gentleman's Agreement* would prove more prophetic than *Home of the Brave* about the solution to the discrimination problem. Having situated the postwar race movies in their blackface past, I want to conclude by pointing them toward their apartheid future.

Gentleman's Agreement recorded a housing victory for a Jewish veteran that the mass of African Americans would not repeat, and *Commentary*'s celebration of a nonfictional success contemporaneous with the movie was a signpost for future trouble. In the late 1940s, a group of veterans waged a struggle to build a cooperative housing development in suburban Philadelphia's exclusive Abington Township. A high percentage of the ex-soldiers were Jewish, and the neighborhood association that opposed the co-op spread stories of a Jewish Communist conspiracy. There were rumors that blacks were to move in as well, but these proved unfounded: the development was restricted to whites. "We wanted to let Negroes in—they're veterans too, you know," explained Robert K. Greenfield, the Philadelphia lawyer who conceived the co-op. "But we've been advised that mortgage investors, unfortunately, will not take Negroes in a mixed project. There are no Negroes in the cooperative."[4]

A *Commentary* letter writer objected to "these pacifying remarks to the country-clubbers." For the veterans group to "fight so intrepidly against anti-Semitism and yet so lightly dismiss Negroes from participating in the project" vitiated the entire enterprise. Greenfield responded that his group "began with the firm determination that there be no discrimination. Every effort was made to finance the project without sacrificing the purpose. Only after every possibility was exhausted did we reluctantly arrive at the conclusion that we must have a 'white' community if we were to have any at all. . . . We would have to limit ourselves to taking on the great problems one at a time."[5]

Taking on the great problem of restrictive covenants against Jews did not open the door for African Americans. Like the contrast between *Gentleman's Agreement* and *Pinky,* the commonality between the Gregory Peck film and Abington Township marks the diverging paths of African Americans and Jews. Abington Township also has another moral, however, to which we must first turn. For the letter writer who protested against the co-op's gentleman's agreement was himself a Jew—a fact that speaks to divisions not just between the Jewish and African American communities, but within them.

Jewish involvement with blacks ran the gamut in the 1940s and 1950s from merchants and landlords who remained in the ghetto as it changed from Jewish to black; to urban and suburban housewives who hired black domestic workers; to Jews in the entertainment business and Norman Mailer's "white Negroes,"[6] whose connection to black culture ranged from making money to changing lives; to urban teachers and social workers whose clientele was becoming ever blacker; to trade unionists, civil rights activists, writers, Communists, and anti-Communists who campaigned for racial equality. Varying institutional positions and points of view produced debates within the Jewish community over racism and Jewish/black relations. *Commentary* participated in those debates, publishing in early issues analyses of the tensions between blacks and Jews by the black social psychologist Kenneth Clark and the young James Baldwin. Both writers addressed black anti-Semitism, but both also spoke about Jewish paternalism and about Jewish Americanization through racism in ways that would have excluded them from *Commentary* two decades later.[7]

The black community was also divided along class, regional, and integrationist/nationalist/accommodationist lines. Although black/Jewish cooperation strongly marked the NAACP and other black civic and political organizations, the occasional anti-Semitic black voice was heard both in the African American press and on the street.[8] Centrifugal forces, moreover, operated even within the black/Jewish alliance, and not always in predictable ways. Thus, although *Home of the Brave* confines African Americans within Hollywood's assimilationist paradigm for Jews, responses to that film did not divide blacks from Jews. Whereas Ralph Ellison and Frantz Fanon indicted the movie, *Crisis* endorsed it. Moreover, indebted to Manny Farber in the *Nation* as well as to Ellison, I am hardly the first Jewish writer made uncomfortable by *Home of the Brave.*

Commentary, which had praised *Gentleman's Agreement*, also criticized the Kramer/Robson film.[9] *Commentary* also identified the racial unconscious in the 1950 movie *No Way Out*, where a black doctor (Sidney Poitier) is menaced by a southern redneck who blames him for the death of his brother. The positive black image exacted its price, argued the reviewers, splitting the African American community into an uncertain lone black professional man dependent on whites, on the one hand, and a menacing, lower-class black mob, on the other.[10]

Commentary and *Crisis* shared the same goals: an end to legal segregation and the integration of minority groups into American life. For a brief period in the late 1940s, however, *Commentary* offered a more radical perspective on race relations. Although strongly anti-Communist from its founding (whereas *Crisis* was pushed belatedly into opposing Henry Wallace), *Commentary* brought together the struggles against Communism abroad and racial injustice at home. Pinky's lawyer also invoked the cold war; the eyes of the world were on American race relations, he told the jury hearing the suit to break Miss Em's will. Pinky's victory, however, compromised the demand for racial equality; *Commentary*'s anti-Communism initially did not.[11]

Home of the Brave was, from *Commentary*'s perspective, an instance of Popular Front culture. *Commentary* and *Partisan Review* in the late 1940s combined modernist art and oppositional politics to create a place to stand outside Popular Front liberalism. The subordination of art to political propaganda produced what the *Home* review called "problem movies." Anti-Communists on the left opposed such cinematic works as insufficiently radical both politically and aesthetically. A movie like *Home*, those critical of the Popular Front charged, only promoted false optimism about racial progress. From the perspective of the New York intellectuals, the reception of *Home* divided not so much blacks from Jews as anti-Stalinists from fellow travelers.[12]

Why did the NAACP organ praise a movie that, in the opinion of the American Jewish Committee magazine, evaded the depth of racial oppression in the United States? It is not sufficient to point to diversity among blacks and Jews to answer that question, for differences within the two groups can only be understood by grasping the fundamental contrast between them. Let us begin with African Americans. The response of *Crisis* to *Home of the Brave* testifies to the constricting force of white supremacy on African American support for racial equality. An integrated organization, the NAACP brought together white liberals and "talented tenth" African Americans. Although the NAACP was radical in demanding full racial equality, it worked primarily through the courts and not the streets, focusing on the removal of legal barriers to individual opportunity. The organization, having forsaken the historic ties of the black middle class to the Republican Party, was strongly prolabor, but it targeted racially discriminatory laws more than economic deprivation as the main barrier to equality. Church based and middle class, the NAACP was suspicious that black popular culture only reinforced the racial stereotypes that made blacks unacceptable to whites.[13]

Crisis, anticipating *Brown*, worried about the damage white supremacy did to black self-esteem. It feared that African Americans would try to avoid racial prejudice simply by remaining in a segregated milieu. Most Negroes lived in a "dis-integrated" world, as one article put it, evoking Du Bois's link between segregation and internal psychic division. "Stroking old wounds, . . . the young Negro" was often "unwilling to undergo the self-discipline and self-denial that are required as part of the integration process."[14] The writer was describing Peter Moss. Unwilling to subject himself to white disapproval, Moss fails (in flashback) to show up at Finch's (all-white) high school graduation party; the doctor opens old wounds to heal them for integration.

To counteract segregation's damage to black self-esteem, *Crisis* continued a century-old African American tradition by featuring successful representative Negro women and men. The magazine filled its pages with pictures of achieving group members—whose absence from *Commentary* signals by comparison the easier road for American Jews. One representative black man who got his picture in *Crisis* was Peter Moss. Stills of the film's protagonist appeared under the headline, "Hollywood Abandons Negro Stereotype in *Home of the Brave*." Presenting in motion pictures a nonmenial, nonbrutish, intelligent black male was a step so radical that it blocked out the cost.[15]

James Edwards also got his picture in *Crisis* as himself, accepting an award for *Home of the Brave* from Justice Meier Steinbrink of B'nai B'rith's Anti-Defamation League. The NAACP had come to terms with *Gone with the Wind* even before Hattie McDaniel received her Academy Award nomination. To object to an integrationist film with a black leading man was a luxury the civil rights organization could not afford.[16]

Underneath the NAACP's apparent approval of *Home*, however, there were signs of distress and subversion. Of the thousands of pictures of successful African Americans *Crisis* published during this period, only James Edwards receiving the B'nai B'rith award is unidentified, as if the magazine was not entirely proud of what it was showing.[17] *Crisis* chose production stills from *Home,* moreover, that brought Moss into close equality with white soldiers. He and Finch stand together in one picture; the other, reversing the racial stereotype, shows Mingo comforting Moss after Finch is killed. *Time* and *Life,* by contrast, depicted a crippled Moss as mammy. (Compare figs. 7.15 and 7.16 with figs. 8.1 and 8.2.) Finally, and strangest of all, *Crisis* used no words of its own to describe *Home of the Brave,* quoting an unidentified source instead. That source noted the shift from anti-Semitism in the play to "Negro discrimination." "The cure was effected," we read between quotation marks, "when Moss realized that he was not guilty. He had not really wished his friend's death. He had only felt what every soldier felt, relief that someone else had been killed rather than himself."[18] Was *Crisis* unwilling to endorse in its own words the film's evasion of racial anger, the price it demanded for integration? Perhaps the NAACP, mouthing what the man wanted to hear, was putting on blackface.

When young blacks took to the streets a decade later, they were rebelling against such NAACP equivocations. Their mass protests, led by blacks and not whites, ultimately challenged integrationist goals as well as accommodationist means. Blacks were no longer willing, wrote the SNCC-become-black-power-leader Stokely Carmichael, to turn the other cheek and be therapy for white Americans.[19] Civil rights tactics may have placed on African Americans the moral burden of redeeming white America. To reduce that project to Uncle Tom, however (even in the Harriet Beecher Stowe / *Body and Soul* version), grossly understated both the tactical militance of mass black nonviolent resistance and its transformative goals. Nonetheless, black power advocates were responding to a white liberal (including Jewish) investment in the redemptive power of blackness, the problematic side of which was already visible on the postwar Hollywood screen.

But in 1949—it would surprise a later generation to realize—militant blacks were more at home in *Commentary* than in the NAACP, for the American Jewish Committee–sponsored journal challenged the integrationist optimism that imprisoned *Crisis.* Rooted in the American Jewish past, however, *Commentary*'s radicalism was temporary; through its vicissitudes one can see the forces that would, from the Jewish side, bring the civil rights period to an end.

A way station for immigrant children moving from 1930s cosmopolitan Marxism back to Jewish identity, *Commentary* joined a revived Jewish consciousness to its fight for civil rights. Whereas *Crisis* featured individual African American achievement rather than celebrating

Figure 8.1. Mossie with his best friend (Lloyd Bridges) in *Home of the Brave*. *Crisis* 56 (June 1949): 180. Courtesy of *Crisis*. © 1949 by United Artists Corp.

collective black (segregated) life, *Commentary* mourned a lost Jewish world destroyed by European genocide and American success. Instead of picturing successful group members, it offered nostalgic evocations of Yiddish culture and debates over the costs of Americanization. Perhaps the journal's ambivalence over Jewish assimilation and its horror at the genocide was expressed consciously in doubts not about the integrationist goal for African Americans but about the ease of its achievement. Whatever the cause, *Commentary* was under no illusions about the obstacles to racial equality. It and not *Crisis* published James Baldwin's attack on accommodationist black leadership and his angry, despairing portraits of Harlem.[20]

Figure 8.2. Mingo (Frank Lovejoy) comforts Mossie in *Home of the Brave*. *Crisis* 56 (June 1949): 180. Courtesy of *Crisis*. © 1949 by United Artists Corp.

Baldwin was on his way to French exile, however, and his departure points to the two historical developments, one in foreign and one in domestic relations—anti-Communism and the racialized northern political economy—that would defeat *Commentary*'s radicalism and make trouble between African Americans and Jews.

Just as the blacklist had a chilling effect on Hollywood filmmaking after 1949, so anti-Communism struck the decisive blow against the Jewish/black civil rights alliance. Nineteen forty-nine was the year of the Alger Hiss and Judith Coplon spy trials. Jews were under suspicion for their disproportionate adherence to the Communist and socialist movements; the desire to prove their patriotism motivated the moguls' capitulation to the Hollywood blacklist, the cooperation between the Jewish prosecutor and the Jewish judge in the atomic spy trial of Ethel and Julius Rosenberg, and perhaps the celebrations of American exceptionalism by the academic children of immigrant Jews. Much further to the right, the FBI saw integration itself as a Communist plot.[21]

Although liberals had initially enlisted anti-Communism in the strug-

gle for racial justice, the cold war ultimately stigmatized the left, subor-
dinating the liberal agenda to the fight against Communist influence.
Anti-Communism deradicalized American politics in general rather than
setting Jews and blacks against each other in particular. Jews and African
Americans provided the core support for Henry Wallace, on one side of
the cold war, and the 1950s NAACP, on the other. The cold war defeat
of the Popular Front blocked neither *Brown v. Board of Education* nor
the Montgomery bus boycott, but it set back civil rights militance
nonetheless.

Whereas HUAC, the Hollywood blacklist, the Truman administration's loyalty program, and Joe McCarthy all put the left on the defensive, the Korean War tipped the balance.[22] The war shifted the liberal
anti-Communist focus from reform imperatives to celebrations of the
United States. That turn to the right was fostered in *Commentary,* to be
sure, by the growing acceptance of Jews in the United States and by an
increasingly uncritical support for the state of Israel that brought together Zionism and American patriotism. But since neither Israel nor
Jewish integration militated against Jewish participation (with *Commentary's* support) in the 1960s civil rights movement, one needs to
stress in 1950 the role of the Korean War.

Commentary regularly published civil rights articles until Truman
sent troops to Korea. Between June and December of 1950, however,
not a single mention of racial injustice appeared. Instead James Rorty
and Winifred Rauschenbusch denied that the mob violence unleashed
against Paul Robeson fans in the Catskills constituted a race riot. American Legion veterans and other local residents, shouting anti-Semitic, antiblack, and anti-Communist epithets, had twice set upon the heavily
Jewish, integrated crowds attending Robeson concerts in Peekskill, New
York. Although Rorty and Rauschenbusch criticized the mob brutality,
they blamed it on Communist provocation rather than anti-Communist
hysteria or local race prejudice. In their sympathetic portraits of the two
veterans who called out the mob, they compared the rioting to the vig-
ilante action that in the 1920s had driven the Ku Klux Klan from Peekskill. Like the Ronald Reagan cold war film *Storm Warning,* Rorty and
Rauschenbusch were enlisting opposition to the Klan in the service of
domestic anti-Communism.[23]

Also like *Storm Warning,* the *Commentary* authors detached anti-Klan
anti-Communism from racial injustice. "The active infection," wrote
Rorty and Rauschenbusch, "was neither anti-Semitism nor fascism, native or imported. It was the Communist virus." *Commentary's* own

postwar link of Nazi anti-Semitism to American Negrophobia was rewritten as a Communist plot, in which—as if *Home of the Brave* were an instance—"the Negro was to be cast in the role that the Jew played in Germany." Robeson's gratitude that "we Negroes owe a great debt to the Jewish people" spoke now not for the civil rights alliance but for the Soviet Union. Not antiracism but anti-Communism was the legacy of the antifascist struggle, for the Communists were trying "to play the same role in weakening this country before a foreign enemy that Nazi agents and their domestic supporters played during World War II."[24]

Cold war liberals continued to support racial equality after Peekskill and Korea. Oscar Handlin, the preeminent historian of immigration and one of the first Jews tenured at Harvard, opposed the appeasement at the 1952 Democratic National Convention of segregationist delegates who refused to support the national ticket. Worrying that northern immigrant groups would stop making common cause with "the Negro," Handlin wanted an authoritative endorsement of what Myrdal was calling "the American creed." What threatened "the struggle for rights that was truly American" was racist mass protests from below like those that, in Handlin's revisionist view, explained American anti-Semitism. For just as equality and not white supremacy was "truly American," so Handlin now attributed the origins of American anti-Semitism not to elite exclusion and Ivy League quotas but to provincial anticapitalism, not to right-wing nativism but to "certain forms of 'grass roots' radicalism." Populism generated the 1920s Ku Klux Klan, according to Handlin, as well as (in the last sentence of his article on anti-Semitism) the *Protocols of the Elders of Zion*.[25] In the reformed *Commentary* perspective, the enemies of the Jews, whether attacking them openly or masquerading as their friends, were to be found on the left. The legacy of the American radical tradition now lay not in the fight for racial justice but in Communism, anti-Semitism, and McCarthyism.

Cold war anti-Communism catalyzed *Commentary*'s suspicion of mass protest, but Handlin's article also pointed to the structural chasm that was opening between blacks and Jews. Handlin and other Jewish historians of the 1950s not only favored civil rights, to be sure; they also broke with the apologia for slavery in the prevailing historiography of the South. Oscar and Mary Handlin decisively reshaped the debate over slavery's origins with their well-supported claim that racism followed from rather than preceded bondage. Their article could be read in hindsight, however, as imagining that racism ended with legal emancipation (or at least would end with the end of Jim Crow) and as sharing the con-

sensus school's turning elsewhere than to white supremacy for its interpretations of American history. The ex-radical Jews who found homes
in northern elite institutions were beginning to celebrate the openness
of America to individual mobility. As the 1950s wore on, *Commentary*
and *Partisan Review* worried less about racial injustice than about what
they saw as Communist and populist assaults on democratic leadership.
By allying Jews with elites and stigmatizing collective action, Handlin
and his cohort were reconciling themselves with America in a way that
would leave radical mass African American protest behind.[26]

Institutionally, moreover, elitist support for civil rights only perpetuated in liberal politics the blackface it condemned in mass culture. For
although immigrant Jews and their children relinquished burnt cork,
many continued to want to speak politically for African Americans. In
the mass actions of the 1960s, however, under the banners first of civil
rights, then of black power, African Americans were speaking for themselves. As the 1960s began, for example, the NAACP was taking legal
action against the International Ladies Garment Workers Union for discrimination in job classifications, wage rates, entrance criteria, and union
leadership. Nathan Glazer, writing in *Commentary*, attributed the contrasting positions in the needle trades of Jews and peoples of color to
their "different capacities to take advantage of the opportunities that are
fairly in large measure open to all."[27]

Glazer spoke not just for individual opportunity, but for group distinctiveness as well. Enjoying the benefits of assimilation, many Jews were
worrying about the loss of community ties. They defended what Glazer
called the "group pattern of American life," where ethnicities could retain "exclusiveness" and live in areas "restricted to their own kind."
African Americans, who had once underpinned Jewish blackface Americanization, were now perceived as a threat to the preservation of postas-
similation Jewish communities. Instead of criticizing Jewish leadership
discrimination against racial minorities, Glazer worried about the threat
to Jewish group distinctiveness from "the Negro" who wants to enter
"the Jewish business, . . . the Jewish union, . . . or the Jewish (or largely
Jewish) neighborhood and school." The New York locals of the ILGWU
were historically Jewish, to be sure, but by the 1960s a majority of their
members were peoples of color. Glazer was updating blackface in the
name of cultural pluralism, for his Jewish leaders represented African
Americans to whom they denied equality. Jazz singers rising with their
people instead of against them, liberal Jewish intellectuals like Glazer and
Handlin wanted to speak both for Jews and for blacks, in the name of

Uncle Sam. Glazer's position exposed the white privilege that, once undergirding the civil rights alliance, was now threatening to blow it up.

A younger, new left generation of Jewish activists, in rebellion against their liberal fathers, gave overwhelmingly disproportionate support to the militant civil rights protests of the 1960s, and SNCC's northern black militants had roots in radical Jewish political communities. But SNCC broke with its Jewish supporters in the late 1960s, embracing black nationalism and opposing Zionism.[28] And on the northern homefront, the rift in New York City between Jewish and African American former allies that had begun in the workplace was consummated in the neighborhood—in the Ocean Hill/Brownsville strike that pitted a largely Jewish teacher's union against largely black neighborhoods, and in conflicts over living space from Canarsie to Crown Heights. Jews not only participated in white flight from expanding black ghettos; they also worried about the preservation of Jewish neighborhoods and schools threatened by Jewish dispersion, on the one hand, and black influx, on the other. By the late 1960s neighborhood conflicts—over bussing and local control of schools; housing, crime, and communal identity; and the presence of Jewish merchants, social workers, and landlords in black slums—were setting African Americans and Jews against each other.* One can take sides in these conflicts, different sides in different struggles. One can also recognize the perpetuation, in spite of the antagonisms, of Jewish/black collaboration—in civil rights organizations and trade unions, and among younger, more secular Jews and middle-class African Americans.

---

*Amidst the high seriousness of the debate over Jewish/black relations, the remake of Roger Corman's low-budget *The Little Shop of Horrors* (1960) has fun with the Jewish investment in black. In the Corman original, the man-eating plant that swallows up Seymour Krelboined is a double of Seymour's devouring Jewish mother. The remake (1986) moves the scene of the crimes from the Los Angeles Jewish to the Harlem black ghetto, and turns the monster into a "mean green mother from outer space." In this rock-and-roll version, the "mother" is a black man—complete with exaggerated blackface lips and the voice of the Four Tops' Levi Stubbs. In both films, a dentist torments Seymour's oral cavity until Seymour feeds him to the plant. But the first Seymour, who remains a slave to his plant until it eats him, never escapes the Jewish family. His successor, on the *Jazz Singer* model, uses the black mouth to win his girl (after whom he has named the plant). Making the ghetto a springboard to the suburbs, this Seymour slays his monster. The final scene of suburban wedding, however, reveals a shadow side, by marrying the ("I'm bad") black criminal to the monstrously reproductive welfare queen: the film ends with little black monster buds (in the form of black bridesmaids) sprouting from the neatly trimmed shrubs. (Thanks to Carol Clover to introducing me to these films.)

From a historical perspective, looking forward from 1949, neither re-crimination nor evidence of cooperation should divert attention from the structural divide that opened decisively in the years after World War II. Abington Township, unnoticed next to the Peekskill riots and the Ko-rean War, points to the problem that would not take center political stage until the late 1960s, when its socioeconomic underpinnings had become fixed to the point of irreversibility. I refer to the forces guaranteeing a segregated North that climaxed after World War II, but whose political effects were delayed for twenty years until the civil rights movement turned northward. For when the locus of racial conflict shifted from the South to the North, it ran up against the wall dividing urban black ghet-toization from Jewish class, neighborhood, and political integration.

Having provided Jewish blackface with a home, the South unified the postwar civil rights movement as well. Only now Dixie served as target rather than lost object of desire. In 1950 a majority of black Americans still lived under state regimes of legalized white supremacy. Making southern segregation its focus, the NAACP emphasized ending legal seg-regation and circulated images of southern dystopia. Although civil rights activists fought northern discrimination as well, they saw the South as the major obstacle to racial equality. World War II had mobi-lized African Americans in uniform and opened up employment for those moving north. Exposés of southern racial atrocities, in reportage and short fiction, made northern integration seem the solution. In the *Crisis* short story "Look Away, Dixie Land," for example, a returning black veteran who once loved the southern soil now associates it with submission. Refusing to adopt a menial front—to put on blackface—he is mutilated by a white shopkeeper as other blacks passively look on.[29]

"Look Away, Dixie Land" inverted the southern paradise of black-face nostalgia, upsetting the regional alliance that was the condition for burnt cork; the result, though, was to make the North look like free-dom. The mass migration of African Americans north, E. Franklin Fra-zier wrote at the end of the war, had destroyed "the [Booker T.] Wash-ington formula" of "biracial organization." "Purely sociological" in a rural environment, segregation in the cities would have to impose itself on all areas of life—work, education, and recreation, as well as residence: and that, Frazier said, was far more difficult. Segregation, he argued, was easily enforceable in a farm economy, where people worked and played where they lived. Such was not the case in the cities. Since Americans were moving from rural to urban areas, it was there that the battle for integration would be won.[30]

Frazier was exactly wrong, for the minority group that achieved full equality in the postwar United States was Jewish, not black. Two-thirds of the American people thought Jews had too much influence during World War II; almost half said they would sympathize with an anti-Semitic campaign, and only 30 percent opposed one. The fantasy of Jewish power reached a high point immediately after the war; beginning in 1947, there was a sharp decline in anti-Semitic attitudes and practices. By 1950 only 10 percent of those polled strongly objected to Jewish neighbors; 69 percent said that it would make no difference at all.[31]

In the years after Jews entered northern neighborhoods, social clubs, and university faculties, the civil rights movement defeated southern legal segregation. It also fostered the emergence for the first time of a substantial northern black middle class. But when the movement shifted north, it confronted just the intractable, materially based racial divisions that Frazier had suggested were essential for the preservation of a biracial society.

Northern blacks had mostly lived in moderately integrated neighborhoods before the mass migration north in the wake of World War I. By 1940, however, African Americans in the urban North inhabited ghettos. "This extreme racial isolation did not just happen," write Douglas Massey and Nancy Denton. "It was manufactured by whites through a series of self-conscious actions and purposeful institutional arrangements that continue today." For example, the 1939 Federal Housing Administration manual warned against areas with "inharmonious racial or nationality groups." "If a neighborhood is to retain stability, it is necessary that properties shall continue to be grouped by the same social and racial classes."[32]

Whereas gentile neighborhoods now admitted Jews, private lenders and the Federal Housing Administration continued to discriminate against African Americans. The Los Angeles office of the FHA had given its lowest rating in 1939 to Boyle Heights because it was "hopelessly heterogeneous," "a melting pot neighborhood . . . literally honeycombed with subversive racial elements." Government mortgage discrimination against black and integrated urban neighborhoods continued after the war, in the face of the federally financed white suburban housing boom. Charles Abrams in *Commentary* warned in the late 1940s against the pattern of government and private collusion to spread segregation, in restrictive covenants, discriminatory FHA mortgage rates, real estate blockbusting to scare out white families, and racist bank lending practices. Although for Abrams blacks and Jews faced a common threat, by 1960,

95 percent of poll respondents had no objection to Jews in their neighborhoods. And even Abrams did not foresee the social formation that would instantiate Baldwin's pessimism, the suburban expansion that created not urban integration but metropolitan apartheid.[33]

The civil rights victories of the 1960s, therefore, failed to reshape the United States in the way the movement had hoped; indeed, the second Reconstruction produced in reaction the racial polarization that has configured American politics for thirty years. As long as pervasive material inequality between whites and peoples of color coexists with formal, legal equality, racialized representations will shadow the language of individual rights, their spiritual "miscegenation" dominating American politics and culture. Thus California governor Pete Wilson, who favors denying citizenship to children born in the United States of "illegal aliens," successfully promoted a 1994 state initiative depriving undocumented immigrants of health and education benefits and requiring nurses, teachers, and other state employees to turn suspects (identifiable by their color) in. Wilson supports in 1996 the "California Civil Rights Initiative" that prohibits the consideration of race in hiring decisions and state college admissions. Racializing politics in the name of color-blindness, contemporary invocations of the first Declaration of Independence continue to capitalize on the second.

Daniel Patrick Moynihan, already troubled thirty years earlier by the disjunction between formal equality and substantive inequality, produced his report "The Negro Family" while serving as assistant secretary of labor in the Lyndon Johnson administration. Even as the Student Nonviolent Coordinating Committee and Martin Luther King Jr. were fighting southern segregation, Moynihan recognized that the effects of slavery, carried north, placed the Negro problem in the middle of the urban ghetto. For Moynihan, however, the legacy of slavery held back African Americans not by restricting modern employment and housing opportunities but in its effect on "the Negro family." "The fundamental problem" explaining black poverty, he wrote, was "that of family structure." And presiding over the "tangle of pathology . . . on the urban frontier" was mammy. Only now that she was attending to black rather than white men, Moynihan gave her and her family a new name—announced boldly in a chapter subheading and repeated on page after page: "Matriarchy." Mammy was now shifting from the positive to the negative pole, from "benevolence, harmless and servile guardianship, and endless love," in Toni Morrison's words, to "insanity, illicit sexuality, and chaos." Deprived of male authority by slavery, according to the Moynihan Report, the black mother was emasculating her young men. The absence of paternal discipline explained the weakness of the work ethic among young males in the ghetto, the demand for "immediate gratification," and the turn to crime.[34]

Although Moynihan cited a number of contemporary social science studies in support of his argument, the single volume most frequently invoked was Stanley Elkins's *Slavery*. Writing when the plantation myth still dominated academic treatments of the antebellum South, Elkins had discredited the institution of slavery by comparing it to the Nazi concentration camp. Indeed, he devoted more pages to Jewish concentration camp victims than to American slaves. Elkins spoke from inside the Jewish/black civil rights alliance. By the mid-1960s that identificatory impulse, the same one that had produced *Home of the Brave,* was generating invidious distinctions between the group whose family structure triumphed over adversity and the group held back by maternal domination.[35]

For Elkins, for Moynihan, and for *Home of the Brave,* blacks continued to carry the psychological wound of slavery. Like the Moynihan Report and *Slavery, Home* had also featured what these documents imagined as an emasculated black man. But *Home* not only showed subtextual desire for the black man as mammy; it also identified the contemporary racist source of his wound. The Moynihan Report went back through the looking glass to find in *Home*'s world the solution.

Although anti-Communism as ideology had only temporarily set back civil rights, it presided over a permanent cold war political economy into which black Americans, like all others, were inserted. That military-industrial complex spoke through Moynihan, from "the largest single source of employment in the nation," the armed forces,[36] to offer an alternative to black matriarchy. Grant Reynolds had charged during World War II that the army "was running a plantation so far as Negroes are concerned." Moynihan, in contrast, proposed that the army repair the damage that the plantation, a "perverted patriarchy,"[37] had done. The fear of maternal influence had organized politics and cultural life after World War II; "The Negro Family" displaced anxiety about patriarchal decline from its mainstream origins to the ghetto. Since "Momism" took on cultural salience with the return of army veterans to the home front, Moynihan naturally enough turned to the army to counteract the influence of the black mother.[38]

In addition to the fact that army jobs, according to Moynihan, were awarded without attention to race, "there is another special quality about military service for Negro men: it is an utterly masculine world. Given the strains of the disorganized and matrifocal family life in which so many Negro youths come of age, the armed forces are a dramatic and desperately needed change: a world away from women, a world run by strong men of unquestioned authority." Where mammy once supported spiritual miscegenation between black and white men, now she stood in the way. Moynihan continued, "The theme of a current Army recruiting poster states it as clearly as can be: 'In the U.S. Army you get to know what it means to feel like a man.' " Uncle Sam wants you, Moynihan was telling young black men: they were wanted for the war in Vietnam.[39]

A few years later (Malcolm X, Martin Luther King Jr., Robert Kennedy, scores of blacks in burning ghettos, and tens of thousands of—disproportionately black—Americans in Vietnam had been killed in the meantime) John A. Williams's documentary novel *Captain Blackman* looked back over the entire history of African Americans in the military from the Revolutionary War to Vietnam. Grueling history gives way to utopian fantasy in the epilogue, where a "nigger" passing as white has risen to the top of the nuclear command structure. As he and his black soldiers cripple the Pentagon and seize control of the White House, the racial passer breaks into Stephen Foster's blackface song "Old Folks at Home." "Way down upon de Swanee Ribber," sings the minstrel in whiteface—words suffice, since everyone knows the music—and the book ends with his voice trailing off, ellipses in the original, "Oh darkies, how my heart grobes weary . . ."[40] The road taking Captain Blackman far from the old folks at home to Moynihan's army is exhausting, one supposes, because it is at once so twisted and so short.

Notes

Chapter 1. Uncle Sammy and My Mammy

1. See Henry Jenkins, *What Made Pistachio Nuts? Early Sound Comedy and the Vaudeville Aesthetic* (New York, 1992), 153–84.

2. Mary White Ovington, *Half a Man: The Status of the Negro in New York* (New York, 1911), 56–59, 70, 80–81. Progressive maternalism names the importance white women reformers placed on biological and social mothering. On the meanings of mammy, see Hortense J. Spillers, "Mama's Baby, Papa's Maybe: An American Grammar Book," *Diacritics* 17 (summer 1987): 65–81; Toni Morrison, ed., *Race-ing Justice, En-gendering Power: Essays on Anita Hill, Clarence Thomas, and the Construction of Social Reality* (New York, 1992). I want to acknowledge here also the comments of Donna Murch, and the clarifications provided by reading in manuscript, after the penultimate draft of my own study was completed, Jeffrey Melnick's *Ancestors and Relatives: The Uncanny Relationship of African Americans and Jews* (Harvard University Press, forthcoming).

3. Israel Zangwill, *The Melting Pot* (New York, [1908] 1914), 207.

4. "From the Managing Editor" and "Rebirth of a Nation, Computer-Style," in "The New Face of America," *Time* 142 (special issue, fall 1993): 2, 66–67. *Time* was looking forward as well as backward, as is evidenced by the publication a year later of Richard J. Herrnstein and Charles Murray's *The Bell Curve: Intelligence and Class Structure in American Life* (New York, 1994) and J. Philip Rushton's *Race, Evolution, and Behavior: A Life History Perspective* (New Brunswick, N.J., 1994), whose theories of quantitatively measurable, hierarchically arranged, pure racial types received favorable notice in the *New York Times Book Review* (Malcolm W. Browne, "What Is Intelligence and Who Has It?" Oct. 16, 1994, 3, 41, 45–46.) *The Bell Curve* would spend weeks on the *New York Times* bestseller list. Thanks to the students in my fall 1993 seminar on racism and anti-Semitism, and especially Gaston Alonse Donate, for directing me to the *Time* and *Newsweek* issues.

5. "New Face of America," 2, 66–67; "The Bloody Odyssey of O. J. Simpson," *Time,* June 27, 1994.

6. "New Face of America," 2, 66–67. See A. Leon Higginbotham Jr., "An Open Letter to Clarence Thomas from a Federal Judicial Colleague," in Morrison, ed., *Race-ing Justice,* 21–25, on *Loving v. Virginia;* and, on *Birth of a Nation,* Michael Rogin, " 'The Sword Became a Flashing Vision': D. W. Griffith's *Birth of a Nation,"* in *"Ronald Reagan," the Movie, and Other Episodes in Political Demonology* (Berkeley, 1987), 190–235.

7. "The Hidden Rage of Successful Blacks," *Newsweek,* Nov. 15, 1993, cover; Elliot Cose, "Rage of the Privileged," ibid., 56–63.

8. Bates is quoted in Mark Whitaker, "White and Black Lies," *Newsweek,* Nov. 5, 1993, 53–54. On *Whoopee!* see below, chapter 5.

9. Goldberg made another mammy movie, *Corrina, Corrina,* after *Made in America;* for a discussion of that film, see below, chapter 4.

10. This advertisement ran for several weeks in November and December 1993 on San Francisco's classical music station, KKHI.

11. Thomas Jefferson, "Autobiography," in *The Life and Selected Writings of Thomas Jefferson,* ed. Adrienne Koch and William Peden (New York, 1944), 25–26; James A. Rawley, *The Transatlantic Slave Trade: A History* (New York, 1981), 311–19, 342–46; Stephen Hopkins, "The Rights of Colonies Examined [1763]," in *Tracts of the American Revolution, 1763–1776,* ed. Merrill Jenson (Indianapolis, 1967), 41–62.

12. Thomas Jefferson, *Notes on Virginia,* in Koch and Peden, eds., *Life and Selected Writings,* 256, 262.

13. Alfred Kazin, "Jews," *New Yorker,* Mar. 7, 1994, 72. See also Hasiah R. Diner, *In the Almost Promised Land: American Jews and Blacks, 1915–1935* (Westport, Conn., 1977). I owe "the stain of shame" to Hasiah Diner, paper at the conference "Blacks and Jews: An American Historical Perspective," Washington University, St. Louis, Dec. 2–4, 1993.

14. Frederick Jackson Turner, *The Frontier in American History* (New York, 1920), 4.

15. On blackface as cross-dressing, see below, chapter 2, with sources cited at note 28.

16. James Baldwin, "On Being 'White' and Other Lies," *Essence,* Apr. 1984, 90–92. Thanks to George Shulman for calling this article to my attention. See also Edmund Morgan, *American Slavery, American Freedom: The Ordeal of Colonial Virginia* (New York, 1975); Peter Kolchin, *Unfree Labor: American Slavery and Russian Serfdom* (Cambridge, Mass., 1987), 31–35; David Roediger, *Toward the Abolition of Whiteness* (New York, 1994), 1–17, 181–98; Theodore Allen, *The Invention of the White Race* (New York, 1994).

17. Cf. Melnick, *Ancestors and Relatives.*

18. As with the surplus value of labor, the extraction of surplus symbolic value is a material process. Eric Lott has grounded it in the expropriation of black sexuality and labor; see his *Love and Theft: Blackface Minstrelsy and the American Working Class* (New York, 1993).

19. On pre-Hollywood cinema, Porter, and *Uncle Tom's Cabin,* see Charles Musser, *Before the Nickelodeon: Edwin S. Porter and the Edison Manufacturing*

Company (Berkeley, 1991); William L. Slout, "*Uncle Tom's Cabin* in American Film History," *Journal of Popular Film* 2 (spring 1973): 137–52; Donald Bogle, *Toms, Coons, Mulattoes, Mammies, and Bucks: An Interpretive History of Blacks in American Films,* 2d ed. (New York, 1989), 3; Thomas R. Cripps, *Slow Fade to Black: The Negro in American Film, 1900–1942* (New York, 1977), 12–14; Robert C. Toll, *Blacking Up: The Minstrel Show in Nineteenth-Century America* (New York, 1974), 1–5; Edward D. C. Campbell Jr., *The Celluloid South: Hollywood and the Southern Myth* (Knoxville, Tenn., 1981), 12–14, 37–39; Janet Staiger, *Interpreting Films: Studies in the Historical Reception of American Cinema* (Princeton, N.J., 1992), 101–23.

20. J. Hoberman, "Our Troubling Birth Rite," *Village Voice,* Nov. 3, 1993, 2–4 (quoted 3). See also David Bordwell, Janet Staiger, and Kristin Thompson, *The Classical Hollywood Cinema: Film Style and Mode of Production to 1960* (New York, 1985), 90–142, 183; Rogin " 'The Sword Became a Flashing Vision.' "

21. J. Hoberman, "Is 'The Jazz Singer' Good for the Jews?" *Village Voice,* Jan. 7–13, 1981, 32; Steve Whitfield, "Jazz Singers," *Moment,* Mar. 1981, 20; Harry M. Geduld, *The Birth of the Talkies* (Bloomington, Ind., 1975), 138, 213n; William K. Everson, *American Silent Film* (New York, 1978), 373–74; J. Douglas Gomery, "Hollywood Converts to Sound: Chaos or Order," in *Sound and the Cinema: The Coming of Sound to American Film,* ed. Evan William Cameron (Pleasantville, N.Y., 1980), 32–33; Bordwell, Staiger, and Thompson, *Classical Hollywood Cinema,* 320–29, 353–56; Thomas Schatz, *The Genius of the System: Hollywood Filmmaking in the Studio Era* (New York, 1988); " 'Gone with the Wind' Champ Again," *Variety,* May 4, 1983, 5. I am indebted to Peter Wollen for adding *Gone with the Wind* to the sequence. The Margaret Mitchell novel on which the film was based has sold more copies than any other book except the Bible (see Jerry Schwartz, "Margaret Mitchell's Atlanta Home Gets a Reprieve," *New York Times,* Dec. 18, 1994, A18).

22. See D. H. Lawrence, *Studies in Classic American Literature* (New York, 1923); Henry Nash Smith, *Virgin Land: The American West as Symbol and Myth* (New York, 1950); Leslie Fiedler, *Love and Death in the American Novel* (New York, 1960); Richard Slotkin, *Regeneration Through Violence: The Mythology of the American Frontier, 1600–1860* (Middletown, Conn., 1973); Winthrop Jordan, *White over Black: American Attitudes Toward the Negro, 1550–1812* (Chapel Hill, N.C., 1969).

23. The western was the most popular genre of 1920s silent and of cold war film, but not during the years of the classic, talking-pictures studio system, roughly 1927–49, covered by this study. On the frontier myth and the western in the industrial age, see Richard Slotkin, *The Fatal Environment: The Myth of the Frontier in the Age of Industrialization, 1800–1890* (New York, 1985), and *Gunfighter Nation: The Myth of the Frontier in Twentieth-Century America* (New York, 1992), 254–57, 347, and passim; Robert B. Ray, *A Certain Tendency of the Hollywood Cinema, 1930–1980* (Princeton, N.J., 1985), 70, 145–46; Richard Koszarski, *An Evening's Entertainment, 1915–1928* (Berkeley, 1990), 182; Lary May, *Screening Out the Past: The Birth of Mass Culture and the Motion Picture Industry* (New York, 1980), 215.

24. Morgan, *American Slavery, American Freedom.* On the enormous vari-

ety of early silent films, out of which precipitated a set of Hollywood genres, see Eileen Bowser, *The Transformation of Cinema, 1907–1915* (Berkeley, 1990).

25. For the preeminent Jewish role in blackface, Hollywood, and Tin Pan Alley, see Neal Gabler, *An Empire of Their Own: How the Jews Invented Hollywood* (New York, 1988); Irving Howe, *World of Our Fathers* (New York, 1976), 562; Lester D. Friedman, "The Conversion of the Jews," *Film Comment* 17 (July–Aug. 1981): 48–50; idem, *Hollywood's Image of the Jew* (New York, 1982), 19; Marc Slobin, "Some Intersections of Jews, Music, and Theater," in *From Hester Street to Hollywood: The Jewish-American Stage and Screen*, ed. Sarah Blacher Cohen (Bloomington, Ind., 1983), 31; Gary Giddins, *Riding on a Blue Note: Jazz and American Pop* (New York, 1981), 5–17, 145–60; and chapter 4, below. "Jew Stars over Hollywood" is an undated pamphlet (St. Louis, Patriotic Tract Society) on display at the Jewish Museum in New York. On Jeffries, Farrakhan, and Muhammad, see *New York Times,* May 12, 1993, A12; May 16, 1993, A20; and Paul Berman, ed., *Blacks and Jews: Alliances and Arguments* (New York, 1984).

26. Diner, *In the Almost Promised Land*, xvi.

27. Abraham Lincoln, speech at Chicago, June 10, 1858, in *Abraham Lincoln: Selected Speeches, Messages, and Letters*, ed. T. Harry Williams (New York, 1957), 91–92.

28. Franz Boas, "Foreword," in Ovington, *Half a Man*, viii.

29. Roemer is quoted in *New York Times,* Mar. 28, 1994, C11, C16. For an extraordinary account of Jewish refugees like Roemer who taught at segregated southern colleges, see Gabrielle Simon Edgcomb, *From Swastika to Jim Crow: Refugee Scholars at Black Colleges* (Malabar, Fla., 1993).

Chapter 2. Two Declarations of Independence

1. Ben Jonson, *The Masque of Blacknesse* and *The Masque of Beautie,* in *Works,* ed. C. H. Herford and Percy Simpson, (Oxford, 1925–63), 7:161–94; John C. Meagher, *Method and Meaning in Jonson's Masques* (Notre Dame, Ind., 1946), 1–3; Anthony Gerard Barthelmy, *Black Face, Maligned Race* (Baton Rouge, La., 1987), 1–19.

2. Immanuel Wallerstein, *The Modern World System* (New York, 1974); Rawley, *Transatlantic Slave Trade,* 1–60, 148–52; Henry Louis Gates Jr., *Figures in Black: Words, Signs, and the "Racial" Self* (New York, 1987), 51–53, 167–75; Wahneema Lubiano, "Black Ladies, Welfare Queens, and State Minstrels: Ideological War by Narrative Means," in Morrison, ed., *Race-ing Justice,* 353; Valerie Harris Smith, *Masks in Modern Drama* (Berkeley, 1984), 12; Susan Manning, *Ecstasy and the Demon: Feminism and Nationalism in the Dances of Mary Wigman* (Berkeley, 1993), 69–71.

The conflict between Christians and Moors contributed to puppet theater in Italy. One of the sources of blackface minstrelsy, and itself containing a black African component, the Italian harlequinade enjoyed popularity in its own right in the nineteenth-century United States. Puppet (marionette) theater used the harlequinade characters. It also staged the triumph of white Christian heroes over black Moorish infidels. These burlesques dramatized feudal love and war or clownish carryings-on between equals rather than the imagined practices of black primitives. Puppet theater is at once less rooted in African or African American culture and less racist than blackface. The comparison between puppet theater and minstrelsy is based on Gates, *Figures in Black*, 51–53; Lott, *Love and Theft*, 38–62; Helen P. Trimpi, *Melville's Confidence Man and American Politics in the 1850s* (Hamden, Conn., 1987), 6–8; exhibits and brochure (1994) of the International Museum of Marionettes, Palermo, Italy; and the June 1994 production of "Orlando Amorato" by the Sicilian marionette theater.

3. Aphra Behn, *Oroonoko* (1688), in *Oroonoko, The Rover, and Other Works*, ed. Janet Todd (New York, 1992). See also Catherine Gallagher, *Nobody's Story: The Vanishing Acts of Women Authors in the Literary Marketplace, 1670–1820* (Berkeley, 1994), 54–85; Paul H. D. Kaplan, *The Rise of the Black Magus in Western Art* (Ann Arbor, 1985); Jonson, *Masques of Blacknesse* and *Beautie*, 169, 173, 183.

4. D. J. Gordon, "The Imagery of Ben Jonson's *The Masque of Blacknesse* and *The Masque of Beautie*," *Journal of the Warburg and Courtauld Institutes* 6 (1943): 130; Gallagher, *Nobody's Story*, 34–48; Sigmund Freud, "The Question of Lay Analysis: Conversations with an Impartial Person" (1926), in *The Standard Edition of the Complete Psychological Works of Sigmund Freud*, ed. James Strachey (London, 1964), 20:212; Jefferson, *Notes on Virginia*, 256–62. On Afro-American trickster reappropriations of the black hole, see Houston Baker, *Blues, Ideology, and Afro-American Literature: A Vernacular Theory* (Chicago, 1984), 3–6, 144–54; and Toni Morrison, *Tar Baby* (New York, 1981).

5. Jonson, *Masque of Beautie*, 183; Barthelmy, *Black Face, Maligned Race*, 3–4 (quoting St. Jerome).

6. Ronald Sanders, *Lost Tribes and Promised Lands* (Boston, 1978), 39–65; Deborah Root, "Speaking Christian: Orthodoxy and Difference in Sixteenth-Century Spain," *Representations* 23 (summer 1988): 118–34; Rawley, *Transatlantic Slave Trade*.

7. Gordon, "Imagery of Ben Jonson," 129 (quoting Jonson); Meagher, *Method and Meaning*, 109. The immediate English imperial project (which produced in other colonial propaganda the conflation between Irish primitives, New World savages, and African blacks) was represented in Jonson's *The Irish Masque at Court*. In that spectacle's "magical thinking," as Elizabeth Fowler puts it, "Irish chieftains are instantly transformed into English earls, throwing off their heavy dialects and mantels, by the metamorphosing presence of James" (Fowler, "The Failure of Moral Philosophy in the Work of Edmund Spenser," *Representations* 51 [summer 1995]: 55).

8. Stephen Greenblatt, *Renaissance Self-Fashioning from More to Shakespeare* (Chicago, 1980); David Suchoff, "The Rosenberg Case and the New York Intellectuals," in *Secret Agents: The Rosenberg Case and the McCarthy Era* (New York, 1995), 155–56 (on Greenblatt); Barthelmy, *Black Face, Maligned Race*, 33–35, 72–76, 167–204; Jordan, *White over Black*, 37–39 (on Othello).

9. Quoted in Alexander Saxton, *The Rise and Fall of the White Republic: Class Politics and Mass Culture in Nineteenth-Century America* (New York, 1990), 166.

10. Gunnar Myrdal, *An American Dilemma: The Negro Problem and Mod-*

ern Democracy (New York, [1944] 1962), 24; cf. Saxton, *Rise and Fall of the White Republic,* 1–18.

11. See, for example, Jordan, *White over Black,* 429–81; James Campbell and James Oakes, "The Invention of Race: Rereading *White over Black," Reviews in American History* 21 (1993): 172–83; Morgan, *American Slavery, American Freedom;* David Brion Davis, *The Problem of Slavery in the Age of Revolution, 1770–1823* (Ithaca, N.Y., 1975); Alexander Saxton, *The Indispensable Enemy: Labor and the Anti-Chinese Movement in California* (Berkeley, 1971) and *Rise and Fall of the White Republic;* Richard Drinnon, *Facing West: The Metaphysics of Indian-Hating and Empire-Building* (Minneapolis, 1980); Robert Blauner, *Racial Oppression in America* (New York, 1972); Ronald T. Takaki, *Iron Cages: Race and Culture in Nineteenth-Century America* (New York, 1979); Michael Rogin, *Fathers and Children: Andrew Jackson and the Subjugation of the American Indian* (New York, 1975) and *"Ronald Reagan," the Movie.*

12. Nathan Glazer and Daniel Patrick Moynihan, *Beyond the Melting Pot: The Negroes, Puerto Ricans, Jews, Italians, and Irish of New York City* (Cambridge, Mass., 1963); Werner Sollors, *Beyond Ethnicity: Consent and Descent in American Culture* (New York, 1986).

13. James Snead, *White Screens/Black Images* (New York, 1994), 60; Milton Gordon, *Assimilation in American Life: The Role of Race, Religion, and National Origins* (New York, 1964).

14. See Sacvan Bercovitch, *The Puritan Origins of the American Self* (New York, 1975); Slotkin, *Regeneration Through Violence;* Turner, *Frontier in American History.*

15. Quoted in Rogin, *Fathers and Children,* 7. On Natty Bumppo, see Slotkin, *Regeneration Through Violence,* 466–517.

16. Harry Levin, *The Power of Blackness: Hawthorne, Poe, Melville* (New York, 1958); Richard Wright, "How Bigger Was Born," introduction to *Native Son* (New York, [1940] 1966), xxxiv. On the role of newly accepted academic Jewish intellectuals in cold war consensus history, a subject returned to at the end of this study, see (implicitly) my *The Intellectuals and McCarthy: The Radical Specter* (Cambridge, Mass., 1967) and (explicitly) *"Ronald Reagan," the Movie,* 275–79.

17. Toni Morrison, *Playing in the Dark: Whiteness and the Literary Imagination* (Cambridge, Mass., 1992), 5–6.

18. See ibid.; Toni Morrison, "Unspeakable Things Unspoken: The Afro-American Presence in American Literature," *Michigan Quarterly Review* 28 (winter 1989): 14–18; Michael Wood, "Life Studies," *New York Review of Books,* Nov. 19, 1992, 7–11; Ralph Ellison, *The Invisible Man* (New York, 1952); Robert Berkhofer, *The White Man's Indian: Images of the American Indian from Columbus to the Present* (New York, 1978); Richard Dyer, "White," *Screen* 29 (autumn 1988): 44–64; Roediger, *Abolition of Whiteness.* I am also indebted to George Lipsitz in seminar discussion at the Humanities Research Institute, University of California, Irvine, Nov. 1992.

19. Toll, *Blacking Up,* 26; Joseph Boskin, *Sambo: The Rise and Fall of an American Jester* (New York, 1986), 70; W. T. Lhamon Jr. "Constance Rourke's Secret Reserve," introduction to Constance Rourke, *American Humor: A Study*

of the National Character (Gainesville, Fla., [1931] 1986), xxiv; Rogin, *Fathers and Children.*

20. F. O. Matthiesen, *The American Renaissance: Art and Expression in the Age of Emerson and Whitman* (New York, 1941); Richard Chase, *The American Novel and Its Tradition* (New York, 1957); R. W. B. Lewis, *The American Adam: Innocence, Tragedy, and Tradition in the Nineteenth Century* (Chicago, 1955); Fiedler, *Love and Death.* See also Michael Rogin, *Subversive Genealogy: The Politics and Art of Herman Melville* (New York, 1983), 15–23, 70–76; David S. Reynolds, *Beneath the American Renaissance* (New York, 1988), 170 (quoted), 174, 205; Toll, *Blacking Up;* Saxton, *Rise and Fall of the White Republic,* 119–80; David R. Roediger, *The Wages of Whiteness: Race and the Making of the American Working Class* (London, 1991); Lott, *Love and Theft.*

21. Arthur Schlesinger Jr., *The Age of Jackson* (Boston 1946), 4–5; idem, *The Disuniting of America* (New York, 1991). Thanks to Kathleen Moran for calling Schlesinger's blackface to my attention.

22. See Lhamon, "Constance Rourke's Secret Reserve," xxxii, xxiv; Rourke, *American Humor,* 95–104; Lott, *Love and Theft,* 56; Toll, *Blacking Up,* 1–30 (minstrel quoted, 1); Saxton, *Rise and Fall of the White Republic,* 118–23.

23. Sollors, *Beyond Ethnicity,* 131–48; Melvin Patrick Ely, *The Adventures of Amos 'n' Andy: A Social History of an American Phenomenon* (New York, 1991); William W. Austin, *"Susanna," "Jeannie," and "The Old Folks at Home": The Songs of Stephen C. Foster From His Time to Ours,* 2d ed. (Urbana, Ill., 1989); Gary Giddins, *Riding on a Blue Note: Jazz and American Pop* (New York, 1981), 5–17; Frank Halliwell, *Halliwell's Filmgoers Companion,* 8th ed. (New York, 1974).

24. Thomas Schatz, *Hollywood Genres: Formulas, Filmmaking, and the Studio System* (New York, 1981), 187; Ethan Mordden, " 'Show Boat' Crosses Over," *New Yorker,* July 3, 1989, 94. On Jolson as the inspiration for Bosco and Mickey Mouse, see Hugh Kenner, *Chuck Jones* (Berkeley, 1994), 24; Susan Willis, *A Primer for Daily Life* (New York, 1991), 130–31.

25. The major examples are Lott, *Love and Theft;* W. T. Lhamon Jr., " 'Ebery Time I Wheel About I Jump Jim Crow': Cycles of Minstrel Transgression from Cool White to Vanilla Ice" (ms., n.d.) and "Constance Rourke's Secret Reserve"; Marjorie Garber, *Vested Interests: Cross-Dressing and Cultural Anxiety* (New York, 1992). Lhamon places himself under the postmodern rubric in his book on the 1950s, *Deliberate Speed: The Origins of a Cultural Style in the American 1950s* (Washington, D.C., 1990), 16–17, 99–101, 200. Lott's proclaimed genealogy is from British cultural studies, but he also invokes poststructuralism. To consider the Americanization of British cultural studies would require a separate essay.

26. The major recent examples are Saxton, *Rise and Fall of the White Republic,* and Roediger, *Wages of Whiteness.* A more compromised position, combining political disapproval with cultural pleasure, is associated with a popular-front orientation. See Toll, *Blacking Up;* Boskin, *Sambo.* These share the orientation of Lawrence Levine's seminal *Black Culture and Black Consciousness* (New York, 1977). My modernist/postmodernist division derives from Marshall Berman, *All That Is Solid Melts into the Air: The Experience of Modernity* (New

York, 1982); and Andreas Huyssen, *After the Great Divide: Modernism, Mass Culture, Postmodernism* (Bloomington, 1987). Saxton and Roediger depart from Frankfurt School and *Partisan Review* modernism, however, in their interpretations of blackface mass culture from the bottom up.

27. I adapt this term from the sexuoeconomic system of Charlotte Perkins Gilman, *Woman and Economics* (New York, [1898] 1966).

28. See Sandra M. Gilbert, "Costumes of the Mind: Transvestism as Metaphor in Modern Literature," in *Writing and Sexual Difference*, ed. Elizabeth Abel (Chicago, 1982), 199–201; Elaine Showalter, "Critical Cross-Dressing: Male Feminists and the Woman of the Year," *Raritan* 3 (fall 1983): 130–49; cf. Judith Butler, *Gender Trouble: Feminism and the Subversion of Identity* (New York, 1990); Garber, *Vested Interests;* Carol Clover, *Men, Women, and Chain Saws: Gender in the Modern Horror Film* (Princeton, N.J., 1992). Cross-dressing celebrations have in turn been challenged in Tania Modleski, *Feminism Without Women* (New York, 1991); and Susan Bordo, *Unbearable Weight: Feminism, Western Culture, and the Body* (Berkeley, 1993). I rely especially on Gaston Alonso Donate, "In Whose Eyes Is What Chic Radical?: A Tootsie Ruminates on Cross-Dressing," *Critical Sense* 3 (spring 1995): 5–35, which provides a much fuller analysis of the literature than the one offered here.

29. See Paul Gilroy, *The Black Atlantic: Modernity and Double Consciousness* (Cambridge, Mass., 1993); Henry Louis Gates Jr., " 'Authenticity,' or the Lessons of Little Tree," *New York Times Book Review*, Nov. 24, 1991, 1, 26–30.

30. Garber, *Vested Interests*, 6–40; also Lhamon, "Constance Rourke's Secrete Reserve," xvi–xxi.

31. Garber, *Vested Interests*, 12, 28, and passim; Jacques Lacan, *Ecrits*, trans. Alan Sheridan (New York, 1977).

32. Cf. David Lloyd, "Race Under Representation," *Oxford Literary Review* 13 (summer 1991): 81.

33. Butler, *Gender Trouble*, 31.

34. Judith Butler, *Bodies That Matter: On the Discursive Limits of "Sex"* (New York, 1993), 231–42.

35. Saidiya V. Hartman, *Performing Blackness: Staging Subjection and Resistance in Antebellum Culture* (Oxford, forthcoming). See also Bertram Wyatt-Brown, "The Mask of Obedience: Male Slave Psychology in the Old South," *American Historical Review* 93 (Dec. 1988): 1228–52.

36. Phillips is quoted in Boskin, *Sambo*, 118. See also William J. Mahar, "Black English in Early Blackface Minstrelsy: A New Interpretation of the Sources of Minstrel Show Dialect," *American Quarterly* 37 (summer 1985): 260–85.

37. Butler, *Bodies That Matter*, 241.

38. Joan Riviere, "Womanliness as a Masquerade" (1929), in *Formations of Fantasy*, ed. Victor Burgin, James Donald, and Cora Kaplan (London, 1986), 35–44; Mary Ann Doane, "Film and the Masquerade: Theorizing the Female Spectator," *Screen* (Sept.–Oct. 1982): 79–82; Butler, *Gender Trouble*, 50–54, 138–46. See also Garber, *Vested Interests*, 142; Modleski, *Feminism Without Women*, 54; and Stephen Heath, "Joan Riviere and the Masquerade," in Burgin, Donald, and Kaplan, eds., *Formations of Fantasy*, 45–53. Cross-dressing, as

a practice that proclaims the distantiation between ascribed identity and role, is sometimes distinguished from masquerade, which is understood as the hiding of that distantiation. That distinction usefully differentiates Butler's drag queens and my blacked-up white men from Riviere's masqueraders. However, I use both terms, *masquerade* and *cross-dressing*, to describe blackface.

39. Modleski, *Feminism Without Women,* 18–22.

40. Cf. Mary C. Watters, *Ethnic Options: Choosing Identities in America* (Berkeley, 1990).

41. Lott, *Love and Theft,* 6–12; Margo Jefferson, "Minstrel Tradition: Not Just a Racist Relic" (review of Lott), *New York Times,* Oct. 27, 1993, B3. See also Sollors, *Beyond Ethnicity,* 131–38; Charles Musser, "Ethnicity, Role-Playing, and American Film Comedy: From *Chinese Laundry Scene* to *Whoopee!* (1894–1930)," in *Unspeakable Images: Ethnicity and the American Cinema,* ed. Lester D. Friedman (Urbana, Ill., 1991), 39–81; Jenkins, *What Made Pistachio Nuts?* 153–84, 198–205, 216–20.

42. George Lipsitz, *Time Passages: Collective Memory and American Popular Culture* (Minneapolis, 1990), 133–60, 262–63; Austin, *"Susanna," "Jeannie," and "The Old Folks at Home,"* 19–20 (Emmett quote); Lott, *Love and Theft,* 39–48.

43. Lott, *Love and Theft,* 25–29; idem, " 'The Seeming Counterfeit': Racial Politics and Early Blackface Minstrelsy," *American Quarterly* 43 (June 1991): 226–27 (Hall quote); Mahar, "Black English in Early Blackface Minstrelsy," 37, 260–85 (quoted 285). Cf. Natalie Z. Davis, "Women on Top," in her *Society and Culture in Early Modern France* (Stanford, 1975); Peter Sahlins, *Forest Rites: The War of the Demoiselles in Nineteenth-Century France* (Cambridge, Mass., 1994).

44. Lhamon, " 'Ebery Time I Wheel About,' " 3–9, and "Constance Rourke's Secret Reserve"; Randall Knoper, *Acting Naturally: Mark Twain in the Culture of Performance* (Berkeley, 1994), 42–46. Cf., for later periods, Lewis Ehrenberg, *Steppin' Out: New York Nightlife and the Transformation of American Culture, 1890–1930* (Chicago, 1981); Lhamon, *Deliberate Speed.*

45. On this last point see Hartman, *Performing Blackness.*

46. Reynolds, *Beneath the American Renaissance,* 450 (quoting Emerson); Carroll Smith-Rosenberg, *Disorderly Conduct* (New York, 1985), 90–108; Rogin, *Fathers and Children,* 2d ed. (New Brunswick, N.J., 1991), xxv.

47. Cf. Roediger, *Wages of Whiteness,* 102–7; Lhamon, " 'Ebery Time I Wheel About,' " 6–7.

48. Lott, *Love and Theft,* 69–75.

49. Lott, *Love and Theft,* 12 (quoted); Saxton, *Rise and Fall of the White Republic;* Roediger, *Wages of Whiteness,* 87.

50. Saxton, *Rise and Fall of the White Republic;* Roediger, *Wages of Whiteness,* 95 (quoting Rawick), 13–14, 116; also Lipsitz, *Time Passages,* 64. Jean H. Baker, *Affairs of Party: The Political Culture of Northern Democracy in the Mid–Nineteenth Century* (Ithaca, N.Y., 1983), 213–57, shares Saxton's perspective. Roediger is indebted to the Marxist interpreters of African American history W. E. B. Du Bois and George Rawick, the latter a follower of the West Indian Marxist C. L. R. James, and to Nathan Huggins, to whose psychologi-

cal interpretation of blackface he adds a class dimension. Roediger avoids the subtextual attraction to blackface found in Jewish writers from the civil rights period, who are fascinated by a practice of which they know they should disapprove. Cf. Roediger, *Wages of Whiteness,* 11–15; George Rawick, *From Sundown to Sunup: The Making of the Black Community* (Westport, Conn., 1972); Nathan Irvin Huggins, *Harlem Renaissance* (New York, 1971), 244–72; Toll, *Blacking Up;* Boskin, *Sambo;* Levine, *Black Culture,* 137–99.

51. Roediger, *Wages of Whiteness,* 104 (quoted). Cf. Shane White, " 'It Was a Proud Day': African American Festivals and Parades in the North, 1741–1834," *Journal of American History* 81 (June 1994): 28–46.

52. Roediger, *Wages of Whiteness,* 108–9; Lott, *Love and Theft,* 25–27, 122, 165–67, 173–81; Fiedler, *Love and Death;* Lawrence, *Studies in Classic American Literature.* T. Walter Herbert, in his examination of Hawthorne family relations, argues that, for middle-class culture as well, strong, sexual women (coded masculine) paid the price for the transgressions of male androgyny (Herbert, *Dearest Beloved: The Hawthornes and the Making of the Middle-Class Family* [Berkeley, 1993]).

53. Roediger, *Wages of Whiteness,* 127; Knoper, *Acting Naturally,* 42–46 (whose position, however, is closer to Lott's than to mine); Charles Neider, ed., *The Autobiography of Mark Twain* (New York, [1917] 1959), 58–62.

54. Saxton, *Rise and Fall of the White Republic,* 43; Austin, *"Susanna," "Jeannie," and "The Old Folks at Home,"* 19, 31, 49; Sean Wilentz, *Chants Democratic: New York City and the Rise of the American Working Class, 1788–1850* (New York, 1984), 171–75, 214–16, 226–27; Walter Hugins, *Jacksonian Democracy and the Working Class* (Stanford, 1960); Lee Benson, *The Concept of Jacksonian Democracy* (New York, 1960); J. Baker, *Affairs of Party,* 213–57.

55. Lott, *Love and Theft,* 105–7, 164–70, 202–9; Austin, *"Susanna," "Jeannie," and "The Old Folks at Home,"* 29 (quoting Taylor); Rourke, *American Humor,* 103.

56. Lott, *Love and Theft,* 201–10; Lhamon, " 'Ebery Time I Wheel About,' " 6; Austin, *"Susanna," "Jeannie," and "The Old Folks at Home,"* 19, 31, 49, 73–76, 99, 189, 233–35, 311; William Taylor, *Cavalier and Yankee: The Old South and the American National Character* (New York, 1961). In these paragraphs I am borrowing the data Lott has brilliantly assembled to reach conclusions at variance with his.

57. Harriet Beecher Stowe, *Uncle Tom's Cabin* (New York, [1852] 1981); Lott, *Love and Theft,* 211–33; Austin, *"Susanna," "Jeannie," and "The Old Folks at Home,"* 233–35; P. Gabriella Foreman, " 'This Promiscuous Housekeeping': Death, Transgression, and Homoeroticism in *Uncle Tom's Cabin," Representations* 43 (summer 1993): 51–72.

58. Lott, *Love and Theft,* 211–33; Linda Williams, "Film Bodies: Gender, Genre, and Excess," *Film Quarterly* 44 (summer 1991): 1–13, and her presentation on *Uncle Tom's Cabin,* Humanities Research Institute seminar, University of California, Irvine, Nov. 1992.

59. Lott, *Love and Theft,* 33.

60. Ibid., 226–33; Roediger, *Wages of Whiteness,* 173–81; David Montgomery, *Beyond Equality: Labor and the Radical Republicans, 1862–1872* (New York, 1967); J. Baker, *Affairs of Party,* 249–58.

61. Austin, *"Susanna," "Jeannie," and "The Old Folks at Home,"* 189, 292; Ely, *Adventures of Amos 'n' Andy,* 28–34; Toll, *Blacking Up,* 144.

62. Perry Miller, *Errand into the Wilderness* (New York, 1956); Bercovitch, *Puritan Origins of the American Self,* and *Rites of Assent* (New York, 1992), 20n, 30n; Louis Hartz, *The Liberal Tradition in America* (New York, 1955).

63. Pierre L. van den Berghe, *Race and Racism: A Comparative Perspective* (New York, 1967); Saxton, *Rise and Fall of the White Republic,* 77–203; Roediger, *Wages of Whiteness,* 59–60.

64. David Nasaw, *Going Out: The Rise and Fall of Public Amusements* (New York, 1993), 45.

65. Warren Goldstein, "Coming Together," *Nation,* Sept. 5–12, 1994, 224–26. See also Ehrenberg, *Steppin' Out;* Michael Rogin, "The Great Mother Domesticated: Sexual Difference and Sexual Indifference in D. W. Griffith's *Intolerance,*" *Critical Inquiry* 15 (spring 1989): 525–30; Nasaw, *Going Out,* 1–2, 45–61, 91–94, 115–16 (quoted 45); Melnick, *Ancestors and Relatives;* Rogin, " 'The Sword Became a Flashing Vision,' " 190–235.

66. Daphne Duval Harrison, *Black Pearls: Blues Queens of the 1920s* (New Brunswick, N.J., 1988), 225, 244; Francis Newton [Eric Hobsbawm], *The Jazz Scene* (Harmondsworth, Eng., 1961), 36; Marshall Stearns, *The Story of Jazz* (New York, 1956), 119–20.

67. Ann Charters, *Nobody: The Story of Bert Williams* (New York, 1970), 10, 19, 28 (quoting Williams); Bert Williams, *"Nobody" and Other Songs,* Folkways Records (1971), RBF602. "Funny Feathers," from the 1990 Vernel Bagneris musical *Further Mo'* (set the same year as *The Jazz Singer,* 1927), blacks up Bert Williams. Bagneris presents a tortured Williams, who comes alive in forcing himself to do a number he hates. (I rely on my memory of the performance. See also Louis Botto, "And Further Mo'," *Village Gate Playbill,* 1990–91 season; and, for the theory of this practice, Hartman, *Performing Blackness.*)

68. For an account of a minstrel troupe set in the years surrounding the Civil War in which white supremacist torture produces a blackface interracial community, see Wesley Brown's remarkable novel *Darktown Strutters* (New York, 1994).

69. Theodore Parker is quoted in Houston A. Baker Jr., "Introduction" to Frederick Douglass, *Narrative of the Life of an American Slave* (New York, 1982), 12–13; Henry O. Osgood, *So This Is Jazz* (New York, 1926), 5n. For the spread of minstrelsy to another part of the British empire, see Richard Waterhouse, *From Minstrel Show to Vaudeville: The Australian Popular Stage, 1788–1914* (Kensington, N.S.W., Austr., 1991).

Chapter 3. Nationalism, Blackface, and the Jewish Question

1. Benedict Anderson, *Imagined Communities* (London, 1983), 74 and passim; Lott, *Love and Theft,* 193–94; Edmund Wilson, *Patriotic Gore: Studies in the Literature of the American Civil War* (New York, 1962).

2. Lhamon, "Constance Rourke's Secret Reserve," xxiii–xxiv.

3. See Toll, *Blacking Up,* 27; Hugh Seton-Watson, *Nations and States* (Lon-

don, 1977), 73; Friedrich Nietzsche, *The Birth of Tragedy from the Spirit of Music*, trans. Walter Kaufman (New York, [1872] 1967); Czeslaw Milosz, "Swing Shift in the Baltics," *New York Review of Books*, Nov. 7, 1993, 12; Austin, *"Susanna," "Jeannie," and "The Old Folks at Home,"* 129–32, 308; Newton, *Jazz Scene*, 32; Bernard Holland, "Dvořák's Spirit Returns to the Iowa He Loved," *New York Times*, Aug. 9, 1993, B1. A fictional account of Dvořák in the United States is Joseph Skvorecky, *Dvořák in Love*, trans. Paul Wilson (London, 1986).

4. Lawrence Buell, "American Literary Emergence as a Postcolonial Phenomenon," *American Literary History* 4 (fall 1992): 411–42; Saxton, *Rise and Fall of the White Republic*, 77–203; Anthony D. Smith, *Theories of Nationalism*, 2d ed. (New York, 1983), 87; Eric Hobsbawm, *Nations and Nationalism Since 1789* (Cambridge, Eng., 1990), 44–45.

5. Anderson, *Imagined Communities*, 28–40; Susan Rodgers, introduction to *Telling Lives, Telling Histories: Autobiography and Historical Imagination in Modern Indonesia* (Berkeley, 1994); Smith, *Theories of Nationalism*, 16–22, 63, 87; Lipsitz, *Time Passages*, 6–9; Hobsbawm, *Nations and Nationalism*, 92; Susan Stewart, "Scandals of the Ballad," *Representations* 32 (fall 1990): 134–56.

6. Lott, *Love and Theft*, 93–94; David Lloyd, *Nationalism and Minor Irish Literature: James Clarence Mangan and the Emergence of Irish Cultural Nationalism* (Berkeley, 1987); Hobsbawm, *Nations and Nationalism*, 46–54.

7. Anderson, *Imagined Communities*, 47–65.

8. Prys Morgan, "From a Death to a View: The Hunt for the Welsh Past in the Romantic Period," in *The Invention of Tradition*, ed. Eric Hobsbawm and Terence Ranger (Cambridge, Mass., 1983), 43–100; Richard Taruskin, " 'Nationalism': Colonialism in Disguise," *New York Times*, Aug. 22, 1993, H24.

9. Austin, *"Susanna," "Jeannie," and "The Old Folks at Home,"* 129, 257; P. H. Scott, *Sir Walter Scott and Scotland* (Edinburgh, 1981). Scott was himself influenced by the Anglo-Irish supporter of union with Britain Maria Edgeworth, whose *Castle Rackrent* (New York, [1800] 1964) invented the (Irish-face) vernacular narrator; see Gallagher, *Nobody's Story*, 239–99. The Scottish clan also served white supremacy when it was transferred to the United States. "The reincarnated souls of the Clansmen of Old Scotland" reborn in the Ku Klux Klan, wrote Thomas Dixon in the novel on which *The Birth of a Nation* was based, produced "one of the most dramatic chapters in the history of the Aryan race" (Dixon, *The Clansman* [Lexington, Ky., (1905) 1970], 2); see also Rogin, " 'The Sword Became a Flashing Vision,' " 190–235. Dixon's Ku Klux Klan resisted national power; *The Birth of a Nation* was closer to Scott in making the Klan a force for national unity.

10. Hugh Trevor-Roper, "The Invention of Tradition: The Highland Tradition of Scotland," in Hobsbawm and Ranger, *Invention of Tradition*, 15–42.

11. Sir Walter Scott, *Old Mortality* (Edinburgh, 1817).

12. Ralph Ellison, "Change the Joke and Slip the Yoke," in his *Shadow and Act* (New York, 1964), 53, 55. See also Margo Jefferson, "Seducified by a Minstrel Show," *New York Times*, May 22, 1994, sec. 2, 1, 40; Huggins, *Harlem Renaissance*, 244–72.

13. Sollors, *Beyond Ethnicity*, 38; John G. Cawelti, *Apostles of the Self-Made Man* (Chicago, 1965), 43.

14. Jean-Christophe Agnew, *Worlds Apart: The Market and the Theater in Anglo-American Thought, 1550–1750* (Cambridge, Mass., 1986), with Hall quoted 97.

15. Cf. Garber, *Vested Interests*, 121.

16. Karen Halttunen, *Confidence Men and Painted Women: A Study of Middle-Class Culture in America, 1830–1870* (New Haven, 1982), 56–152.

17. Daniel Lerner, *The Passing of Traditional Society: Modernizing the Middle East*, rev. ed. (New York, 1964), 49–53. On Lerner, see also Smith, *Theories of Nationalism*, 89–91; Greenblatt, *Renaissance Self-Fashioning*, 224–27, 236. Thomas Haskell, in an argument reminiscent of Lerner's, explains antislavery in terms of the expansion of the marketplace. Haskell's marketplace, though, is uniquely productive not of sympathy but of increased recognition of interdependence and responsibility for injustices far away. Haskell and his critics appear in Thomas Bender, ed., *The Anti-Slavery Debate: Capitalism and Abolitionism as a Problem in Historical Interpretation* (Berkeley, 1992).

18. Halttunen, *Confidence Men and Painted Women;* Miles Orvell, *The Real Thing: Imitation and Authenticity in American Culture, 1880–1940* (Chapel Hill, N.C., 1989); David Brion Davis, *The Slave Power Conspiracy and the Paranoid Style* (Baton Rouge, La., 1969). My own earlier treatments of the relationships between American self-making, mistrust, and masquerade are in *Fathers and Children*, 256–58, and *Subversive Genealogy*, 3–5, 236–56.

19. Neil Harris, *Humbug: The Art of P. T. Barnum* (Boston, 1973), 3–29. Lott, *Love and Theft*, 72–78, offers a class- rather than nation-based interpretation of Barnum.

20. This is precisely the point at which Greenblatt ends *Renaissance Self-Fashioning* and Jordan begins *White over Black*

21. Smith, *Theories of Nationalism*, xiii–xiv, 210; Hobsbawn, *Nations and Nationalism*, 19–20, 30–32, 39. A recent major work of scholarship that bases itself on the distinction between consensual and primordial nationalism—or "individualistic-libertarian" versus "ethnic" and "collectivistic-authoritarian"—is Liah Greenfeld, *Nationalism: Five Roads to Modernity* (Cambridge, Mass., 1992), 3–17 (for the theory) and 387–484 (for the application to the United States). For Greenfeld, racism is an attribute of German national identity, not American. In her celebratory account of American nationalism, the Civil War ends the contradiction between freedom and slavery, and therefore between black and white. Black Americans disappear from her postbellum United States; she turns to immigrants instead, congratulating ethnic pluralism for resisting the national uniformity that afflicts the French. But the repressed origins of the United States in white supremacy return when Greenfeld begins her own section on the United States, for her epigraphs taken together invoke an American starting point that absorbs ethnicity into (the white) race. She quotes John Adams—"It is of great importance to begin well"—and George Bancroft—"Our land is . . . the recipient of the men of all countries. . . . Our country stands, therefore, more than any other, as the realization of the unity of the race" (387).

22. Hector St. John Crevecoeur, *Letters from an American Farmer* (New

York, [1782] 1963); Turner, *Frontier in American History;* Sollors, *Beyond Ethnicity.* Cf. Michael Zuckerman, "The Fabrication of Identity in Early America," in his *Almost Chosen People: Oblique Biographies in the American Grain* (Berkeley, 1993), 21–54. On the making of a French nation, see Eugen Weber, *Peasants into Frenchmen: The Modernization of Rural France, 1870–1914* (Stanford, 1976).

23. Sollors, *Beyond Ethnicity,* 131–48. See also Bercovitch, *The Puritan Origins of the American Self* (New York, 1975). I borrow the term "choosing people" from Sara Beshtel and Alan Graubard, *Saving Remnants: Feeling Jewish in America* (New York, 1992).

24. Kenneth Cmiel, " 'A Broad Fluid Language of Democracy': Discovering the American Idiom," *Journal of American History* 79 (Dec. 1992): 930.

25. Anderson, *Imagined Communities,* 136–38; Hobsbawm, *Nations and Nationalism,* 44–45, 89, 95–108, 130; Arno Mayer, *Why Did the Heavens Not Darken? The "Final Solution" in History* (New York, 1990), 64–89; Carl Schorske, *Fin-de-Siècle Vienna: Politics and Culture* (New York, 1980), 116–207; Takaki, *Iron Cages,* 14–15; Reginald Horsman, *Race and Manifest Destiny: The Origins of American Racial Anglo-Saxonism* (Cambridge, Mass., 1981).

26. Crevecoeur, *Letters from an American Farmer,* 168–73, 194–218.

27. Sollors, *Beyond Ethnicity,* 131–48.

28. Lott, *Love and Theft,* 94–97, 148–49; Roediger, *Wages of Whiteness,* 133–56.

29. Allen, *Invention of the White Race,* 169–84 and passim; Lott, *Love and Theft,* 94–97, 148–49; Nicholas B. Canny, "The Ideology of English Colonization: From Ireland to America," *William and Mary Quarterly,* 3d ser., 30 (1973): 575–98; Lloyd, *Nationalism and Minor Irish Literature,* 206 (Carlyle quote); L. Perry Curtis, *Apes and Angels: The Irishman in Victorian Caricature* (Washington, D.C., 1971), vii–x, 1–30. The turn to Israel by American Jews a century later, post- rather than pre-ethnic blackface, followed rather than threatened Jewish Americanization.

30. Lott, *Love and Theft,* 94–97, 148–49; Roediger, *Wages of Whiteness,* 133–44; Joe Lee, "The Irish Migration" (lecture at the University of California, Berkeley, Oct. 6, 1994); Melnick, *Ancestors and Relatives;* Douglas C. Riach, "Blacks and Blackface on the Irish Stage, 1830–60," *American Studies 7* (fall 1981): 231–42.

31. Allen, *Invention of the White Race;* Lee, "Irish Migration."

32. Michael Mayer, "A Musical Facade for the Third Reich," in *"Degenerate Art": The Fate of the Avant-Garde in Nazi Germany,* ed. Stephanie Barron (New York, 1991), 180; John Rockwell, "Jazz Was Sin, Jewishness Worse," *New York Times,* Apr. 25, 1993, H29, H35. For the derivation of jazz from the relations between blacks and Jews, see below, chapter 4. Thanks to Françoise Vergès for discovering the *Jonny spielt auf* poster.

33. Donna Murch suggested in seminar discussion that that difference is visible in the two versions, since the German poster is more embedded in the racialized black body, the American more a signifier of theatricality.

34. Rockwell, "Jazz Was Sin," H29.

35. Wilson is cited in Rogin, *"Ronald Reagan," the Movie*, 94; Oscar Jaszi, *The Dissolution of the Hapsburg Monarchy* (Chicago, [1929] 1964). See also Seton-Watson, *Nations and States*, 164–67.

36. Hannah Arendt, *The Origins of Totalitarianism*, new ed. (New York, [1951] 1973), 10–25, 56–68; idem, "The Jew as Pariah," in *The Jew as Pariah: Jewish Identity and Politics in the Modern Age*, ed. Ron H. Feldman (New York, 1978), 67–90; Ernst Pawel, *The Nightmare of Reason: A Life of Franz Kafka* (New York, 1984); Seton-Watson, *Nations and States*, 164–65, 389–92; Benjamin Harshav, *Language in Time of Revolution* (Berkeley, 1993), 68–69; Schorske, *Fin-de-Siècle Vienna*, 116–207; Zygmunt Bauman, *Modernity and the Holocaust* (Ithaca, N.Y., 1989), 50–59; Peter Pulzer, *The Rise of Political Anti-Semitism in Germany and Austria* (New York, 1964), 138–39; Frederic V. Grunfelt, *Prophets Without Honour: A Background to Freud, Kafka, Einstein, and Their World* (New York, 1979); Hans Rogger, *Jewish Policies and Right-Wing Politics in Imperial Russia* (Berkeley, 1986), xii, 22.

37. Arendt, *Origins of Totalitarianism*, 11–53, 222–302; George L. Mosse, *Confronting the Nation: Jewish and Western Nationalism* (Hanover, N.H., 1993), 1–10, 146–60; Steven Beller, *Vienna and the Jews, 1867–1938: A Cultural History* (Cambridge, Eng., 1989); Bauman, *Modernity and the Holocaust*, 50–51. Distinguishing racism from earlier nationalism, Arendt (*Origins*, 222–302) shows how racism destroyed the European nation-state. Across the ocean, it supported the American nation.

38. Beller, *Vienna and the Jews*, 201–6; Mayer, *Why Did the Heavens Not Darken?* vii–xi, 39–63; Schorske, *Fin-de-Siècle Vienna*, 116–46, 181–98; Rogger, *Jewish Policies and Right-Wing Politics*, 18–19.

39. Hans Rogger, "Conclusion and Overview," in *Pogroms: Anti-Jewish Violence in Modern Russian History*, ed. John D. Klier and Shlomo Lambrose (New York, 1992), 351–62; Rogger, *Jewish Policies and Right-Wing Politics*, 3–12; Bauman, *Modernity and the Holocaust*, 34–39.

40. Beller, *Vienna and the Jews*, 193. Hitler reports his encounter with the Jew in *Mein Kampf*, trans. Ralph Manheim (Boston, 1943), 56–61. See also Bauman, *Modernity and the Holocaust*, 34–39.

41. Douglas A. Massey and Nancy A. Denton, *American Apartheid: Segregation and the Making of the Underclass* (Cambridge, Mass., 1993), 18–19 and passim. Although Massey and Denton do not say so, and provide no data to test the hypothesis, it is likely that Indians, Chinese Americans, and Mexican Americans were also ghettoized in various times and places in the United States.

42. Hitler, *Mein Kampf*, 17, 137–39, 286, 304–5, 439–40.

43. Mayer, *Why Did the Heavens Not Darken?* 45–46, 60, 74–77; Arendt, *Origins of Totalitarianism*, 52; Stephen Steinberg, *The Ethnic Myth: Race, Ethnicity, and Class in America*, 2d ed. (Boston, 1989), 90–91; Edna Bonacich, "A Theory of Middleman Minorities," *American Sociological Review* 38 (Oct. 1973): 583–94; Robert Cherry, "Middlemen Minority Theories: Implications for Black-Jewish Relations," *Journal of Ethnic Studies* 17 (winter 1990): 117–38.

44. Beller, *Vienna and the Jews*, 141 (quoting Gomperz), 130, 202–3; Zangwill, *Melting Pot*.

45. Beller, *Vienna and the Jews*, 162. See also, on Jews and German culture,

Arthur Schnitzler, *The Road into the Open*, trans. Roger Byers (Berkeley, 1992); Stefan Zweig, *The World of Yesterday*, trans. Harry Zohn (New York, 1943); Grunfelt, *Prophets Without Honor*.

46. Sollors, *Beyond Ethnicity*, 66; Mosse, *Confronting the Nation*, 143–44. Modernist Central European high culture influenced American mass culture through the arrival of émigré film professionals in Hollywood. To cite an early, related example, Joseph Urban, a (Catholic, not Jewish) Viennese expatriate, was the stage and set designer most responsible for the modern look of New York commercial culture in the early twentieth century. Adapting European modernism to American capitalism, wrote Gregory F. Gilmartin, "in America Urban found a surrogate for the centralized state in the notion of commercial culture." Urban, who gave Ziegfeld's Follies its stage look, also did the sets and stage design for *Show Boat*. In Hollywood, he was the house art director for William Randolph Hearst's film studio. See Gregory F. Gilmartin, "Joseph Urban," in *Inventing Times Square: Commerce and Culture at the Crossroads of the World*, ed. William R. Taylor (New York, 1991), 271–83 (quoted 274); Richard Koszarski, *An Evening's Entertainment, 1915–1928* (Berkeley, 1990), 286.

47. Arendt, *Origins of Totalitarianism*, 50–68; idem, "Jew as Pariah," 65–71; idem "Portrait of a Period," in *Jew as Pariah*, 112–21; Schorske, *Fin-de-Siècle Vienna*, 3–10, 116–207, 279–319; Schnitzler, *Way into the Open;* Zweig, *World of Yesterday*, 1–91; Joseph Roth, *The Radetzky March*, trans. Eva Tucker (London, 1974); Erich von Stroheim, dir., *The Wedding March* (1927).

48. Walter Benjamin, "Theses on the Philosophy of History," in *Illuminations*, ed. Hannah Arendt (New York, 1968), 256; also Zangwill, *Melting Pot*, 207; Stephen Greenblatt, *Marvelous Possessions: The Wonder of the New World* (Chicago, 1991), 128. On these matters generally I have benefited from Austin, *"Susanna," "Jeannie," and "The Old Folks at Home";* and Giddins, *Riding on a Blue Note*, 5–17 (and everything else Giddins writes; see, for example, "The Way We Weren't," *Village Voice*, Feb. 28, 1995, 56).

49. Cherry, "Middlemen Minority Theories," 117; Charles Herbert Stember et al., *Jews in the Mind of America* (New York, 1966), 9, 53–55, 125–39, 159–67.

50. See Londa Schiebinger, "Skeletons in the Closet: The First Illustrations of the Female Skeleton in Nineteenth-Century Anatomy," *Representations* 14 (spring 1986): 42–82.

51. On anti-Semitism as parricide or body-destruction, see, for example, Norman Cohn, *Warrant for Genocide: The Myth of the Jewish World-Conspiracy and the Protocols of the Elders of Zion*, 1st ed. (London, 1967), 251–74; Sigmund Freud, *Moses and Monotheism*, in *Standard Edition* 23:3–140; Philip Roth, "Imagining Jews," in *Reading Myself and Others* (New York, 1975), 215–56; Michael Rogin, "On the Jewish Question," *democracy* 3 (spring 1983): 105–14; Sander Gilman, *The Jew's Body* (New York, 1991), 81–82 and passim (quoted 126); Garber, *Vested Interests*, 224–29.

52. Otto Weininger, *Sex and Character* (New York, 1906); Danilo Kis, *Hourglass*, trans. Ralph Manheim (London, [1974] 1990), 55; Sander Gilman, *Difference and Pathology: Stereotypes of Sexuality, Race, and Madness* (Ithaca, N.Y., 1985), and *Jew's Body*, 136–37 (quoting Weininger); J. Geller, "Juden-

zopf/Chinesenzopf: Of Jews and Queues" (ms., 1993), 8 (quoting Jung); Rogin, "On the Jewish Question," 110–14 (on Freud's family romances); Hutchins Hapgood, *The Spirit of the Ghetto: Studies of the Jewish Quarter of New York* (Cambridge, Mass., [1902] 1967), 13–38; Henry Roth, *Call It Sleep* (New York, 1934); Garber, *Vested Interests,* 224–32; Bauman, *Modernity and the Holocaust,* 31–60.

53. Sollors, *Beyond Ethnicity,* 67–69, 172–73; 182–83; Koszarski, *An Evening's Entertainment,* 43–50.

Chapter 4. Blackface, White Noise

1. Musser, *Before the Nickelodeon,* 254.

2. On early cinema generally, see, among many other sources, ibid.; Nasaw, *Going Out,* 134–53, 166; John Fell, ed., *Film Before Griffith* (Berkeley, 1983); Miriam Hansen, *Babel and Babylon: Spectatorship in American Silent Film* (Cambridge, Mass., 1991), 23–125.

3. Musser, *Before the Nickelodeon,* 242–44; Bordwell, Staiger, and Thompson, *Classical Hollywood Cinema,* 183; Bowser, *Transformation of Cinema,* 96; Campbell, *Celluloid South,* 12–14, 37–39; Staiger, *Interpreting Films,* 101–23.

4. See, for example, Musser, *Before the Nickelodeon,* 212–30; Tom Gunning, "Weaving a Narrative: Style and Economic Background in Griffith's Biograph Films," *Quarterly Review of Film Studies* 6 (winter 1981): 12–25; idem, "The Cinema of Attractions: Early Film, Its Spectator, and the Avant-Garde," in *Early Cinema,* ed. Thomas Elsaesser (London, 1990), 56–62; Noel Burch, "Narrative/Diegesis—Thresholds, Limits," *Screen,* July–Aug. 1982, 16–33; Staiger, *Interpreting Films,* 101–23; Hansen, *Babel and Babylon,* 90–125.

5. Koszarski, *An Evening's Entertainment,* 184.

6. Sergei Eisenstein, *Film Form* (New York, 1949), 197.

7. This paragraph and the next derive from Rogin, " 'The Sword Became a Flashing Vision.' " Koszarski, *An Evening's Entertainment,* is quoted 214.

8. Bordwell, Staiger, and Thompson, *Classical Hollywood Cinema,* 87–112; Robert Sklar, "Oh! Althusser!: Historiography and the Rise of Cinema Studies," in *Resisting Images: Essays on Cinema and History,* ed. Robert Sklar and Edwin Musser (Philadelphia, 1990), 19–32; Gabler, *Empire of Their Own.* (Even De-Mille was half Jewish, but he did not come from a Jewish milieu.)

9. Sklar, "Oh! Althusser!" 19–32; Kathy Peiss, *Cheap Amusements: Working Women and Leisure in Turn-of-the-Century New York* (Philadelphia, 1986), 149–62; Roy Rosenzweig, *Eight Hours for What We Will: Workers and Leisure in an Industrial City, 1870–1920* (New York, 1983), 191–215; Lizabeth Cohen, *Making a New Deal: Industrial Workers in Chicago, 1919–1939* (New York, 1990), 120–29; May, *Screening Out the Past,* 167–241; Stuart Ewen and Elizabeth Ewen, *Channels of Desire: Mass Images and the Shaping of American Consciousness* (New York, 1982), 88–96; George Mitchell, "The Consolidation of the American Film Industry, 1915–1920," *Cine-tracts* 2 (spring–summer 1979): 28–36, 63–70; Robert C. Allen, "Motion Picture Exhibition in Manhattan, 1906–1912: Beyond the Nickelodeon," in Fell, ed., *Film Before Griffith,*

162–73; Ben Singer, "Manhattan Nickelodeons: New Data on Audiences and Exhibitors," *Cinema Journal* 34 (spring 1995): 5–35; Hansen, *Babel and Babylon*, 64 (Zukor quote).

10. See Fiedler, *Love and Death*.

11. Quoted in William M. Tuttle Jr., *"Daddy's Gone to War": The Second World War in the Lives of America's Children* (New York, 1993), 155.

12. *"The Jazz Singer" Souvenir Program*, in *Souvenir Programs of Twelve Classic Movies, 1927–1941*, ed. Miles Kreuger (New York, 1977), 1–20; Mordaunt Hall, "Al Jolson and the Vitaphone," *New York Times*, Oct. 27, 1927, 24; *Variety*, Oct. 12, 1927, 16.

13. Jonathan D. Tankel, "The Impact of *The Jazz Singer* on the Conversion to Sound," *Journal of the University Film Association* 30 (winter 1979), 210–26; Larry Swindell, "The Day the Silents Stopped," *American Film* 3 (Oct. 1977): 24–31; Andrew Sarris, "The Cultural Guilt of Musical Movies," *Film Comment* 13 (Sept.–Oct. 1977): 39–41; Audrey Kupferberg, "The Jazz Singer," *Take One* 6 (Jan. 1978): 28–32.

14. J. Hoberman, "Is 'The Jazz Singer' Good for the Jews?" *Village Voice*, Jan. 7–13, 1981, 1, 31–33; Gabler, *Empire of Their Own*, 134–45; "Jews in the Movies," *Film Comment* 17 (July–Aug. 1981): 34–48; Steve Whitfield, "Jazz Singers," *Moment* 6 (Mar.–Apr. 1981): 19–25; Friedman, *Hollywood's Image of the Jew*, 48–53; Patricia Erens, *The Jew in American Cinema* (Bloomington, Ind., 1984), 70–110; Slobin, "Some Intersections of Jews, Music, and Theater," 31–69.

15. Cf. Frantz Fanon, *Black Skin, White Masks*, trans. Charles Lam Markmann (New York, [1952] 1967), and Jean Genet, *The Blacks: A Clown Show*, trans. Bernard Frechtman (London, [1954] 1960), on the asymmetrical inversion of whites in blackface.

16. Tankel, "Impact of *The Jazz Singer*," 23; Gabler, *Empire of Their Own*, 43.

17. Swindell, "Day the Silents Stopped," 28.

18. Sarris, "Cultural Guilt of Musical Movies," 41.

19. See, for example, Paula Fass, *The Damned and the Beautiful: American Youth in the 1920s* (New York, 1977), 22.

20. Robert L. Carringer, ed., *The Jazz Singer* (Madison, Wis., 1979), 144–45; Newton, *The Jazz Scene*, 275. Newton was Eric Hobsbawm, who, putting on blackface, borrowed his nom de plume from the African American jazz trumpeter Frankie Newton.

21. R. E. Sherwood, "The Jazz Singer," *Life*, Oct. 27, 1927, 24. See also Gabler, *Empire of Their Own*, 150; Friedman, *Hollywood's Image of the Jew*, 48.

22. Hoberman, "Is 'The Jazz Singer' Good for the Jews?" 32; Hoberman is the first to make this point.

23. *"Jazz Singer" Souvenir Program*, 6. See also Hoberman, "Is 'The Jazz Singer' Good for the Jews?" 31; Robert Carringer, "Introduction: History of a Popular Culture Classic," in Carringer, ed., *Jazz Singer*, 11, 24; Gabler, *Empire of Their Own*, 139–41; Herb G. Goldman, *Jolson: The Legend Comes to Life* (New York, 1988), 42–43, 120, 183.

24. Gabler, *Empire of Their Own*, 1–183 (quoted 3–4). See also Hoberman, "Is 'The Jazz Singer' Good for the Jews?" 32; May, *Screening Out the Past*,

167–79. Griffith had also chosen a (symbolic) story of parricide, *Judith of Bethulia*, as his first full-length feature; see Rogin, " 'The Sword Became a Flashing Vision,' " 202–3.

25. *"Jazz Singer" Souvenir Program*, 9; Hoberman, "Is 'The Jazz Singer' Good for the Jews?" 31.

26. Barry Paris, "The Godless Girl," *New Yorker*, Feb. 13, 1989, 55–7, 67–68 (quoted 57). Cf. Gabler, *Empire of Their Own*, 123–24, 136–37.

27. Paris, "Godless Girl," 57; Gabler, *Empire of Their Own*, 124–37; Goldman, *Jolson*, 101, 151; Kupferberg, "Jazz Singer," 30; Carringer, ed., *Jazz Singer*, 18, 140; J. Douglas Gomery, "The Coming of Sound: Technological Change in the American Film Industry," in *The American Film Industry*, rev. ed., ed. Tino Balio (Madison, Wis., 1985), 236–39.

28. Thanks to Aliza Bresky for the characterization of Yom Kippur. The anarchist ball is described in Ronald Sanders, *The Downtown Jews: Portrait of an Immigrant Generation* (New York, [1969] 1987), 99–100; and Diner, *In the Almost Promised Land*, 33. On Sam Warner's death, see Gabler, *Empire of Their Own*, 42–3; Paris, "Godless Girl," 58, 62; George Morris, "Opening Night," *Take One* 6 (Jan. 1978): 32. Basquette played in *The Younger Generation* a variation on the deathbed performances in life and in *The Jazz Singer*: she was the Jewish daughter who marries a writer of popular songs and is reconciled with her father only on his deathbed. The makers of an earlier intermarriage film, *The Passover Miracle* (1914), received rabbinical permission to film a synagogue service. Setting a precedent for *The Jazz Singer*, they timed their film release to coincide with that holiday. Yom Kippur is not Passover, however, nor was *The Passover Miracle* rebellious, since its prodigal was returning permanently to the ghetto. See Erens, *Jew in American Cinema*, 43–44.

29. Hoberman, "Is 'The Jazz Singer' Good for the Jews?" 1, 31–32. See also Christine Gledhill, "The Melodramatic Field: An Investigation," in *Home Is Where the Heart Is: Studies in Melodrama and the Woman's Film*, ed. Christine Gledhill (London, 1987), 9, 30.

30. Louis B. Mayer, Samuel Goldwyn, Harry Cohn, Jack Warner, and David O. Selznick all abandoned Jewish for younger gentile women. The studios continued to make occasional Jewish generational-conflict films for a few years after *The Jazz Singer*, but that movie marks the apogee of the Hollywood immigrant film. See Gabler, *Empire of Their Own*, 142–49; Carlos Clarens, "Moguls— That's a Jewish Word," *Film Comment* 17 (July–Aug. 1981): 35; Otto Friedrich, *City of Nets* (Glasgow, 1986), 220–21, 354–56; Patricia Erens, "Mentshlekhkayt Conquers All: The Yiddish Cinema in America," *Film Comment* 12 (Jan.–Feb. 1976): 48, and *Jew in American Cinema*, 138, 162; J. Hoberman, "Yiddish Transit," *Film Comment* 17 (July–Aug. 1981): 36.

31. Peter Rose, *Mainstream and Margins: Jews, Blacks, and Other Americans* (New Brunswick, N.J., 1983), 67. See also Carringer, ed., *Jazz Singer*, 21; Sampson Raphaelson, "The Day of Atonement," in ibid., 147–67; Sampson Raphaelson, *The Jazz Singer* (New York, [1925] 1935).

32. Harry Warner planned a film about anti-Semitism; he made *The Jazz Singer* instead. Where silent films depicted anti-Semitism, they located it in Rus-

sia, not the United States. See Friedman, *Hollywood's Image of the Jew,* 46–47; Erens, *Jew in American Cinema,* 54–57, 73.

33. Hannah Arendt, "The Jew as Pariah: A Hidden Tradition," in *The Jew as Pariah,* ed. Ron H. Feldman (New York, 1978); Robert A. Burt, *Two Jewish Justices: Outcasts in the Promised Land* (Berkeley, 1988).

34. For the older historiography, see John Higham, *Strangers in the Land* (New Brunswick, N.J., 1955); William G. Leuchtenberg, *The Perils of Prosperity, 1914–1932* (Chicago, 1958); William Preston, *Aliens and Dissenters* (Cambridge, Mass., 1963); Robert K. Murray, *Red Scare* (Minneapolis, 1955). More recent interpretations include Fass, *The Damned and the Beautiful;* Richard Fox and T. J. Jackson Lears, eds., *The Culture of Consumption* (New York, 1983).

35. Arnold Shaw, *The Jazz Age: Popular Music in the 1920s* (New York, 1987), 7–8, 14; F. Scott Fitzgerald, "May Day," in *Tales of the Jazz Age* (New York, 1922), viii, 87 (the complete story is on 61–125).

36. That same shift from radical politics to aesthetics defined the Harlem Renaissance, and it is encapsulated in the changed meaning of the term "the New Negro." See Henry Louis Gates Jr., "The Trope of a New Negro and the Reconstruction of the Image of the Black," *Representations* 24 (fall 1988): 129–55.

37. Fitzgerald, "May Day," 77; Kathleen Blee, *Women of the Klan: Racism and Gender in the 1920s* (Berkeley, 1991), 40, 168; Lee J. Levinger, *The Causes of Anti-Semitism in the United States* (Philadelphia, 1925), 9–15, 94; David Levering Lewis, *When Harlem Was In Vogue* (New York, 1981), 44; Michael Selzer, ed., *"Kike!" A Documentary History of Anti-Semitism in America* (New York, 1972), 117 (for Committee on Immigration quote); Slotkin, *Gunfighter Nation,* 198–202, 699 (for Stoddard quote); John Higham, "American Anti-Semitism Historically Reconsidered," in Charles Herbert Stember et al., *Jews in the Mind of America* (New York, 1966), 240–51; Jack Salzman, ed., *Bridges and Boundaries: African Americans and American Jews* (New York, 1992), 175.

38. Quoted in David H. Bennett, *The Party of Fear* (Chapel Hill, N.C., 1988), 204.

39. Sarris, "Cultural Guilt of Movie Musicals," 39. My description of Jolson in blackface is indebted to Lemuel Johnson and Anne Norton.

40. Quoted in Thomas Elsaesser, "Film History and Visual Pleasure," in *Cinema Histories, Cinema Practices,* ed. Patricia Mellenkamp and Philip Rosen (Frederick, Md., 1984), 57–58.

41. *"Jazz Singer" Souvenir Program,* 15.

42. Toll, *Blacking Up,* 274; Robert C. Allen, *Vaudeville and Film: A Study in Media Interaction* (New York, 1980); Whitfield, "Jazz Singers," 20; Hugo Munsterberg, *The Film: A Psychological Study—The Silent Photoplay in 1916* (New York, [1916] 1970), 7; J. Douglas Gomery, "Problems in Film History: How Fox Innovated Sound," *Quarterly Review of Film Studies* 1 (Aug. 1976): 315–30; idem, "The Coming of Sound," 229–51.

43. Tankel, "Conversion to Sound," 22–23; Geduld, *Birth of the Talkies,* 120–26, 143–49; Gabler, *Empire of Their Own,* 135–36; Carringer, ed., *Jazz Singer,* 15–16; Goldman, *Jolson,* 146.

44. Bordwell, Staiger, and Thompson, *Classical Hollywood Cinema,* 177, 189–93; Charles Wolfe, "Vitaphone Shorts and *The Jazz Singer,*" *Wide Angle*

12 (summer 1990): 58–78. Wolfe's splendid article, which emphasizes frontal performance, denies that there is shot–reverse shot editing in the scene where Jack meets Mary. Repeated viewings support, I believe, my language in the text.

45. Carringer, ed., *Jazz Singer,* 61. A decade later a Jolson film took the risk. "If I didn't have this black on, I'd kiss you," Al Howard (Jolson) says to Dot (Jolson's wife, Ruby Keeler) at the end of *Go Into Your Dance.* "Don't let a little black stop you," she replies.

46. Carringer, *Jazz Singer,* 61, 78–80, 83, 136; *"Jazz Singer" Souvenir Program,* 1; *Pittsburgh Courier,* Apr. 21, 1928, 13; Raphaelson, *Jazz Singer,* 107. Cf. Garber, *Vested Interests,* 12. I have quoted Jack's letter from the movie intertitle, which differs slightly from the version reprinted in the shooting script. *Father and Son* (1913) contains the first name change in immigrant Jewish film, according to Erens, *Jew in American Cinema,* 52.

47. Bowser, *Transformation of Cinema,* 179; also 245–48.

48. Thomas Elsaesser, "Social Mobility and the Fantastic: German Silent Cinema," *Wide Angle* 5 (1982): 15–17, 24–25. See also Otto Rank, *The Double: A Psychoanalytic Study,* trans. Harry Tucker Jr. (New York, [1925] 1979), 4–7.

49. See Heide Schlüpmann, "The First German Art Film: Rye's *The Student of Prague,*" in *German Film and Literature: Adaptations and Tranformations,* ed. Eric Rentschler (New York, 1986), 9–24.

50. *"Jazz Singer" Souvenir Program,* 15; "Al Jolson: America's Minstrel Man," *Coronet,* May 1948, in Jolson file, Margaret Herrick Library, Motion Picture Academy of Arts and Sciences, Hollywood, Calif. [hereafter cited as MPAAS]; Cripps, *Slow Fade to Black,* 138; W. E. B. Du Bois, *The Souls of Black Folk* (Chicago, 1903), 2.

51. Carringer, ed., *Jazz Singer,* 61, 62, 136; Gabler, *Empire of Their Own,* 136. *"Jazz Singer" Souvenir Program* has Jakie singing in "his best darkey manner" (4).

52. *"Jazz Singer" Souvenir Program,* 14; Carringer, ed., *Jazz Singer,* 23; Raphaelson, "Day of Atonement," 151.

53. My summary comes from the movie; the shooting-script blackface line is in Carringer, ed., *Jazz Singer,* 133. On the moving-picture cathedral in the 1920s, see May, *Screening Out The Past,* 147–66; on island communities, see Robert Wiebe, *The Search for Order, 1877–1920* (New York, 1967); on the jazz singer as religious figure, see Slobin, "Some Intersections of Jews, Music, and Theater," 36–69.

54. Quoted in Bennett, *Party of Fear,* 204.

55. Howe, *World of Our Fathers,* 562 (quoted); Giddins, *Riding on a Blue Note,* 144–55; MacDonald Smith Moore, *Yankee Blues: Musical Culture and American Identity* (Bloomington, Ind., 1985), 1–3, 70–71, 131–60 (Tasker quoted 160); Michael Freedland, *So Let's Hear the Applause* (London, 1984), 22–23 (*Variety* quote). See also Friedman, *Hollywood's Image of the Jew,* 19; Goldman, *Jolson,* 40; Cripps, *Slow Fade to Black,* 223–24; Marilyn Berger, "Irving Berlin, Nation's Songwriter, Dies," *New York Times,* Sept. 23, 1989, 1, 7–8; Philip Furia, "Irving Berlin: Troubadour of Tin Pan Alley," in Taylor, ed., *Inventing Times Square,* 194; Shaw, *Jazz Age,* 47; Isaac Goldberg, *George Gershwin: A Study in American Music* (New York, 1931), 18, 278.

56. Isaac Goldberg, "Aaron Copland and His Jazz," *American Mercury* 12 (Sept. 1927): 63–64; *Baltimore Afro-American,* Sept. 10, 1927, 9. Cf. Diner, *In the Almost Promised Land,* 112–15.

57. Higham, "American Anti-Semitism Historically Reconsidered," 250–51; Diner, *In the Almost Promised Land;* Lewis, *When Harlem Was in Vogue,* 100–102, 148.

58. Howe, *World of Our Fathers,* 563.

59. Ralph Ellison accused Howe of "appearing . . . in blackface" by playing the loyal son of Richard Wright, prescribing the kind of (social protest) fiction that the reprobates Ellison and James Baldwin should write. See Ellison, "The World and the Jug," in *Shadow and Act,* 109–11, 124.

60. This is the claim of Ruth Perlmutter, "The Melting Pot and the Humoring of America: Hollywood and the Jew," *Film Reader* 5 (1982), 248.

61. Goldberg, *George Gershwin,* 41. Howe quotes the equation sympathetically in *World of Our Fathers,* 563.

62. Melnick, *Ancestors and Relatives;* William R. Taylor, "Broadway: The Place That Words Built," in Taylor, ed., *Inventing Times Square,* 212–31. Thirties gangster films and screwball comedies provide the major exceptions to the absence of urban, ethnic, native-born America from the classical Hollywood screen. Although those genres marginalize Jews and blacks, a book about them would suggest rather a different political and aesthetic conjunction between Hollywood and the United States than the one outlined in the present volume. See, for example, Robert Sklar, *City Boys: Cagney, Bogart, Garfield* (Princeton, N.J., 1992).

63. David Levering Lewis, "Parallels and Divergencies: Assimilation Strategies of Afro-American and Jewish Elites from 1910 to the Early 1930s," *Journal of American History* 71 (1974): 544–45. See also Diner, *In the Almost Promised Land,* xii, xvii, 239 (quoted).

64. Carl Engel, "Jazz: A Musical Discussion," *Atlantic Monthly,* Aug. 1922, 182–89. The Gershwin brothers' four violinists were Mischa Ellman, Jasha Heifetz, Tascha Teubel, and Alexander Jacobsen; see Melnick, *Ancestors and Relatives.* On orientalism, blacks, and Jews in general, and for the examples cited in this paragraph, see Joel Williamson, *The Crucible of Race: Black/White Relations in the American South Since Emancipation* (New York, 1984), 111–14; Edward Said, *Orientalism* (New York, 1978); Rogin, "Great Mother Domesticated," 527–28; Lewis, *When Harlem Was in Vogue,* 29, 187–88; Rudolph Fisher, "The Caucasian Storms Harlem," *American Mercury* 11 (Aug. 1927): 393–94; Goldberg, "Aaron Copland and His Jazz," 63; Moore, *Yankee Blues,* 131–36; Hapgood, *Spirit of the Ghetto,* 155; Henry T. Sampson, *Blacks in Blackface: A Sourcebook on Early Black Musical Shows* (Metuchen, N.J., 1980), 6.

65. Raphaelson, "Day of Atonement," 152–53; Fass, *The Damned and the Beautiful,* 482.

66. Raphaelson, "Day of Atonement," 152.

67. Lewis, *When Harlem Was in Vogue,* 44 (Harding quote); Goldman, *Jolson,* 113.

68. "The Jazz Singer," *Variety,* 16. See also Goldman, *Jolson,* 35–36; Gilbert

Seldes, "The Daemonic in the American Theater," in *The Seven Lively Arts* (New York, [1924] 1957), 175–77. Cf. Giddins, *Riding on a Blue Note*, 17.

69. Gilbert, "Costumes of the Mind," 199–201; Showalter, "Critical Cross-Dressing." Cf. Robert J. Stoller, "A Contribution to the Study of Gender Identity," *International Journal of Psychoanalysis* 45 (1964): 220–25; idem, "The Sense of Maleness," *Psychoanalytic Quarterly* 34 (1965): 207–18; Fred Schaffer, "Male Political Hysteria" (seminar paper, University of California, Berkeley, 1987); and above, chapter 2. On the relation between mixed gender and mixed genre, see W. J. T. Mitchell, *Iconology: Image, Text, Ideology* (Chicago, 1986), 104–15.

70. Rank, *The Double*, 4–7, 11, 33, 73. The student's rescue of the count's daughter from a runaway horse, which initiates their tragic romance, is replayed as the tramp's comic fantasy.

71. Erens, *Jew in American Cinema*, 2–3, 47–49; Sanders, *Downtown Jews*, 257–360; Huggins, *Harlem Renaissance*, 298; Furia, "Irving Berlin," 201.

72. Huggins, *Harlem Renaissance*, 298; Cripps, "The Movie Jew as an Image of Assimilation," *Cinema Journal* 4 (summer 1981): 193–203. *The Jazz Singer* appeared before *Green Pastures;* identifying thematic commonality, not historical influence, my interpretation of *Green Pastures* is taken from the 1936 film. White historians universally blamed black dissoluteness for the failure of Reconstruction, with *Birth of a Nation* offering the popular, graphic version. Hence *Green Pastures* was a possible allegory.

73. Siegfried Kracauer, "The Mass Ornament" (1927), *New German Critique* 5 (spring 1975): 67–68. On "The Mass Ornament," see also Patrice Petro, *Joyless Streets: Women and Melodramatic Representation in Weimar Germany* (Princeton, N.J., 1989), 65–66.

74. Petro, *Joyless Streets*, 110–21, 155–58; Jim Pines, *Blacks in Film: A Study of Racial Themes and Images in the American Film* (London, 1975), 17, 19; Williamson, *Crucible of Race;* Fass, *The Damned and the Beautiful*, 482. Jolson invented a blackface trickster servant, Gus, for his Broadway shows; Gus was the name of the lower-class rapist in *Birth of a Nation*.

75. Goldman, *Jolson*, 65, 69; *"Jazz Singer" Souvenir Program*, 6–7; Huggins, *Harlem Renaissance*, 251–56; Seldes, "Daemonic in the American Theater," 178.

76. Carringer, ed., *Jazz Singer*, 120.

77. Friedman, *Hollywood's Image of the Jew*, 23, 50.

78. Rank, *The Double*, 75.

79. Martha Fineman, comment at Center for Twentieth Century Studies, University of Wisconsin, Milwaukee.

80. Perlmutter, "Melting Pot," 249; Wolfe, "Vitaphone Shorts," 76.

81. Sigmund Freud, *Beyond the Pleasure Principle*, in *Standard Edition* 20:8–11.

82. Miles Krueger, ed., *The Movie Musical from Vitaphone to 42nd Street as Reported in a Great Fan Magazine* (New York, 1975), 4; John Higham, *Send These to Me: Immigrants in Urban America* (Baltimore, 1984), 180–87; Steinberg, *Ethnic Myth*, 228.

83. Sophie Tucker, *Some of These Days: The Autobiography of Sophie Tucker*

(Garden City, N.Y., 1945), 2, 112; Jean-Paul Sartre, *Nausea*, trans. Lloyd Alexander (New York, [1938] 1959), 22, 178; Denis Hollier, *Politique de la prose: Jean-Paul Sartre et l'an quarante* (Paris, 1982); Shaw, *Jazz Age*, 168, 176, 203; Whitfield, "Jazz Singers," 20, 22; Howe, *World of Our Fathers*, 561.

84. Shaw, *Jazz Age*, 63; Al Young, "I'd Rather Play a Maid Than Be One," *New York Times Book Review*, Oct. 15, 1989, 13–14; Bogle, *Toms, Coons, Mulattoes, Mammies, and Bucks*, 63, 72; Nella Larsen, *Quicksand* (New Brunswick, N.J., [1927] 1988); Phyllis Rose, *Jazz Cleopatra: Josephine Baker in Her Time* (New York, 1989), 44; Daphne Duval Harrison, *Black Pearls: Blues Queens of the 1920s* (New Brunswick, N.J., 1988), 3–4, 87–88, 179–93, and passim; Rosetta Reisz, liner notes to *Mean Mothers*, Rosetta Records, RR 1300; Hazel Carby, "It Just Be's Dat Way Sometime: The Sexual Politics of Women's Blues," *Radical America* 20 (Apr. 1986): 6–13; Giddins, *Riding on a Blue Note*, 5; Rosa Henderson, "Oh Papa Blues" (1924), and Frances Hereford, "Midnight Mama" (1928), both on *The Blues, 1923–1937*, BBC Records, RFB 683; Sara Martin, "Mean Tight Mama" (1928), *The Immortal King Oliver*, Milestone Records, MLP 2006; Bessie Smith, "Reckless Blues" (1925), *Bessie Smith: The Collection*, CBS Records, 7461-44441; Ma Rainey, "Oh Papa Blues" (1928), *Blues: Ma Rainey*, Riverside Records, RLP 12–108; Hattie McDaniel (with Dentist Jackson), "Dentist Chair Blues" (1929), *Female Blues Singers, Vol. M*, Fantasy Records, SHN-4029.

85. *Women's Railroad Blues* and Rosetta Reisz liner notes, Rosetta Records, RR 1301; Hattie McDaniel, "I Thought I'd Do It" (1927), and Ethel Waters, "No Man's Mama" (1925), with Rosetta Reisz liner notes, *Big Mamas*, Rosetta Records, RR 1306; Ethel Waters, "Get Up Off Your Knees" (1928), *The Blues, 1923–1937*, BBC Records, RFB 683.

86. Zelda Fitzgerald quoted in Nancy Milford, *Zelda* (New York, 1970), 123; thanks to Harry Stecopoulos for calling this comment to my attention. See also Spillers, "Mamma's Baby, Papa's Maybe," 79–80; Ernst Kris, *Psychoanalytic Explorations in Art* (New York, 1952).

87. See Goldman, *Jolson*, 4, 74, on Jolson and his mother. For the link between Kol Nidre and "My Mammy," as for so much in my approach here, I am indebted to Norman Jacobson; however, he would (I am fairly sure) like to be held no more responsible for the analysis than would Cantor Rabinowitz for Jack's music.

88. Rourke, *American Humor*, 95–104.

89. Hoberman, "Is 'The Jazz Singer' Good for the Jews?" 31.

90. Shaw, *Jazz Age*, 41–44; Goldman, *Jolson*, 102; Goldberg, *Gershwin*, 3; Slobin, "Some Intersections of Jews, Music, and Theater," 35 (quoting Raphaelson); Tucker, *Some of These Days*, 34, 38, 62, 139; Leroi Jones [Amiri Baraka], *Blues People: Negro Music in White America* (New York, 1963), 99.

91. For the jazz/speech analogy, see Reed Dickerson, "Hot Music: Rediscovering Jazz," *Harper's*, Apr. 1936, 567–74. Among many examples of the denigration of African American jazz, see Seldes, *Seven Lively Arts*, 67–109; "King Jazz and the Jazz Kings," *Literary Digest*, Jan. 30, 1926, 37–42; Don Knowlton, "The Anatomy of Jazz," *Harper's*, Apr. 1926, 578–85; Henry O. Osgood, *So This Is Jazz* (New York, [1926] 1978); Isaac Goldberg, "Jazz," *Forum*, Apr.

1932, 232–36. Cf. Moore, *Yankee Blues;* Krin Gabbard, *Jamming at the Margins* (University of Chicgo Press, forthcoming), chap. 1. James Lincoln Collier's revisionist interpretation of the reception of jazz, valuable as it is, ignores the racial question in the 1920s; see Collier, *The Reception of Jazz in America: A New View* (Brooklyn, N.Y., 1988). The wish to identify jazz with American freedom by burying the race question also mars the beginning of S. Frederick Starr, *Red and Hot: The Fate of Jazz in the Soviet Union* (New York, 1983). See also the discussion of Paul Whiteman's *The King of Jazz,* below, chapter 5.

92. William T. Shultz, "Jazz," *Nation,* Oct. 25, 1922, 438.

93. Ulrich B. Phillips, *Life and Labor in the Old South* (New York, 1929).

94. Goldman, *Jolson,* 102; Shaw, *Jazz Age,* 109; Austin, *"Susanna," "Jeannie," and "The Old Folks at Home,"* ii, 331; *Oxford English Dictionary,* c.v. "Jazz."

95. Alan Lomax, *Mister Jelly Roll: The Fortunes of Jelly Roll Morton, New Orleans Creole and "Inventor of Jazz,"* 2d ed. (Berkeley, [1950] 1973), xv, 78, 99–100.

96. Gunther Schuller, *Early Jazz: Its Roots and Musical Development* (New York, 1968); Lewis, *When Harlem Was in Vogue,* xv, 171; Newton, *Jazz Scene,* 9, 34, 37, 42, 67, 155–56; Baker, *Blues, Ideology, and Afro-American Literature,* 121; Cripps, *Slow Fade to Black,* 225–28, 253; Paul Whiteman selections, *Bix Beiderbecke, Bix Lives!* Bluebeard Records, 6845-1-RB; Sampson, *Blacks in Blackface,* 54, 133; Samuel B. Charters and Leonard Kunstadt, *Jazz: A History of the New York Scene* (New York, 1981), 246; Paul Oliver, *The Meaning of the Blues* (New York, 1963), 78–82, 260, 329, and Richard Wright's "Foreword" to that volume, 9.

97. Schuller, *Early Jazz,* 252. See also Newton, *Jazz Scene,* 201–2.

98. Raymond Williams, *The Country and the City* (London, 1973); T. J. Clark, *Image of the People: Gustave Courbet and the Second French Republic, 1848–1851* (Greenwich, Conn., 1973), 140–54.

99. Neil Leonard, *Jazz and the White Americans* (Chicago, 1962), 11; Ehrenberg, *Steppin' Out.*

100. Thanks to Michael Fried and Ruth Leys for this perception.

101. D. W. Winnicott, "Transitional Objects and Transitional Phenomena," in *Playing and Reality* (London, 1971), 1–25.

102. Ray, *A Certain Tendency of the Hollywood Cinema,* 29.

103. Sholem Aleichem, *From the Fair,* trans. Carl Leviant (New York, 1985), xi. See also Benjamin Harshav, *The Meaning of Yiddish* (Berkeley, 1990), 108.

104. Garber, *Vested Interests,* 12, 34, 50.

105. See Geza Roheim, *Magic and Schizophrenia* (Bloomington, Ind., 1955); Kaja Silverman, *The Acoustic Mirror: The Female Voice in Psychoanalysis and Cinema* (Bloomington, Ind., 1988), 8–9, 14–24, 45, 52–54, 72–86; Margaret Homans, *Bearing the Word: Language and Female Experience in Nineteenth-Century Women's Writing* (Chicago, 1986).

106. Gorky is quoted in Judith Mayne, "Dracula in the Twilight," in Rentschler, ed., *German Film and Literature,* 37–38.

107. "Hon. Will H. Hays, President of the Motion Picture Producers and Distributors of America, Welcomes Vitaphone, 1926," in *The Dawn of Sound,* ed. Mary Lee Bandy (New York, 1989), 17.

108. Geduld, *Birth of the Talkies,* 123; Peter Chamisso, *Peter Schlemihl,* trans. Sir John Bowring (Columbia, S.C., 1993); Lotte Eisner, *The Haunted Screen* (Berkeley, 1973), 73; Hall, "Al Jolson and the Vitaphone," 24 (for "Mr. Jolson's shadow"); Cripps, *Slow Fade to Black,* 47 (for racist joke).

109. Bogle, *Toms, Coons, Mulattoes, Mammies, and Bucks,* 20–90; Evan William Cameron, introduction to *Sound and the Cinema,* xii–xiii; Bordwell, Staiger, and Thompson, *Classical Hollywood Cinema,* 245–48, 257–58, 302; Gledhill, "Melodramatic Field," 39; Burch, "Narrative/Diegesis—Thresholds, Limits," 19–20; André Bazin, "The Myth of Total Cinema," in *What Is Cinema?* trans. Hugh Gray (Berkeley, 1967), 1:17–40; Geduld, *Birth of Talkies,* 100–101; Gomery, "Hollywood Converts to Sound," 26–33; idem, "Coming of Sound," 234–35; Sarris, "Cultural Guilt of Musical Movies," 41.

110. Hansen, *Babel and Babylon;* Dana Polan, *Power and Paranoia: History, Narrative, and the American Cinema, 1940–1950* (New York, 1986); Jenkins, *What Made Pistachio Nuts?* 96–97 and passim; Rogin, "Great Mother Domesticated," 510–55.

111. Jane Feuer, "The Self-Reflective Musical and the Myth of Entertainment," in *Genre: The Musical,* ed. Rick Altman (London, 1981), 160.

112. Wolfe, "Vitaphone Shorts," 65; Altman, ed., *Genre: The Musical.*

113. Elton Mayo, *The Social Problems of an Industrial Civilization* (Boston, 1945).

114. Kupferberg, "Jazz Singer," 29.

115. Credit Adrienne MacLean for discovering Jolson under the blackface. The photograph can be found in the *Mammy* folder in the stills archive of the Museum of Modern Art, New York.

Chapter 5. Racial Masquerade and Ethnic Assimilation in the Transition to Talking Pictures

1. Sanders, *Downtown Jews,* 104–9.

2. The quotations are from, respectively, Herbert Ward, "Life Among the Congo Savages," *Scribner's,* Feb. 1890, 135, 152–54, 186; and Jacob A. Riis, "How the Other Half Lives: Studies Among the Tenements," *Scribner's,* Dec. 1889, 655, 657, 659. See also Frederick E. Hoxie, "Exploring a Cultural Borderland: Native American Journeys of Discovery in the Early Twentieth Century," *Journal of American History* 79 (Dec. 1992): 969–95; Sanders, *Downtown Jews,* 197–204; Amy Kaplan, *The Social Construction of American Realism* (Chicago, 1988), 109 (Dreiser quote); Curtis, *Apes and Angels.* Sanders identifies Stanley as the author of the article Cahan translated, but Stanley's *Scribner's* article (see note 3) was in fact published the year after the first issue of the *Arbeiter Zeitung.* Ward's travel account, which centers on cannibalism, as Stanley's does not, must be the essay in question. It appeared one month before Cahan's translation. At the same time that Stanley and Ward were reporting from Africa and Riis from the Lower East Side, *Scribner's* also published John G. Bourke's "The American Congo" (May 1894, 590–610), on Mexico. (Thanks to Gaston Alonse Donate for this reference.)

3. Henry M. Stanley," "The Pygmies of the Great African Forest," *Scribner's,*

Jan. 1891, 3, 8, 17. Stanley's *In Darkest Africa,* published in 1890, was a best-seller. On Stanley, see Jeremy Bernstein, "A Critic at Large," *New Yorker,* Dec. 31, 1990, 93–101; and Maria Torgovnick, *Gone Primitive: Savage Intellects, Modern Lives* (Chicago, 1990), 26–33.

4. Jonathan Frankel, *Prophecy and Politics: Socialism, Nationalism, and the Russian Jews, 1862–1917* (New York, 1981), 411 (quoting Cahan), 466–67, 507–8.

5. See Mark Slobin, "From Vilna to Vaudeville: Minikes and *Among the Indians,*" *Drama Review* 24 (Sept. 1980): 17–26; James R. Barrett, "Americanization from the Bottom Up: Immigration and the Remaking of the Working Class in the United States, 1880–1930," *Journal of American History* 79 (Dec. 1992): 1006.

6. Abraham Cahan, *The Rise of David Levinsky* (New York, [1917] 1960), 194, 526, 530. See also Sanders, *Downtown Jews,* 435–48.

7. Raphaelson, *Jazz Singer,* and *"Accent on Youth" and "White Man"* (New York, 1935). (Raphaelson copyrighted *White Man* in 1926 under the title *Harlem Nights.* He could never get it produced.)

8. Hannah Arendt, *Rahel Varnhagen: The Life of a Jewish Woman* (New York, 1974), 204, 208, 214, 219, 225. See also Hanna Pitkin, "Conformism, House-keeping, and the Attack on the Blob," in *Feminist Interpretations of Hannah Arendt,* ed. Bonnie Honig (University Park, Pa., 1995), 51–64.

9. The novel *Imitation of Life,* which centers on the relations between a Jewish employer and her black servant, was influenced by Hurst's relationship with the black writer Zora Neale Hurston. The film converted the Jewish woman into a gentile (played by Claudette Colbert). Hurst also wrote the screenplay for the Jewish generational-conflict film *The Younger Generation* (1929). On Hurst and Hurston, see Gay Wilentz, "White Patron and Black Artist: The Correspondence of Fannie Hurst and Zora Neal Hurston," in *The Library Chronicle* (Austin, Tex., 1986), 21–43. Thanks to Elizabeth Abel for this reference.

10. Raphaelson, *Accent on Youth;* William Paul, *Ernst Lubitsch's American Comedy* (New York, 1983), 20–21, 207, 294. Raphaelson also wrote the screenplays for *Design for Living, Ninotchka,* and *Heaven Can Wait.*

11. Cahan, *Rise of David Levinsky,* 529.

12. See Melnick, *Ancestors and Relatives.*

13. We will return to the civil rights film's version of that contrast in chapter 7.

14. Nasaw, *Going Out,* 167–68.

15. See chapter 4, above; and Gabler, *Empire of Their Own;* May, *Screening Out the Past;* Hansen, *Babel and Babylon,* 64 (Zukor quote).

16. Michael North, *The Dialect of Modernism: Race, Language, and Twentieth-Century Literature* (New York, 1994), 198, lists six 1928 blackface films, to which I have added *The Singing Fool.* North gets his list from William Torbert Leonard, *Masquerade in Black* (Metuchen, N.J., 1986).

17. *Washington Star,* May 5, 1930, and Carl Johnson, *Paul Whiteman: A Chronology* (ms.), 20, both in the Paul Whiteman Collection, Williamsiana Collections, Williams College Archives, Williamstown, Massachusetts; Jenkins, *What Made Pistachio Nuts?* 155. Thanks to William Nestrick for lending me his copy of *The King of Jazz.*

18. See Carroll Smith-Rosenberg, "Dis-Covering the Subject of the 'Great Constitutional Discussion,' 1786–1789," *Journal of American History* 79 (Dec. 1992): 841–73.

19. *Takao Ozawa v. United States,* 260 U.S. 178, cited in Ronald T. Takaki, *Strangers from a Different Shore: A History of Asian Americans* (Boston, 1989), 208; Said, *Orientalism;* William K. Everson, undated program notes, *Old San Francisco* file, Clippings Collection, Pacific Film Archive, University Art Museum, University of California, Berkeley; Norman K. Dorn, "San Francisco from Gold Rush to '06—Warner Bros. Film Revival," *San Francisco Chronicle,* Sept. 9, 1973, "Sunday Date Book" sec., 15, ibid.; Gina Marchetti, *Romance and the "Yellow Peril": Race, Sex, and Discursive Strategies in Hollywood Fiction* (Berkeley, 1993), 2–4, 18–19; Nick Browne, "American Film Theory in the Silent Period: Orientalism as Ideological Form," *Wide Angle* 11 (Oct. 1989), 26–30 (quoted 30); Matthew Bernstein, *Walter Wanger: "Independent" in Hollywood* (Berkeley, 1994), 44–46, 186–91; Rogin, "Great Mother Domesticated," 522–28; Hansen, *Babel and Babylon.*

20. Saxton, *Indispensable Enemy.*

21. Ana M. Lopez, "Are All Latins from Manhattan? Hollywood, Ethnography, and Cultural Colonialism," in Friedman, ed., *Unspeakable Images,* 406–13 ("wily senoritas" is at 406–7); Erens, *Jew in American Cinema,* 64–164.

22. Sollors, *Beyond Ethnicity;* Michel Foucault, *The History of Sexuality,* vol. 1: *An Introduction,* trans. Robert Hurley (New York, 1978), 124.

23. *"Jazz Singer" Souvenir Program,* 13. Oland played the villainous Cesare Borgia in the first feature with Vitaphone sound effects, *Don Juan.* He would go on to star as a Eurasian warlord in Josef von Sternberg's *Shanghai Express* (where he rapes a Chinese woman [Anna May Wong] and brands a white man) and as the sinister Fu Manchu. Relevant to the substitution of Mongol for mogul is the presence of an old, wealthy, German and Sephardic Jewish community in San Francisco, a city where yellow peril fears took the place of anti-Semitism. The substitution of Spanish aristocrats for Latino workers has its analogue in the German Jewish wish not to be made guilty by association with the more recent Jewish immigration from Eastern Europe. See Higham, *Send These to Me,* 164–66.

24. Takaki, *Strangers from a Different Shore,* 102.

25. Riis, "How the Other Half Lives," 155.

26. See William F. Wu, *The Yellow Peril: Chinese Americans in American Fiction, 1850–1940* (Hamden, Conn., 1982); Takaki, *Strangers from a Different Shore,* 14, 41, 121–23. For the identification of the specific 1927 pulp novel by Allie Lowe Miles from which Darryl Zanuck wrote the screenplay for *Old San Francisco,* see Dorn, "San Francisco from Gold Rush to '06," 15.

27. Review of *Old San Francisco,* June 29, 1927, in *Variety Film Reviews, 1907–1980* (New York, 1983), vol. 3, n.p.

28. The godless girl was Sam Warner's widow, Lina Basquette.

29. Cf. Lawrence W. Levine, *Highbrow/Lowbrow: The Emergence of Cultural Hierarchy in America* (Cambridge, Mass., 1988), 171–84, 197–200.

30. Mordaunt Hall, review of *Old San Francisco,* June 22, 1927, in *New York Times Film Reviews* (New York, 1970), 1:372.

31. Lott, *Love and Theft.*

32. Paul Whiteman and Mary Margaret McBride, *Jazz* (New York, 1926), 122; and see above, chapter 4.

33. Seldes, *The Seven Lively Arts*, 98–100; emphasis in the original.

34. "King Jazz and the Jazz Kings," *Literary Digest*, Jan. 30, 1926, 37–42; Whiteman and McBride, *Jazz*, 3–4, 17, 176, 265; Osgood, *So This Is Jazz*. See also William Weaver, "Jazz in Jackets: Cultural Commodification in the Jazz Age" (seminar paper, Johns Hopkins University, 1988); I am indebted to Weaver's paper, and to his comments on a draft of this chapter.

35. Whiteman and McBride, *Jazz*, 15, 19, 27–28, 122–27, 178, 237.

36. Shaw, *Jazz Age*, 47–53.

37. Goldberg, *George Gershwin*, quoted 136; Creighton Peet, "The Movies," *Outlook and Independent*, May 14, 1930, 72; Whiteman and McBride, *Jazz*, 94–99. "We enslaved the Negroes's body; he helped to liberate our soul," wrote Goldberg (*Gershwin*, 47).

38. Whiteman and McBride, *Jazz*, 178–79.

39. *Washington Star*, May 10, 1930, in Whiteman Collection, Williams College.

40. "Porky in Whackyland" can be found cross-referenced under Jolson in the Film and Television Archive, University of California, Los Angeles.

41. *Wall Street Journal*, May 5, 1930; *New York Post*, May 5, 1930; *Brooklyn Eagle*, May 5, 1930, all in Whiteman Collection, Williams College.

42. Goldberg, "Aaron Copland and His Jazz," 63–64.

43. Peet, "Movies," 72.

44. Richard Dana Skinner, review of *The King of Jazz*, *Commonweal*, May 21, 1930, 80; Peet, "Movies," 72; review of *The King of Jazz*, *Variety*, May 3, 1930, in *Variety Film Reviews*, vol. 3, n.p.; review of *The King of Jazz*, *Nation*, May 28, 1930, 633; review of *The King of Jazz*, *Time*, May 12, 1930, 64.

45. Barrett, "Americanization from the Bottom Up," 996; Erens, *Jew in American Cinema*, 61; "The Melting Pot," in American Film Institute, *Catalogue: Feature Films, 1911–1920* (Berkeley, 1988); Mordaunt Hall, review of *The King of Jazz*, May 30, 1930, in *New York Times Film Reviews* 1:623; Whiteman and McBride, *Jazz*, 15; "King of Jazz," *Photoplay*, June 1930, 56, in Anthony Slide, ed., *Selected Film Criticism, 1921–1930* (Metuchen, N.J., 1982) 157.

46. Sollors, *Beyond Ethnicity*, 75–99; Whiteman and McBride, *Jazz*, 17.

47. See above, chapter 4. Box office figures are from Everson, *American Silent Film*, 373–74.

48. Cf. Edward Baron Turk, *Child of Paradise: Marcel Carné and the Golden Age of French Cinema* (Cambridge, Mass., 1989), 310–11.

49. Jolson and his young dancer wife, Ruby Keeler, called the son they adopted after the release of *The Singing Fool* Sonny Boy. When Keeler left Jolson, she took the child with her. A story circulated that when Sonny Boy later saw Jolson and was asked if he knew who he was, the child replied, "A Jew." See *American Weekly*, May 7, 1933, Jolson file, MPAAS; Goldman, *Jolson*, 222, 229.

50. Richard Koszarski, "On the Record: Seeing and Hearing Vitaphone," in Bandy, ed., *Dawn of Sound*, 18; Bordwell, Staiger, and Thompson, *Classical Hollywood Cinema*, 3–39; Tony Berman, *"Jolson Sings Again," Classic Images*, Mar. 1986, 51.

51. André Bazin, "The Ontology of the Photographic Image," in *What Is Cinema?* 1:9–16. See also "Hon. Will H. Hays . . . Welcomes Vitaphone, 1926," 17.

52. Nasaw, *Going Out*, 233; Hansen, *Babel and Babylon*, 245–94.

53. Sollors, *Beyond Ethnicity*, 131–48; Charles Musser, "Ethnicity, Role-Playing, and American Film Comedy: From *Chinese Laundry Scene* to *Whoopee!* (1894–1930)," and Ella Shohat, "Ethnics-in-Relation: Toward a Multicultural Reading of American Cinema," both in Friedman, ed., *Unspeakable Images*, 62, 230, 245; Eddie Cantor, as told to David Freedman, *My Life Is in Your Hands* (New York, 1928). (I am indebted to Mark Slobin for directing me to this source.) *Whoopee!* is also an early example of the male buddy film, pairing a straight, macho man with a clownish feminized cross-dresser (Dean Martin and Jerry Lewis, Bing Crosby and Bob Hope). See Rebecca Bell-Mettereau, *Hollywood Androgyny* (New York, 1985), 23.

54. Sollors, *Beyond Ethnicity*, 132–38; Sarah Blacher Cohen, "Introduction," in Cohen, ed., *From Hester Street to Hollywood*, 2; Cantor, *My Life Is in Your Hands*, 82; Musser, "Ethnicity, Role-Playing, and American Film Comedy," 64.

55. Musser, "Ethnicity, Role-Playing, and American Film Comedy," 62, 43; ad for *Whoopee!*, *New Yorker*, Oct. 4, 1930, 87.

56. Cantor, *My Life Is in Your Hands*, 29–30; Lott, *Love and Theft*.

57. Cantor, *My Life Is in Your Hands*, 44. Ruby Keeler appeared in the Broadway production of *Whoopee!*, and Jolson sang from the audience in her first performance (the incident is borrowed for *The Jolson Story*) to ease her stage fright. Jolson later withdrew Keeler from the show in anger at a Cantor parody of "My Mammy." See *American Weekly*, Dec. 9, 1928, and *Motion Picture Magazine*, Nov. 1947, in Jolson file, MPAAS.

58. Cantor, *My Life Is in Your Hands*, 113–15, 122–23, 159–60; Jenkins, *What Made Pistachio Nuts?* 153–84; William D. Routt and Richard J. Thompson, "Keep Young and Beautiful: Surplus and Subversion in *Roman Scandals*," *Journal of Film and Video* 42 (spring 1990): 17–35. Thanks to Vivian Sobchack for this reference.

59. James Fenimore Cooper, *The Pioneers* (New York, 1823).

60. Cf. Sollors, *Beyond Ethnicity*, 102–38.

61. Otto Friedrich, *City of Nets* (Glasgow, 1987), 354–56; Routt and Thompson, "Keep Young and Beautiful," 24–27; Jenkins, *What Made Pistachio Nuts?*

62. Lenny Bruce's Jewish/goyish monologue is legendary. I heard it in Chicago, ca. 1960. Musser, "Ethnicity, Role-Playing, and American Film Comedy," celebrates ethnic performance as a vehicle for American self-making. Although I have learned and borrowed from Musser's rich essay, which I read after completing a draft of this chapter, he takes a sunnier view of the material.

63. No African American put on Jewface in a Hollywood film, to my knowledge, until Eddie Murphy's Jewish barber in *Coming to America*. (Thanks to Ed Guerrero for telling me about it.) When Spike Lee turned the Jewish blackface tables in *Mo' Better Blues* (1990), with barbed, comic ethnic stereotypes of two brothers in the entertainment business, Josh and Joe Flatbush, the outcry about anti-Semitism sounded in a historical vacuum. See Caryn James, "Spike Lee's

Jews and Charges of Racism," *New York Times,* Aug. 16, 1990, B1, B3; "Spike Lee Film Under Fire," *San Francisco Chronicle,* Aug. 7, 1990, E1.

64. Cantor, *My Life Is in Your Hands,* 40, 44, 186–87; Jenkins, *What Made Pistachio Nuts?,* 90.

65. Cantor, *My Life Is in Your Hands,* 292–95.

66. Charles Musser ("Ethnicity, Role-Playing, and American Film Comedy," 66–67) described the barbershop quartet, inspiring me to see *Animal Crackers* again and discover that the Marx Brothers had already written this chapter. That *Animal Crackers* was in part a deliberate parody of *My Life Is in Your Hands* is indicated by Chico's Irish chiropodist tune, "My fayt is in your hands."

Chapter 6. New Deal Blackface

1. Erwin Leiser, *Nazi Cinema* (New York, 1974), 80–82; David Stuart Hull, *Film in the Third Reich: Art and Propaganda in Nazi Germany* (Berkeley, 1969), 205.

2. Leiser, *Nazi Cinema,* 82 (quoting *The Rothschilds*).

3. David Welch, *Propaganda and the German Cinema, 1933–1945* (Oxford, 1987), 285–90. See also *Triumph of the Will,* Leni Riefenstahl's film of the 1934 Nuremberg Nazi Party Congress; and Moishe Postone, "Anti-Semitism and National Socialism: Notes on the German Reaction to 'Holocaust,' " *New German Critique* 19 (winter 1980): 97–115.

4. Hull, *Film in the Third Reich,* 215–16; Welch, *Propaganda and the German Cinema,* 285.

5. Angrily obsessed with the success of *Gone with the Wind,* Goebbels tried until the end of the war to make a German equivalent. *Kolberg,* also directed by Harlan, is said to be Goebbels's answer to the Selznick production. I have not seen *Kolberg,* and rely on visual evidence for *Die goldene Stadt's* indebtedness to *Gone with the Wind.* See Hull, *Film in the Third Reich,* 179, 182, 212, 218. In preparation for the 1996 Olympics, to be held in Atlanta, the German corporation Daimler-Benz is planning to buy and restore the apartment building where Margaret Mitchell wrote *Gone With the Wind.* See Jerry Schwartz, "Margaret Mitchell's Atlanta Home Gets a Reprieve," *New York Times,* Dec. 16, 1994, 18.

6. *"Gone with the Wind" Souvenir Program,* in *Souvenir Programs of Twelve Classic Movies.*

7. Carlton Jackson, *Hattie: The Life of Hattie McDaniel* (New York, 1990), 35, 46–48.

8. Bette Davis, whose role in *Jezebel* anticipates Scarlett O'Hara, briefly initiates a subversive bond with her slaves; see Edward Villaluz Guerrero, "The Ideology and Politics of Black Representation" (Ph.D. diss., University of California, Berkeley, 1989).

9. Taylor Branch, *Parting the Waters: America in the King Years* (New York, 1988), 54–55.

10. See Ely, *Adventures of Amos 'n' Andy.*

11. Gunther Schuller, *The Swing Era: The Development of Jazz, 1931–1945*

(New York, 1989), 8. See also David Stowe, *Swing Changes: Big Band Jazz in New Deal America* (Cambridge, Mass., 1994), 121–30; Jake Bowers, "Benny Goodman: An Exploration of the Role of Race in the Representation of the 'King of Swing' " (seminar paper, University of California, Berkeley, 1994).

12. See Schatz, *Genius of the System*, 243, 261; Gerald Early, *The Culture of Bruising: Essays on Prizefighting, Literature, and Modern American Culture* (Hopewell, N.J., 1994), 280–85; Snead, *White Screens/Black Images*, 47–66; Doris Kearns Goodwin, *No Ordinary Time—Franklin and Eleanor Roosevelt: The Home Front in World War II* (New York, 1994), 218.

13. Joel Williamson's powerful *The Crucible of Race* (New York, 1984) distinguishes progressive paternalism from racist savagery, locating Griffith and his supporter, Woodrow Wilson, in the former camp; but the Thomas Dixon/Griffith collaboration on *Birth*, the character of that film, and Williamson's own account of Dixon trouble the distinction he is trying to maintain. See my " 'The Sword Became a Flashing Vision.' "

14. Jackson, *Hattie*, 41–43.

15. Ibid., 49–51; Patricia Storace, "Look Away, Dixie Land," *New York Review of Books*, Dec. 19, 1991, 24–37; John D. Stevens, "The Black Reaction to *Gone with the Wind*," *Journal of Popular Film* 2 (fall 1973): 367; Al Young, "I'd Rather Play a Maid Than Be One," *New York Times Book Review*, Oct. 15, 1989, 14. Carleton Moss will play an important role in chapter 7, below. His mistake is reported in Jackson.

16. Jackson, *Hattie*, 95.

17. Ibid., xii, 12–16, 65–71, 95, 122.

18. Roediger, *Wages of Whiteness*; Ely, *Adventures of Amos 'n' Andy*, 64–96. Repeating the pattern of *The Jazz Singer*, Selznick's determination to make the great American epic, *Gone with the Wind*, was in part a rebellion against his Jewish mogul father-in-law, Louis B. Mayer. Selznick was on the way to leaving his Jewish wife, Mayer's daughter, for the younger gentile actress, Jennifer Jones. See Schatz, *Genius of the System*, 332–39.

19. Jane Feuer, "The Self-Reflective Musical and the Myth of Entertainment," in Altman, ed., *Genre: The Musical*, 160.

20. Jim Kitses, *Horizons West: Anthony Mann, Budd Boetticher, Sam Peckinpah—Studies of Authorship Within the Western* (London, 1969), 8. See also Schatz, *Hollywood Genres*; John G. Cawelti, "*Chinatown* and Generic Transformation in Recent American Films," in *Film Theory and Criticism: Introductory Readings*, 3d ed., ed. Gerald Mast and Marshall Cohen (New York, 1985), 515.

21. Don Carle Gilette, "Burnt Cork the Sincerest Form of Flattery," Los Angeles *Times*, July 31, 1977, in Jolson file, MPAAS.

22. Robin Wood, "Ideology, Genre, Author," in Mast and Cohen, eds., *Film Theory*, 475–85; Vivian Sobchack, "Child/Alien/Father: Patriarchal Crisis and Generic Exchange," *Camera Obscura* 15 (1986): 6–34.

23. The importance of the social problem film in the Progressive Era is indicated in Koszarski, *An Evening's Entertainment*, 187. Nor did the genre disappear in the depression decade, which generated *I Am a Fugitive from a Chain Gang* (1932), *Wild Boys of the Road* (1933), and *The Grapes of Wrath* (1940). However, even taking notice of the unprecedented sight of black prisoners on

Fugitive's chain gang and in *Sullivan's Travels* (1941), no 1930s social problem film foregrounded race; indeed, almost all made it invisible.

24. Opening title of *The Younger Generation*.

25. Erens, *Jew in American Cinema*, 43–97, 140–45; Cripps, *Slow Fade to Black*, 269; Daniel J. Leab, *From Sambo to Superspade* (Boston, 1975), 116; Wolfe, "Vitaphone Shorts"; Toll, *Blacking Up*, 1–5. The Italian immigrant Frank Capra directed *The Younger Generation*. The movie imitates Samuel Goldfish's name change to Goldwyn by having the parvenu son change his name from Morris Goldfish to Maurice Fish. Was David Lodge quoting this film when he named the protagonist of *Changing Places: A Tale of Two Campuses* (New York, 1978), modeled on one-time Berkeley English professors Stanley Fish and Larzer Ziff, Morris Zapp?

26. Campbell, *Celluloid South;* Warren French, ed., *The South and Film* (Jackson, Miss., 1981); Bogle, *Toms, Coons, Mulattoes, Mammies, and Bucks*, 26–90; Cripps, *Slow Fade to Black*, 254–96, 357–59; Altman, ed., *Genre: The Musical*. As Cripps points out, sound also gave African Americans musical access to the screen. King Vidor's first sound film was the all-black *Hallelulah* (1929).

27. Mark Roth, "Some Warners Musicals and the Spirit of the New Deal," in Altman, ed., *Genre: The Musical*, 42–46; Rick Altman, "A Semantic/Syntactic Approach to Film Genre," in *Film Genre Reader*, ed. Barry Keith Grant (Austin, Tex., 1986), 34–35. *Gold Diggers of 1933* and *42nd Street* were, unlike *The Jazz Singer*, musical comedies. "The Kentucky Hillbillies," who speak with New York accents, try to get a job in the *Gold Diggers* show. "You know 'Your Old Kentucky Home'?" asks the producer. "You bet." "Then go back to it. Your mammy's waiting for you."

28. Geoffrey Perrett, *Days of Sadness, Years of Triumph: The American People, 1939–1945* (Madison, Wis., 1985), 243; Furia, "Irving Berlin," 208; " 'Gone with the Wind' Champ Again," *Variety*, May 4, 1983, 15. Thirties comedian comedies, descended from vaudeville and driven by virtuoso performances rather than plot, also often featured blackface, usually in musical numbers. Eddie Cantor was the major film blackface comedian, and examples of the genre that employ blackface include his *Whoopee!* (1931), *Palmy Days* (1931), *Roman Scandals* (1933), and *Ali Baba Goes to Town* (1937), as well as Bert Wheeler and Robert Woolsey's *Diplomaniacs* (1933) and the Marx Brothers' *Day at the Races* (1937). See Jenkins, *What Made Pistachio Nuts?*

29. Ray, *A Certain Tendency of the Hollywood Cinema*, 130, 287; Doug McLelland, *From Blackface to Blacklist: Al Jolson, Larry Parks, and "The Jolson Story"* (Metuchen, N.J., 1987), 79; Robert Edelman, "*Home of the Brave*," in *McGill's Survey of Cinema, 2d series*, ed. Frank V. McGill (Englewood Cliffs, N.J., 1981), 3:1047; J. Douglas Gomery, "Al Jolson," in *Actors and Actresses*, James Vinson (Chicago, 1986), 335–36; Don Miller, "Films on TV," *Films in Review*, July 1962, in *Jolson Story* file, MPAAS; undated, unidentified clipping, in *Jolson Sings Again* file, Pacific Film Archive, University Art Museum, University of California, Berkeley. Frank Capra's *It's a Wonderful Life* shared Academy Award attention with *The Jolson Story* and *Best Years of Our Lives*, but it did not have their box office success. It was two decades before Hollywood had a better year at the box office than 1946.

30. On *Duel in the Sun,* see Schatz, *Genius of the System,* 405–7. *Duel in the Sun* was released the same year as *Gilda,* and the far subtler, more powerful, less degraded persona and performance of Rita Hayworth, compared to those of Jennifer Jones, are partly explained by the absence of Hayworth's half-Mexican parentage from the diegesis of the film.

31. *Body and Soul,* discussed in chapter 7, a social problem boxing film focusing on the Jewish/African American bond rather than race prejudice per se, comes at the beginning of the cycle, which continued with *No Way Out* (1950), Sidney Poitier's first film; there are few other examples (the 1955 *Blackboard Jungle* is one) until the end of the decade, with Stanley Kramer's successor to *Home of the Brave, The Defiant Ones* (1958), and Douglas Sirk's remake of *Imitation of Life* (1959). Although the black man wrongly accused of murder in *Intruder in the Dust* is "the keeper of . . . our conscience" (the actual criminal is a parricide), *Intruder in the Dust* is the only one of these films that does not entirely fit within the category of civil rights blackface that I will be analyzing. Cf. Ellison, *Shadow and Act,* 279–80. The problem picture continued to enjoy box office success in the 1950s, more than it had in the 1930s, but race was almost never the problem. See Ray, *A Certain Tendency of the Hollywood Cinema,* 144.

32. Joy Gould Boyum, *Wall Street Journal,* Sept. 8, 1975, in *Jolson Story* file, MPAAS.

33. Riv Ellen Prel, "Anxiety and Intimacy: Making American Jewish Families in the 1930s" (paper presented at the meeting of the American Studies Association, Nov. 6–9, 1992, Costa Mesa, Calif.); Glazer and Moynihan, *Beyond the Melting Pot.*

34. I do not mean to identify the civil rights film with the perspective of all Jews fighting for civil rights. When in the next chapter I refer to the "Jewish solution" to the problem of discrimination, I mean that imagined for Jews by Hollywood civil rights films. Many Jews in the 1940s endorsed neither the separation of Jewish achievement from radical, collective struggle nor Hollywood's form of the Jewish/black homology. Nonetheless, as we shall see, these movies expose trouble in the civil rights perspective and the Jewish/black alliance that goes beyond motion pictures.

35. See Larry Rogin lecture reported in Ray Kochler, "Labor Educator Cites '34 Lesson," *Reading Times,* Nov. 10, 1984, 17, 32; Snead, *White Screens/Black Images,* 31.

36. See Snead, *White Screens/Black Images,* 47–66.

37. Jackson, *Hattie,* 23; Dudley Nichols and Lamar Trotti, "Irving Cobb's Judge Priest in *The Band Played Dixie,*" Apr. 2, 1934, screenplay manuscript in Lilly Library, Indiana University, Bloomington.

38. Nichols and Trotti, "Irving Cobb's Judge Priest"; Huggins, *Harlem Renaissance,* 260. Louis Armstrong, elected an honorary member of the New Orleans Pelicans baseball team, got in trouble in this period for momentarily forgetting himself and boasting about a forthcoming game: "We're going to take them like Grant took Richmond." See Stanley P. Hirshon, "Jazz, Segregation, and Desegregation," in *A Master's Due: Essays in Honor of David Herbert Donald,* ed. William J. Cooper et al. (Baton Rouge, La., 1985), 235.

39. Bernard Wolfe, "Uncle Remus and the Malevolent Rabbit," *Commen-*

tary 8 (July 1949): 31. On *Blonde Venus,* see Snead, *White Screens/Black Images,* 71–73.

40. Bogle, *Toms, Coons, Mulattoes, Mammies, and Bucks,* 63.

41. Goodwin, *No Ordinary Time,* 15 (on Warm Springs); Saxton, *Rise and Fall of the White Republic,* 165–82 (on Democratic Party minstrelsy).

42. Boskin, *Sambo,* 88 (USO quotation); David Lardner, "Democracy and Burnt Cork," *New Yorker,* July 3, 1943, 38.

43. *Variety,* Nov. 19, 1949, Sept. 17, 1950; *Motion Picture Herald,* Sept. 29, 1949; *Los Angeles Times,* Oct. 24, 25, 28, 1950; *Hollywood Citizen News,* Oct. 24, 1950; *Los Angeles Examiner,* Oct. 25, 1950; all in Jolson file, MPAAS.

44. Karl Marx, *Capital* (New York, 1906), 1:82–83; Sigmund Freud, "Fetishism," in *Collected Papers,* ed. and trans. James Strachey, Joan Riviere, and Alix Strachey (London, 1959), 5:199; Garber, *Vested Interests,* 121, 209, 249–50; Ellen Willis, *A Primer for Daily Life* (New York, 1991), 124–25.

45. "Film Actors Learn the Origins of 'Ham,' " *Columbia Pictures News,* undated [1946] clipping, in *Jolson Story* file, MPAAS; Gates, *Figures in Black,* 235–46; Ellison, "Change the Joke and Slip the Yoke," 45–59.

46. Wolfe, "Uncle Remus and the Malevolent Rabbit," 32.

47. Jim Collins, "Towards Defining a Matrix of the Musical Comedy: The Place of the Spectator Within the Textual Mechanisms," in Altman, ed., *Genre: The Musical,* 137–43; Carol J. Clover, "Dancin' in the Rain," *Critical Inquiry* 21 (summer 1995): 739, note 47.

48. Unidentified clipping, Sept. 17, 1930, in *Big Boy* file, MPAAS.

49. Al Jolson, "Maaaaam-my! Maaaaamy! The Famous Mammy-Singer Explores His Native(?) Sunny Southland," *Vanity Fair,* Apr. 1925, in Jolson file, MPAAS. Cf. the discussion in North, *Dialect of Modernism,* 7.

50. *American Weekly,* Dec. 9, 25, 1928, in Jolson file, MPAAS.

51. Robert Benchley, *Vanity Fair,* in Jolson file, MPAAS; Seldes, "The Daemonic in the American Theater," 166, 175–83.

52. See Jenkins, *What Made Pistachio Nuts?* 153–84.

53. Lipsitz, *Time Passages,* 39–76.

54. David Wyman, *The Abandonment of the Jews: America and the Holocaust* (New York, 1984); Al Jolson, "The Best Role I Ever Had," *Coronet,* Aug. 31, 1946, and "AL JOLSON DIES," *Los Angeles Times,* Oct. 24, 1950, in Jolson file, MPAAS. Forty years after Jolson's death, one New York Jew remembered a friend mourning the entertainer because "he was a good Jew." The reminiscer had also loved *The Jolson Story* as a child, but he preferred to celebrate Jolson not for "sectarian" reasons but because "he sang 'Mammy' like nobody's business" (quoted in Sara Beshtel and Alan Graubard, *Saving Remnants: Feeling Jewish in America* [New York, 1992], 41).

55. Mary Ann Doane, "Dark Continents; Epistemologies of Racial and Sexual Difference in Psychoanalysis and the Cinema," in *Femmes Fatales: Feminism, Film Theory, Psychoanalysis* (New York, 1991), 231–33; Jackson, *Hattie,* 31.

56. Martha Wolfenstein, "The Emergence of Fun Morality," *Journal of Social Issues* 7 (Nov. 1951): 15–25; Arlie Hochschild, *The Managed Heart: Commercialization of Human Feeling* (Berkeley, 1983). Elmer Rice, whose urban

drama of ethnic types, *Street Scene,* was scripted for Hollywood by Lillian Hellman, adapted *Holiday Inn* for the screen.

57. Lipsitz, *Time Passages,* 53.

58. *American Weekly,* Dec. 9, 1928, in Jolson file, MPAAS; Goldman, *Jolson,* 274.

59. Among many other sources, see Barbara Ehrenreich, *The Hearts of Men: American Dreams and the Flight from Commitment* (Garden City, N.Y., 1983). Gussie's promotion of Wham looks backward to Louise Beavers's role as the pancake maker Aunt Delilah in the 1934 *Imitation of Life* (see chapter 5), and forward to Whoopi Goldberg in the 1994 *Corrina, Corrina* (see chapter 4). When mammy returned to the 1950s screen, in Douglas Sirk's 1959 remake of *Imitation of Life,* she served to reproach the white career woman (see chapter 7).

60. *Life,* July 5, 1943, 8–10, 80–90. See also Boskin, *Sambo,* 89–90.

61. Undated *New York Age* clippings in author's possession.

62. Ely, *Adventures of Amos 'n' Andy,* 160–93; Cripps, *Slow Fade to Black.*

63. *Baltimore Afro-American,* May 12, 1928; *Amsterdam News* (New York), May 2, 1928, 6; *Pittsburgh Courier,* June 25, 1927; Floyd C. Covington, "The Negro Invades Hollywood," *Opportunity,* Apr. 1929, 111–13. See also Cripps, *Slow Fade to Black,* 40, 106, 219; Lewis, *When Harlem Was in Vogue,* 98, 163, 182.

64. Grabbard, *Jamming at the Margins,* chap. 5; "Duke's Music for Amos 'n' Andy," *Amsterdam News,* July 7, 1930, in Allon Schoerer, ed., *Harlem on My Mind* (New York, 1968), 131. On the *Chicago Defender* parade, see Ely, *Adventures of Amos 'n' Andy,* 4.

65. Ely, *Strange Adventures of Amos 'n' Andy,* 125, 167; *Amsterdam News,* May 2, 1928, 6; Cripps, *Slow Fade to Black,* 257.

66. Perrett, *Days of Sadness, Years of Triumph,* 11; Ely, *Adventures of Amos 'n' Andy,* 202–44; Marjorie P. Lasky, "Off-Camera: A History of the Screen Actor's Guild During the Era of the Studio System" (Ph.D. diss., University of California, Davis, 1992), 278–79, 301–9, 315; Boskin, *Sambo,* 198–200; *Motion Picture Herald,* Mar. 15, 1947, in Jolson file, MPAAS.

67. Jackson, *Hattie,* 95–120; Dalton Trumbo, "Blackface, Hollywood Style," *Crisis* 50 (Dec. 1943): 365–67, 378; John Lovell Jr., "Negro Drama: Double Take," *Crisis* 54 (Nov. 1947): 336; L. D. Reddick, "Educational Programs for the Improvement of Race Relations: Motion Pictures, Radio, the Press, Libraries," *Journal of Negro Education* 13 (summer 1944): 372.

68. Phil Carter, "It's Only Make Believe," *Crisis* 53 (Feb. 1946): 44.

69. Boskin, *Sambo,* 198; Snead, *White Screens/Black Images,* 81; Jackson, *Hattie,* 95–120; Ely, *Adventures of Amos 'n' Andy,* 160–245.

70. *Motion Picture Herald,* Mar. 15, 1947, in *Jolson Story* file, MPAAS.

71. Cf. Jane Feuer, *The Hollywood Musical* (Bloomington, Ind., 1982), 102–8; Lipsitz, *Time Passages;* Lhamon, *Deliberate Speed,* 23, 31–99; Nasaw, *Going Out,* 245–48. On Jerry Lewis I am indebted to material provided by George Lipsitz.

72. Cf. Leo Braudy, *The World in a Frame* (Garden City, N.Y., 1976), 238–39.

73. Goldman, *Jolson*, 230–31; McLelland, *From Blackface to Blacklist*, 87; Alan Williams, "The Musical Film and Recorded Popular Music," in Altman, ed., *Genre: The Musical*, 147–50.

74. The real Jolson was in this scene, too, as an anonymous member of the audience of actors watching (along with the man playing him) the man playing him; see Braudy, *World in a Frame*, 238–39.

75. Columbia Pictures could easily have made Parks-as-Jolson look older than Parks-as-Parks. In this period of the biopic and the life story, great attention was paid to the use of makeup to suggest aging. Compare the two Larry Parkses in *Jolson Sings Again* to, for example, Bette Davis and Claude Rains as they grow old in *Mr. Skeffington* (discussed in chapter 7).

76. Goldman, *Jolson*, 285.

77. Jacques Lacan, "The Mirror Stage as Formative of the Function of the I as Revealed in Psychoanalytic Experience," in *Ecrits*, 1–7.

78. My analysis of Freed's career adds race to the illuminating account in Schatz, *Hollywood Genres*, 193–220, esp. 193–4, 207–8, 220.

79. Cf. "Black Up for That Blackout on Broadway" with the Jimmy Rushing/Count Basie number "Lose the Blackout Blues," recorded in Hollywood almost simultaneously with the release of the movie. Rushing's version can be heard on *Stars of the Apollo Theater*, CBS Records 67203.

80. See James Naremore, *The Films of Vincente Minelli* (New York, 1993), 51–70.

81. *Singin' in the Rain* was the only musical and one of only two talkies (the other was *Citizen Kane*) to rank in a 1976 poll of film critics and historians among the top ten "most important and unappreciated" American films. Film critics in the 1982 *Sight and Sound* fiftieth-anniversary poll ranked *Singin' in the Rain* the fourth best film of all time, behind *Citizen Kane, Rules of the Game,* and *The Seven Samurai.* See Koszarski, *An Evening's Entertainment*, 317–18; Peter Wollen, *Singin' in the Rain* (London, 1992), 9. Wollen himself offers a splendid appreciation of *Singin' in the Rain,* stressing the film's roots in Popular Front culture.

82. "Pulling the Plug on Lina Lamont," an unpublished paper written a decade ago, first alerted me to the anti-ethnic theme in *Singin' in the Rain.* I regret being unable to remember the author, or to discover a publication.

83. The discussion that follows—what could be more appropriate?—steals from the brilliant analysis in Clover, "Dancin' in the Rain," 722–47.

84. Michael North begins his recent *The Dialect of Modernism* (3–8)—I discovered after writing this chapter—with the whitening of *Singin' in the Rain.* Although his fine discussion compares the film with its source, *The Jazz Singer,* North does not discuss the film's indebtedness to black dance. That is the core of Clover's analysis (see note 83), which I do not repeat here.

85. Schatz, *Hollywood Genres*, 215–16.

86. Wollen, *Singin' in the Rain*, 55.

87. Cf. Silverman, *Acoustic Mirror*, 45–57; Mollie Haskell, *From Reverence to Rape: The Treatment of Women in the Movies* (New York, 1987), 189–230; Sarah Grimke, *Letters on the Equality of the Sexes and the Condition of Women* (Boston, 1838).

Chapter 7. "We Could Cross These Racial Lines"

1. Sarah Blacher Cohen, "Yiddish Origins and Jewish-American Transformations," in Cohen, ed., *From Hester Street to Hollywood,* 12–13; Erens, *Jew in American Cinema,* 125–85; Sklar, *City Boys,* 81.

2. "They Won't Forget," *Variety Film Reviews,* June 30, 1937.

3. Gregg Mitchell, *The Campaign of the Century* (New York, 1992), 415–16.

4. Cripps, *Making Movies Black,* 30–94; Sklar, *City Boys,* 138. Thanks to Amy Kaplan for alerting me to *Mr. Skeffington.*

Hangmen Also Die, the 1943 Fritz Lang/"Bert Brecht"/Hanns Eissler collaboration that fictionalizes the hunt for the man who killed Reinhard Heydrich, contains but a single reference to a "Jew" (as among those Czechs taken hostage); in this film, the "inferior race" persecuted by the Nazis is Czech. (To be sure, it would not have been known to the filmmakers that Heydrich was in charge of the final solution, and he was better known in 1943 for the massacre of the inhabitants of the Czech village of Lidice than for his extermination of Jews; nonetheless, *Hangmen Also Die* is evidence for the fact that, like the country's political institutions, Hollywood turned away from Nazi anti-Semitism in its characterization of the war.)

5. Samuel J. Rosenthal, "Golden Boychik: Star-Audience Relations Between John Garfield and the Contemporary American Jewish Community" (master's thesis, Annenberg School of Communication, University of Pennsylvania, 1993), 25.

6. Review of *Humoresque, Variety,* Dec. 15, 1946. There was at least one more generational-conflict film in the late 1940s, *The House of Strangers* (1949). In that film Jewish actors played members of an Italian American family.

7. On Hollywood and HUAC, see Larry Ceplair and Steven Englund, *The Inquisition in Hollywood: Politics in the Film Community, 1930–1960* (Berkeley, 1983), 421 and passim; Victor Navasky, *Naming Names* (New York, 1980); Rogin, *"Ronald Reagan," the Movie,* 27–30. Unlike Lee, Revere, and Polonsky, Rossen and Garfield were not blacklisted. Garfield's struggle to appear as a cooperative witness before HUAC while refusing to name names ended with his death in 1952. The next year Rossen testified before the committee and was allowed to continue making movies. See Sklar, *City Boys,* 183–88; Rosenthal, "Golden Boychik," 90, 131–32.

8. Erens, *Jew in American Cinema,* 125–85. Garfield first starred as a Jew in *Humoresque,* but I have already discussed the elimination of Jewishness from that film. To be fair to Rossen's role in *They Won't Forget,* he was working from a novel of the same title that had already Christianized Leo Frank.

9. The films are *Pinky, Lost Boundaries, Home of the Brave, Intruder in the Dust* (all 1949), and *No Way Out* (1950); *Pinky* and *Home of the Brave* are discussed below. On *Crossfire,* see Rogin, *"Ronald Reagan," the Movie,* 255–57.

10. Cripps, *Making Movies Black,* 214.

11. Enterprise Studios was an independent production company set up by Garfield; it made two films before the blacklist, *Body and Soul* and the Polonsky/Garfield production *Force of Evil.* According to Polonsky, film studios worried about suits from people with the same name as movie villains. Bob Roberts

was Garfield's agent. Saying "I won't sue you," he suggested the use of his own name (Abraham Polonsky, telephone interview, Apr. 18, 1995). See also Michael Shepler, *"Body and Soul,"* in *McGill's Survey of Cinema, 1st Series,* ed. Frank V. McGill (Englewood Cliffs, N.J., 1980), 1:195–97. When Tim Robbins named his 1992 political satire *Bob Roberts,* he was surely referencing *Body and Soul.*

12. Augmenting the documentary effect, Shimin Rishkin was played by a Jewish comedian of the same name. See Rosenthal, "Golden Boychick," 99.

13. Polonsky interview.

14. Ibid.; Tuttle, *"Daddy's Gone to War,"* 184; Early, *Culture of Bruising;* Shepler, *"Body and Soul,"* 195–6. For instruction in boxing history, I am indebted to conversations with Early and with Norman Jacobson.

15. Early, *Culture of Bruising,* 10–38, 91; Harry Carpenter, *Masters of Boxing* (New York, 1964), 55.

16. Garfield's first Hollywood role was in a Fannie Hurst screenplay, *Four Daughters* (1938). In his last role onstage, in the 1951 Broadway revival of *Golden Boy,* he finally got to play Joe Bonaparte. Since Bonaparte was torn between boxing and the violin, he united the roles split for Garfield between *Body and Soul* and *Humoresque.* On Garfield and *Golden Boy,* see Sklar, *City Boys,* 82; Rosenthal, "Golden Boychik," 31, 131.

17. The Jewish boxer Benny Leonard had beaten the black fighter Kid Chocolate (I learned from Norman Jacobson) for the lightweight crown in the 1920s. Thanks to Isabelle Rogin for a discussion about the play and film of *Golden Boy.*

18. Leslie Fiedler, "Come Back to the Raft Ag'in, Huck Honey!" *Partisan Review,* June 1948 (reprinted in *An End to Innocence* [Boston, 1952]), and *Love and Death.* Cf. Lott, *Love and Theft.*

19. Lewis Ehrenberg, "Impressions of Broadway Night Life," in Taylor, ed., *Inventing Times Square,* 176; Billie Holiday, "Strange Fruit," and liner notes, *Billie Holiday,* Commodore Records CCK 7001, and *Lady in Autumn: The Best of the Verve Years,* Polygram 849 43614; Polonsky interview (Polonsky did not attend the Los Angeles concert, however). Thanks to Jonathan Buchsbaum for first alerting me to the opening shot.

20. Early, *Culture of Bruising,* 37.

21. Although *Body and Soul* was Robeson's first film, and although he traveled in the same circles as the makers of the Garfield film, the source of that movie's title may rather have been an obscure 1931 James Cagney movie, also *Body and Soul.* Polonsky could not remember in 1995 from which earlier film the title of his was taken. See Polonsky interview; Sklar, *City Boys,* 279; Snead, *White Screens/Black Images,* 113; Martin Bauml Duberman, *Paul Robeson* (New York, 1988), 77. Thanks to Jane Gaines and Stephen Best for the Micheaux connection.

22. On "Body and Soul," the music, see *The Smithsonian Collection of Classic Jazz,* selected and annotated by Martin Williams, Columbia Records P6 11891 (Washington, D.C., 1973), side 4 and p. 24; Billie Holiday, "Body and Soul," *Lady in Autumn,* Polgram 849 43614; Polonsky interview. Polonsky does not remember the music as an important issue in the film. Holiday had recorded with the Teddy Wilson orchestra in the late 1930s.

23. *New York Times,* Mar. 28, 1994, C11, C16 (quote).

24. James Baldwin, "The Image of the Negro," *Commentary* 5 (Apr. 1948): 379–80; Bogle, *Toms, Coons, Mulattoes, Mammies, and Bucks,* 213–15.

25. Cf. Musser, "Ethnicity, Role-Playing, and American Film Comedy," 39–81; Hortense Powdermaker, *Hollywood: The Dream Factory* (Boston, 1950); Philip Rieff, *The Triumph of the Therapeutic* (New York, 1966).

26. Dorn, "San Francisco from Gold Rush to '06"; Cripps, *Making Movies Black,* 55; Elliot Cohen, "Mr. Zanuck's *Gentleman's Agreement*," *Commentary* 5 (Jan. 1948): 51–56; "Ladies, What Would You Do?" *Life,* Oct. 17, 1949, 112–15. Thanks to Herbert Hill for the reminder about 20th Century Fox.

27. Connie McFealy, "*Pinky,*" in McGill, ed., *McGill's Survey of Cinema, 1st ser.* 3:1346.

28. Ralph Ellison, "The Shadow and the Act," in *Shadow and Act,* 279–80; Roland Barthes, *Mythologies,* trans. Annette Lavers (New York, 1972), 129. Ellison was the first to bring together the four 1949 films for analysis, and I am indebted throughout to "The Shadow and the Act."

29. Baldwin, "Image of the Negro," 379–80; Ellison, *Shadow and Act,* 278–79.

30. Chester Himes, "To End All Stories," *Crisis* 55 (July 1948): 205–7, 220.

31. Loren Berlant, "National Brands/National Body: *Imitation of Life,*" in *Comparative American Identities: Race, Sex, and Nationality in the Modern Text,* ed. Hortense J. Spillers (New York, 1991), 110–41.

32. Joel Williamson, *New People* (New York, 1980), 142–70.

33. See the essays in Gledhill, ed., *Home Is Where the Heart Is.*

34. Arthur Laurents, *Home of the Brave* (New York, 1945). Laurents would go on to write the libretto for *West Side Story.*

35. *Time,* May 9, 1949, 100; John Mason Brown, *Saturday Review of Literature,* June 11, 1949, 26–27. For the contrary view, see Manny Farber, *Nation,* May 21, 1949, 590. See also *Variety,* May 4, 1949, in *Variety Film Reviews,* 8.

36. Daniel James, "A New Coalition in U.S. Politics," *Jewish Frontier* 19 (Nov. 1952): 5–9; Ted Poston, "The Race Riots in Cicero," *Jewish Frontier* 18 (Aug. 1951): 5–10 (6 quoted). See, from *Crisis,* Jacob Panken, "A Northern Judge Looks at the South," 54 (Feb. 1947): 42; untitled, 53 (Sept. 1946): 276; "What Happened at Columbia," 53 (Apr. 1946): 110–11; Joseph H. Genrie, "Roosevelt College and Democracy," 55 (Feb. 1948): 45–46; untitled, 54 (Oct. 1947): 297. And from *Commentary,* see Felix S. Cohen, "The People vs. Discrimination," 1 (Mar. 1946): 17–22; Malcolm Ross, "The Outlook for a New FEPC," 3 (Apr. 1947): 301–8; Charles Abrams, "Homes for Aryans Only," 3 (May 1947): 421–27; Maurice J. Goldbloom, "The President's Civil Rights Report," 4 (Dec. 1947): 559–67; Felix S. Cohen, "Alaska's Nurenberg Laws," 6 (Aug. 1948): 136–38; James A. Wechsler and Nancy F. Wechsler, "The Road Ahead for Civil Rights," 6 (Oct. 1948): 297–304; Charles Abrams, "The Segregation Threat in Housing," 7 (Feb. 1949): 123–26.

37. Panken, "A Northern Judge Looks at the South," 60; Harold P. Reese, "The Klan's 'Revolution of the Right,' " *Crisis* 54 (July 1946): 202–3; Kenneth Clark, "Candor About Negro-Jewish Relations," *Commentary* 1 (Feb. 1946) 8–14; James Baldwin, "Previous Condition," *Commentary* 6 (Oct. 1948):

334–42; idem, "The Death of the Prophet," *Commentary* 9 (Mar. 1950): 257–61. Baldwin's first story addressed the problem of friendship between an African American and a Jew; in the second story, a Jewish boy, by introducing the protagonist to the movies, initiates his rift with his fundamentalist preacher father. (Baldwin retells that story as autobiography, indicating his father's anti-Semitism, in *The Fire Next Time* [New York, 1963], 53–54.) The deathbed confrontation between unforgiving father and terrified son offers an unredemptive version of *The Jazz Singer*.

38. See Lewis, "Parallels and Divergencies," 543–64.

39. Roy Wilkins, "Still a Jim Crow Army," *Crisis* 53 (Apr. 1946): 106–8 (quoting army report); Richard Polenberg, *One Nation Divisible: Class, Race, and Ethnicity in the United States Since 1938* (New York, 1980), 76, 112–14. However, blacks and whites did work together in the Army Corps of Engineers, and *Bataan*'s black soldier among whites was precedent for *Home*. See Cripps, *Making Movies Black*, 72. Challenged by white southern support for the segregationist States Rights Party, and by African American and Jewish support for Henry Wallace, Truman owed his 1948 victory to massive black majorities in Cleveland, Chicago, and Los Angeles. See Polenberg, *One Nation Divisible*, 108.

40. Tom Schatz, presentation on the war film to the Film Group, Humanities Research Institute, University of California, Irvine, Nov. 11, 1992; Clayton R. Koppes and Gregory D. Black, *America Goes to War* (New York, 1987).

41. Quoted in Polenberg, *One Nation Divisible*, 47.

42. Cripps, *Making Movies Black*, 22, 106–8, 125, 222–23.

43. The two adolescents were Tom Schatz and myself. Watching *Home of the Brave* again forty years later with Tom Schatz and Carol Clover decisively influenced my understanding of the film. See also Clover, *Men, Women, and Chain Saws*.

44. Mary Ann Doane, *The Desire to Desire: The Woman's Film of the 1940s* (Bloomington, Ind., 1987); Siegfried Kracauer, "Psychiatry for Everything and Everybody," *Commentary* 5 (Mar. 1948): 222–28. James Agee (*Nation*, Nov. 19, 1946, 536–37) reviewed a doctor/female-divided-self film, *The Dark Mirror*, alongside *The Jolson Story*, perhaps sensing the invasive doubling that doctor/female-patient movies share with blackface. Doane associates *Home of the Brave* with the medical-discourse subgenre of the postwar woman's film in "Dark Continents," 295.

45. Schatz, seminar on the war film; Rebecca Plant, "The Menace of Momism: Psychiatry and the Anti-Woman Backlash in the Post–World War II Era" (seminar paper, Johns Hopkins University, 1992), 16–21; Polan, *Power and Paranoia;* Kaja Silverman, *Male Subjectivity at the Margins* (New York, 1992), 52–90.

46. Silverman, *Male Subjectivity at the Margins*, 52–54, 63–90; Mary Ovington, *Half a Man* (New York, 1911); Manny Farber, "Films," *Nation*, Aug. 21, 1949, 590–91; Frantz Fanon, *The Wretched of the Earth*, trans. Constance Farrington (New York, 1961). During the black/Jewish Crown Heights conflict of the early 1990s, there were New York City police who called Mayor David Dinkins a "nigger" and who carried signs announcing that his "true color" was "yellowbellied" (see Elliot Cose, *The Rage of a Privileged Class* [New York, 1993], 28).

47. Although Fanon interprets racial oppression psychoanalytically, he cites *Home of the Brave* to illustrate his distrust of most "talk of psychoanalysis in connection with the Negro" (Fanon, *Black Skin, White Masks,* 150–51). Fanon had yet to develop his *Wretched of the Earth* alternative. "Whites don't want you to be angry," observed Basil Patterson half a century after *Home of the Brave* (quoted in Cose, *Rage of a Privileged Class,* 31).

48. Clover, *Men, Women, and Chain Saws,* 18.

49. Richard M. Clurman, "Training Film for Democrats," *Commentary* 8 (Aug. 1949): 182; Robert Hatch, "Good Intention," *New Republic,* May 16, 1949, 22; Fiedler, "Come Back to the Raft Ag'in, Huck Honey!"; Ellison, *Shadow and Act,* 51. Two recent critical and popular successes that offer variations on the caretaking, feminizing theme are *Driving Miss Daisy* (1990) and *The Crying Game* (1992).

Until he visited amputees in military hospitals during World War II, Franklin Roosevelt only once let himself be seen publicly as unable to walk. Dedicating a new building at Howard University, FDR agreed to show his solidarity with the black students who, as the president of Howard put it, "had been so crippled themselves." See Goodwin, *No Ordinary Time,* 532–33.

50. " 'Jolson Sings Again,' " *Life,* Sept. 12, 1949, 96; Gabler, *Empire of Their Own,* 351–86; Sklar, *City Boys,* 220–21; Navasky, *Naming Names;* Eric Bentley, ed., *Thirty Years of Treason: Excerpts from Hearings Before the House Committee on Un-American Activities, 1938–1968* (New York, 1971), 299; Garber, *Vested Interests,* 224. Thanks to Leo Braudy for suggesting I look at Parks's HUAC testimony.

51. Bentley, ed., *Thirty Years of Treason,* 309–40. While Parks was naming names before HUAC, in a futile effort to save his career, Gene Kelly left the country for a year and a half to avoid the blacklist. When he returned, he was given clearance to continue to make movies. See Wollen, *Singin' in the Rain,* 43–51.

52. Bentley, ed., *Thirty Years of Treason,* 340–45.

53. Clurman, "Training Film for Democrats," 183; Lipsitz, *Time Passages,* 64–65; Edelman, *"Home of the Brave,"* 1047.

54. See Peter Brooks, *The Melodramatic Imagination: Balzac, Henry James, Melodrama, and the Mode of Excess* (New Haven, Conn., 1976), applied to American racial melodrama in Linda Williams's presentation to the Film Group, Humanities Research Institute, University of California, Irvine, Nov. 18, 1992.

55. Perrett, *Days of Sadness, Years of Triumph,* 37.

56. Abram Kardiner and Lionel Ovesey, *The Mark of Oppression* (New York, 1951); Stanley Elkins, *Slavery: A Problem in American Institutional and Intellectual Life* (Chicago, 1959); Lee Rainwater and William Yancey, *The Moynihan Report and the Politics of Controversy* (Cambridge, Mass., 1967). Elkins labels his contribution "the damage hypothesis" in his third edition ([Chicago, 1976], 267–70). He described the army genesis of *Slavery* to me in personal conversation. For Ralph Ellison, the flight from acts of racial injustice to psychological shadows produces a phantom Negro in the white mind, the shadow who substitutes for actual black Americans. Ellison is turning the white supremacist trope of the black as "shadow" on its head. See *Shadow and Act,* 277–78. For Ellison's critique of Elkins, see " 'A Very Stern Discipline': An In-

terview with Ralph Ellison," *Harper's,* Mar. 1967, 76–95, and *Shadow and Act,* 303–17.

57. Schatz, in his seminar on the war film, differentiated World War II from Vietnam War movies on this score.

58. J. Wilvey, *Crisis* 53 (Sept. 1946): 281.

59. For *Crisis* analyses of the Jim Crow army, see especially Wilkins, "Still a Jim Crow Army," 106–8; and three pieces by Grant Reynolds, "What the Negro Soldier Thinks About This War," 51 (Sept. 1944): 289–91, 299, "What the Negro Soldier Thinks About the War Department," 51 (Oct. 1944): 316–18, 328, "What the Negro Soldier Thinks," 51 (Nov. 1944): 342–43, 353. See also Amy Kaplan, "Black and Blue on San Juan Hill," in *Cultures of Imperialism,* ed. Amy Kaplan and Donald Pease (Chapel Hill, N.C., 1993), 219–36; Saxton, *Rise and Fall of the White Republic,* 370–76.

60. Reynolds, "What the Negro Soldier Thinks About the War Department," 317, and "What the Negro Soldier Thinks About This War," 289. Kramer's shooting title for *Home* was *High Noon.* The film Kramer and Fred Zinneman finally called *High Noon* was his allegorical attack on Hollywood for refusing to stand behind those targeted by HUAC; nonetheless, the antipopulism of the Gary Cooper film was foreshadowed by *Home.* See Robert Warshaw, *The Immediate Experience: Movies, Comics, Theater, and Other Aspects of Popular Culture* (New York, 1975), 148–49.

61. Reynolds, "What the Negro Soldier Thinks," 353. See also Goodwin, *No Ordinary Time,* 523–24. "The Port Chicago Mutiny" was finally being filmed half a century later, with Harry Belafonte as director; see "A Film Turns the Tables on Race Relations," *New York Times,* Feb. 6, 1995, B4.

62. Reynolds, "What the Negro Soldier Thinks," 353; Max Lerner, *Crisis* 55 (May 1948): 155.

Chapter 8. Conclusion

1. Quoted in Cheryl Greenberg, "Class Tensions and the Black/Jewish Alliance, 1930–1960" (paper delivered at the Organization of American Historians, Atlanta, 1994), 17.

2. Laurence Thomas, "Group Autonomy and Narrative Identity: Blacks and Jews," in Berman, ed., *Blacks and Jews,* 287.

3. For the distinction between solidarity at work and neighborhood ethnic particularism, see Ira Katznelson, *City Trenches: Urban Politics and the Patterning of Class in the United States* (New York, 1981).

4. Morton M. Hunt, "The Battle of Abington Township," *Commentary* 9 (Mar. 1950): 234–43.

5. See the letters from Elwyn Silverman and Robert K. Greenfield, *Commentary* 9 (June 1950): 585–86, and 10 (Sept. 1950): 286, respectively.

6. Norman Mailer's notorious defense of the hipster as "white Negro" was originally published in *Dissent* (summer 1957). It is reprinted in Mailer, *Advertisements for Myself* (New York, 1959), 311–31.

7. Like Negroes, wrote Baldwin, "Jews must try to cover their vulnerability

by a frenzied adoption of the customs of the country; and the nation's treatment of Negroes is unquestionably custom." As for the Negro, "in his dilemma he turns first upon himself and then upon whoever most represents to him his own emasculation. . . . A society must have a scapegoat. . . . Georgia has the Negro and Harlem has the Jew" (James Baldwin, "The Harlem Ghetto," *Commentary* 6 [Feb. 1949]: 168–70). See also Clark, "Candor About Negro-Jewish Relations," 8–14; and Greenberg, "Class Tensions and the Black/Jewish Alliance."

8. See Arnold M. Rose, *The Negro's Morale* (Minneapolis, 1949), 128–40.

9. "Hollywood Abandons Negro Stereotype in *Home of the Brave*," *Crisis* 56 (June 1949): 180; Manny Farber, "Films," *Nation,* Aug. 21, 1949, 590–91; Clurman, "Training Film for Democrats," 181–83.

10. Martha Wolfenstein and Nathan Leites, "The Unconscious vs. the 'Message' in an Anti-Bias Film," *Commentary* 10 (Oct. 1950): 388–90.

11. My characterization of *Commentary* is the result of reading the magazine from its inception in November 1945 through 1951. For the repudiation of Henry Wallace by *Crisis,* see "Editorial," 55 (Feb. 1948): 41; "For or Against Wallace," 55 (Apr. 1948): 106; untitled, 55 (Aug. 1948): 245–47; "Editorial," 55 (Dec. 1948): 361.

12. Diana Trilling assaulted *Gentleman's Agreement,* the book, on those grounds in *Commentary;* in Elliot Cohen's movie review, distaste for the Popular Front may have been overridden by what Cohen thought was good for the Jews. No such inhibition protected *Home of the Brave* once the black soldier replaced the Jew, and *Commentary*'s negative response to the sentimental male bonding was also inflected by homophobia. See Diana Trilling, "*Gentleman's Agreement,*" *Commentary* 3 (Mar. 1947): 290–92, and letter, 3 (Apr. 1947): 386–88; Elliot Cohen, "Mr. Zanuck's *Gentleman's Agreement,*" *Commentary* 5 (Jan. 1948): 51–56; Clurman, "Training Film for Democrats," 181–82. For critiques of Popular Front culture, see Warshaw, *Immediate Experience;* Leslie Fiedler, *An End to Innocence* (Boston, 1952). Andrew Ross attacks the anti-Stalinist left's hostility to popular culture, from a latter-day Popular Front perspective, in *No Respect: Intellectuals and Popular Culture* (New York, 1989). For the political evolution of the New York intellectuals, see (among many other sources) Alan Wald, *The Rise and Decline of the Anti-Stalinist Left from the 1930s to the 1980s* (Chapel Hill, N.C., 1987).

13. Cf. Lewis, "Parallels and Divergencies," 543–64; Clayborne Carson, "The Politics of Relations Between African-Americans and Jews," in Berman, ed., *Blacks and Jews,* 131–43.

14. Lester B. Granger, "Does the Negro Want Integration?" *Crisis* 58 (Feb. 1951): 76.

15. "Hollywood Abandons Negro Stereotype," 56, 180. See also Gates, "Trope of a New Negro."

16. Untitled, *Crisis* 57 (Jan. 1950): 8; Stevens, "Black Reaction to *Gone with the Wind*," 361–72; Cripps, *Making Movies Black,* 18–23.

17. *Crisis* made up for that oversight a few months later with a lead essay on Edwards; see Duane Valentry, "Local Boy Makes Good," *Crisis* 56 (Nov. 1949): 313, 354–55.

18. "Hollywood Abandons Negro Stereotype," 180; "Movie of the Week," *Life*, May 23, 1949, 143–44; "*Home of the Brave*," *Time*, May 9, 1949, 100.

19. Stokely Carmichael, "What We Want," *New York Review of Books*, Sept. 22, 1966, 5–8. SNCC, the Student Nonviolent Coordinating Committee, was the most important militant civil rights group of the early 1960s.

20. Baldwin, "Image of the Negro," "Harlem Ghetto," and "Too Late, Too Late," *Commentary* 7 (Jan. 1949): 97–99.

21. See Sklar, *City Boys*, 203–15; Wollen, *Singin' in the Rain*, 43–51; Gabler, *Empire of Their Own*, 326–86; Ronald Radosh and Joyce Milton, *The Rosenberg File: A Search for Truth* (New York, 1983), 277–79, 352–55, 428–30; Rogin, "*Ronald Reagan*," *the Movie*, 275–79; Suchoff, "The Rosenberg Case and the New York Intellectuals," 155–69.

22. In my first book, *The Intellectuals and McCarthy*, I argued that because the New York intellectuals supported the Korean War, they overlooked its role in spreading the domestic anti-Communist hysteria.

23. James Rorty and Winifred Rauschenbusch, "The Lessons of the Peekskill Riots," *Commentary* 10 (Oct. 1950): 309–23. See also Rogin, "*Ronald Reagan*," *the Movie*, 261–62.

24. Rorty and Rauschenbusch, "Lessons of the Peekskill Riots," 312, 320, 321; see also letters, *Commentary* 10 (Dec. 1950): 595–96. *Crisis* (56 [Oct. 1949]: 213), by contrast, although it attacked "Communists and their stooges," wrote that Paul Robeson "had as much right to sing 'Ole Man River' at the lakeside picnic grounds in Peekskill, New York, as he had to warble 'The Song of the Warsaw Ghetto' several months ago . . . in Moscow's Gorky Park."

25. Oscar Handlin, "Party Maneuvers and Civil Rights Realities," *Commentary* 14 (Sept. 1952): 228–36, and "How U.S. Anti-Semitism Really Began," *Commentary* 11 (June 1951): 541–48. My *Intellectuals and McCarthy* was an attack on this view. On "the American creed," see Myrdal, *An American Dilemma*.

26. Oscar Handlin and Mary F. Handlin, "Origins of the Southern Labor System," *William and Mary Quarterly*, 3d ser., 7 (Apr. 1950): 199–223. See also Rogin, *Intellectuals and McCarthy*, and "*Ronald Reagan*," *the Movie*, 275–79.

27. Nathan Glazer, "Negroes and Jews: The New Challenge to Pluralism," *Commentary* 38 (Dec. 1964): 29–34. For the discussion in this paragraph and the next I rely especially on Herbert Hill, "Blacks and Jews: The Labor Context" (paper delivered at the conference "Blacks and Jews: The American Historical Perspective," Washington University, St. Louis, Dec. 2–4, 1993). Hill, a Jewish radical, was labor secretary of the NAACP during the ILGWU conflict. See also Carson, "The Politics of Relations Between African-Americans and Jews," 138–39.

28. See Clayborne Carson, "Blacks and Jews in the Civil Rights Movement: The Case of SNCC," in Salzman, ed., *Bridges and Boundaries*, 36.

29. Babette Stiefel, "Look Away, Dixie Land," *Crisis* 53 (Aug. 1946): 207, 217–19.

30. E. Franklin Frazier, "Significant Study of Negro Urban Life," *Crisis* 53 (Jan. 1946): 25–26.

31. Beshtel and Graubard, *Saving Remnants,* 65; Stember et al., *Jews in the Mind of America,* 8, 53–57, 102–5, 125–64, 377–85.

32. Massey and Denton, *American Apartheid,* 2–57 (quoted 2, 51–52 [FHA quote]; table at 46).

33. Lipsitz, *Time Passages,* 37 (quoting FHA); Abrams, "Segregation Threat in Housing," 123–24; Massey and Denton, *American Apartheid.*

34. Daniel Patrick Moynihan, "The Negro Family: The Case for National Action" (1965), in Rainwater and Yancey, *Moynihan Report,* 44, 55, 56, 75, 76, 80–81, 84–86; Toni Morrison, "Introduction: Friday on the Potomac," in Morrison, ed., *Race-ing Justice,* xv. (On the demonization of the black mother in contemporary political discourse, see also in that volume Nell Irvin Painter, "Hill, Thomas, and the Use of Racial Stereotype," 200–214; Christine Stansell, "White Feminists and Black Realities: The Politics of Authenticity," 251–68; and Wahneema Lubiano, "Black Ladies, Welfare Queens, and State Minstrels: Ideological War by Narrative Means," 323–63.) This is hardly the place to elaborate the subsequent influence of the Moynihan Report. Although the now senior senator from New York remains himself one of only eleven Senate members who continue to support welfare entitlements for the children of unwed mothers, he observed on the thirtieth anniversary of his original report that the high percentage of children born out of wedlock "marked such a change in the human condition that biologists would talk of a 'speciation'—the creation of a new species." Children of two-parent families and the offspring of black matriarchs, Moynihan was suggesting, would no longer belong to a single human race. *Speciation* is the Darwinian word for the evolution of a population that (the wish?) cannot interbreed with the species from which it developed. The senator was regressing from explanations of racial inequality that used social scientific theories of culture to the biological language of scientific racism. See Todd S. Purdum, "The Newest Moynihan," *New York Times Magazine,* Aug. 7, 1994, 36; *New York Times,* Sept. 3, 1994, 22; Robert Pear, "Moynihan Promises Something Different on Welfare," *New York Times,* May 14, 1995, A13.

35. Moynihan most often cited *Slavery* by quoting from the introduction to the paperback edition, which was written by his own co-author on *Beyond the Melting Pot,* Nathan Glazer. See Elkins, *Slavery;* and Moynihan, "Negro Family," 49, 51, 61–62.

36. Moynihan, "Negro Family," 86.

37. "Perverted patriarchy" is Elkins's term for slavery in the United States (*Slavery,* 104).

38. See Rogin, *"Ronald Reagan," the Movie,* 236–71.

39. Moynihan, "Negro Family," 86, 88–89. In another turn of the screw, Moynihan was proposing to subject African American men to the total institution that, Elkins reported (see above, chapter 7, n. 56), had led him to see the similarity between slavery and the concentration camp. Moynihan's claim that the "United States Armed Forces" treated the black man "not as a Negro equal to any white, but as one man equal to any man in a world where the category 'Negro' and 'white' do not exist"—extraordinary on its face given the history of the Jim Crow military—was also contradicted by his own data. He attributed the lower percentage of African Americans in the armed forces than in the pop-

ulation as a whole to their high failure rate on the army intelligence test; his data, however, in fact showed that blacks were *over* represented in the army compared to their proportions in the population. What brought the total figure down was the scarcity of blacks in the marines and, especially, the notoriously color-conscious navy. See "Negro Family," 86–88.

Is it the result of coincidence or irony, the personal or the historical unconscious, that the end of *Blackface, White Noise* can be read as retracting the advertisement for the MIT Press volume containing the Moynihan Report that (as Gaston Alonse Donate reminds me) appeared on the back cover of my first book, *The Intellectuals and McCarthy*?

40. John A. Williams, *Captain Blackman* (Garden City, N.Y., 1972), 336. Thanks to Amy Kaplan for introducing me to this novel. Would either Moynihan or Williams, far-seeing as they were, have imagined General Colin Powell commanding the American armed forces during the Gulf War or contemplating a run for the Presidency?

Films Cited

Abie's Irish Rose, dir. Victor Fleming (Paramount, 1929)

Abie's Irish Rose, dir. Edward A. Sutherland (United Artists, 1946)

Al Jolson in a Plantation Act (Warner Bros., 1926)

An American in Paris, dir. Vincente Minnelli (MGM, 1951)

Animal Crackers, dir. Victor Heerman (Paramount, 1930)

Babes in Arms, dir. Busby Berkeley (MGM, 1939)

Babes on Broadway, dir. Busby Berkeley (MGM, 1941)

The Band Wagon, dir. Vincente Minnelli (MGM, 1953)

Bataan, dir. Tay Garnett (MGM, 1942)

The Battle of Elderbush Gulch, dir. D. W. Griffith (Biograph, 1913)

The Best Years of Our Lives, dir. William Wyler (Goldwyn, 1946)

Big Boy, dir. Alan Crosland (Warner Bros., 1930)

The Birth of a Nation, dir. D. W. Griffith (Epoch, 1915)

Blackboard Jungle, dir. Richard Brooks (MGM, 1955)

Blazing Saddles, dir. Mel Brooks (Warner Bros., 1974)

Blonde Venus, dir. Josef von Sternberg (Paramount, 1932)

Bob Roberts, dir. Tim Robbins (Paramount, 1992)

Body and Soul, dir. Oscar Micheaux (Micheaux Film Corp., 1924)

Body and Soul, dir. Alfred Santell (Warner Bros., 1931)

Body and Soul, dir. Robert Rossen (Enterprise Studios, 1947)

Breaking Point, dir. Michael Curtiz (Warner Bros., 1950)

Bullets over Broadway, dir. Woody Allen (Miramax, 1994)

317

Cabin in the Sky, dir. Vincente Minnelli (MGM, 1943)

Check and Double Check, dir. Melville Brown (RKO, 1930)

Coming to America, dir. John Landis (Paramount, 1988)

Corrina, Corrina, dir. Jessie Nelson (New Line Cinema, 1994)

Crossfire, dir. Edward Dmytryk (RKO, 1947)

The Crying Game, dir. Neil Jordan (Miramax, 1992)

Dances with Wolves, dir. Kevin Costner (Orion, 1990)

Dark Mirror, dir. Robert Siodmak (Universal, 1946)

Dark Victory, dir. Edmund Goulding (Warner Bros., 1939)

A Day at the Races, dir. Sam Wood (MGM, 1937)

The Defiant Ones, dir. Stanley Kramer (United Artists, 1958)

Design for Living, dir. Ernst Lubitsch (Paramount, 1933)

Diplomaniacs, dir. William Selter (RKO, 1933)

Disraeli, dir. Alfred E. Green (Warner Bros., 1929)

Dixie, dir. Anthony Mann (Paramount, 1943)

Driving Miss Daisy, dir. Bruce Beresford (Warner Bros., 1989)

Don Juan, dir. Alan Crosland (Warner Bros., 1926)

Duel in the Sun, dir. King Vidor (Selznick, 1946)

The Eddie Cantor Story, dir. Alfred E. Green (Warner Bros., 1953)

The Emile Zola Story, dir. William Dieterle (Warner Bros., 1937)

Emperor Jones, dir. Dudley Murphy (Britain, 1933)

The First Auto, dir. Roy Del Ruth (Warner Bros., 1926)

The Fights of Nations (American Mutoscope and Bioscope, 1907)

Forrest Gump, dir. Robert Zemeckis (Paramount, 1994)

42nd Street, dir. Lloyd Bacon (Warner Bros., 1933)

Gentleman's Agreement, dir. Elia Kazan (Twentieth Century Fox, 1947)

The Ghost Goes West, dir. René Clair (United Artists, 1935)

Gilda, dir. Charles Vidor (Columbia, 1946)

Go into Your Dance, dir. Archie L. Mayo (Warner Bros., 1935)

The Godless Girl, dir. Cecil B. DeMille (C. B. DeMille Productions, 1928)

Gold Diggers of 1933, dir. Mervyn Le Roy (Warner Bros., 1933)

Golden Boy, dir. Rouben Mamoulian (Columbia, 1938)

Die goldene Stadt, dir. Veit Harlan (Ufa, 1942)

Gone with the Wind, dir. Victor Fleming (MGM, 1939)

The Grapes of Wrath, dir. John Ford (Twentieth Century Fox, 1940)

The Great Dictator, dir. Charles Chaplin (United Artists, 1940)

The Great Train Robbery, dir. Edwin S. Porter (Edison, 1903)

Green Pastures, dir. Marc Connelly and William Keighley (Warner Bros., 1936)

The Guilt of Janet Ames, dir. Henry Levin (Columbia, 1947)

Hallelulah, dir. King Vidor (MGM, 1929)

Hangmen Also Die, dir. Fritz Lang (United Artists, 1943)

Heaven Can Wait, dir. Ernst Lubitsch (Paramount, 1943)

High Noon, dir. Fred Zinneman (United Artists, 1952)

Holiday Inn, dir. Mark Sandrich (Paramount, 1942)

Home of the Brave, dir. Mark Robson (United Artists, 1949)

House of Strangers, dir. Joseph L. Mankiewicz (Fox, 1949)

Humoresque, dir. Frank Borsage (Cosmopolitan, 1920)

Humoresque, dir. Jean Nogelesco (Warner Bros., 1946)

I Am a Fugitive from a Chain Gang, dir. Mervyn Le Roy (Warner Bros., 1932)

The Idle Class, dir. Charles Chaplin (First National, 1921)

I Dream of Jeannie, dir. Alan Dwan (Republic, 1952)

I Love to Singa (Warner Bros., 1936)

Imitation of Life, dir. John M. Stahl (Universal, 1934)

Imitation of Life, dir. Douglas Sirk (Universal, 1959)

Intolerance, dir. D. W. Griffith (Griffith, 1916)

Intruder in the Dust, dir. Clarence Brown (MGM, 1949)

It's a Wonderful Life, dir. Frank Capra (RKO, 1946)

The Jazz Singer, dir. Alan Crosland (Warner Bros., 1927)

The Jazz Singer, dir. Michael Curtiz (Warner Bros., 1952)

The Jazz Singer, dir. Richard Fleischer (AFO, 1980)

Jezebel, dir. William Wyler (Warner Bros., 1938)

Jolson Sings Again, dir. Henry Levin (Columbia, 1949)

The Jolson Story, dir. Alfred E. Green (Columbia, 1946)

Judge Priest, dir. John Ford (Warner Bros., 1934)

Judith of Bethulia, dir. D. W. Griffith (Biograph, 1914)

Jud Süss, dir. Veit Harlan (Terra, 1940)

Just Around the Corner, dir. David Butler (Twentieth Century Fox, 1938)

The King of Jazz, dir. John Murray Anderson (Universal, 1930)

Kolberg, dir. Veit Harlan (Ufa, 1945)

Kramer vs. Kramer, dir. Robert Benton (Columbia, 1979)

Levisky's Holiday (1913)

The Life of an American Fireman, dir. Edwin S. Porter (Edison, 1902)

The Little Colonel, dir. David Butler (Twentieth Century Fox, 1935)

The Little Shop of Horrors, dir. Roger Corman (Film Group, 1960)

Little Shop of Horrors, dir. Frank Oz (Warner Bros., 1986)

The Littlest Rebel, dir. David Butler (Twentieth Century Fox, 1935)

Lost Boundaries, dir. Alfred M. Werker (De Roademont, 1949)

Made in America, dir. Richard Benjamin (Warner Bros. 1993)

Mammy, dir. Michael Curtiz (Warner Bros., 1930)

Meet Me in St. Louis, dir. Vincente Minnelli (MGM, 1944)

The Melting Pot, dir. James Vincent and Oliver D. Bailey (Cort Film, 1915)

Mister Blandings Builds His Dream House, dir. H. C. Potter (RKO, 1948)

Mister Skeffington, dir. Vincent Sherman (Warner Bros., 1944)

Mo' Better Blues, dir. Spike Lee (Forty Acres and a Mule, 1990)

Monkey Business, dir. Norman Z. McLeod (Paramount, 1931)

Ninotchka, dir. Ernst Lubitsch (MGM, 1939)

Nosferatu, dir. F. W. Murnau (Prana-Film, 1922)

Nothing but a Man, dir. Michael Roemer (Cinema V, 1963)

No Way Out, dir. Joseph L. Mankiewicz (Twentieth Century Fox, 1950)

Now, Voyager, dir. Irving Rapper (Warner Bros., 1942)

Odds Against Tomorrow, dir. Robert Wise (United Artists, 1959)

Old San Francisco, dir. Alan Crosland (Warner Bros., 1927)

Palmy Days, dir. Edward A. Sutherland (Goldwyn, 1931)

Paris Blues, dir. Martin Ritt (United Artists, 1961)

The Passover Miracle (1914)

Pilot Number 5, dir. George Sidney (MGM, 1943)

Pinky, dir. Elia Kazan (Twentieth Century Fox, 1949)

Porky in Whackyland, dir. Carl W. Stalling (Warner Bros., 1938)

Pulp Fiction, dir. Quentin Tarantino (Miramax, 1994)

Rhapsody in Blue, dir. Irving Rapper (Warner Bros. 1945)

Roman Scandals, dir. Frank Tuttle (Goldwyn, 1933)

Say It with Songs, dir. Lloyd Bacon (Warner Bros., 1929)

The Shanghai Express, dir. Josef von Sternberg (Paramount, 1932)

The Sheik, dir. George Melford (Famous Players/Lasky, 1921)

Show Boat, dir. James Whale (Universal, 1936)

Show Boat, dir. George Sydney (MGM, 1951)

Silver Streak, dir. Arthur Hiller (Twentieth Century Fox, 1976)

Singin' in the Rain, dir. Gene Kelly and Stanley Donen (MGM, 1951)

The Singing Fool, dir. Lloyd Bacon (Warner Bros., 1928)

The Singing Kid, dir. William Knightly (Warner Bros., 1936)

Song of the South, dir. Wilfred Jackson (Walt Disney, 1946)

A Star Is Born, dir. George Cukor (Warner Bros., 1954)

Storm Warning, dir. Stuart Heisler (Warner Bros., 1950)

The Story of Vernon and Irene Castle, dir. H. C. Potter (RKO, 1937)

Street Scene, dir. King Vidor (United Artists, 1931)

The Student from Prague, dir. Stellan Rye (Deutsche Bioscop, 1913)

The Student from Prague, dir. Henrik Galeen (H. R. Sokol-Film, 1926)

Sullivan's Travels, dir. Preston Sturges (Paramount, 1941)

Swanee River, dir. Sidney Lanfield (Twentieth Century Fox, 1939)

Swing Time, dir. George Stevens (RKO, 1936)

Symphony of Six Million, dir. Gregory La Cava (RKO, 1932)

The Ten Commandments, dir. Cecil B. DeMille (Famous Players-Lasky, 1923)

They Won't Forget, dir. Mervyn Le Roy (Warner Bros., 1937)

This Is the Army, dir. Michael Curtiz (Warner Bros., 1943)

To Be or Not to Be, dir. Ernst Lubitsch (MGM, 1942)

The Triumph of the Will, dir. Leni Riefenstahl (Ufa, 1934)

Trouble in Paradise, dir. Ernst Lubitsch (Paramount, 1932)

Uncle Tom's Cabin, dir. Edwin S. Porter (Edison, 1902)

Uncle Tom's Cabin, dir. William Robert Daley (World, 1914)

The Wedding March, dir. Erich von Stroheim (Paramount, 1927)

Whoopee!, dir. Thornton Freeland (Samuel Goldwyn, 1930)

Wild Boys of the Road, dir. William Wellman (First National, 1933)

With Bosco in Africa (Warner Bros., 1929)

Wonderbar, dir. Lloyd Bacon (Warner Bros., 1934)

The Younger Generation, dir. Frank Capra (Columbia, 1929)

Index

Other books by Michael Rogin

The Intellectuals and McCarthy: The Radical Specter

(with John L. Shover) *Political Change in California: Critical Elections and Social Movements, 1890–1966*

Fathers and Children: Andrew Jackson and the Subjugation of the American Indian

Subversive Genealogy: The Politics and Art of Herman Melville

Ronald Reagan the Movie, and other Episodes in Political Demonology

Index:	Do Mi Stauber
Composition:	Com-Com
Text:	10/13 Galliard
Display:	Galliard
Printing and binding:	Haddon Craftsmen

Singing Kid
(Cab Calloway)
Holiday Inn - Astaire/ Crosby

Rooney/Kelly - 1178h

Dixie
Rhapsody in Blue
Swanee River
Got into your dancee
GW Mr Blandings Bud House
his Dream House

A Star is Born.
Sing'n in the Rain.